Ruth Richards, one of the world's leaders in the study of creativity, has assembled an enormously valuable compendium of leading-edge research on the nature of creativity and its relationship to learning, spirituality, art, social justice, and the search for meaning. The amazing insights brought forth by this broad array of distinguished writers and thinkers lead us to the inescapable conclusion that the study of creativity is the "high ground" for a new and deeper understanding of the cognitive process. This is an essential resource for anyone interested in new ways of thinking about how we transform ourselves and the world.

—**Michael Grady, MFA,** *Chair, Department of Arts and Consciousness,*
*John F. Kennedy University, Berkeley, CA*

This collection assembled by Dr. Ruth Richards represents a remarkable range of ideas, characterized by sound scholarship, beautifully written prose, and surprise. The book itself embodies the essence of creativity in its presentation, and its breadth and thoroughness destine it to become a multidisciplinary classic.

—**Jeanne Achterberg, PhD,** *Professor of Psychology, Saybrook Graduate School,*
*San Francisco, CA; Senior Editor of the* Journal of Complementary and Alternative Therapy;
*author of* Imagery in Healing: Shamanism and Modern Medicine *and* Woman as Healer

In this book, Ruth Richards has synthesized an important dialogue that invites a broad readership. By viewing everyday creativity in a multifaceted mirror, we are invited to more clearly see the complexity of who we are; how we image ourselves; what we may become; and how to open ourselves to life, spirit, and transformation. This book speaks to anyone who is interested in the human capacity for transformation. The core creativity it addresses applies to spiritual experience as well as to survival and adaptation. It is excellent to see a book tackle everyday creativity at this level.

—**Nik Warren, PhD,** *President of AHIMSA* (nonviolence *in Sanskrit*)*, an interfaith*
*organization dedicated to encouraging dialogues and public forums that bridge spirituality,*
*science, and society; editor of* Dimensions of Unity: Dialogues of Spirituality, Science,
and Society

Too often the term *creativity* is narrowly used to describe the individual gifted in the arts, the scientist who develops a new theory, or the inventor of cutting-edge technology. *Everyday Creativity and New Views of Human Nature* illustrates the point that creativity is inherent in every person and is, in reality, an organic part of life itself. It drives home the message that the life well lived is a creative one—and the creativity inherent in life itself transforms the person in return. Creativity heals lives individually and has the potential to transform society as a whole.

—**Marie A. DiCowden, PhD,** *founder and CEO, The Biscayne Institutes of Health & Living,*
*Miami, FL; author/editor of* Humanizing Health Care *and* The Colors of Prayer by Heart

This book offers a fresh approach to the significance of creativity in the lives of all of us at every age and stage of our development. Although the product of everyday creativity is a goal, readers will see that the process of being creative can have transforming psychological benefits. This volume includes the best contributing authors in the field and great editing by Ruth Richards.

—**Delmont Morrison, PhD,** *University of California, San Francisco, and*
**Shirley Linden Morrison, MA,** *Notre Dame de Namur University, Belmont, CA;*
*coauthors of* Memories of Loss and Dreams of Perfection

This impressive book brings together a variety of fascinating essays on both personal and social aspects of creativity. The essays are authored by distinguished scholars and draw on academic research yet are written in such a clear and engaging manner that they are accessible to a wide audience. The book will be of great interest not only to scholars and students but also to anyone who wants to learn more about creativity from some of the world's experts on the subject.

—**Dennis Kinney, PhD,** *Research Psychologist, McLean Hospital, Belmont, MA;*
*Associate Professor in Psychology, Harvard Medical School, Boston, MA*

This fascinating volume presents important and unusual perspectives on creativity. Drawing extensively on systems perspectives, the authors provide us with a broader and richer approach to the phenomenon of creativity in all its permutations and manifestations.

—**Alfonso Montuori, PhD,** *Professor, California Institute of Integral Studies,*
*San Francisco, CA; coeditor of* Social Creativity *and* Creators on Creating; *coauthor*
*of* From Power to Partnership: Creating the Future of Love, Work, and Community

# EVERYDAY CREATIVITY

### and New Views of Human Nature

# EVERYDAY CREATIVITY

## and New Views of Human Nature

### Psychological, Social, and Spiritual Perspectives

Edited by Ruth Richards

Foreword by Mihaly Csikszentmihalyi

American Psychological Association
Washington, DC

Published by
American Psychological Association
750 First Street, NE
Washington, DC 20002
www.apa.org

To order
APA Order Department
P.O. Box 92984
Washington, DC 20090-2984
Tel: (800) 374-2721
Direct: (202) 336-5510
Fax: (202) 336-5502
TDD/TTY: (202) 336-6123
Online: www.apa.org/books/
E-mail: order@apa.org

In the U.K., Europe, Africa, and the Middle East, copies may be ordered from
American Psychological Association
3 Henrietta Street
Covent Garden, London
WC2E 8LU England

Typeset in Goudy by World Composition Services, Inc., Sterling, VA

Printer: Maple-Vail Book Manufacturing, Binghamton, NY
Cover Designer: Naylor Design, Washington, DC
Technical/Production Editor: Tiffany L. Klaff

The opinions and statements published are the responsibility of the authors, and such opinions and statements do not necessarily represent the policies of the American Psychological Association.

**Library of Congress Cataloging-in-Publication Data**

Everyday creativity and new views of human nature : psychological, social, and spiritual perspectives / Ruth Richards, editor ; foreword by Mihaly Csikszentmihalyi ; with Fred Abraham ... [et al.].—1st ed.
   p. cm.
Includes bibliographical references and index.
ISBN-13: 978-0-9792125-7-4
ISBN-10: 0-9792125-7-X
1. Creative ability. 2. Creative ability—Social aspects. I. Richards, Ruth. II. Abraham, Frederick David.

BF408.E896   2007
153.3'5—dc22                                                                 2006103319

**British Library Cataloguing-in-Publication Data**
A CIP record is available from the British Library.

*Printed in the United States of America*
*First Edition*

To my daughter
Lauren Jo Richards-Ruby
and to all of us as we learn, develop, dream,
and seek life's possibilities

# CONTENTS

# CONTRIBUTORS

**Frederick David Abraham, PhD,** Blueberry Brain Institute, Waterbury, VT; formerly, University of California, Los Angeles, and Silliman University, the Philippines; neuroscientist, psychologist; cofounder, Society for Chaos Theory in Psychology and the Life Sciences; coauthor, *A Visual Introduction to Dynamical Systems Theory for Psychology*

**Mike Arons, PhD,** State University of West Georgia, Carrollton; former Chair of Humanistic Psychology; philosopher, founded fourth program in humanistic psychology; worked with Abraham Maslow

**James R. Averill, PhD,** University of Massachusetts, Amherst; psychologist with interests in emotions and creativity across cultures; writings include the book *Voyages of the Heart*

**Allan Combs, PhD,** California Institute of Integral Studies, San Francisco, CA; neuropsychologist, consciousness researcher, systems theorist; books include *Radiance of Being*

**Mihaly Csikszentmihalyi, PhD,** C. S. and D. J. Davidson Professor of Psychology and Management; Director, Quality of Life Research Center, Claremont Graduate School, Claremont, CA

**Riane Eisler, JD,** President, Center for Partnership Studies, Pacific Grove, CA; cultural historian, evolution theorist, human rights and peace activist; award-winning author of *The Chalice and the Blade, The Power of Partnership,* and *The Real Wealth of Nations*

**S. J. Goerner, PhD,** Director, Integral Science Institute, Chapel Hill, NC; past president of the Society for Chaos Theory in Psychology and Life Sciences, Pewaukee, WI; psychologist, computer scientist; books include *After the Clockwork Universe*

**Stanley Krippner, PhD,** Saybrook Graduate School, San Francisco, CA; received 2002 American Psychological Association Award for

Distinguished Contributions to the International Advancement of Psychology; expert in dreamwork and creativity, altered states, and shamanism; books include *The Mythic Path* (with David Feinstein)

**David Loye, PhD,** cofounder, Institute for Partnership Studies, Pacific Grove, CA; formerly at University of California, Los Angeles, School of Medicine and Princeton University; social psychologist, futurist, systems theorist, creator of The Darwin Project; books include *Darwin's Truth*

**Steven R. Pritzker, PhD,** Saybrook Graduate School and Research Center, San Francisco, CA; prizewinning Hollywood writer in earlier years with credits including *The Mary Tyler Moore Show*; coeditor of *The Encyclopedia of Creativity* (with Mark A. Runco)

**Ruth Richards, MD, PhD,** Saybrook Graduate School and Research Center, San Francisco, CA; McLean Hospital and Harvard Medical School; coauthor of *The Lifetime Creativity Scales* and coeditor of *Eminent Creativity, Everyday Creativity, and Health*

**Mark A. Runco, PhD,** California State University, Fullerton, and Norwegian School of Economics and Business Administration; editor of *Creativity Research Journal*; coeditor of *The Encyclopedia of Creativity* (with Steven Pritzker); Past President of American Psychological Association Division 10 (Society for the Psychology of Aesthetics, Creativity, and the Arts)

**David Schuldberg, PhD,** University of Montana, Missoula; psychologist, clinician, and researcher in chaos theory and in issues of creativity and mental health whose studies have helped bring these areas together

**Louise Sundararajan, PhD, EdD,** Rochester Regional Forensic Unit, Rochester, NY; psychologist and philosopher with interest in relations between emotion, creativity, and spirituality, including Eastern and Western views

**Tobi Zausner, PhD,** C. G. Jung Institute, New York, NY; artist, psychologist, and art historian with expertise in creativity and health and archetypal imagery; author of *When Walls Become Doorways: Creativity and the Transforming Illness*

# FOREWORD

MIHALY CSIKSZENTMIHALYI

Much has been written about creativity in the past few decades. We have learned a great deal about how great artists and scientists go about their work, about what motivates them, about their childhood, and even about their old age. As usually happens with the advancement of science, all this knowledge keeps suggesting new questions. One of the most central questions being, so what does what we learn about these outstanding creative individuals tell us about our own lives—about the everyday, small "c" creativity that goes into raising our children, surviving in our jobs, and making life rich and interesting? Many scholars have asked that question, but few have even begun to speculate what an answer to it might look like.

In this collection, Ruth Richards and her collaborators have finally taken the plunge and produced a stimulating, thought-provoking kaleido-scope of views about what everyday creativity can involve for people, both individually and together. Readers will come across many scintillating gems along the way. At the same time, as is often the case with pioneering ventures, readers may also find what time will show to be false starts. Because this volume is in itself a creative product, it is useful to remember an oft-repeated definition of creativity: It dwells on the edge that separates chaos from order. Whereas most scholarly books on creativity might err by staying safely on the side of order, this volume tends to venture occasionally into the possibility of chaos. That is the risk one must take when creativity is at stake.

However, this is certainly not a pop-psych or how-to book. It is not easy reading because of the variety of perspectives it presents and vocabularies it uses. Yet for those individuals who are serious about understanding how to live their lives more creatively, and for those who wish to study and understand everyday creativity, there are enough budding ideas to build on and exciting hints to explore to keep one busy for a lifetime. And as with all good books, it is what the reader brings and adds to it that will make this book a great one.

# ACKNOWLEDGMENTS

We contributors were all delighted that this book found a home with the American Psychological Association. We are grateful to Lansing Hays for seeing its potential and accepting the project, and to two anonymous reviewers for their astute suggestions for the volume. In the development phase, it was an honor to work with Ron Teeter, who stands with only one other editor this writer has known in helping authors bring forth important material that might never have appeared otherwise. I am not the only contributor to say so.

The cover design struck us as beautiful and elegantly simple. Anne Woodworth Gasque and her staff deserve many creative accolades. In the production phase Tiffany Klaff and her copyeditors did excellent work—careful, thorough, sensitive to nuance, and timely in keeping us on track. I would also like to thank the others at APA Books whose names we don't know, but who have assisted, and continue to assist, in various ways.

As volume editor, I would also like to thank Kathleen Drucker Spivack, Pulitzer nominee, editor with whom I've worked, friend, inspiration, and source of golden poetry and prose. In several ways, she has helped this project come to realization. Finally, I am well aware that we all have dear family and friends who have supported our work and our intentions, and whose own identities, suggestions, examples, and hopes, too, are interwoven in various ways with what one reads here. Heartfelt thanks to you all.

# EVERYDAY CREATIVITY

### and New Views of Human Nature

# INTRODUCTION

RUTH RICHARDS

If I had to define life in a word, it would be Life is creation.
—Claude Bernard

We humans are often "everyday creative," or we would not even be alive. To cope with changing environments, we improvise, we flexibly adapt, we try this and that. At times, we change the environment to suit us— whether we are making a living, raising a child, feeding the family, writing a report, or finding our way out of the woods when lost. Far from being a minor or specialized part of our lives, our everyday creativity—our originality of everyday life—is, first of all, a survival capability. It is also a universal capability.

But, as this book suggests, our everyday creativity offers us more: It offers a dynamic process and a powerful way of living. When developed, it can open all of us to new depths, richness, and presence. This book brings together a variety of eminent thinkers and writers, who offer new and sometimes speculative perspectives on how creativity can enter our lives in unsuspected ways, from the prosaic to the dramatic. They offer as well a renewed appreciation of creativity—as a process, a force, a strategy, even a vehicle for societies at a difficult, and perhaps decisive point, in human history.

Our human creativity, it is suggested, can affect our health and well-being, personal growth and development, our creativity together, and even the evolution of cultures. It can also, as our multidisciplinary thinkers suggest,

3

offer new views of ourselves in this complex and interdependent world, and reasons for being on this earth in the first place. Here is hope indeed, in a troubled age.

*Everyday Creativity and New Views of Human Nature* is not just about personal growth or social change, but about transformation—offering new views of who we are, individually and together, and new ways of being in the world, and affecting it. When the authors say "new," this also means new in every age, and new for each of us; ways of engaging life we must come into for ourselves, while discovering a freshness and a wonder we could not have imagined beforehand.

Our chapter contributors tell us in many forms, and in many contexts, that we humans have only begun to discover what is possible. If indeed our capacity for creativity in our daily lives can offer new pathways to human unfolding and fulfillment—both individually and together—then people need to hear about this, and assess the possibilities for themselves. That is the reason for this book.

## EVERYDAY CREATIVITY IS ABOUT MORE THAN THE ARTS

Contrary to the earlier view, some people think that our creativity is mainly about the arts and, furthermore, that it is an activity largely reserved for "geniuses" and certain widely recognized people—at least if it is to be taken seriously. For them, everyday creativity seems an "extra," set apart from the rest of life. People who believe this are depriving themselves of their creative birthright. "I'm not creative!" one hears people say, even emphatically, next explaining they cannot draw a portrait or a likeness (Richards, 1990, in press). Not the point! How much of life these people may be missing by leaving their creativity underdeveloped.

We use our everyday creativity throughout our lives, at work and leisure, whether making a sale, organizing a benefit, counseling a client, helping the kids do homework, or planning a winter vacation (Cropley, 1990; Kinney, Richards, & Southam, in press; Richards, Kinney, Benet, & Merzel, 1988). Furthermore, when everyday creativity is, in fact, about aesthetic concerns, it is not just about writing poetry or singing in a choir, but also about helping one's child with a school display, writing a letter to the editor, rearranging a room, or landscaping the yard. In truth, our creativity is less about Activity A or B, than a way of approaching life which can expand our experiences and options, and even deeply affect who we are—and can become.

Seen as a process, and even a way of life, our everyday creativity offers whole new ways of thinking, of experiencing the world, and experiencing ourselves. It can pull blinders from our eyes, and bring us alive, making us more conscious participants in our lives, aware of the dynamic of life moving about us (see Franck, 1993; Loori, 2004; Nachmanovitch, 1990; Richards, 2006). It can offer us joy, energy, and challenge. Colors become brighter, and sounds become sweeter. The smallest moments—a raindrop, a gust of air—offer wonder. We may even have a chance for fundamental transformation.

## IDENTIFYING EVERYDAY CREATIVITY

How does one identify everyday creativity? Formally, this involves meeting just two criteria, now widely accepted, as defined by the remarkable creativity researcher, the late Frank X. Barron (1969), namely: *originality* and *meaningfulness*. There needs to be something new, in other words—whether a concrete product, behavior, or idea. In addition, the *product*—one of Mooney's "four Ps of creativity"—should not be random, accidental, or idiosyncratic. It should communicate to others. Still, an identified "accident" might qualify as creative if it meets the two criteria. The mishap of a broken jar of jam on the floor is probably not creative. Yet seeing, appreciating, and photographing its accidental pattern of deep red and sparkling glass might still be. There is newness and the intent to show an artistic effect. (Kinney et al., in press; Richards et al., 1988; Shansis et al., 2003).

In addition, in this book, originality can be assessed against different baselines, for different purposes. A creative outcome may be new on a global scale, or to a particular reference group, or to a domain or area of endeavor, or simply to one's own personal experience (Beghetto & Kaufman, in press; Runco, 1996; Richards, 1981). It depends on one's purpose.

This is not to overlook the other three of Mooney's "four Ps" of creativity (Richards, 1999) which are often less stressed than creative product. One can also speak of the creative *process*, *person*, and *press* of the environment (environmental factors that help or hinder creativity). It is process, above all, that is a focus in this book—as it leads to the various products (or gets derailed along the way). Our concern lies mostly with the benefits and possibilities for us personally, as we go through our day, while discovering how experience can be different if we live life more openly and innovatively. With everyday creativity, it is not so much what one does as how one does it.

## EVERYDAY CREATIVITY IS NOT NEW—
## BUT IS IT SOMETIMES OVERLOOKED?

Everyday creativity is not a new idea. It has diverse precursors, including the work of psychologists, psychiatrists, philosophers, educators, and other scientists and artists interested in origins of originality or newness in human experience. Philosopher and educator John Dewey's (1934/1980) views of aesthetics focus on process, and the richness and immediacy of all of life. Dewey spoke of "an aesthetic in the raw," intertwined with how we live each day—often overlooked by modern culture, "where what (we) know as art is relegated to the museum or gallery" (p. 6). Consider that the

> mechanic engaged in his job, interested in doing well and finding satisfaction in his handiwork, caring for his materials and tools with genuine affection, is artistically engaged. The difference between such a worker and the inept and careless bungler is as great in the shop as it is in the studio. (p. 5)

Dewey also mourned the removal from everyday life, and from the community, of the sacred, noting that, for many, "an aura of mingled awe and unreality encompasses the 'spiritual' and the 'ideal' while 'matter' has become by contrast a term of depreciation" (p. 6). Yet a child may find unsurpassed wonder in a cloud, a rainbow, a drop of dew. Can we not return awe, wonder, and deeper meaning to our lives? (See also Loori, 2004; Richards, 2001; Schneider, 2004.)

Clinicians, meanwhile, had their own concerns with originality, viewed both as process and clinical indicator, emerging from less healthy origins. Sigmund Freud, father of psychoanalysis, as well as neo-Freudians such as Lawrence Kubie, saw clients' innovative ideas and productions as transformations of unconscious or preconscious thoughts and conflicts toward a more settled homeostasis (Richards, 1981). Humanistic and transpersonal psychologists, by contrast, looked to ongoing growth-oriented aspects of the person (Taylor & Martin, 2001), with creativity as a central part of humans' continuing development (Arons & Richards, 2003), as in work on creativity by Carl Rogers (1961) or Abraham Maslow (1968). Maslow's self-actualizing creativity is of particular interest, although not identical to everyday creativity, and will be discussed more elsewhere.

In an entirely different domain, flexible, original human adaptations, as a survival capability can be connected with the "phenotypic plasticity" of evolutionary biologists such as Theodosius Dobzhansky (1962). Here our human creativity or ingenuity, possessed by all humans, is relevant to our genetic or "genotypic" endowment, manifesting "phenotypically" in diverse and flexible responses to environmental conditions, within the bounds of our genetic inheritance.

Many psychologists joined in the scientific and laboratory study of creativity, spurred by J. P. Guilford's (1950) Presidential Address to the American Psychological Association, bemoaning the lack of scientific attention to creativity. Concern was not about creative functioning of the rare few, but about better developing a universal and natural resource in our youth and populace. J. P. Guilford (1967), E. Paul Torrance (1962, 1988), Frank Barron (1969, 1995), and Ravenna Helson (1971; Helson, Roberts, & Agronick, 1995) are just a few well-known names. Some researchers sought distinct creative abilities, and individual differences, especially Guilford, with his "structure of intellect" model, and also Torrance with his related verbal and figural "divergent thinking" tests for fluency, flexibility, originality, and elaboration.

Other psychologists, such as Barron, Helson, Donald MacKinnon, Harrison Gough, and others at the Institute of Personality Assessment and Research at the University of California, Berkeley, went beyond ability to include more general and nonintellective characteristics of the creative person; it is of interest that they found similar patterns across domains, related more directly to the personality (Barron & Harrington, 1981; Helson, 1999). Two examples of these are: *openness to experience*, and *tolerance of ambiguity*, about which one shall hear more in this book.

A long-standing debate still continues about the extent to which creative characteristics are domain-specific (e.g., varying from artists to scientists) or involve similar features across different domains—with the most likely resolution being that there is some of each (see Sternberg, Grigorenko, & Singer, 2004, and selected chapters in this book).

Other researchers have since developed additional theories, measures, and research programs relevant to everyday creativity (e.g., Richards et al., 1988; Runco, 1999; Runco & Pritzker, 1999), building on what has gone before. In fact, the literature on creativity has expanded, filling volumes. It has led to the launching of periodicals such as *the Journal of Creative Behavior*, *The Creativity Research Journal*, and the newer journal for Division 10 of the American Psychological Association, *Psychology of Aesthetics, Creativity, and the Arts*, as well as the publication of the *Encyclopedia of Creativity*.

Now, into the 21st century, one of the characteristics mentioned earlier as important to creativity, openness to experience, is highlighted as a factor in the "five factor theory of personality" (Costa & Widiger, 1994). The new positive psychology (Peterson, 2006), too, has been reawakening interest in our more healthy and universal capacities, and these certainly include our day-to-day creativity.

If everyday creativity is not a new idea, it still seems downplayed compared with other life concerns. It is likely that many of us know intuitively what our own everyday creativity is (or feels like), even if we have not learned to look for it or name it. In view of this, it becomes even more important to ask why the creativity we take seriously is widely considered exclusive to eminent or exceptional people—just think about media coverage of famous artists, actors, authors, inventors, public figures—in preference to the creativity we all can manifest. Do we let a few famous people carry the creative ball for the rest of us?

And creativity is not without a moral dimension. One is reminded, sometimes, of how easily human creativity can be used for harmful and destructive purposes. What makes the difference? C. Rogers (1961) and others (e.g., Barron, 1969; Pennebaker, 1995; Richards, 2006) remind us that a continued and open process, tapping deep unconscious sources, tends toward health, and Maslow (1971) shows that one's values can even change toward more universal benefit and contribution at higher levels of self-actualizing creativity. Others (Feinstein & Krippner, 1997; Singer, 2006) remind us that our guiding life stories and images can also be changed. A special issue of the *Creativity Research Journal*, edited by Howard Gruber and Doris Wallace (1993) further explores creativity in the moral domain. How to live our humanistic or spiritual values in our creative life and work is a general concern among contributors to *Everyday Creativity and New Views of Human Nature*, and of many religious and secular leaders (e.g., Carter, 2001; Dalai Lama, 1991; Minh Duc, 2000; Nhat Hanh, 1992; Tarthang Tulku, 1991; also see Badiner, 1990; Rothberg, 2006; Scholl, 1995; Whitmyer, 1994).

Because of all this, multiple and potential factors that contribute to— or discourage—everyday creativity are considered in this book, all of which may play a role to varying degrees. To mention one, there can be powerful inner and outer blocks, or obstacles, to our creativity (Amabile, 1996; Montuori & Purser, 1999; Richards, 2006). If, at times, we find it "hard to get started," there may also be outside systems and even self-organizing forces that prefer we don't get started either. Their power can be surprising.

Yet meanwhile, talent and innovation are increasingly being sought at all levels of work, in a global information age (Florida, 2005; Richards, in press). An aging population, in addition, may start awakening to new evidence of creativity's healing properties. One may find renewed energy behind opening the blocks to developing one's creativity. In some opinions, there may be a new creative age coming (Florida, 2002; Naisbitt & Aburdene, 1990); if not, it is at least a time for opportunity and change.

## BENEFITS OF CREATIVITY—SOME BACKGROUND

Why can one say creativity is good for people? Here are some highlights. For instance, as a result of multiple studies and the use of rigorous methodology, research on expressive writing is particularly notable. Such writing connects to improvements in health, both physical and psychological, as seen later in this volume. It has, remarkably enough, even been linked to stronger immune function—enhancing resistance to disease (Lepore & Smyth, 2002; Pennebaker, Kiecolt-Glaser, & Glaser, 1988). Might the soaring popularity of blogs on the Internet have anything to do with such health benefits?

One also finds numerous anecdotes, examples, and research reports about other arts medicine approaches, and in many areas including grief and loss, eating disorders, mood disorders, coping with cancer, HIV, and other illnesses, as well as toward enhancing personal growth and well-being (Levine & Levine, 1999; Richards, 2004; N. Rogers, 1993; Runco & Richards, 1998; Schlitz, Amorok, & Micozzi, 2005; Wiseman, 1986; Zausner, 2007). It is ironic, and sad too, that many still do not connect creativity with health.

Turning from arts to creative orientations and attitudes, it is striking that older people who think more divergently and innovatively and remain interested, open and curious, tend to be more comfortable with aging, illness, and death. Here are valuable findings for the baby boomers as they age. These elder citizens also show a fuller involvement with life (Smith & van der Meer, 1990; Adams-Price, 1998; Adler, 1995). Or looking at children and their penchant for fun, play, and fantasy, how interesting to discover this is time well spent—enhancing social and emotional, as well as intellectual development, and bringing greater sense of control over one's life, and the mastery of fears (Richards, 1996; Russ, 1993; Scales, Almy, Nicolopoulou, & Ervin-Tripp, 1991; Singer, Golinkoff, & Hirsh-Pasek, 2006). Play can be considered part of everyday creativity and, furthermore, has been called the "cornerstone of the imagination" (Van Hoorn, Nourot, Scales, & Alward, 1993, p. 25). We adults could certainly play more ourselves (see Nachmanovitch, 1990).

Resilient creative coping may help with immediate difficulties (Albert & Runco, 1986; Flach, 1990; Goertzel & Goertzel, 1962; Richards, 1990, 1998; Runco & Richards, 1998) and, beyond that, yield more lasting benefits for personal growth, even progressing over the years (Helson et al., 1995). The lower aggression found among more versus less creative children (Dudek & Verrault, 1989) is an appealing example.

Of particular interest is when creativity previously fueled by "deficiency needs" as per Maslow (1968; see Rhodes, 1990; Storr, 1988), such as needs for safety, love and esteem, becomes in itself a force for change and growth, increasing a creator's intrinsic motivation. Take a troubled young person who finds refuge and self-esteem in a science lab, and then continues on with the work for the thrill of discovery. Especially in the arts, there may be a growing awareness of more universal themes—so that now the troubled young person is writing creatively about conflict at home, and empathizing broadly with a similarly disaffected teenage cohort. Sometimes a need develops to contribute from these insights to the broader culture (Jamison, 1993; Ludwig, 1995; Morrison & Morrison, 2006; Rhodes, 1990; Rothenberg, 1990; Runco & Richards, 1998; Zausner, 2007), in forms which can help everyone.

It has been said this movement from deficiency-motivated creativity is more likely for persons open to experience (Rhodes; 1990; C. Rogers, 1961). The progression can be particularly significant when leading to self-actualizing creativity (Maslow, 1971), and even for some, to expanded states of consciousness, peak experiences, an oceanic awareness, and other transpersonal states and experiences which are sometimes reported (see also Miller & Cook-Greuter, 2000; N. Rogers, 1993).

It is also useful to ask how culture and its "health" interact with creativity. What, first of all, does "health" even mean here? This has been debated by varied scholars (myself and others in Runco & Richards, 1998), and is important for Part II of this book. Some people, at least, would think sustainable, participatory, and peaceful qualities, with ability to adapt and develop as needed, would be among signs of a healthy culture. We do know that cultural receptivity to, and support of, creativity, and presence of rich resources and like-minded others, can stimulate creativity in general, in specific domains, and even when it is fairly private and personal (Amabile, 1996; Csikszentmihalyi, 1988, 1996; Montuori & Purser, 1999; Richards, 1981). Whether on a remote island, or in the center of town, one is still effectively an open system embedded in a social-global context, subtly and multiply influenced by others and the surrounds (Barron, 1995; Montuori & Purser, 1996; Richards, 1996).

Can cultural factors account for "golden ages" when creativity flourishes? What about Greece, early Rome, the Renaissance. Arieti (1976) posits the positive coming together of three cycles, economic, social, and political. His focus was on exceptional creativity, and not necessarily everyday creativity. However, as some chapters in this volume suggest, the two may be related. At the negative extreme, Simonton (1990) found political disruption often hurts creativity (as with anarchy). Yet two types seemed to boost it, albeit a generation later: political fragmentation and civil disturbance. Is this another instance of creative and resilient response to conflict?

Turning this around, how may individual creativity affect society? Altered social conditions or a change of paradigm may be led by changes in an early adopting group. Ray and Anderson's (2000) compelling subpopulation called the "cultural creatives" are seen by some as harbingers of change, as noted later—perhaps 25% of our society, interestingly 40% men, and 60% women, with a social conscience, rejecting materialism, more interested in green values and sustainability, and looking for new ways to live, with a subgroup deeply committed to spirituality and personal growth.

Although not particularly well organized, the "cultural creatives" can help seed change in the larger culture, through spreading their interest in new lifestyles, and departures from the mainstream. Still, we North Americans face strong obstacles to group creativity and collaborative change. It has been said (Stewart & Bennett, in Montuori & Purser, 1999) that "in the American self, there is a remarkable absence of community, tradition, and shared meaning which impinge upon perception and give shape to behavior" (p. 15).

Another model considers that more people today are mobile, or fairly mobile, and have flexible work conditions, and can live more complex and creatively stimulating lives. Some younger people, in particular, may deliberately seek out such stimulation. Concurrently, the "demand for talent-intensive skills is rising" and "the proportion of workers doing jobs that call for complex skills has grown three times as fast as employment" ("The Search for Talent," 2006). Within this growing creative ethos, Florida (2002), identifies a separate subgroup, the *creative class*, based on "the ability to create meaningful new forms" (p. 5), estimated at above 30% of the workforce, who can also help open up things up, and bring change. In fact, because dynamic factors are involved, this can happen rather quickly (Florida, 2005).

How interesting that some of these like-minded individuals are tending to cluster together. Florida's data shows geographical areas of greater and lesser concentration of the creative class, with the top five large cities being Washington, DC, Raleigh-Durham, Boston, Austin, and San Francisco. Advantages include the so-called three Ts of economic development: *technology*, *talent*, and *tolerance*.

One might suggest these also provide, among other things, opportunity, community, and openness.

If the earlier "golden ages" were based on the coming together, at a given time and place, of more fertile conditions, now more mobile and proactive creators may themselves seek out the more welcoming cities with such conditions, at the same time increasing these cities' appeal. It may happen with countries as well. In Florida's (2005) *Flight of the Creative Class*, the top six countries for these creatives are: The Netherlands, Australia, Sweden, Switzerland, Denmark, and Norway (Florida, 2005). Countries farther from the cutting edge—or losing talent to others—may scramble to duplicate some of the advantages. New Zealand is another nation on the ascent. It is interesting that creativity, at all levels, is one of its top governmental priorities (Clark, 2002). Will community—and social creativity—gel more with creative migration? This is worth further attention.

Finally, apart from all this, the present discussion reminds us that everyday creativity is far from an optional "extra." Our creativity may increasingly become a primary driver for much that happens in our world, and with us.

# ABOUT THIS VOLUME

The idea for this book first took form while I was involved in planning an APA symposium with learned colleagues who had given much thought to the nature and importance of creativity: Mike Arons, Stanley Krippner, Steven R. Pritzker, and David Schuldberg. What a group of visionaries! We all believed creativity in daily life was far from understood, its power poorly recognized, its healthy effects only beginning to be known, and the forces aligned against it huge. This had remained the case despite years of creativity research in psychology and allied fields. The thought came naturally, "What about a book?" To develop and frame the issues in the broadest interdisciplinary way, I added other visionary and creative scholars from allied fields. The focus became one, not so much on creative outcome, but on creative process, on what we humans actually do and experience, and what helps and hinders us, as well as on what the act of creating can do for us, the creative person, in turn.

Another important precursor to the present book was *Eminent Creativity, Everyday Creativity, and Health*, a book I coedited earlier, with Mark A. Runco (1998), on the health benefits of creativity. That volume considered both eminent and everyday creators, and personal and social creativity. It focused on issues of creativity and illness, resilient response to conflict, health maintenance and personal growth, with "health" issues broadly defined. The present volume, *Everyday Creativity and New Views of Human Nature* goes further beyond everyday creativity based on "deficiency" needs (see section earlier) to consider our positive and developing selves, our potential for transformation (e.g., Mezirow, 1991), and the larger untapped future of our human potential.

*Everyday Creativity and New Views of Human Nature* not only addresses us *Homo sapiens*, but also prehuman evolution as well, and even moves forward in time to speculate about the cyberworlds we may yet create, in fact with surprising consequences for gender and other polarities, and creativity itself. It looks not only at conflict and creative coping, but also at fuller mind-body-spirit integration with a deeper potential for healing and growth, and further human development. In so doing, the focus turns more to process and the sorts of orientations that can guide creative lives. Some contributors, in fact, even see such creative orientations as ones which can influence—and may have influenced down through history—not only health and personal development, but also even biological and cultural evolution.

Contributors to the present book include major voices in the psychology and social psychology of creativity, including two Editors-in-Chief of the *Encyclopedia of Creativity*, one also the Editor-in-Chief of the *Creativity Research Journal*. Contributors are also experts in Jungian, humanistic, and developmental psychology, Eastern philosophy, Western psychiatry, neuropsychology and consciousness studies, education, art history, cultural history, systems science, "chaos" theory, and more. They are often authors or editors of influential books, and steady contributors to the creativity literature.

I was interested indeed to discover that, for several of us, creativity also represented a path—a personal route to something better and more powerful in our lives. For different contributors, this path led to some combination of better health and well-being, a stress-free, relaxed and more immediate presence in our world, greater awareness of our interconnection, with enhanced concern and caring for others, and greater awe and awareness of beneficial forces beyond the mundane, with enhanced life meaning, and spirituality.

I was also intrigued to find that we, as a group, believed strongly that creativity had much more to offer socially in a troubled world—an aspect that has been vastly underrepresented in a literature focused on individuals. Should not the study of creativity have something to suggest about living more peacefully in an age of terrorism and violence? About wars that ravage dozens of nations? About the real weapons of mass destruction, falling each day into more and more hands? Or the poisoning of our air, water, and food, or global warming, overpopulation, starvation, and rampant disease around the world? What about the complexities and faster pace of modern life, aligned with higher rates of substance abuse, mental disorders, mindless escape, alienation, loneliness, and meaninglessness among the very youth who will succeed us and could help save us? If our creativity cannot assist us in such urgent matters, we might ask why we are studying creativity in the first place.

Nor did contributors to *Everyday Creativity and New Views of Human Nature* believe that personal and social focuses were opposed. It was very much the opposite. "Who we are," this group believes, leads naturally into our intentions and actions. We may well start with ourselves. "Peace in oneself, peace in the world," wrote Zen Master Thich Nhat Hanh.

*Everyday Creativity and New Views of Human Nature* has three parts, focusing on our human creativity both individually and together, with a final section for integration and conclusions. Part I, Creativity and Our Individual Lives, considers individuals—our well-being, potential for new and transformative understandings, and openings to richness, immediacy, and profundity of experience. It draws on multidisciplinary sources, including the psychology of consciousness, art history, cross-cultural studies, philosophy, systems science, and chaos theory. There is a focus on creative process, which is not at all new in the literature—consider for example the work of Csikszentmihalyi (1990, 1996), Gruber (Gruber & Davis, 1988), C. Rogers (1961), and others, including clinical and educational psychologists.

In my chapter, I suggest that obstacles to our everyday creativity can at times be serious, unexpected, and quite surprising. Beginning with "writer's block" and moving outward from there, one finds these obstacles can be both internal and external, conscious and unconscious, and individual and group derived, while also being subtle and sometimes self-organizing. I illustrate important health benefits from being creative, ones we may forfeit if we minimize our potential—including greater openness, nondefensiveness, and enhanced comfort and acceptance of the idiosyncrasies of self and others. The abnormal, after all, is not always pathological. Health benefits may occur, in part, from overcoming some of these obstacles, supported by such findings, for example, as enhanced working memory. We may also be more in touch with our mind–body continuum, and perhaps even with expanded capacities we are only beginning to anticipate.

Looking further at process, David Schuldberg shows us rhythms and patterns of our life we do not always recognize, as we maneuver in a world based on complex dynamical systems (or chaos theory). We can learn to see more fully in terms of process and change. We can stay relatively balanced, and creatively ready to respond to new openings, even if we are not fully in control, within the "somewhat complicated systems" (SCS) we encounter. Using common examples, Schuldberg nicely introduces concepts from chaos theory, including chaotic attractors and "sensitivity to initial conditions." Remember that the famed "butterfly effect" can throw all into disarray but can also open the door to creative opportunity. If we bravely face uncertainty, as part of "living well," we may also find the pleasure of "new vitality, creativity, and surprise."

Tobi Zausner looks at healing and creativity from the dual perspective of making visual art and viewing it. Art making has often helped people heal, and at times it has even changed lives. Zausner shows this for Henri Matisse, Albert Pinkham Ryder, and Maud Lewis. Matisse, for example, found art as a young adult during recurrent appendicitis, leading to a new career and opportunities, and in the end, providing great works of art for the public. One also sees how the viewer of art is in some sense cocreator, dialoguing with it, and completing the artist's intention. In addition, art can tap into powerful archetypes, or deep organizing principles of the unconscious mind, through symbols and images, potentially bringing new awarenesses. Religious works can be designed for spiritual elevation and, in some traditions and practices, even for transformation. The viewing of art can and should change the viewer and, as such, Zausner says, it can be very much a creative act.

Mark Runco shows that our personal creativity—even if original only to us—is a vitally important factor in the way we live our lives. Are we finding new interpretations and creating new understandings about the world and ourselves? Are we, furthermore, consciously taking initiative to innovate proactively in life, seeing problems and needs, and not taking the status quo for granted, or are we mindlessly going along with what we are given, and what we expect? Such issues are discussed in terms including Piaget's accommodation and assimilation, and three central aspects of personal creativity: *interpretation*, *discretion*, and *intentionality*. Implications include a natural personal and creative development, and a possible progress toward self-actualization.

Steven Pritzker looks at the surprising amount of creativity that is possible during the seemingly passive activity of television watching. It is worth noting that Dr. Pritzker, prior to obtaining his PhD, was a prizewinning Hollywood sitcom writer, committed to social relevance and viewer learning, for programs such as *The Mary Tyler Moore Show*. This chapter focuses on process and flow, as defined by Csikszentmihalyi, and its possible manifestations in audience creativity. Contrary to popular belief, one's creativity can be active, even for someone who is quietly being attentive to a source of information. Television viewers can be focused, involved, and participatory. Viewing can raise questions, bridge defenses, and create opportunities for new learning on clinical, personal, and social issues, with implications for therapists, clients, and the rest of us, with applications through videotherapy and teletherapy.

Finally, Part I ends with a big challenge to all of us, from Allan Combs and Stanley Krippner, in a chapter that also bridges into Part II, Creativity and Society. Is what each of us sees and experiences really what is manifestly present, or is this just a small slice of an already biased picture, one that is hugely culturally constructed, as well as personally biased? As with a fish in water, we may not even know what we are swimming in. Short of a fully enlightened mind, our human fate may be shaped by historically evolving "'structures' of consciousness [that] act like colored lenses through which unalloyed consciousness is constrained." Our arts and our belief systems reflect different eras of human collective understanding, according to views also consistent with certain Eastern wisdom traditions. The cultural patterns are now said to be changing, with a subset of people moving toward a more open and multiperspectival "integral consciousness," with advantages for creativity, mutual understanding, and living better together.

Part II of this book involves social creativity—including issues of complexity, collaboration, contextual relativity, cultural difference, inclusiveness, and creative systems evolving from the ground up (vs. more hierarchical models). Important changes in our value systems could accompany a greater social valuing of creativity. The section begins with a look backward at "the lost Darwin" and goes forward into varied visions of the future with more proactive roles for our human creativity, and in which humans and cultures may yet evolve.

David Loye's chapter will evoke surprise and shock for readers who first discover that part of Darwin's theory of evolution has not been passed down to us. Through historical reconstruction and textual analysis, Loye illustrates how the second part of Darwin's theory, "the lost Darwin," has been downplayed, diminishing vital concerns including cooperation, love, and moral sensibility. Of humans, and "survival of the fittest," Darwin said in *The Descent of Man* (1871) that, as far as "the highest part of our nature is concerned, there are other agencies more important" (pp. 403–404). There are implications for dominant Western views of biological and cultural evolution. Toward a more open and creative understanding now, Loye supports interdisciplinary and systems science inquiry, to fulfill the promise of Darwin's full theory of evolution.

In a different look at human possibility, Mike Arons notes a singular fact most of us do not consider: Among all creatures, only we humans stand upright. Arons looks at the brain evolving toward *Homo sapiens*, and then for us humans, at our outward reaching (vs. homeostasis-seeking) and increasing creative urge. To Arons, upright posture is both a reflection of and a metaphor for our creative possibility, always a little off balance by its nature, while dynamic, risk taking, and striving for new heights. He also shows how this is also reflected in our language. We humans are stabilized as much as we can be, not by further physical factors—after all, while standing, we still need to keep our balance—but by the mind and creative spirit. Arons suggests that, it is in mind–body–spirit integration that human beings find the greatest balance and harmony. The upright, as metaphor, also fits with creative traits such as tolerance of ambiguity, and with possibilities of Maslow's peak experiences.

As we humans try to stay balanced and make our way within our constructed realities, how often do we consider that what we call creativity, too, is highly culturally conditioned? To illustrate this, Louise Sundararajan and James R. Averill take us on an enchanted voyage into the subtleties of emotional creativity and the poetry of John Keats from the West and Ssu-k'ung T'u from the East. They look at the relative importance of novelty and authenticity, plus how this interacts culturally with differentiation and involvement, both through analysis of poetry and relevant research data. The journey takes us all the way from Western creative uniqueness to Eastern transcendence. We humans can, of course, expand our own possibilities beyond one chosen or inherited orientation, and to our great benefit.

S. J. Goerner calls for more individual and collective creativity, integrated into better collaborative learning structures, in the face of a seemingly (and hopefully) imminent paradigm shift, from what is called an Enlightenment worldview to an ecosystem or web-based worldview. Integral science provides a basis for the complex, systems-based processing and interactions that are required. Our charge as individuals includes cooperation and stewardship, to sustain family, community, and the larger global environments and cultures, while we live our individual lives. Societies can be viewed as learning communities and "knowledge ecologies," very much, at best, honoring diversity and creative uniqueness, while usefully pooling information, to enter into larger considerations.

Looking ahead, via futuristic science fiction, and feminist and postmodern analysis, with a touch of chaos and systems theory, Fred Abraham posits a new twist to the usual creativity scholarship. He addresses our cyberworld, both separate from us and increasingly embedded within our own organisms, and its future consequences for both our manifest and virtual realities, as well as traditional gendered roles. Following the evolution of the human brain, he shows the growing importance of creativity, now including the spawning of artificial offspring and cyberrealms in which creativity can become even more important. In such a cyberculture, troubling false dichotomies and differences may be transcended, including some concerning gender and related polarities.

Finally, cultural historian Riane Eisler, looking both back and forward, characterizes the nature and origins of our current "dominator" social context, and indicates how it can repress, and limit, not only our social development, but also—recognizing the social shaping of human development—some of the vital qualities of the human brain and psyche that provide potential for progress and creativity. Relevant too are gender issues and suppression of the feminine, important both for social progress and men and women's fullest creative development. However, Eisler asserts, we humans have the power to recreate society ourselves, consciously, deliberately, and humanely. For the future, Eisler shows natural roles for consciousness, creativity, and caring, in a more heterarchical and "partnership" societal context that can be nurturing, sustainable, peaceful, and participatory. It can represent a new and vital step for human development and cultural evolution. And it can reclaim the power of love.

Part III provides conclusions and an integration and in the form of 12 potential benefits of living creatively, and ties the concerns of the book to those of the psychology of creativity and allied fields.

Overall, this book intends to challenge you, the reader—in a lively and engaging way—to look more broadly at our human creativity without, and more deeply at our creativity within, to discover new capacities and approaches to living, both individually and together, while unfolding our human and creative potential. In presenting this collection on everyday creativity, we the contributors hope you will find something here that stimulates your own new visions for humanity and our future, while helping make your own life lighter, richer, healthier, and more joyful and meaningful.

# REFERENCES

Adams-Price, C. E. (Ed.). (1998). *Creativity and successful aging: Theoretical and empirical approaches*. New York: Springer-Verlag.

Adler, L. P. (1995). *Centenarians: The bonus years*. Santa Fe, NM: Health Press.

Albert, R. S., & Runco, M. A. (1986). The achievement of eminence. In R. J. Sternberg & J. E. Davidson (Eds.), *Conceptions of giftedness* (pp. 332–357). New York: Cambridge University Press.

Amabile, T. M. (1996). *Creativity in context*. New York: Westview Press.

Arieti, S. (1976). *Creativity: The magic synthesis*. New York: Basic Books.

Arons, M., & Richards, R. (2003). Two noble insurgencies. Creativity and humanistic psychology. In K. J. Schneider, J. F. T. Bugental, & J. F. Pierson (Eds.), *The handbook of humanistic psychology: Leading edges in theory, research, and practice* (pp. 127–142). Thousand Oaks, CA: Sage.

Badiner, A. H. (Ed.). (1990). *Dharma gaia: A harvest of essays in Buddhism and ecology*. Berkeley: Parallax Press.

Barron, F. (1969). *Creative person and creative process*. New York: Holt, Rinehart & Winston.

Barron, F. (1995). *No rootless flower: An ecology of creativity*. Cresskill, NJ: Hampton Press.

Barron, F., & Harrington, D. (1981). Creativity, intelligence, and personality. *Annual Review of Psychology, 32*, 439–476.

Beghetto, R. A., & Kaufman, J. C. (in press). Toward a broader conception of creativity: A case for "mini-c" creativity. *Psychology of Aesthetics, Creativity, and the Arts*.

Carter, J. (2001). *Living faith*. New York: Three Rivers Press.

Clark, H. (2002). Prime minister's statement to parliament. Retrieved February 11, 2005, from http://www.executive.govt.nz/minister/clark/innovate/speech.htm

Costa, P. T., & Widiger, T. A. (1994). *Personality disorders and the five-factor model of personality*. Washington, DC: American Psychological Association.

Cropley, A. J. (1990). Creativity and mental health in everyday life. *Creativity Research Journal, 3*, 167–178.

Csikszentmihalyi, M. (1988). Society, culture, and person: A systems view of creativity. In R. J. Sternberg, (Ed.), *The nature of creativity* (pp. 325–339). New York: Cambridge University Press.

Csikszentmihalyi, M. (1990). *Flow: The psychology of optimal experience*. New York: HarperPerennial.

Csikszentmihalyi, M. (1996). *Creativity: Flow and the psychology of discovery and invention*. New York: HarperCollins.

Dalai Lama (1999). *Ethics for a new millennium*. New York: Riverhead Books.

Darwin, C. (1871). *The descent of man*. Princeton: Princeton University Press.

Dewey, J. (1980). *Art as experience*. New York: Perigree Books. (Original work published 1934)

Dobzhansky, T. (1962). *Mankind evolving*. New Haven, CT: Yale University Press.

Dudek, S., & Verrault, R. (1989). The creative thinking and ego functioning of children. *Creativity Research Journal, 2*, 64–86.

Feinstein, D., & Krippner, S. (1997). *The mythic path*. New York: Tarcher.

Flach, F. (1990). Disorders of the pathways involved in the creative process. *Creativity Research Journal, 3*, 158–165.

Florida, R. (2002). *Rise of the creative class*. New York: Basic Books.

Florida, R. (2005). *Flight of the creative class*. New York: HarperBusiness.

Franck, F. (1993). *Zen seeing, Zen drawing: Meditation in action*. New York: Bantam Books.

Goertzel, V., & Goertzel, M. (1962). *Cradles of eminence*. Boston: Little, Brown.

Gruber, H., & Davis, S. N. (1988). Inching our way up Mount Olympus: The evolving-systems approach to creative thinking. In R. J. Sternberg (Ed.), *The nature of creativity* (pp. 243–270). New York: Cambridge University Press.

Gruber, H., & Wallace, D. B. (Eds.). (1993). Special issue: Creativity in the Moral Domain. *Creativity Research Journal, 6* (1&2).

Guilford, J. P. (1950). Creativity. *American Psychologist, 5*, 444–454.

Guilford, J. P. (1967). *The nature of human intelligence*. New York: McGraw-Hill.

Helson, R. (1971). Women mathematicians and the creative personality. *Journal of Consulting and Clinical Psychology, 36*, 210–220.

Helson, R. (1999). Institute of Personality Assessment and Research. In M. A. Runco & S. R. Pritzker (Eds.), *Encyclopedia of Creativity* (Vol. 2, pp. 71–79). San Diego, CA: Academic Press.

Helson, R., Roberts, B. W., & Agronick, G. S. (1995). Enduringness and change in the creative personality and the prediction of occupational creativity. *Journal of Personality and Social Psychology, 69*, 1173–1181.

Jamison, K. R. (1993). *Touched with fire: Manic-depressive illness and the artistic temperament*. New York: Free Press.

Kinney, D., Richards, R., & Southam, M. (in press). Everyday creativity, its assessment, and The Lifetime Creativity Scales. In M. A. Runco (Ed.), *Handbook of creativity*. Cresskill, NJ: Hampton Press.

Lepore, S. J., & Smyth, J. M. (Eds.). (2002). *The writing cure: How expressive writing promotes health and emotional well-being*. Washington, DC: American Psychological Association.

Levine, S. K., & Levine, E. G. (Eds.). (1999). *Foundations of expressive arts therapy: Theoretical and clinical perspectives*. London: Jessica Kingsley.

Loori, J. D. (2004). *The Zen of creativity: Cultivating your artistic life*. New York: Ballantine Books.

Ludwig, A. (1995). *The price of greatness*. New York: Guilford Press.

Maslow, A. (1968). *Toward a psychology of being*. New York: Van Nostrand.

Maslow, A. (1971). *The farther reaches of human nature*. New York: Penguin.

Mezirow, J. (1991). *Transformative dimensions of adult learning*. San Francisco: Jossey-Bass.

Miller, M. E., & Cook-Greuter, S. R. (Eds.). (2000). *Creativity, spirituality, and transcendence*. Stamford, CT: Ablex Publishing.

Minh Duc, T. (2000). Dam Luu: An eminent Vietnamese Buddhist nun. In K. L. Tsomo (Ed.), *Innovative Buddhist women: Swimming against the stream* (pp. 104–120). Richmond, Surrey, England: Curzon Press.

Montuori, A., & Purser, R. E. (1996). Context and creativity: Beyond social determinism and the isolated genius. *Journal of Humanistic Psychology, 36*(2), 34–43.

Montuori, A., & Purser, R. E. (Eds.). (1999). *Social creativity* (Vol. 1). Cresskill, NJ: Hampton Press.

Morrison, D., & Morrison, S. L. (2006). *Memories of loss and dreams of perfection: Unsuccessful childhood grieving and adult creativity*. Amityville, NY: Baywood Publishing.

Nachmanovitch, S. (1990). *Free play: Improvisation in life and art*. New York: Tarcher.

Nhat Hanh, T. (1992). *Touching peace: Practicing the art of mindful living*. Berkeley, CA: Parallax Press.

Naisbitt, J., & Aburdene, P. (1990). *Megatrends 2000*. New York: Avon Books.

Pennebaker, J. W. (Ed.). (1995). *Emotion, disclosure, and health*. Washington, DC: American Psychological Association.

Pennebaker, J. W., Kiecolt-Glaser, J. K., & Glaser, R. (1988). Disclosure of trauma and immune function: Health implications for psychotherapy. *Journal of Consulting and Clinical Psychology, 56*, 239–245.

Peterson, C. (2006). *A primer in positive psychology*. New York: Oxford University Press.

Ray, P. H., & Anderson, S. R. (2000). *The cultural creatives: How 50 million people are changing the world*. New York: Three Rivers Press.

Rhodes, C. (1990). Growth from deficiency creativity to being creativity. *Creativity Research Journal, 3*, 287–289.

Richards, R. (1981). Relationships between creativity and psychopathology: An evaluation and interpretation of the evidence. *Genetic Psychology Monographs, 103*, 261–324.

Richards, R. (1990). Everyday creativity, eminent creativity, and health. *Creativity Research Journal, 3*, 300–326.

Richards, R. (1996). Does the lone genius ride again? Chaos, creativity, and community. *Journal of Humanistic Psychology, 36*(2), 44–60.

Richards, R. (1998). Everyday creativity. In H. S. Friedman (Ed.), *The Encyclopedia of Mental Health* (Vol. 1, pp. 619–633). San Diego, CA: Academic Press.

Richards, R. (1999). Four Ps of creativity. In M. A. Runco & S. R. Pritzker (Eds.), *Encyclopedia of creativity* (Vol. 1, pp. 733–742). San Diego, CA: Academic Press.

Richards, R. (2001). A new aesthetic for environmental awareness: Chaos theory, the natural world, and our broader humanistic identity. *Journal of Humanistic Psychology, 41*(2), 59–95.

Richards, R. (2004, March). *The arts and self-expression in mental health.* Invited presentation, at the Carter Presidential Center as part of the Conversation Series, Atlanta, GA.

Richards, R. (2006). Frank Barron and the study of creativity: A voice that lives on. *Journal of Humanistic Psychology, 46*, 352–370.

Richards, R. (in press). Everyday creativity and the arts. *World Futures.*

Richards, R., Kinney, D., Benet, M., & Merzel, A. (1988). Assessing everyday creativity: Characteristics of the Lifetime Creativity Scales and validation with three large samples. *Journal of Personality and Social Psychology, 54*, 476–485.

Rogers, C. (1961). *On becoming a person.* Boston: Houghton Mifflin.

Rogers, N. (1993). *The creative connection: Expressive arts as healing.* Palo Alto, CA: Science & Behavior Books.

Rothberg, D. (2006). *The engaged spiritual life.* Boston: Beacon Press.

Rothenberg, A. (1990). Creativity, mental health, and alcoholism. *Creativity Research Journal, 3*, 179–201.

Runco, M. A. (1996). Personal creativity: Definition and developmental issues. *New Directions for Child Development, 72*, 3–30.

Runco, M. A. (1999). Appendix II: Tests of Creativity. In M. A. Runco & S. R. Pritzker (Eds.), *Encyclopedia of creativity* (Vol. 1, pp. 755–760). San Diego, CA: Academic Press.

Runco, M. A., & Pritzker, S. R. (1999). *Encyclopedia of creativity* (Vols. 1 & 2). San Diego, CA: Academic Press.

Runco, M. A., & Richards, R. (Eds.). (1998). *Eminent creativity, everyday creativity, and health.* Greenwich, CT: Ablex Publishing.

Russ. S. (1993). *Affect and creativity: The role of affect and play in the creative process.* Hillsdale, NJ: Erlbaum.

Scales, B., Almy, M. C., Nicolopoulou, A., & Ervin-Tripp, S. (1991). *Play and the social context of development in early care and education.* New York: Teachers College Press.

Schneider, K. J. (2004). *Rediscovery of awe.* St. Paul, MN: Paragon House.

Schlitz, M., Amorok, T., & Micozzi, M. S. (Eds.). (2005). *Consciousness and healing: Integral approaches to mind-body medicine.* St. Louis, MO: Elsevier.

Scholl, S. (Ed.). (1995). *Common era: Best new writings on religion* (Vol. 1). Ashland, OR: White Cloud Press.

Search for talent, the (2006, 7–13 October). *The Economist,* p. 11.

Shansis, F., Fleck, M., Richards, R., Kinney, D., Izquierdo, I., Mattevi, B., et al. (2003). Desenvolvimento da versao para o Portugues das Escalas de Criatividade ao Longo da Vida (ECLV) [Development of the Portuguese language version of The Lifetime Creativity Scales]. *Revista de Psiquiatria do Rio Grande do Sul, 25*(2), 284–296.

Simonton, D. K. (1990). Political pathology and social creativity. *Creativity Research Journal, 3,* 85–99.

Singer, D. S., Golinkoff, R. M., & Hirsh-Pasek, K. (Eds.). (2006). *Play = learning: How play motivates and enhances children's cognitive and social-emotional growth.* New York: Oxford University Press.

Singer, J. (2006). *Imagery in psychotherapy.* Washington, DC: American Psychological Association.

Smith, G. J. W., & van der Meer, G. (1990). Creativity in old age. *Creativity Research Journal, 3,* 249–264.

Sternberg, R., Grigorenko, E., & Singer, J. (2004). *Creativity: From potential to realization.* Washington, DC: American Psychological Association.

Storr, A. (1988). *Solitude: A return to the self.* New York: Ballantine Books.

Tarthang Tulku. (1991). *Skillful means: Patterns for success* (2nd ed.). Berkeley, CA: Dharma Publishing.

Taylor, E., & Martin, F. (2001). Humanistic psychology at the crossroads. In K. Schneider, J. F. T. Bugental, & J. F. Pierson (Eds.), *The handbook of humanistic psychology: Leading edges in theory, research, and practice* (pp. 21–27). Thousand Oaks, CA: Sage.

Torrance, E. P. (1962). *Guiding creative talent.* Englewood Cliffs, NJ: Prentice Hall.

Torrance, E. P. (1988). The nature of creativity as manifest in its testing. In R. J. Sternberg (Ed.), *The nature of creativity* (pp. 43–75). New York: Cambridge University Press.

Van Hoorn, J., Nourot, P., Scales, B., & Alward, K. (1993). *Play at the center of the curriculum.* New York: Macmillan.

Whitmyer, C. (1994). *Mindfulness and meaningful work: Explorations in right livelihood.* Berkeley, CA: Parallax Press.

Wiseman, A. S. (1986). *Nightmare help: A guide for adults from children.* Berkeley, CA: Ten Speed Press.

Zausner, T. (2007). *When walls become doorways: Creativity and the transforming illness.* New York: Harmony Books.

# I
## CREATIVITY AND OUR INDIVIDUAL LIVES

# 1

# EVERYDAY CREATIVITY: OUR HIDDEN POTENTIAL

## RUTH RICHARDS

What (the creator) feels ... is joy, joy defined as the emotion that goes with heightened consciousness, the mood that accompanies the experience of actualizing one's own potentialities.

—Rollo May

Our everyday creativity is not only good for us but also one of the most powerful capacities we have, bringing us alive in each moment, affecting our health and well-being, offering richness and alternatives in what we do, and helping us move further in our creative and personal development. We may nonetheless resist our own creativity and, even at times without knowing it, resist or suppress the creativity of others as well. How and why does this happen? What precisely are we giving up? If we are more consciously aware of what we are losing, might we respond differently?

First, *everyday creativity* is not what many people expect from the word *creativity*. To them, creativity is about arts, or maybe sciences, or at least about special fields of endeavor. Sometimes it is about special people as well, such as famous artists, best-selling novelists, or groundbreaking scientists (Richards, Kinney, Benet, & Merzel, 1988). Such creativity is not primarily about us.

Indeed, everyday creativity is about everyone, throughout our lives; it is fundamental to our survival. It is how we find a lost child, get enough to eat, and make our way in a new place and culture. It is not so much what we do as how we do it, whether this is at work or at leisure. With our everyday creativity, we adapt flexibly, we improvise, and we try different options, whether we are raising our child, counseling a friend, fixing our home, or planning a fundraising event. Our "originality of everyday life" as is manifested in new *products*—including concrete creative outcomes, behaviors, or ideas—need only involve two criteria, after Frank Barron (1969): originality and meaningfulness to others. In this chapter, we also address the other three "Ps" of creativity originally described by Mooney (see Richards, 1999c)—the *process* and *person* aspects, as well as the *press* of the environment. The person and process aspects, in particular, incorporate features of who we are and how we approach our days that facilitate this "originality of everyday life."

If most people know intuitively what their everyday creativity is—and my colleagues and I have found this to be so, in teaching creativity classes, once the spotlight is turned on these activities—then why does our creativity not get more attention? Are we just so accustomed to it that our everyday creativity provides a backdrop whose presence is assumed and then quickly forgotten?

This chapter suggests there is even more to it. Our everyday creativity may often be overlooked—either consciously or unconsciously, for a purpose. One may talk about the three "U's": Our creativity is often underrecognized, underdeveloped, and underrewarded, in schools, at work, and at home. Why is it, after all, that in so many schools students are trying to get 100% on someone else's test and not making up more questions of their own? Why, at work, aren't we always greeted with big smiles when we knock on the boss's door and suggest a more efficient way of doing something? Why, at home, may hapless parents—including parents who try to encourage creativity—be bowled over by sudden spurts of incorrigible and insistent originality, all too often at the worst time?

In this chapter, we look first at some background on the nature of everyday creativity, including reasons why some of its health benefits may not be well known. Next we consider obstacles which can get in the way of our creative impulses and expression, including both conscious and unconscious factors within ourselves and out in the world, individually and together. Here, the discussion includes one unconventional example of creative discovery, intended to challenge one's open-mindedness, while raising experientially the issue of these outside obstacles to innovation. Next, the chapter considers the benefits of everyday creativity that we may forfeit if we are too readily deterred, including advantages for our physical and psychological health, our well-being, and the ability to appreciate the creativity of others.

## IF THIS CREATIVITY IS SO HEALTHY, WHY DON'T WE KNOW MORE ABOUT IT?

If everyday creativity is so positive and good for us, and even woven throughout our lives, why we do we not hear more about it? Why is this creativity in some ways our "hidden potential"? The situation may seem puzzling. Next I present a little background on the sources of everyday creativity as well as issues that arose as Dennis Kinney and I, along with colleagues Maria Benet and Ann Merzel, at Harvard Medical School and McLean Hospital, first began to study it.

First, everyday creativity should not be seen as a new idea. It is, for one, a fundamental survival capability. How, then, can it be forgotten? Our creativity can help us find something to eat when starving, talk our way out of a life-threatening situation, or perhaps, as a child, deal with a scary monster (Kinney, Richards, & Southam, in press; Richards, Kinney, Benet, et al., 1988; Richards, 1999d).

Everyday creativity, by one name or another, can be linked back to John Dewey's (1934) writings about innovative education and aesthetic appreciation, and is also consistent with the "phenotypic plasticity" noted by evolutionary biologists such as Theodosius Dobzhansky (1962), regarding the wide and flexible range of our human manifestations within our genetic potential. At its higher levels, everyday creativity can be related to the quality described by Abraham Maslow (1968) as "self-actualizing" (SA) creativity, distinct from "special talent" creativity. Echoing Rollo May's (1975) quote that opened this chapter, Maslow (1968) said that, with SA creativity, we are motivated to actualize our potentials and talents, "toward fuller knowledge of and acceptance of (our) own intrinsic nature" (p. 25; see also Arons & Richards, 2001). Maslow (1968) found that SA creativity "sprang much more directly from the personality and . . . showed itself widely in the ordinary affairs of life. . . . like a tendency to do *anything* creatively: e.g., housekeeping, teaching, etc." (p. 137). It operates beyond survival and "deficiency" needs, moving us toward realizing our higher human potential, and even forwarding our ongoing development.

This point is crucial, because we are no longer talking about a single creative feat, skill, or one good new idea, but, rather, about major life alterations that can catapult us to a new developmental level with, perhaps, unknown potentials we only now suspect. Can practicing our creativity possibly be so powerful? It is a question one should take seriously. In his interviews, Maslow (1971) found that self-actualizing people seemed happier, more fulfilled and at peace, not grasping, worried, striving, and were "motivated in other higher ways" (p. 289). They could focus on larger endeavors, and on what Maslow called "being values," such as *truth, goodness, beauty, justice*, or *aliveness* (as process). In their work, these creators showed devotion to a calling, task, or vocation, all of which benefit others and embody such "being values."

If it can bring not only innovation, but happiness and self-development, why, then, is this creative capacity not more celebrated? There seems to be a story here. First, the term *creativity* is often applied largely to the arts (Richards, in press), which is, in fact, how I got involved in this area myself. Yet, the arts tend to be marginalized in our scientific society, especially in our public schools. Engaging in the arts is viewed by some people as a leisure activity that is not terribly significant on a larger scale (unless it involves a famous person), a bit of dabbling, perhaps in paint. If one wants more serious art, it is implied, one should go to a museum. Meanwhile, the rest of one's real-life originality, or what we call everyday creativity, may not even be recognized as such, or named, and, thus, may not only remain underdeveloped but be forgotten.

In other cases, the term *creativity* may carry negative implications. It is ironic that work I have done with Dennis Kinney and colleagues at McLean Hospital and Harvard Medical School (Richards, 1997; Richards, Kinney, Lunde, & Benet, 1988) has been cited to support this negativity, although we, the researchers, think it is quite the opposite. We investigated the possibility that everyday creativity might carry a "compensatory advantage" linked to a personal or family history of bipolar "spectrum" mood disorders—prevalent and painful disorders which run in families. Such a compensatory role for creativity may actually be quite positive, a resource for resilience and coping—and sometimes for a broader giving back to society—and, thus, acting in the service of health. Could such a "compensatory advantage" even help, we researchers asked, to explain the persistence of these painful mood disorders down through the generations?

The complex details of this research will not be explored further here, except to say that we did find—in rigorous research that controlled for rater bias and other sources of error—a "compensatory advantage" for everyday creativity. It is of interest that this was part of a curvilinear relationship, as we researchers expected, and not related to the most serious mood disorders. Our various findings were linked to others' work (see edited volume, Runco & Richards, 1998). The everyday creativity picture was also healthier than that widely reported for "eminent creativity." We later found much milder but compelling suggestions of a possible "compensatory advantage" related to schizophrenic symptomatology as well, an area which deserves further study (Kinney et al., 2000–2001).

Earlier work by other investigators focused largely on eminent, or socially recognized, creators in specific fields such as visual arts or fiction writing. This is a different research question. For the research in the present chapter, we researchers needed to develop and validate a new measure, the

Lifetime Creativity Scales (LCS; Richards, Kinney, Benet, et al., 1988). This involved developing rating scales based on interview data about real-life creative accomplishments at work and leisure—information we needed even to be able to ask our research questions. It is interesting to note that this measure and our mental health applications actually ended up featured in *The New York Times* Tuesday "Science Times" section (Goleman, 1988).

In using the LCS, we were interested in a variety of people, chosen only for either having or being related to someone with a mood disorder. Their "originality of everyday life" was of interest to us, no matter in which way it happened to emerge. This posed an assessment challenge. We had to be there to see it, or we would miss the patterns of interest, for example, within families. We used only two criteria, originality and meaningfulness (Richards, Kinney, Benet, et al., 1988), although we included accomplishments ranging from the fully unique to those that were relatively unusual in a particular setting. We did not look at what Runco (1996; chap. 4, this volume) calls "personal creativity" or which Beghetto and Kaufman (in press) call "mini-c" creativity, regarding accomplishments new primarily to the person (See also Richards [1981], on issues of defining creativity).

To our great surprise, we discovered something about ourselves. Over literally years of working with the LCS, our eyes were opened. At the start, we thought we knew what everyday creativity was, but in some cases, we had not even begun to see it. This was despite our good intentions, hard work, and supposed open-mindedness. New possibilities were often revealed for the first time in multirater trials to establish interrater reliability, and resulted in extensive discussions. We ended up crediting research participants whose ingenuity might have been less visible previously. These included a single mother who made many clothes on a tight budget, a father who modified a special wheelchair for his disabled child, an amateur archaeologist who made special finds on his digs, or an unusual auto mechanic who created his own tools. We even held seminars on special topics, for instance, on the circumstances of World War II resistance fighters who bravely and ingeniously brought endangered persons to safety.

Among other things, this work brought us new insights into two phenomena. First was the difficulty of honoring an area of human functioning (here, everyday creativity) before it has been clearly identified and named. I have had many happy and, sometimes, ecstatic college students in creativity courses, after they have finally (and seemingly all at once) realized how truly original and innovative they had been for a long time—for example, in raising a child, renovating a home, or resolving conflicts at the office. This discovery was really a moment of insight in the process of raising consciousness.

Second, we also gained new insight into the origins of some negative attributions about creativity. Certain people, we found, at a deep and unquestioning level, link together "creativity and madness" (Becker, 1978). They are concerned that creativity, by its nature, may cause or reflect severe mental disturbance; they may sometimes actually worry about the status of people they know who are also highly creative (or perhaps about themselves).

What else, some people wonder, might secretly be wrong with these creators? They may not even consider that the appearance of creativity can be positive and helpful. Problems go with problems, they unconsciously assume. In view of how many people have a mood disorder running in their family or who have experienced a mood disorder themselves, it behooves researchers to look more carefully at the evidence (e.g., Runco & Richards, 1998). Beyond this, some people are not aware that the phenomenon of "mood disorders and creativity" in all its complexity, is just one pattern among many, that—and this is basic—there are "many roads to creativity" (Richards, 1981, 1997). Finally, it is worth noting that negative views of the effects of creativity could not be further from the patterns Abraham Maslow (1968) reported for his self-actualizing creative people.

We submit that some seemingly discrepant results for health and illness all fit together nicely, as shown elsewhere (see Richards, 1981, 1997, 2000–2001; Richards & Kinney, 1990; Runco & Richards, 1998; Schuldberg, 1994), where creativity generally plays a more positive role toward resilient coping; this will be readdressed shortly. In the meantime, let us be aware of this important tendency that can turn certain people away from creativity: a sweeping (and usually inaccurate) tendency to pathologize it.

## IDENTIFYING MAJOR OBSTACLES TO OUR CREATIVITY

This section goes further to consider types of both inner and outer obstacles to our everyday creativity, as found within ourselves or as imposed on us by other people or cultures. Examples of each type are given subsequently. Some are more commonly known than others. They tend to concern two of the four "Ps," the creative person and the process.

### Inner Obstacles

Here, three examples are considered—situations in which one can "get in one's own way" when creating.

### Example 1. Writer's Block

In this common example, we are working late writing a paper but when our mind suddenly goes blank. We worry if what we are doing is right. Most of us have had "writer's block" at one time or another. This particular example is not about intellectual obstacles such as perceptual or functional cognitive blocks or habits (Dodds & Smith, 1999), but rather the emotional and psychological agony that strikes us when our mind feels paralyzed or blank. There can be many causes (Davis, 1999), but a common scenario, and final common pathway for varied causes, involves the appearance our ever-present critic, disrupting our creative state of mind. "That is not good enough!" says the critic. Another piece of crumpled paper gets thrown in the basket.

### Example 2. Keep It Buried/Pandora's Box

Consider some specific reasons we may stop, or feel stopped from, creating, for instance, when there is something we do not want to see or know. We need to "keep it away" from us. It is below consciousness— perhaps it is fear, depression, anger, anxiety, or doubt—and we are defending against recognizing this material (Barron, 1969; Pennebaker, 1995). Some people may even start fearing for their mental health. Then suddenly we decide we will do it, and take that creative risk anyway, altering our mental state, diffusing our attention, and saying in theory "let's see it." We are asking a vague uneasiness to show itself, perhaps in a frightening (or magnificent) form. It is a risk, because there is no control, and it can be difficult. Yet, one can also learn to find affective pleasure in the challenge (Richards, 1997, Russ, 1999).

Oddly enough, the forbidden thought, when recognized and understood, can often be a special part of our creative palette. And it may not be that different from our neighbor's censored thought either—we are, after all, human. Here is a rich Pandora's box of our mind: our worst fears, the Jungian Shadow, and the other restricted contents within. Are we afraid perhaps for our egos (and a challenge to our fixed views of self)? Are there ways we must change in perspective if we are to comfortably be more open within ourselves?

### Example 3. Pathologizing Creativity

As presented earlier, do we sometimes fear that creativity is in itself "abnormal" and potentially dangerous? Will we become weird and crazy from being creative? Why are "geniuses" sometimes suspected of being bizarre, even when they appear normal, or out of touch with the usual customs and manners of mainstream society? Consider the stereotype some people have of the "mad" scientist with wild hair, or the absent-minded professor, who stumbles into a wall.

One important possibility is that this is not solely about "them," but a bit about "us," our own fear of our less than conscious selves, of seeing what is not unconscious in our own minds, and which may rise to the surface, creating anxiety, as Freud said. There is also the related issue of not being in control (Richards, 1997, in press; Runco & Richards, 1997; Schuldberg, 1994).

It is also possible, eventually, to become comfortable with this process. Consider the following examples:

- There is a long tradition of research supporting the relationship between eminent or exceptional creativity, particularly in the arts, and mood disorders in families as well as individuals (Jamison, 1993; Ludwig, 1995; Runco & Richards, 1997). This has received much popular attention, compared with the research on everyday creativity. Artists, writers, and other creative individuals are the usual focus, chosen for their exceptional and celebrated creativity, placing them far from the average creator, or patient, to begin with.

- It is important to reemphasize that the status of creator as patient tells us nothing about the positive or negative value of the creativity to this creator. First, however ill they were, at worst, the highest creativity was most often reported, for eminent and everyday creators alike, during milder and more functional mood states, particularly mild mood elevations (Jamison, 1989; Jamison, Gerner, Hammen, & Padesky, 1980; Richards & Kinney, 1990). This fits with the ability to access rich mental material while adapting it to real-world needs (Runco & Richards, 1997). Also, a critical point is that we do not know how these artists and writers would have done without their creative outlet. Things might well have been more difficult. There is more than one possible pattern; a five-part typology giving possible direct and indirect relations between creativity and mental health problems is useful here (Richards, 1981, 1999e). One can even talk about "occupational drift" such that artistic creators, for example, locate job situations that will tolerate and allow their unusual ways of functioning (Kinney et al., in press; Richards, 1981).

- Research on everyday creativity, as already mentioned, supports a curvilinear relationship between creativity and diagnosis of bipolar mood disorders. This is consistent with a "compensatory advantage," in which the highest creativity appears with relatively milder overall dysfunction or, surprisingly, even none at all, for normal relatives carrying family risk factors (Richards, 1997; Richards, Kinney, Lunde, et al., 1988). This complex subject cannot be further developed here; but one may suggest that some milder and often manageable features of dysfunction may (under the right conditions) start a creative ball rolling, which can subsequently, and perhaps paradoxically, bring unusual advantages for resilient creative coping and health (Runco & Richards, 1997). Yet, unfortunately, even when the real message is about health, some people just remember the part about illness.

- Highly creative writers who were studied at the University of California, Berkeley Institute of Personality and Research, scored in the top 15% of every psychopathology scale on the (Minnesota Multiphasic Personality Inventory ([MMPI]; Barron, 1969). This was not because they manifested all, or even any, of the diagnoses corresponding to the MMPI scale categories. These same creative writers also scored unusually high on ego strength, defined in terms of the healthy trait of adapting to reality (Barron, 1969, 1995). This is a striking anomaly; the ego strength measure usually correlates negatively with the psychopathology scales. This suggests that the writers were open to, and could sample from, their less conscious depths for their own practical purposes, and could pull it all together. They were masters of the unknown, and did not fear Pandora's box. As creativity researcher Barron (1969) said,

> It appears that creative individuals have a remarkable affinity for what in most of us is unconscious and preconscious . . . to find hints of emerging form in the developmentally more primitive and less reasonable structured aspects of his own mental functioning. (p. 88)

Barron (1963) also concluded, in one of his more famous quotes, that "the creative person is both more primitive and more cultivated, more destructive and more constructive, occasionally crazier and yet adamantly saner, than the average person" (p. 234).

We thus need to ask if we are projecting our own fears on our stereotype of an "eccentric" or "bizarre" creative person, a creative person who, per Barron (1968), may in some ways actually be healthier than the average individual. Meanwhile, in avoiding the unspoken fears of our less rational self, we may well be blunting our own creativity and, ironically, a road to health. In looking within our own minds, we could open up a lot of difficult unconscious material. Yet doing this creatively, and then transforming it, could bring insight and healing and, in the long run, a greater internal wholeness, and peace.

## Outer Obstacles

Now we turn to the last of the four "Ps," the press of the environment for or against creativity. The true creator can at times be seen as a threat—

an agent of change, a provocateur, even a troublemaker. An example is the employee who wants to reorganize the office, or change a report's focus. "We don't have time for this right now," says the disconcerted manager.

Another example deserves further thought: A child with a good idea—a really good idea—who finds that adults do not have time to hear it. The child brings it up again and again, but cannot get through to adults. "Who has time?" think the hassled parents—parents who will, if someone asks them, say they value creativity. There is a delicate balance here, because stimulating creativity is not about unchecked freedom either, and this is often a hard call.

Studies by researchers such as Westby and Dawson (1995), or Getzels and Jackson (1962), show that some teachers too—teachers who think they are honoring their students' creativity—do not always follow through. These kids may be difficult, and who has time, anyway, in an overcrowded classroom?

*Example 1. Do Teachers Really Want Creative Students?*

There are many ways to squelch creativity (e.g., Davis, 1999). Research suggests some adults do not even recognize the creative person—in this case, who the more creative kids are. Not to say they are pathologizing them, but it is a factor worth considering. Westby and Dawson (1995), for example, developed a research-based list of traits typical of "more creative" versus "less creative" kids. Among others, less creative children were found to be sincere, appreciative, responsible, and reliable. The more creative children made up rules as they went along, were more emotional, impulsive, and nonconforming. The researchers then presented the list to teachers and asked them to indicate which traits they considered to be typical of more rather than less creative children.

Among the most notable discrepancies, teachers believed features of less creative children to be more strongly linked with creativity than those which were related to more creative children. In fact the opposite is the case. "Emotional" and "nonconforming" are more apt to be identified with higher creativity in the research literature than "sincere" and "reliable." Of course, there is nothing wrong with being sincere and reliable. However, traits more typical of creative kids, such as being impulsive and making up the rules, are not always the easiest traits to deal with in a classroom. In fact, when teachers described features of their "favorite" student, these were in many ways opposite to the traits found in the creative student, both in this study and elsewhere (Getzels & Jackson, 1962). Here is, once again—and despite some adults' best intentions—evidence of negative reactions that may confront the more creative young person.

*Example 2. When Creativity is Suppressed by Conscious and Unconscious Group Forces*

Creative innovations can be more than just trouble, they can appear dangerous, especially to the status quo. Some surprising subcultural reactions may even be unconscious and self-organizing. We turn again to the "4th P," the press of the environment. One ominous example of the "muzzling of scientific diversity" is a true story, detailed in Howard Bloom's (2000) book, *Global Brain*. (See also chap. 7, this volume, on suppression of Darwin's full theory.)

The protagonist is Dr. Gilbert Ling, a biochemist, who found a viable alternative to the popular theory of the sodium pump for cell membrane transport. For a time, this ingenious new alternative theory had support and garnered interest and attention. Initially, Dr. Ling was acclaimed, offered a new job as head of his own lab, and began lecturing around the world. He was hailed by Nobel Laureate Albert Szent-Gyorgyi, as "one of the most inventive biochemists I have seen" (Bloom, 2000, p. 184).

The tide turned, however, and many scientists took exception to Dr. Ling's work. The Federation of American Societies for Experimental Biology planned a debate at the 1967 annual meeting, to be broadcast widely on closed-circuit television. Six proponents of the sodium pump were invited to take part. Not one person accepted the invitation, although all were invited a whole year ahead.

What followed was not a normal process of peer review, which is healthy and useful, with open discussion of strengths and problems, and which can conclude with the success of one theory over another. Instead, there was a subtle marginalizing of the scientist's work. What does it mean when a student feels pressure to exclude Dr. Ling's theory from his own reporting? One German graduate student performed an experiment supportive of Dr. Ling's theory, but was told by his superior that "in spite of his evidence, membrane pump theories were correct and Dr. Ling's had been disproved" (Bloom, 2000, p. 188). Consider, too, a graduate student at the University of Pennsylvania who was surprised when Dr. Ling's model came up only briefly and was then ignored in his biophysical chemistry class. He later spoke with the professor, who said nervously, "If I consider Dr. Ling, I'll hear repercussions, and my position is threatened. . . . I have a wife and children" (Bloom, 2000, p. 188). Such censure may seem hard to believe.

Dr. Ling protested and finally became part of a seven person committee formed by a Texas congressman to examine the "creativity smothering peer review processes used by government agencies" (Bloom, 2000, p. 188). He testified before Congress on various identified obstacles. Still, the story gets worse. Dr. Ling's funding was later cut and his resources and "subcultural" base, including his graduate students, began to dwindle. Nonetheless, Dr. Ling persisted with his work and continues today. If he is right, let us hope we will still discover it is so.

Yet, remember, it is not a question of whether a creative scientist is right or wrong. It is about whether the scientist encounters free interplay of ideas (and objective consideration of relevant research data) rather than blind suppression of minority views. How freely can one think? How fairly can the merits of one's position be tested? It is through open, critical, and creative dialogue that our individual mind, group mind, and culture, will learn and grow.

*Example 3. Attempt to Stop Suppression of Open Scientific Discourse*

Dr. Serge Lang was a mathematical theorist, and member of the National Academy of Sciences who had worked at Yale for many years but passed away in 2005. In addition to mathematics, Dr. Lang was known for his challenges to scientists who seemed sloppy or unscrupulous (Chang & Leary, 2005), and for his opposition to biased coverage of research. In 1998, Dr. Lang wrote a book called *Challenges*, which included the claim that he had "systematic evidence of suppression and manipulation of letters to the editors in some of the major scientific journals such as *Science, Nature, Chemical and Engineering News, The Lancet,* and *The New York Times*" (Coulter, n.d., ¶ 3). In this example, too, the issue remains whether we value and evaluate creative science on its own merits, or can be swayed, or biased, by other factors, perhaps at times unconsciously.

Dr. Lang later landed on the unpopular side of a controversy himself when he sided with a large group of skeptics who doubted AIDS was caused by the HIV virus. He wanted certain evidence to be considered. Yet even the *Daily Californian*, at the University of California, Berkeley, would not print an editorial that Dr. Lang wrote on the problem, so Dr. Lang ran it as an advertisement. He said it was a "sad state of affairs when universities (including Yale and UC) do not provide natural academic forums which would make advertisement in the *Daily Cal* unnecessary" (Lang, 1997, p. 12).

Was Dr. Lang mistaken? Was he right? Does it matter? How do we decide which creative voices should be heard? Do we, as a general practice, honor all voices based on the quality of the science involved, or lean at times toward situations in which we like what someone says? As mentioned, a subtle test of our own open-mindedness will come up a little later in this chapter.

The first step toward more open inquiry is conscious awareness, followed by group action if there is unfairness, with commitment to open discourse. The many social influences on what one calls creativity need to be recognized

(Bloom, 2000; Montuori & Purser, 1999). Such awareness, in a population, could help head off the dreadful distortions that unconscious "group mind" has been known to perpetrate throughout history, even leading to major abuses of human rights and freedom. In general, everyday creativity, with its attendant personal qualities of open, questioning awareness, nonconformity, and willingness to challenge the mainstream, can help. But remember that, even for the highly creative person, it is not always easy to do this.

## IF WE REJECT OR DEVALUE CREATIVITY, WHAT MAY WE FORFEIT?

Although creativity in others, or ourselves, is not always comfortable to live with, there are definite advantages to creative activity for our health, well-being, and the ability to appreciate creatively the innovations of others. Here are three examples of health benefits, one straightforward, one more unusual in creativity literature, and one which is intended to challenge us and our open-mindedness. (See also chap. 3, this volume.)

### Can Everyday Creativity Improve Our Health and Well-Being?

*Example 1. Expressive Writing*

There is particularly good research on the benefits of expressive writing for physical and psychological health, especially in the studies of Pennebaker (1995) and colleagues (Lepore & Smyth, 2002). In the usual design, college students were asked, on four different days, to write about something so traumatic that they had never told anyone about it. They were to focus on their deepest thoughts and feelings. Meanwhile a control group wrote about something more neutral, such as their shoes (Pennebaker, Kiecolt-Glaser, & Glaser, 1988).

The findings were remarkable. In one study, over 6 weeks, the first (expressive writing) group made fewer student health center visits, compared with the control group. Although the expressive writing subjects were initially more depressed, 3 months later, compared with the control students, they were significantly happier. Furthermore, comparing blood tests from the beginning of the study and then 6 weeks later, the expressive writing group showed evidence of a stronger immune response on measures of T-cell function compared with the control group. Within the expressive writing group, there were also relative benefits: Students who disclosed more, from beginning to follow-up, showed greater drops in systolic blood pressure and heart rate than did those who disclosed less.

It is notable that our bodies, our immune systems, can respond to our writing, to what we creatively do with our mind. However, many people in Western culture still adhere to a mind–body dichotomy dating back to

Descartes, and have trouble thinking that our mental activity could positively affect our bodies, never mind contribute to related advances in complementary and alternative, or mind–body medicine (Freeman & Lawlis, 2001). It does make sense that immune boosting could help us resist disease and even lengthen our lives. Research seems at minimum to suggest that creativity is related to successful aging and longevity (Adler, 1995; Langer, 1989; Smith & van der Meer, 1997). Here is when our creativity may finally be taken seriously in the future—if we have solid proof that it can help us to live longer.

Consider one of the participants with a history of early abuse (although one should note that recovery from such abuse usually takes much longer than this), who shared the effects of her writing experience. This example involves one's inner obstacles. She said at the study's follow-up, "Before when I thought about it, I'd lie to myself. . . . Now I don't feel like I even have to think about it because I got it off my chest. . . . I really know the truth" (p. 300).

Research on *working memory* and expressive writing (Klein, 2002) shows that when poorly organized and fragmented structures—which can be highly accessible, even intrusive—become more coherent and organized, working memory is freed. There is also improved problem solving, coping, and health. Looking more closely, Sundararajan and Richards (2005) showed that the pattern is more complex than the nostrum that "writing is good." Conscious, controlled, deliberate processing of emotions through writing is different from nonconscious processing called "emotionality." Although both can yield health improvements, the first also leads eventually to a lowered reactivity, along with improved cognitive function.

Let us also remember that some of us may not even have brought certain difficult experiences fully to consciousness until we process them creatively. With processing, we become more accepting and open to our experience. We can control our experience, at least symbolically, rather than vice versa. Finally, it is worth noting that repression, suppression, and over-conforming to group norms can pose health risks (e.g., Singer, 1990; Wickramasekera, 1998). Consider by contrast the consequences if we, as a culture, became more open, direct, accepting, in touch with nonconscious material, and did not pathologize others' "weirdness" quite so much. Might we find the healthy ideal to be, again, after Barron (1963): "The creative person is both more primitive and more cultivated, more destructive and more constructive, occasionally crazier and yet adamantly saner, than the average person" (p. 234).

*Example 2. Creating Mental Imagery for Physical Healing*

Here we look further at mind–body healing, in which creativity can again play a role. One's mental imagery is usually private, but this makes it no less everyday creative, at least if it is original and useful. As such, mental imagery can be useful in healing.

One's mental imagery involves more than just visualization. It is a thought process that invokes and uses the senses: seeing, hearing, touching, and so forth (Freeman & Lawlis, 2001). It is significant that when we imagine something, our brains can react just as if we were encountering the situation itself (see also chap. 3, this volume.) This potential provides us with real power. Among other things, imagery has been used to alter immune and cardiovascular function and enhance relaxation. Yet mainstream medicine has been resistant to such mind–body medicine benefits.

Images are a special language, and we can creatively use *attention* and *intention*, remarkably, to communicate within ourselves. Healing effects include increasing immune response and blood flow in an area of one's body. Finding one's own most meaningful images, and what they mean to us, can be particularly effective (Achterberg, 2002; Freeman & Lawlis, 2001; Rossman, 2000, 2003). We can learn to bridge from our conscious mind to other parts of our being. Carl Jung (in Rossman, 2003) felt imagery could bring us as close as anything to unconscious experience. These are creative capabilities indeed.

In one example of the use of guided imagery for healing, a group of cancer patients were asked to imagine a descent down a tunnel or staircase toward the "cancer presence" (Locke & Colligan, 1986). One patient found "that search led to increasingly smaller rooms and finally to a small cavelike chamber, where the search by the light of the crystal illuminated a small worm, the cancer, which burned with a mysterious fire" (Locke & Colligan [1986], p. 156). He then worked to put out that fire.

We do not know the outcome for this particular man, although some participants in this group did well. One researcher wondered if specific images were really central, or whether it was merely the fact that the "cancer patients were doing something" (Locke & Colligan [1986], p. 158). Whatever the case may be, there is a growing literature on consciousness and healing (Dossey, 1999; Schlitz, Amorok, & Micozzi, 2005) to consider.

It is also important to note that, while the use of imagery may "cure" at times, at other times it may "heal," that is, restore "the client's physical, mental, emotional, or spiritual capacities, as contrasted with . . . surmounting a disease" (Krippner & Achterberg, 2000, p. 359). Indeed, it is important not to "blame the victim" if someone does not recover. People get sick for many reasons, and some illnesses may be more modifiable than others. The use of imagery is important if it can improve one's odds while bringing new comfort, wholeness, meaning, and peace; it is a positive use of one's creative mind.

Still, it seems significant that certain cancer patients "who lived longer than expected" appeared to be, overall, more creative, and flexible, with greater psychological strength, and could even be something of a nuisance at times to those who were treating them (Krippner & Achterberg, 2000). Such survivors have appeared both more assertive and more flexible (Rossman, 2003). The combination is the key; they knew both when to agitate and when to go with the flow.

It seems worth wondering—and also studying—what life would be like if people were more consciously aware and able to influence various mental states, images, expectations as well as related beliefs—and indeed inner stories that can shape our existence (Feinstein & Krippner, 1997). What if we were better able to modulate such activity, so that it clearly and truly affected our health? Surely, then, our everyday creativity would be taken more seriously.

*Example 3. Pushing the Borders of the Known: Healing at a Distance*

How open-minded are we? Remember the story of Dr. Ling from earlier in this chapter. Now, consider a treatment in which a healer in one place is said to affect someone's health status in a different location. Even with knowledge of the new physics and the "quantum mechanical wave function" stretching to infinity many are loathe to think people could actually, with their creative minds, have an effect on someone far away and a healthy effect at that. It seems worth giving this possibility an open-minded try. Such thinking was not a problem for Einstein, who made the following statement:

> A human being is part of the whole . . . a part limited in time and space. He experiences his thoughts and feelings as something separate from the rest—a kind of optical delusion of his consciousness. This delusion is a kind of prison for us." (Dossey, 2001, p. 15)

If healing at a distance has validity, it will require a paradigm shift for psychology and the healing arts, and some modifications to our mainstream models of reality. To be sure, meta-analyses of distance-healing research show effects to be highly significant (Schlitz & Braud, 1997). Yet, some people wonder if ordinary factors were not missed that explain findings in more conventional ways—or if only the positive (and not negative or nonsignificant) studies were reported. There are disbelievers who will persist in rejecting these findings no matter what. Yet, mainstream interest is growing. The American Psychological Association published an edited book titled *Varieties of Anomalous Experience* (Cardeña, Lynn, & Krippner, 2000), which included anomalous healing, and provided an excellent model of critical thinking.

It is notable that one respected research team in Hawaii (Achterberg et al., 2005) has shown brain changes in functional magnetic resonance imaging (fMRI) during distance healing, using experienced healer–client pairs, separated and shielded fully from each other. There were both healing "on" periods and "off" periods and the schedule was unknown beforehand to the participants. Strong significant effects were found during the first or healing periods compared with the control periods on fMRI assessments.

Again, one is not asked automatically to believe this, but only to read about it critically and keep an open mind. For example, one large study has been cited as counterevidence by Benson et al. (2006) at Harvard. This was a multicenter randomized trial, involving intercessory prayer in cardiac bypass patients. In this case, there was no significant difference in postoperative complications for a prayed-for group versus a non-prayed-for control group. However this study, in turn, can be critiqued as being unlike true prayer. By contrast, Achterberg et al. (2005) used healer–client pairs who shared an empathic emotional bond, and employed methods such as sending "healing energy," good intentions, or prayer, that the healers had used for more than 20 years. Indeed, the fMRI machine is also a remarkably objective observer of response. The point here is not to opt for one position over another, but to carefully critique these and related studies (Schlitz et al., 2005) while applying solid research principles apart from either automatic skepticism or wishful thinking. An additional question: If our mental healing power far exceeds what we think is possible, and in just this way, would we really want to know?

## Can a Creative Style in Itself Enhance Our Well-Being?

Here the focus turns again to the creative process and the creative person, and what one can experience when being creative. Can ongoing creative activity make our human experience more vivid, real, enjoyable, and meaningful from moment to moment? Can it further our creative and personal development? If we take an open systems model of creativity, where our mutual influence on each other and our environment is dynamic and ongoing (e.g., Marks-Tarlow, 1999), and if we look at process more than product, we see some potential advantages (Richards, 1999c, 2001, in press). In summary, this includes our becoming more

- spontaneous, free: Abraham Maslow (1971) said of the "self-actualizing" creative people he studied that they were more "spontaneous, effortless, innocent, easy, [and had] a kind of freedom from stereotypes and clichés" (p. 138). They were more like children, in many activities of daily life.
- creatively developing: Maslow's (1971) "self-actualizers" also appeared more mature, with a higher purpose, doing work that seemed like a calling, acting from beyond "deficiency" needs (personally focused needs such as love, acceptance, or respect) toward "being" needs, involving more universal caring and a

greater good, a difference which has also been applied to creative activity (Rhodes, 1990).

- consciously aware: Creative persons can be more mindfully attuned to what is happening; more consciously aware in the moment, rather than leading a habit-bound routinized life (Langer, 1989; Richards, 1999a, 1999b, 2001, 2006).
- open to experience: Highly creative people show traits such as "tolerance for ambiguity," and "preference for complexity," and the ability to enjoy and "play" with elements (Barron, 1969, 1995; Rogers, 1961). These and other traits are found in highly creative persons across fields, and such "core" creative personality traits remain effective predictors of creativity, decades after they were first assessed (Feist & Barron, 2003). In addition, it seems worth speculating that such sensitive creators will relish the new, as a general rule, but not jump to conclusions. Hence they are at once both less and more independent than others.
- resilient when shaken up or destabilized—sometimes even enjoying and seeking this challenge or change: Here indeed is resilience, the ability to cope creatively with change and disappointment, and even at times to thrive, rather than to be decimated. This sometimes involves spending time willingly on the creative "edge of chaos," raising the odds in favor of sudden change, and transforming difficulty into opportunity (Richards, 1997, 1999b; Zausner, 1996).
- original, almost as a habit: On the basis of studies of well-known creators across fields, Frank Barron suggested originality was habitual with highly creative persons (Barron, 1969, 1995; Barron & Harrington, 1981). Rather than being focused only on one domain, their creativity seemed to involve specific attitudes and behaviors across fields: a cognitive style, almost a way of life, a more open and flexible manner that generated new perspectives. It is significant that in studies of families showing patterns of both creativity and mood disorders (Andreasen, 1987; Richards, Kinney, Benet, et al., 1988) relatives' creativity was expressed in a range of different areas—mathematics, teaching, entrepreneurship, and so on, and not just in a single discipline such as music in one family, or math in another. Finally, although some people speak of discrete abilities in creativity (Gardner, 1993), one might question if these abilities are always at the unique and distinctive core of the creative act. Amabile's (1996) distinction between creativity-relevant skills versus task-motivation and domain-relevant skills is also relevant here.

- able to live more vividly in the moment, and not in the past or future: Imagine being creatively involved, moving in the flow of life, and using all your capacities so that creator and task come together. One's senses are acute, and everything feels more vivid and alive (Csikszentmihalyi, 1993). Consider instructions from a book on Chinese brush painting: "paint with joy, with the sheer pleasure of singing life's song. Paint with love and kindness for the materials and the subject portrayed, becoming one with both" (Cassettari, 1987, p. 7). Sekida (1977) called this "a total involvement with some object or activity" (p. 42).
- appreciative of our fundamental interdependence, along with our complex effects on each other and the world: The highly creative and self-aware person has the potential to be more aware of life's flow, the nature of change, and our interdependency. Creators may, as their careers progress, move more toward "being" creativity from "deficiency" creativity, as noted above. They become increasingly more concerned with universal themes and a greater good, rather than with only their own personal issues (e.g., Rhodes, 1990; Richards, 1997).

Overall, if we were more involved in such creative moments and endeavors, and if we were living a more creative life, might we feel more alive, enjoy life more, act less neurotically from our own self-serving motives, and know ourselves better, with corresponding health benefits? Might we feel a greater connection with others and moved to share our own creativity?

## Might We Become Better Appreciators, as Well as Initiators, of Creativity?

Beyond our roles as initiators of creativity, humans have important functions as appreciators of creativity, as people who further the "metabolism of the new" (Richards, 1997) in a culture by relishing novelty, processing innovations actively, and encouraging the flow of innovation to others who will spread its influence further (Arons & Richards, 2001; Richards, 1999b). Although some are more attracted to novelty than others, this function still applies to everyone. (See also chaps. 3 & 5, this volume.) Ray and Anderson's (2000) work identifies the group now called the "cultural creatives," a dispersed subgroup in this country, albeit equal in population to that of France. Through their creative appreciation and participation, the "cultural creatives" are helping move the values and orientation of this country in ways that include more simple, sustainable, connected, and engaged living, and toward greater personal and spiritual development (see also chaps. 10 & 12, this volume).

*Example 1. Role of Everyday Creativity in Identifying Eminent Creativity*

If the customer is always right (or even often right), one may suggest that an eminent or exceptional level of creativity vitally depends on what serves the rest of us, for it to be noticed, first of all, and then to survive and thrive. Exceptional innovation will not occur then be celebrated in a vacuum. It will have social relevance and, further, may be supported and carried onward as a function of the level of everyday creativity in the populace that accepts it, and creatively adapts it to make it "theirs" (Richards, 1997). This is an active creative function, although it may not always appear so.

Some tend to think of "the lone genius" (Richards, 1996) as a solitary person, who is isolated, standing apart from others, and who single-handedly challenges norms and advances culture while metaphorically (or literally) sitting alone on top of a hill. Consider instead an *open systems* view of genius, involving the give and take that we all experience routinely from each other and our surroundings, a metabolism of information along with air, water, food, and other resources. When I hear another person speak, my brain is altered—accessing memories, sending new chemical signals, likely growing new dendrites.

Our so-called genius (who may still be a hermit on a mountain) should be very much in tune with some current trends in some area, with "what's in the air," and perhaps in the literature, meanwhile seeing a little farther than most. Let us say his or her insight provides an Ah-Ha! experience for many of us who encounter this, pulling things together in ways that bring new pleasure or relief (and more complex brain organization, as well; Csikszentmihalyi, 1993). For this, we may reward the "genius" with acclaim (Richards, 1996). Yet, we too, and our own creativity, have played a part in this evolving system (Montuori & Purser, 1996; Richards, 1996).

What is key is that the eminent creator is actually responsive to others (at least, as others will react, later on). The fate of the innovation depends on the audience, on us, especially the more creative forefront of this audience, which enjoys innovation, and may consider new ideas more open-mindedly. The readers of this book are likely in such a forefront.

Creative appreciation is often not included along with visibly active creating. Yet it does take creative processing to dialogue with the innovation (see chaps. 3 & 5, this volume, on art and on television viewing, respectively). Each person's "conversation" is different, a unique encounter. Working with Dennis Kinney and colleagues at Harvard Medical School, we found that "creative appreciation" was significantly correlated with everyday creative accomplishment (Richards, Kinney, Benet, et al., 1988). This does make sense if both processes involve original thinking and creative enjoyment.

An example of an artist being "tuned in" to his appreciative audience occurred at the end of the first part of the Martin Scorsese (2005) television special, "No Direction Home," a program about songwriter and performer, Bob Dylan. Two of the commentators noted Dylan's ability to connect with his audience: "He articulated what the rest of us wanted to say but couldn't say" and, with respect to Jung's collective unconscious and the universal archetypes to which we may all deeply relate, "Bobby . . . tapped into it."

The responsive "others" may be renowned critics—a limited elite—or they may be everyone. Here lies a discussion about domain and field. Bob Dylan's work changed music and he (and we) were also changed. The point is this: The "genius" level creator operates and succeeds in a larger context which is cocreated with a creatively minded public.

*Example 2. Systems Perspective on Appreciating Creativity Within an Evolving Culture*

Art critic Suzi Gablik (1997) has written about art in a systems context, as an expression of the voice of the community and part of an ongoing dialogue in which the viewer is also an active participant. She speaks of a "connective aesthetics," based in the vigorously active engagement of artist and community. Everyone contributes in some way, and everyone is changed. Often this interplay is hidden, but sometimes we can make it visible, and one museum show deliberately attempted to do this.

In 1999, I had the privilege of speaking at an unusual Oakland Museum of California show, *What Is Art For? William T. Wiley & Mary Hull Webster & 100 Artists*. The show highlighted the emergence of art from the wisdom and voice of the community, while showing some of the personal and social functions art can serve in helping the community heal, grow, and thrive. An individual goes to the museum and is changed; then the person acts upon this change out in the world. The *What Is Art For?* show hailed our ongoing mutual influence, and artistic interaction, whether through making art or viewing it.

My particular talk encompassed art and healing, and art and growth, in the context of creative surprise and insight linked to chaos theory (see also chaps. 2 & 3, this volume). The talk, along with a series of slides, was really the glue holding together a marvelous mosaic of performing and speaking parts from therapists, artists, and teachers Dassie Hoffman, Elias Katz, Christine Kerr, Ilene Serlin, Marti Southam, and Margie Torres. (Our group, together, was one of the "100 Artists.") These presenters, representing movement therapy, studio art, art and disabilities, and occupational therapy, showed that "we are all artists," while also being part of a larger evolving picture. They highlighted the interactions between themselves and their clients and students, and the mutual discovery and impact of creativity in their work together. Against a backdrop, and off to the side, during much of the event, dancers Dassie, Ilene, and Margie did an interactive improvisational dance reflecting what was going on in the moment while showing that art, even then, was generating reaction, and hence more art. At times performers involved the audience as well, once in a hilarious segment on humor and creativity, where people physically acted out issues toward new insights, or at the end, where the dancers led audience and performers in an undulating spiral dance of celebration that circled the room, uniting the group, and tying everything together.

I was asked to write a short statement for a book to accompany the show (Richards, 1999b), Dorothy Nissen's edited, *What Good Is Art?* Fortunately, my young daughter, Lauren, provided the inspiration and the key idea as I started work on this, demonstrating again our ongoing mutual influence and how we all play our separate parts. Lauren suggested the idea of text and subtext, and the almost fractal structure where word patterns are echoed at different magnifications (see Arons & Richards, 2001), after I had started working on "We Are All Creative . . ."

WE ARE ALL CREATIVE
and we are all artists whether we are viewing art or making it. We are open systems
EVOLVING AT THE EDGE OF CHAOS
in resonance with each other
IN OUR EVERYDAY LIVES.
Our artists are our helpmates, bringing us images, metaphors, and meanings that speak to our depths,
And call forth new visions.
WE SEE WORLDS
unimagined
AND HOPE
at last for this one. We find understanding
AND BEAUTY AND
the bridging of conflict and distance which heralds
OUR DEEPER SELF.
We are transformed in turn and
WE SPREAD THE VISION THROUGH OUR
own unique expressions be they in conversation or painting. Our museums serve as
NERVE CENTERS
humming with life and concentrating the streams
OF THIS EVOLVING MIND
while mixing in the bright new colors of the viewer,
OF YOU.

### Where Has Our Creativity Gone? How Do We Get It Back?

To conclude, it is useful to review some of what we lose if we shy away from our creativity and opt for safety, conformity, or the status quo. At best, our everyday creativity can be

- everywhere: It is not only about arts but also about new and flexible innovations throughout our lives.
- beneficial: It makes us more alive, healthier, helps us grow and connect with our world, both in creating and appreciating creativity.
- freed from obstruction: We can be open, nondefensive, beyond self-serving distortions, more integrated, with the freeing of working memory, opening to mind–body healing, inner unity, and more.
- overall, a happy path: It is a creative path of growth and further development that feels good, opens us to inspiration, brings us deeper self-knowledge, adds more meaningful contributions to the world, creates an openness and ease, resilience and power, self-awareness in a greater system, and a more mature knowledge tempered by childlike fun and joy.

How odd it may seem, considering the benefits, that we do not stress everyday creativity more in schools, homes, businesses, healthcare settings, senior centers, and centers for personal growth and development. Why, one may ask again, is our creativity so hidden or diminished (or underrecognized, underdeveloped, and underrewarded)?

Reasons touched upon here include seven important aspects of everyday creative activity that need clarification:

1. It is not an optional "extra" for all but certain famous people, but, rather, is an essential capability for survival and ongoing development.
2. It is not limited to special areas such as the arts, but, rather, it can be found in all parts of life.
3. It is not merely a light and pleasant diversion, but, rather, is a vital enterprise involving deep commitment, concentration, risk taking, and sometimes personal transformation.
4. Although sometimes unsettling, it is not fundamentally an enterprise that unsettles and evokes pathology, but, rather, is one that can open, integrate, and heal.
5. It is not an endeavor focused only on end products, but, rather, involves a healthy way of approaching life, which connects

us more meaningfully to our world, whether we are actively creating or appreciating the creativity of others.

6. It is not an activity set apart from much of our being, but, rather is one that reaches deep into mind, body, and spirit, and can help heal us, revealing a profound mind–body connection we are only beginning to understand.

7. It is not a neutral or safe activity, that risks little, but, rather, can be a potentially dangerous enterprise offering disruption and change—including personal reorganization, and potential threats to society's status quo. Against these forces of change may be arrayed powerful obstacles, internal and external, conscious and unconscious. But we cannot address them unless we know why our creativity may be eclipsed and "hidden" to begin with.

Far from being trivial, or light and fluffy, or strictly constrained to special domains, and only intermittently of relevance, our everyday creativity represents a pervasive and dynamic way of being and knowing, and of encountering the world. If it offers profound and sometimes painful new insights, at the same time it brings us delight, healing, new purpose, growth, and ongoing potential for personal development. Let us not give up our creative birthright, or let it lie "hidden," when our everyday creativity offers new life and hope for each of us in a troubled world.

## REFERENCES

Achterberg, J. (2002). *Imagery in healing: Shamanism and modern medicine.* Boston: Shambhala.

Achterberg, J., Cooke, K., Richards, T., Standish, L. J., Kozak, L., & Lake, J. (2005). Evidence for correlations between distant intentionality and brain function in recipients: A functional magnetic resonance imaging analysis. *Journal of Alternative and Complementary Medicine, 11,* 965–971.

Adler, L. P. (1995). *Centenarians: The bonus years.* Santa Fe, NM: Health Press.

Amabile, T. (1996). *Creativity in context.* Boulder, CO: Westview Press.

Andreasen, N. (1987). Creativity and psychiatric illness: Prevalence rates in writers and their first-degree relatives. *American Journal of Psychiatry, 144,* 1288–1292.

Arons, M., & Richards, R. (2001). Two noble insurgencies: Creativity and humanistic psychology. In K. J. Schneider, J. F. T. Bugental, & J. F. Pierson (Eds.), *Handbook of humanistic psychology* (pp. 127–142). Thousand Oaks, CA: Sage.

Barron, F. (1963). *Creativity and psychological health.* Princeton, NJ: Van Nostrand.

Barron, F. (1968). *Creativity and personal freedom.* Princeton, NJ: Van Nostrand.

Barron, F. (1969). *Creative person and creative process.* New York: Holt, Rinehart & Winston.

Barron, F. (1995). *No rootless flower: An ecology of creativity.* Cresskill, NJ: Hampton Press.

Barron, F., & Harrington, D. (1981). Creativity, intelligence, and personality. *Annual Review of Psychology, 32,* 439–476.

Becker, G. (1978). *The mad genius controversy: A study in the sociology of deviance.* Beverly Hills, CA: Sage.

Beghetto, R., & Kaufman, J. C. (in press). Toward a broader conception of creativity: A case for "mini-c" creativity. *Psychology of Aesthetics, Creativity, and the Arts.*

Benson, H., Dusek, J., Sherwood, J. B., Lam, P., Bethea, C. F., Carpenter, W., et al. (2006). Study of the therapeutic effects of intercessory prayer (STEP) in cardiac bypass patients: A multicenter randomized trial of uncertainty and certainty of receiving intercessory prayer. *American Heart Journal, 151,* 934–942.

Bloom, H. (2000). *Global brain: The evolution of mass mind from the Big Bang to the 21st century.* New York: Wiley.

Cardeña, E., Lynn, S. J., & Krippner, S. (2000). *Varieties of anomalous experience: Examining the scientific evidence.* Washington, DC: American Psychological Association.

Cassettari, S. (1987). *Chinese brush painting techniques.* London: Angus & Robertson.

Chang, K., & Leary, W. (2005, September 25). Serge Lang, 78, a gadfly and mathematical theorist, dies. *The New York Times,* p. 27.

Coulter, H. (n.d.). In suppress studies/research quotes. Retrieved September 27, 2005, from http://www.whale.to/a/suppress_q.html

Csikszentmihalyi, M. (1993). *The evolving self: A psychology for the third millennium.* New York: HarperCollins.

Davis, G. (1999). Barriers to creativity and creative attitudes. In M. A. Runco & S. R. Pritzker (Eds.), *Encyclopedia of creativity* ( Vol. 1, pp. 165–174). San Diego, CA: Academic Press.

Dewey, J. (1934). *Art as experience.* New York: Putnam.

Dobzhansky, T. (1962). *Mankind evolving.* New Haven, CT: Yale University Press.

Dodds, R. A., & Smith, S. M. (1999). Fixation. In M. A. Runco & S. R Pritzker (Eds.), *Encyclopedia of creativity* (Vol. 1, pp. 725–728). San Diego, CA: Academic Press.

Dossey, L. (1999). *Reinventing medicine.* New York: HarperCollins.

Dossey, L. (2001). How healing happens: Exploring the nonlocal gap. *Alternative Therapies, 8*(2), 12–15 , 103–110.

Feinstein, D., & Krippner, S. (1997). *The mythic path.* New York: Tarcher.

Feist, G., & Barron, F. (2003). Predicting creativity from early to late adulthood: Intellect, potential, and personality. *Journal of Research in Personality, 37,* 62–88.

Freeman, L. W., & Lawlis, G. F. (2001). *Mosby's complementary and alternative medicine: A research-based approach.* St. Louis, MO: Mosby.

Gablik, S. (1997). *Conversations before the end of time: Dialogues on art, life, and spiritual renewal*. London: Thames & Hudson.

Gardner, H. (1993). *Creating minds: An anatomy of creativity seen through the lives of Freud, Einstein, Picasso, Stravinsky, Eliot, Graham, and Ghandhi*. New York: Basic Books.

Getzels, J. W., & Jackson, P. W. (1962). *Creativity and intelligence: Explorations with gifted students*. New York: Wiley.

Goleman, D. (1988, September 13). A new index illuminates the creative life. *The New York Times*, pp. C1, C9.

Jamison, K. R. (1989). Mood disorders and patterns of creativity in British writers and artists. *Psychiatry, 52*, 125–134.

Jamison, K. R. (1993). *Touched with fire: Manic-depressive illness and the artistic temperament*. New York: Free Press.

Jamison, K. R., Gerner, R., Hammen, C., & Padesky, C. (1980). Clouds and silver linings: Positive experiences associated with primary affective disorders. *American Journal of Psychiatry, 137*, 198–202.

Kinney, D. K., Richards, R., Lowing, P., LeBlanc, D., Zimbalist, M., & Harlan, P. (2000–2001). Creativity in offspring of schizophrenics and controls. *Creativity Research Journal, 13*(1), 17–26.

Kinney, D. K., Richards, R., & Southam, M. (in press). *Everyday creativity, its assessment, and The Lifetime Creativity Scales: Handbook of Creativity*. Cresskill, NJ: Hampton Press.

Klein, K. (2002). Stress, expressive writing, and working memory. In S. J. Lepore & J. M. Smyth, (Eds.), *The writing cure: How expressive writing promotes health and emotional well-being* (pp. 135–155). Washington, DC: American Psychological Association.

Krippner, S., & Achterberg, J. (2000). Anomalous healing experiences. In E. Cardeña, S. J. Lynn, & S. Krippner (Eds.), *Varieties of anomalous experience: Examining the scientific evidence* (pp. 353–395). Washington, DC: American Psychological Association.

Lang, S. (1998). *Challenges*. New York: Springer-Verlag.

Lang, S. (1997, March 1). Dissent from the "HIV/AIDS" orthodoxy. *Scienza e Democrazia/Science and Democracy*. Retrieved September 27, 2005, from http://www.Dipmat.unipg.it/~mamone/sci-dem

Langer, S. (1989). *Mindfulness*. Reading, MA: Addison Wesley.

Lepore, S. J., & Smyth, J. M. (2002). *The writing cure: How expressive writing promotes health and emotional well-being*. Washington, DC: American Psychological Association.

Locke, S. E., & Colligan, D. (1986). *The healer within*. New York: Dutton.

Ludwig, A. (1995). *The price of greatness*. New York: Guilford Press.

Marks-Tarlow, T. (1999). The self as dynamical system. *Nonlinear Dynamics, Psychology, and the Life Sciences, 3*, 311–345.

Maslow, A. (1968). *Toward a psychology of being*. New York: Van Nostrand.

Maslow, A. (1971). *The farther reaches of human nature*. New York: Penguin.

May, R. (1975). *The courage to create*. New York: Norton.

Montuori, A., & Purser, R. (1996). Context and creativity: Beyond social determinism and the isolated genius. *Journal of Humanistic Psychology, 36,* 34–43.

Montuori, A., & Purser, R. (1999). *Social creativity* (Vol. 1). Cresskill, NJ: Hampton Press.

Pennebaker, J. W. (1995). *Emotion, disclosure, and health*. Washington, DC: American Psychological Association.

Pennebaker, J. W, Kiecolt-Glaser, J. K., & Glaser, R. (1988). Disclosure of traumas and immune function: Health implications for psychotherapy. *Journal of Consulting and Clinical Psychology, 56,* 239–245.

Ray, P., & Anderson, S. R. (2000). *The cultural creatives: How 50 million people are changing the world*. New York: Three Rivers Press.

Rhodes, C. (1990). Growth from deficiency creativity to being creativity. *Creativity Research Journal, 3,* 287–299.

Richards, R. (1981). Relationships between creativity and psychopathology: An evaluation and interpretation of the evidence. *Genetic Psychology Monographs, 103,* 251–324.

Richards, R. (1996). Does the lone genius ride again? *Journal of Humanistic Psychology, 36,* 44–60.

Richards, R. (1997). When illness yields creativity. In M. A. Runco & R. Richards (Eds.), *Eminent creativity, everyday creativity, and health*. Stamford, CT: Ablex Publishing.

Richards, R. (1999a). The subtle attraction: Beauty as a force in awareness, creativity, and survival. In S. W. Russ (Ed.), *Affect, creative experience, and psychological adjustment* (pp. 195–219). Philadelphia: Brunner/Mazel.

Richards, R. (1999b). We are all creative . . . In D. Nissen (Ed.), *What good is art: Artists respond to the questions: What is art for? What are museums for? What are you for? and (sometimes) what is art?* Oakland, CA: The Oakland Museum of California.

Richards, R. (1999c). The "Four Ps" of creativity. In M. A. Runco & S. R. Pritzker (Eds.), *Encyclopedia of creativity* (Vol. 1, pp. 733–742). San Diego, CA: Academic Press.

Richards, R. (1999d). Everyday creativity. In M. A. Runco & S. R. Pritzker (Eds.), *Encyclopedia of creativity* (Vol. 1, pp. 683–687). San Diego, CA: Academic Press.

Richards, R. (1999e). Affective disorders. In M. A. Runco & S. R. Pritzer (Eds.), *Encyclopedia of creativity* (Vol. 1, pp. 31–43). San Diego, CA: Academic Press.

Richards, R. (2001). A new aesthetic for environmental awareness: Chaos theory, the beauty of nature, and our broader humanistic identity. *Journal of Humanistic Psychology, 41*(2), 59–95.

Richards, R. (2000–2001). Creativity and the schizophrenia spectrum: More and more interesting. *Creativity Research Journal, 13,* 111–132.

Richards, R. (2006). Frank Barron and the study of creativity: A voice that lives on. *Journal of Humanistic Psychology, 46*, 352–370.

Richards, R. (in press). Everyday creativity and the arts. *World Futures.*

Richards, R., & Kinney, D. K. (1990). Mood swings and creativity. *Creativity Research Journal, 3*, 203–218.

Richards, R., Kinney, D. K., Benet, M., & Merzel, A. P. C. (1988). Assessing everyday creativity: Characteristics of the Lifetime Creativity Scales and validation with three large samples. *Journal of Personality and Social Psychology, 54*, 476–485.

Richards, R., Kinney, D. K., Lunde, I., Benet, M., & Merzel, A. P. C. (1988). Creativity in manic-depressives, cyclothymes, their normal relatives, and control subjects. *Journal of Abnormal Psychology, 97*, 281–288.

Rogers, C. (1961). *On becoming a person.* Boston: Houghton Mifflin.

Rossman, M. L. (2000). *Guided imagery for self-healing.* Tiburon, CA: New World Library.

Rossman, M. L. (2003). *Fighting cancer from within.* New York: Holt.

Runco, M. A. (1996). Personal creativity. *New Directions for Child Development, 72*, 3–30.

Runco, M. A., & Richards, R. (1997). *Eminent creativity, everyday creativity, and health.* Stanford, CT: Ablex Publishing.

Russ, S. (Ed.). (1999). *Affect, creative experience, and psychological adjustment.* Philadelphia: Brunner/Mazel.

Schlitz, M., Amorok, T., & Micozzi, M. S. (2005). *Consciousness and healing: Integral approaches to mind-body medicine.* St. Louis, MO: Elsevier.

Schlitz, M., & Braud, W. (1997). Distant intentionality and healing: Assessing the evidence. *Alternative Therapies in Health and Medicine, 3*(6), 62–73.

Schuldberg, D. (1994). Giddiness and horror. In M. Shaw & M. A. Runco (Eds.), *Creativity and affect* (pp. 87–101). Norwood, NJ: Ablex Publishing.

Scorsese, M. (Director). (2005, 20 September). *Bob Dylan: No direction home.* [Television broadcast.]. Hollywood, CA: Paramount Studios.

Sekida, K. (Ed. & Trans.). (1977). *Two Zen classics: Mumonkan and Hekiganroku.* New York: Weatherhill.

Singer, J. L. (1990). *Repression and dissociation: Implications for personality theory, psychopathology, and health.* Chicago: University of Chicago Press.

Smith, G. J. W., & van der Meer, G. (1997). Creativity in old age. In M. A. Runco & R. Richards (Eds.), *Eminent creativity, everyday creativity, and health* (pp. 333–353). Stamford, CT: Ablex Publishing.

Sundararajan, L. L., & Richards, J. A. (2005, August). *Expressive writing and health: Insights from a finer-grained language analysis.* Paper presented at the 113th Annual Convention of the American Psychological Association, Washington, DC.

Westby, V. L., & Dawson, E. L. (1995). Creativity: Asset or burden in the traditional classroom? *Creativity Research Journal, 8,* 1–10.

Wickramasekera, I. (1998). Secrets kept from the mind, but not the body and behavior. *Independent Practitioner, 18,* 38–42.

Zausner, T. (1996). The creative chaos: Speculations on the connection between non-linear dynamics and the creative process. In W. Sulis & A. Combs (Eds.), *Nonlinear dynamics in human behavior: Studies of nonlinear phenomena in life science* (Vol. 5, pp. 343–363). Singapore: World Scientific.

# 2

# LIVING WELL CREATIVELY: WHAT'S CHAOS GOT TO DO WITH IT?

DAVID SCHULDBERG

There had come the realization that the genome wasn't the monolithic data bank plus executive team devoted to one project—keeping oneself alive, having babies—that I had hitherto imagined it to be. Instead, it was beginning to seem more a company boardroom, a theater for a power struggle of egotists and factions. . . . I was an ambassador ordered abroad by some fragile coalition, a bearer of conflicting orders from the uneasy masters of a divided empire. . . . Given my realization of an eternal disquiet within, couldn't I feel better about my own inability to be consistent in what I was doing, about my indecision in matters ranging from daily trivialities up to the very nature of right and wrong?
—W. D. Hamilton (1995, pp. 133–134)

The "bricoleur" [improviser, handyperson] is adept at performing a large number of diverse tasks; but, unlike the engineer . . . the rules of his game are always to make do with "whatever is at hand," that is to say with a set of tools and materials which is always finite and . . . bears no relation to the current project, or indeed to any particular project . . . the "bricoleur" . . . derives his poetry from the fact that he does not confine himself to accomplishment and execution: he "speaks" not only *with* things . . . but also through the medium of things: giving an account of his personality and life by the choices he makes between the limited possibilities. The "bricoleur" may not ever complete his purpose but he always puts something of himself into it.
—Levi-Strauss (1966, pp. 17–21)

Living creatively is an intrinsic part of everyday life, a core component of living well. In this chapter, the term *creativity* means coming up with solutions to life's problems, solutions that are both novel and useful. Sometimes the problem is an aesthetic one—in which case the result is artistic creativity—and at other times the solutions are practical and homely, forgotten when they have served their purpose. This chapter emphasizes thinking about "the good life" as a path and not an outcome, something constructed from attainable and ordinary actions; living well and creating beauty inhabit and emerge from activities that are literally mundane. This chapter also argues that certain types of theoretical models, those derived from the flourishing field of nonlinear dynamical systems theory (sometimes called chaos theory), can help us understand how little processes of living well are involved with the grander themes of human nature. A variation on the chaos perspective—referred to as a *Somewhat-Complicated Systems* (SCS) approach—provides concepts that can illuminate human potentialities in a new way.

Living well (for oneself) and doing good (for others) are not simple activities, although they involve the ordinary and worldly, not the metaphysical. Living well proceeds from small, sometimes easily accomplished activities. Small models of the processes used to approach the good life can be assembled from simple systems that are completely mechanistic and deterministic. Such little systems go far toward describing how people work with the small-scale, microscopic details of their days. Yet, despite their economy, these models are not simplistic; they can also embody the reality that day-to-day lives emerge into something big and special. This transformation from the humble to the magnificent has implications for defining a "good life," for ethics, for spiritual practice, and for understanding what it means to be innovative. The interactions and aggregations of our small daily activities come together into larger agglomerations that are—technically speaking—complex, sometimes characterized by what is called *chaos*. This leads to a new view of human nature as something approximate, contextual, and determined, yet full of vitality, promise, and surprise.

The concepts of the everyday and ordinary are at the heart of this chapter and this book. Is it possible to find some of the most beautiful and even exalted aspects of human life in ordinary activities? Is the seemingly simple conduct of daily life somehow more complex, deeper, richer in its implications, than it seems? People tend to talk about the everyday with ambivalence. The ordinary sometimes doesn't seem grand enough; perhaps the moments that make us most human should be more special than the present one. Words referring to the everyday reflect this tension; the terms in Table 2.1 suggest how the "daily" can have a negative tinge.

## WHAT'S CHAOS GOT TO DO WITH IT? SIMPLICITY, COMPLEXITY, AND THE SOMEWHAT-COMPLICATED SYSTEMS PROGRAM

It is difficult to define "living well;" it is often described by what it is not, something that also happens with accounts of "good," "God," and

TABLE 2.1.
Synonyms for "Everyday"

| Valence | Characteristic |
|---------|----------------|
| Positive | New, promising |
| | Novel, fresh |
| | Innovative |
| | In the present moment |
| | Populist |
| Neutral | Daily, quotidian |
| | Regular |
| | Plain, simple, unornamented |
| | Ordinary |
| | Sparse |
| Negative | Humdrum |
| | Mundane, banal, not special |
| | Boring, bland |
| | Unvarying, repetitive |
| | Habitual |
| | Common, lowbrow |
| | Worldly, secular |

even "health." Living well is what Wittgenstein (1953) called a family resemblance concept, entwining separate threads having to do with happiness, relationships, social engagement, authenticity, meaning, satisfaction, adjustment, consistency, regulation, and ethical integrity. Although a good life proceeds from myriad daily activities, the idea is baffling when one tries to account for it from a larger, unified perspective. This conceptual confusion can be eased if we first lower our gaze and view the good life as an ever-changing process composed of small steps, rather than as an ultimate state or outcome.

Creativity, spiritual meaning, and many of life's finer aspects do indeed exist in the everyday; I believe that the best things in life can be found in simplicity. In the words of the Shaker hymn: "Tis a gift to be simple." However, if we look deeper, simple things reveal an intricacy in their structure and texture, and the goods that we seek are linked in complicated ways. There are also fundamental nonlinearities in the relationships that connect our positive attributes—and their contexts—with positive outcomes: More and more of a good thing is generally not better and better. Moreover, we are constantly changing, as are the situations we inhabit.

To consider these dynamic relationships, to include time as a variable in models of the good life, is to view life as composed of what I call SCS. These are simply small nonlinear dynamical systems; they represent little models, built from psychological-level variables that change with time, contain nonlinear relationships, and, when coupled together, form the building blocks of larger, more intricate systems. A brief introduction to the larger chaos theory point of view will clarify its relevance to this chapter's concerns. (See chaps. 10 & 7, this volume, for views on self-organization and systems science.)

## Introduction to Nonlinear Dynamical Systems (Chaos) Theory

The nonlinear dynamical systems approach is an extension of the general systems theory, cybernetics, and living systems theory of the 1940s, 1950s, and 1960s, with earlier roots in physiologist Walter Cannon's (1929) "homeostasis," the political philosophy of the Greeks, and more ancient nonwestern traditions of holism and flux. Chaos theory is innovative in its emphasis on nonlinearity in systems, on nonequilibrium states, and because nonlinear equations (e.g., those governing the famous three-body problem in physics) often lack exact solutions (and are only amenable to approximations from long computer calculations). This makes it difficult to predict and control even deterministic systems. It is worthwhile to look at both the large-scale, macroscopic behavior of SCS, viewed from the outside, as well as the small-scale microscopic mechanics of their construction on the inside. Both perspectives have implications for living well creatively.

## Macroscopic Properties of Behavior in Nonlinear Dynamical Systems and Somewhat-Complicated Systems

The large-scale behaviors of nonlinear dynamical systems in general and SCS in particular, are commonly described as paths or trajectories. These refer to a system's motion through the life-space and are related to the currently popular idea of narratives, although the term *narrative* can also imply a more limited set of story structures, genres, and styles as well as the idea of dramatic progress, even in tragedy. In contrast, SCS can follow interesting, quirky, even maddening trajectories far from simple and uplifting stories of progress, triumph, or even homeostasis. Everyday paths are complex and unpredictable. SCS represent a type of small nonlinear dynamical system, and they too can produce behavior characterized by technically defined chaos. And what is chaos? In contrast to nontechnical definitions involving extreme and even frightening disorder, chaos, in a mathematical sense, refers to behavior of a system that is bounded yet never repeating, deterministic yet unpredictable. These features also define "*strange attractors*." Attractors in general are regions in a space defining a system's behavior where it tends to go and tends to stay. Strange attractors are bounded regions of the space where the system is never in exactly the same place and moving in the same direction twice, where behavior is contained but ever novel.

Chaotic systems also exhibit extreme sensitivity to initial conditions and small nudges from the environment. Two systems that are, at one moment, close together but not in identical places may end up different later on. This is the meaning of the famous *butterfly effect*, and also corresponds to our understanding and experience that small things can make big and lasting differences in our lives (e.g., a child finds an understanding adult; a grown-up has a chance encounter). Being apparently determined and following sequences moment to moment where one thing causes another (e.g., the movements of a clock's mechanism or electricity across a circuit board), how we live also seems highly contingent and unpredictable.

Strange attractors are also related to the popular nested and repeating fractal patterns that depict their structures. These patterns sometimes demonstrate an odd and striking visual organization, with patterning across many scales and magnifications as well as a type of orderly beauty that has emerged from a system that is nevertheless difficult to forecast and guide. Another characteristic of systems in or near chaos is "*emergence*," in which new kinds of order appear from old systems.

An example of these phenomena is provided by a friend of mine, a consultant who receives a usually reliable but variable stream of referrals. She commented that the difference between experiencing work as heaven or as hell, between over- and underwork, is "four clients." She loves the intellectual challenge of her consulting, and therefore it is "heaven." However, with too many clients, she is drained by the job; too few and she worries about the office rent. Exhaustion is narrowly separated from stimulation and then from anxiety (Csikszentmihalyi, 1998).

The consultant is aware that there is an optimal number of appointment hours per week. Yet, how should she control her work load? Living well in this example involves saying "yes," "no," and "later" to erratic inputs from the outside. Because referral flow is somewhat unpredictable, it is tempting to blame the consultant's dilemmas on its influx and outflow: "If only I would get a few more clients." However, the external environment is really not at the root of intractable problems such as this. Well-being would still be a hard problem even if the outside world were relatively uniform and even unchanging.

What is occurring really involves the inherent instability and the difficulty of steering an SCS. Optimality is elusive and healthy regulation never represented by standing still. There is not even a dynamic equilibrium; if the environment has ever been capricious, the consultant will never completely recover, even after life is temporarily pacified: A snafu is forever. This example is also characterized by a nonnarrative form, a story that circles and repeats, with subtle and sometimes unfathomable meanings. It is neither a heroic narrative of progress and triumph, nor a bracing account of stability. Instead, it might be called "working woman's blues."

This example also contains something like a possible strange attractor. As I noted earlier, an attractor is a place in "phase space" where a system will settle or linger. A strange attractor in a chaotic system is a region where the system never returns to exactly the same place and direction of motion, while still staying within bounds. The consultant's work load is fluctuating but constrained; she rarely meets with fewer than 5 or more than 30 clients per week. Yet, her work life is also never repeating, always new in its challenges. Every week, every day is different. "Strangeness" is present if her client load never exactly repeats itself (by being in a particular place—with a particular combination of number of clients and the difficulty of their problems—while also changing in a particular direction). There may also be fractal-like symmetries, similarities, patterns, and flavors across weeks, days, seasons, and larger periods of her career.

## Microscopic Properties of Somewhat-Complicated Systems

What about the nuts and bolts of SCS, their smaller internal mechanisms? The most important defining characteristic of an SCS is an internal nonlinear relationship linking means and ends, independent and dependant variables. Nonlinearity can also be a consequence of delay in response, of time lag between changes in a causal variable and the resultant effects. There are pauses following a change in diet or lifestyle, the administration of a drug, or the implementation of a therapy.

People also pursue multiple, sometimes contradictory goals, deploying multiple, often conflicting, strategies. Living well is a set of modular processes. It emerges from relatively independent but coupled subsystems that have different agendas and sometimes only weak connections to and dim awareness of each other, never mind our valuing of consistency and integration. We can imagine the consultant in the example torn between one part of her trying to build her business and another favoring cutting back, two opposing modules.

The good life has many variables, both independent and dependant, and subsystems do influence each other. (I believe that they are generally loosely coupled.) These interactions of strategies, and the couplings among outcomes, can also introduce important nonlinearities into our seeking the things we want. The view of human nature inherent in SCS includes acknowledgement that people are ambivalent and multifaceted. As Walt Whitman (1855/1999) said, "Very well, then, I contradict myself; (I am large—I contain multitudes)" (Lines 1322–1323). These multitudes interact and contribute to healthy chaos.

## Chaos and Health

The possible connections between chaos and everyday life are underscored by contemporary interest in relationships between chaos and health. Despite psychology and medicine's historic interest in stability and consistency, there are longstanding suggestions that variability might be an essential part of well-being (Larson, Csikszentmihalyi, & Graef, 1980). Cardiologist Ary Goldberger and his coworkers (Goldberger & Rigney, 1989) went further and suggested that—as one example—the healthy heartbeat, far from being regular and strictly rhythmic, contains chaotic irregularities that actually determine the organ's health and the individual's survival. Goldberger has developed empirical evidence that it is extreme regularity, not irregularity, which predicts imminent cardiac death. This "healthy chaos" position is controversial, and there are counterexamples within cardiology as well as ones referring to other physical and mental disorders (see Abraham, Abraham, & Shaw, 1990, pp. 111–112). Nevertheless, this approach promises a picture of our human natures in which the properties of variability—rather than stability and coherence—define personal identity and well-being.

## Complexity From Simplicity

SCS (Schuldberg, 2002) is used specifically to refer to a subset of nonlinear dynamical systems particularly useful for understanding human-scale processes. As I noted earlier, these are small model systems that are constructed from variables at the psychological or behavioral level, and that include nonlinearity in either dose–response relationships or in the connections among subsystems. Human nature can be modeled by simple structures. Yet, relatively simple systems—when they are coupled in combination and sometimes in opposition—can produce extremely interesting, literally complex and chaotic, results. These SCS are simple in construction and complex in behavior. There has likely been a high evolutionary premium on mechanisms such as these that combine elementary structure and richness of function, and SCS provide useful building blocks for more complicated social and biological processes.

In my home town people are often in the position of leaving for work somewhat late on cold winter mornings without having time to warm up their cars properly. In this imperfect world, pursuing an already less-than-optimal lifestyle by rushing into town with a still-cold engine, how fast should one drive until the car warms up? First, one can argue that—because the engine is cold and the oil is still thick—one should proceed slowly. This puts a minimal load on the machinery and keep its parts rubbing at a low speed, at least until the oil gets warm. This is my spouse's position on the matter. Second, there is a contrasting argument that urges one to keep the engine revved high. At a low speed the oil pump turns slowly, the pressure of the cold, thick oil is low, and its circulation is poor. Thus, it is a good idea to keep engine speed high to ensure proper lubrication throughout the engine. This is the position of the famous Volkswagen *Idiot Book*. Given the ultimate goal of maintaining the longevity and health of one's vehicle, these define two competing strategies, "drive slow" and "drive fast."

When the pedal hits the metal, the rules collide head-on. One solution is to drive at a moderate speed, neither quickly nor slowly. Some would say that this is what Aristotle would have done if he had neglected to warm up his car. Yet, as Aristotle knew, such a compromise strategy is not guaranteed to be the best, or even a very good, strategy. A behavioral estimation of a sort of optimum can also occur dynamically and in real time, motorically if you will; rather than thinking the situation through in advance and deciding that 32 miles per hour is best, the driver can start out and more or less settle on a speed. For others, the strategies maintain an ongoing dynamic tension; a third driver might drive more erratically, slowing down and then speeding up again. Alternating behavior represents yet another fluctuating outcome from an SCS, living well as best it can; these are among the infinite possibilities between the poles of steady "slow" or "fast," possibilities that at times might lead to highly original solutions.

### The Creativity of the Everyday

This chapter's conception of the everyday is tied to Ruth Richards' (1998) notion of "*everyday creativity*." Richards and her colleagues (Richards, Kinney, Benet, & Merzel, 1988) sought to measure creativity as an attribute not only of the greatest geniuses but also of lesser mortals; they wanted to detach creative behavior from societal recognition, fame, and eminence. Everyday creativity implies continua, the idea that geniuses (and, it turns out, madmen and -women) are a lot like everybody else. Both ordinary and extraordinary, creativity shows up in most people, but it continues to amaze; the features of genius and madness occur in the normal as well as in the extreme ranges of people's behaviors and characteristics. This contrasts with more romantic pictures (Sass, 2000–2001) of the creative person as genius, freak, "primitive," vessel for the divine, or monster.

### "Somewhat-Complicated Systems" Use Small-Scale Improvisation

SCS (and nonlinear dynamical systems in general) are creative at two levels. At the microscopic or everyday level they rely on heuristics, humble rules of thumb that provide pretty good strategies for living in a world of uncertainty and noise, obscured and incomplete data. Because the future is unknowable and not completely controllable, one must live by improvisation and bricollage, using the wrong spare parts to effect repairs and generally not bringing exactly the correct tools to any job. Because we are living life forward in time without a full understanding of its end, we are (paraphrasing Kierkegaard) condemned to improvise. Thus, small-scale innovation occurs constantly.

These heuristic procedures, which lack guarantees for their outcomes, nevertheless provide the opportunities and the methods for successful problem solving. For example, I live in Montana, in a communitarian town in a high social-capital state that, as I already noted, has cold winters. It is not unusual to return to the parking lot at the end of the day to a dead battery. To get the help needed to drive home, the heuristic of starting to walk back toward my office carrying a set of booster cables generally suffices in this situation, although it has no guarantees. (A card from AAA serves as backup.) The strategies of daily life—and, after repeated use, the strategy just described may seem manipulative and indirect—are imperfect, aggregated from limited rules of thumb. This is part of an SCS view of human nature.

We do not give away life's power, order, or beauty when we embrace its inexactness. Life is computational, in the sense that we live incrementally a step at a time, but it is not "analytic," in the sense that we can solve it out in advance: We live via algorithms but cannot compute an optimal or guaranteed solution for tomorrow's problems today. Day by day we engage in satisficing (Simon, 1979), not maximizing, and we must use selective strategies (Marsiske, Lang, Baltes, & Baltes, 1995). "Satisficers," people who attempt to find "good enough" solutions rather than an elusive best, are also more happy and satisfied with their lives than maximizers (Schwartz et al., 2002), who live closer to rational choice theory. This is one reason that the choices provided for us as U.S. consumers can tyrannize and not necessarily lead to happiness (Schwartz, 2004).

### Somewhat-Complicated Systems Also Have Large-Scale Creative Dynamics

SCS can also be creative in their larger scale macroscopic behaviors. Some researchers (Richards, 1996; Schuldberg, 1999; Zausner, 1996) have suggested that the creative act itself arises from systems that are either chaotic or at the "edge of chaos." Frank Barron (1995) proposed an "ecology of creativity" of dynamic systems (Richards, 2006) and spoke eloquently of the relationships between order, disorder, and chaos in originality. Chaotic processes are robust and constantly original and can be highly adaptive and responsive. They also resist rigid entrapment by the external environment, avoiding conformity and slavish imitation. In addition, the fractal properties of strange attractors, reflecting the infinite possibilities within these bounded systems, can demonstrate both simplicity and beauty; Richards (2001) and others have discussed how viewers tend to find their patterns pleasing (Zausner, 1996). The drip paintings of Jackson Pollock, sometimes criticized as disorganized, evince a high level of fractal structure (Taylor, Micolich, & Jonas, 1999) distinct from random splatters.

Fractals exhibit self-similarity across scales, an example being the characteristic branching of a tree from trunk to branches to twigs to twiglets, and this may well account for some of what is meant by "style." Thus, different people will have distinct styles of cold-weather driving, and the consultant mentioned earlier will sometimes recognize a particular kind of "one of those weeks" in her business. Style generally entails the recognizability of an artist's work—or someone's personality and behavior—across different products, places, pieces, periods, phases of a career, and small and large artistic works or behavior samples. Fractal patterns can also include compression of larger patterns into smaller ones; this was a component of psychedelic designs of the 1960s and 1970s and helps account for the intrinsic aesthetic properties of "miniatures" (Levi-Strauss, 1966).

Self-similarity is also related to the phenomena of *"parallel process"* in clinical and similar situations, experienced, for example, in adults' visits home to their own parents. When young adults (older ones, too) spend time with their families of origin, they may experience, first, some regression to their own childhoods, followed by a rapid recapitulation of early periods and former genres from their archaic family lives. Psychotherapy relies on this miniaturization, using a small subset (often the Fifty Minute Hour) of the totality of everyday life to observe, formulate, understand, and intervene, to effect changes and evaluate them. This represents an important isomorphism of healing generalization, from the little clinical hour to the big life. Similarly, today may be taken to represent a miniature of our larger, "whole" life. Yet, in another sense, the everyday is not miniature at all; it is writ large and is indeed what our real lives are made of. It is generally in little things that we can see and appreciate the style and aesthetics of a particular life. In a practical sense living well is ever before our eyes and in our hands, not somewhere off in the distance.

Not mind-bogglingly complicated, SCS have behaviors big enough to encompass important phenomena of the good life. Chaos provides a way to reconcile small and large as well as the value of both change and consistency. People have long been aware that others can be consistent in their variation, describing them as "erratic," "labile," "flighty," "unstable," "responsive," "unpredictable," or "stolid." Chaotic variability provides an updated picture of moving systems as ordered, recognizable, and even beautiful in their patterned changes and uncertainty, reflecting their always original and self-renewing natures.

# MORE IMPLICATIONS OF THE CHAOS IN DAILY SYSTEMS

Chaos theory has consequences for questions about free will; it helps reconcile determinism with freedom. A deterministic system in a chaotic regime is unpredictable and hard to control because small adjustments, unintentional twitches, and external influences can have big downstream effects. I find this position compatible with the phenomenological textures of daily life. Yet, questions remain concerning the necessity of the will, the role of intentionality, and the processes of initiating action. What do we do to live well? How, exactly, can we attain well-being? Where do I start?

## Everyday Spirituality

Focusing on how life is lived in the everyday leads to a vision of the links between the mundane and the spiritual. This occurs through recognition of the larger implications of each moment, the sacredness of the everyday, and the creativity, even risk and uncertainty, associated with the most ordinary activities of daily living. Jesus' teachings champion common people, and meditative disciplines and practices (e.g., Zen) refer both technically and philosophically to our most basic human actions: breathing, paying attention, sitting, listening, and walking (Nhat Hanh, 1995). The pursuit of creativity also meets spirituality when it invokes and invites spark and inspiration.

This is how the everyday connects to grander themes: What we do on a daily basis, the seemingly small strategies, behaviors, thoughts, feelings, and relationships of the day, all can serve to grow human capital, the potential for art and the reality of beauty. Activities of daily life are the keys to everyday spirituality in practices that emphasize the here and now, mindfulness, and immanence (see Hughes, 2003). And, because of its focus on "ordinary people" as opposed to elites, this point of view implies intrinsic value for every life and leads to notions of human universals, universal rights, and social justice.

## Everyday Psychopathology and Positive Psychology

The themes of ordinary, "normal" life are also connected to those of psychopathology and abnormality. This is evident in Richards' (2000–2001) and her coworkers' research on links between creativity, cyclothymia, and also schizotypal traits, and in my own work as well (Schuldberg, 2000–2001). To view normal, even exemplary functioning and pathology as inhabiting continua unifies illness and health, complementing a similar kinship between the composer of symphonies and the repairer of automobiles. Both psychopathology and creativity are components of "normal" life.

It is important to note that Richards (2000–2001; Kinney, Richards, Lowing, Leblanc, & Zimbalist, 2000–2001) and her colleagues have proposed curvilinear (inverted-U) relationships linking psychopathological character-istics and everyday creativity, implying there are important SCS at work here as well. A related question concerns the generality or specificity of creativity: Is there one continuum from less creative to more, or are there many dynamic and creative subsystems? Are there specific modules for particular types of madness that can produce or enhance certain kinds of genius?

Parallel movements in both psychology and medicine are now attempt-ing to correct overly negative, pathological emphases in past theorizing, research, and clinical practice in the health and mental health fields. Positive psychology (Seligman, 2002) and wellness approaches in medicine grapple with emphasizing strengths, reinforcing positive functioning, and under-standing virtues. The search for the positive has also been a component of past programs, including the World Health Organization's redefinition of health in 1946, the 1960s community mental health movement, interest in "positive mental health" (Jahoda, 1958), and in humanistic psychology. Finding a positive approach to human functioning is fraught with problems involving how to avoid being too Pollyannaish, to preserve optimism along with personal nuance and complexity. How can we not oversimplify? How can we be positive without sinking into sterile "positivism?"

An SCS approach illuminates both the sources and a resolution for these puzzlements. Positive psychology faces deep difficulties from nonlinear-ity, the fact that our virtues aren't generally virtuous at every level and intensity, or universal across contexts (Chang & Sanna, 2003). Creativity and living well, as well as illness and health, are also in continual flux and present constantly moving targets. Whereas we can sometimes point to an artistic accomplishment or a finished creative solution, well-lived life is generally defined by paths, not destinations and goals. Even the most mun-dane daily tasks are dynamic; the mechanics of just standing there involve constant swaying, and these movements are only slightly different from those of falling down. Positive functioning, although emerging from simple systems, is complex and subtle.

## Engagement and the Will: Active Versus Passive Forms of Life

An SCS approach also raises questions about the differences between active and more passive approaches to living originally and well. For example, developments in robotic walking (Alexander, 2005) emphasize implementa-tion of passively responsive elements, in contrast to mechanisms that expend energy to control every component of gait. Similarly, in realizing realistic computer animations, passive elements can yield the best simulated movement. This highlights the issue of how much of life is lived via near-effortless adaptation rather than acts of will, or how much we rely on dissipative systems that use up energy to work. In a creative life one may pick moments to intervene consciously and others to coast, or still others (as in musical or dramatic improvisation) to remain deliberately open to, and then to use, the accidents of the moment. As in the winter driving example from earlier, an SCS can still be complex and difficult even with only minimal interference from the outside; active coping has constrained and often unpredictable effects. To what extent, then, are inspiration and creative activity willed versus received? In expert performance and musical improvisation, not every move is thought out in advance, although one might begin with a theme, a melody, or an idea; and, one must also get oneself to the piano and sit down.

## Simplicity and Its Dark Side: A Sparse Approach to Life and Its Pitfalls

This next example illuminates implications of simplicity and is drawn from the life and writings of William S. Burroughs, beat author and philosopher. Burroughs outlined an approach to everyday life that emphasizes minimizing effort. This practice, which he called "*DO EASY*" (DE), has some similarities to Zen, and it is defined as "doing whatever you do in the easiest most relaxed way you can manage which is also the quickest and most efficient way" (Burroughs, 1966/1973, p. 58). He provides an example as his fictional protagonist:

> "washes up and tidies his small kitchen. . . . Knives forks and spoons flash through his fingers and tinkle into drawers. Plates dance onto the shelf. He touches the water taps with gentle precise fingers and just enough pressure considering the rubber washers inside. Towels fold themselves and fall softly into place. As he moves he tosses crumpled papers and empty cigarette packages over his shoulder and under his arms and they land unerringly in the wastebasket as a Zen master can hit the target with his arrow in the dark. . . . With one fluid rippling cast the sheets crinkle into place and the blankets follow tucked in with fingers that feel the cloth and mattress. In two minutes the flat is dazzling." (pp. 57–58)

Burroughs also exemplifies some pitfalls of an "easy" approach and shows how contemplative passivity can be a vice. One potential problem involves substance abuse. Burroughs was a heroin addict during part of his life, and some of his other writing shows how this can represent a misguided form of seeking the soul. Substance use can be a form of experimental introspection, in which independent variables (in this case blood levels of substances and rituals surrounding self-administration) are manipulated and the effects are self-observed in self-absorbing detail. As Burroughs wrote,

"Junk is a cellular equation that teaches the user facts of general validity" (1977, p. xvi). The solipsistic aesthetic of apprehending the kinetics of chemicals, of living the differential equations of dose, diffusion, and the complex mechanics of drug action—as they ripple out from blood to brain into social world and cosmos—can lead the person badly astray. Nevertheless, Burroughs wrote: "I have never regretted my experience with drugs. . . . When you stop growing you start dying. An addict never stops growing" (p. xv).

Although DE and substance abuse can have a lot in common, illustrating how spirituality and addiction can sometimes be confused with one another, there are important differences. They both represent radically simplified practices, attentiveness to feedback between will and consciousness, awareness of the links between behavior and perception, and the seeking of happiness and even enlightenment in small and regular daily heuristics. However, they have distinct results; the two practices yield radically different lives later on.

It is not always easy to determine what the macro consequences will be that will emerge from the intentional use of specific micro strategies. A special type of trajectory involves discontinuous change, for better or worse, for example the precipitous "falling off the wagon" of a relapsing alcoholic taking a drink or "a-ha!"experiences in psychotherapy. Such sudden and sometimes startling changes are now popularly referred to as *tipping*, and more technically as *catastrophes* (see Gladwell, 2002; Guastello, 1995). Small movements can produce sudden and large effects, sometimes wondrously transformative and creative, sometimes perverse and unintended.

## Making a Better World

This brings us back to earlier questions concerning activity and engagement with the larger environment. How can one learn from DE and still be connected to the big picture? Seligman (2002) discusses engagement as a component of positive psychology, and Thich Nhat Hanh (1975) combines meditation with involvement in everyday (and political) activity in "engaged Buddhism." Even emphasizing the harmony of going with the flow, we must include room for making a better world, for activism and organizing (Nakamura & Csikszentmihalyi, 2003). The creative "gift" may involve heuristic knowledge about how, when, and where to nudge a moving system just a little, to good effect. Although beyond the scope of this chapter, it is worthwhile to touch on how to go about making a better world.

First the bad news: There are limits to our own control over the diverse SCS at play in our lives; the path to betterment is circuitous and indirect, beset by perverse effects and unintended consequences. The procedures we use to attain our ends are inexact, messy, contradictory, and generally inefficient. Thus, it is disconcerting and difficult to approach the seemingly intractable tasks of changing ourselves and others. However, the good news is that the trajectories of expert performance, improvisation, and social activism may well be chaotic, surprising, and unexpectedly important in scope and effect, even as they proceed from simple beginnings. We must start on our small approximations and then be ready to travel the wider vistas that they open up for us. It is important to note that there are also limits to efficiency as a virtue. Seeking too much of it can be tied up with desires to optimize and maximize, and this can get us into big trouble, just as the simplicity of DE can.

The environmental writer William McKibben (2004) discussed this when he noted that, through the mid-20th century, Americans listening to the radio had to hear more and different kinds of music and other programming than they necessarily wanted to or enjoyed, because of their access to only a limited number of stations. This unchosen diversity and sharing of one's airwaves with many other people broadened horizons and contributed to democratic life, despite—actually precisely because of— exposing people to media content that they would not choose voluntarily. Now, with satellite radio and iPod™, this inconvenience is no longer necessary. One can efficiently and narrowly inhabit whatever microscopic, isolated, comfortable, and nontaxing niche market pleases the individual most; this experience-narrowing efficiency contrasts with the positive "broaden and build" processes mentioned in the next section and suggests that we should now take a different approach, using more rough-hewn heuristic processes in seeking our ends.

## Chaos Rules: Complexity-Based Interventions

This chapter proposes viewing human nature as malleable but only indirectly steerable. In medicine, psychotherapy, and political change the goals are to shape human trajectories, I hope for the better, perhaps starting with our own trajectory. Despite centuries of healing science and lore, political practice and political science, spiritual teaching and technique, we lack universally practical and generally applicable ideas of how to characterize, categorize, and unify the improvement of trajectories: There are simply no simple panaceas, and an intuitive creative solution may sometimes bring the best reward.

We will never have a completely mature technology of behavioral or health engineering, but we do have many useful tools. These available strategies are wonderfully diverse and contradictory: A psychotherapist may advise a client to "go slow" or "go fast," and—in this situation, if not in the case of giving cold-weather driving advice—both strategies can work well. Positive psychology's study of how to live well, for example research on "broaden and build" strategies that use upwardly spiraling positive emotions and widening horizons of experience (Fredrickson, 2001), will also benefit from dynamic, SCS formulations.

## WHAT'S NEW WITH HUMAN NATURE

Do this chapter's pictures of chaos, creativity, and the everyday really constitute a new view of human nature? Seeing people and the rest of the natural world as changeable goes back at least to Heraclitus, and Aristotle's approach to moderation foreshadows the nonlinearity of virtues (Chang & Sanna, 2003). However, I believe that we are on the verge of a new approach that rests on rethinking what is implied by determinism. Chaotic systems, deterministic and unpredictable at the same time, can help us understand everyday human nature in its beauty and also its terror: It is lovely, and sometimes comprehensible on a small scale, but it is hard to steer.

This also helps us to downsize our lingering and persistent modernist notions of rationality, large-scale knowability, and control. Rational choice models are not only untrue to the emotional and "irrational" bases of much of our economic decision making but also fail to take into account the fact that choices take place in the face of noise, missing data, limited attentional and computational capacity, and a stubbornly opaque future. We are always guessing, estimating, and improvising, with uncertain outcome. "Bounded rationality" (Simon, 1979) represents the best we can do. Creativity is also intimately and inextricably braided throughout the mundane work and play of daily life. We have no alternative but to be innovative, no matter how simple the building blocks we start with. Of all the possible, inevitable— even tragic—fates for us as human beings, constant creativity is not a bad one.

## CONCLUSION

Keith Richards is the seemingly immortal guitarist and coleader of the Rolling Stones, arguably the best rock and roll band in the world even as its core members are now in their 60s. Bandmate, guitarist Ron Wood (The Rolling Stones, 2003), says of him, "Keith brings the air of raggedness, which we'd be lost without." Watching Richards as he plays sometimes presents an odd picture, especially when he is also singing: He can appear, moment-to-moment, not to know where he is going to put his hand on the neck of his guitar, chord to chord, from phrase to phrase. And, he is playing songs that he has played and played (perhaps for more than 40 years), songs that he is likely to have composed. Richards's occasional apparent (and it is probably only apparent) puzzlement in the course of expert performance has something to teach the rest of us: Old music is new, sometimes even baffling.

This chapter has emphasized the position of the solitary actor creating and self-actualizing as an SCS, with relatively little input from the environment. This, of course, is an insufficiently relational simplification, and better models will need to be developed to address this.

Richards describes engaging with Ron Wood, his coguitarist, in what they call "the ancient form of weaving," a process in which these two virtuoso musicians, neither clearly identified as playing lead nor playing rhythm, perform and invent music. Thinking about SCS and the chaos they can make will help us as we continually learn and rediscover different "ancient forms of weaving" and use them to get by, to make beauty and meaning in our own ragged lives.

## REFERENCES

Abraham, F. D. (with Abraham, R. H., & Shaw, C. D.). (1990). *A visual introduction to dynamical systems theory for psychology*. Santa Cruz, CA: Dakota Press.

Alexander, R. M. (2005, April 1). Walking made simple. *Science, 308*, 58–59.

Barron, F. (1995). *No rootless flower: An ecology of creativity*. Cresskill, NJ: Hampton Press.

Burroughs, W. S (1973). *Exterminator*. New York: Penguin Books. (Original work published 1966)

Burroughs, W. S. (1977). *Junkie*. New York: Penguin Books.

Cannon, W. B. (1929). Organization for physiological homeostasis. *Physiological Reviews, 9*, 399–431.

Chang, E. C., & Sanna, L. J. (Eds.). (2003). *Virtue, vice, and personality: The complexity of behavior*. Washington, DC: American Psychological Association.

Csikszentmihalyi, M. (1998). *Finding flow: The psychology of engagement with everyday life*. New York: Basic Books.

Fredrickson, B. L. (2001). The role of positive emotions in positive psychology: The broaden-and-build theory of positive emotions. *American Psychologist, 56*, 218–226.

Gladwell, M. (2002). *The tipping point: How little things can make a big difference*. New York: Little, Brown.

Goldberger, A. L., & Rigney, D. R. (1989). On the non-linear motions of the heart: Fractals, chaos, and cardiac dynamics. In A. Goldbeter (Ed.), *Cell to cell signaling: From experiments to theoretical models* (pp. 541–549). San Diego, CA: Academic Press.

Guastello, S. J. (1995). *Chaos, catastrophe, and human affairs: Applications of nonlinear dynamics to work, organizations, and social evolution*. Mahwah, NJ: Erlbaum.

Hamilton, W. D. (1995). *Narrow roads of gene land: The collected papers of W. D. Hamilton, Volume 1: Evolution of Social Behaviour*. New York: W. H. Freeman.

Hughes, G. A. (2003). *Transcendence and history: The search for ultimacy from ancient societies to postmodernity*. Columbia, MO: University of Missouri Press.

Jahoda, M. (1958). *Current concepts of positive mental health*. New York: Basic Books.

Kinney, D. K., Richards, R., Lowing, P. A., LeBlanc, D., & Zimbalist, M. E. (2000–2001). Creativity in offspring of schizophrenic and control parents: An adoption study. *Creativity Research Journal, 13*(1), 17–25.

Larson, R., Csikszentmihalyi, M., & Graef, R. (1980). Mood variability and the psychosocial adjustment of adolescents. *Journal of Youth and Adolescence, 9*, 469–490.

Levi-Strauss, C. (1966). *The savage mind*. Chicago: University of Chicago Press.

Marsiske, M., Lang, F. R., Baltes, P. B., & Baltes, M. M. (1995). Selective optimization with compensation: Life-span perspectives on successful human development. In R. A. Dixon, & L. Bäckman (Eds.), *Compensating for psychological deficits and declines: Managing losses and promoting gains* (pp. 35–79). Mahwah, NJ: Erlbaum.

McKibben, W. (2004, March). *Thinking local: What comes next for our economy and culture*. Paper presented at the President's Lecture Series faculty-student seminar, University of Montana.

Nakamura, J., & Csikszentmihalyi, M. (2003). The construction of meaning through vital engagement. In C. L. M. Keyes & J. Haidt (Eds.), *Flourishing: Positive psychology and the life well-lived* (pp. 83–104). Washington, DC: American Psychological Association.

Nhat Hanh, T. (1975). *The miracle of mindfulness*. Boston: Beacon Press.

Nhat Hanh, T. (1995). *Living Buddha, living Christ*. New York: Riverhead Books.

Richards, R. (1996). Beyond Piaget: Accepting divergent, chaotic, and creative thought. In M. A. Runco (Ed.), *Creativity from childhood through adulthood: The developmental issues* (New Directions for Child Development, No. 72) (pp. 67–86). San Francisco: Jossey-Bass.

Richards, R. (1998). Creativity, everyday. In M. A. Runco & S. R. Pritzker (Eds.), *Encyclopedia of creativity* (Vol. 1; pp. 619–633). New York: Wiley.

Richards, R. (2000–2001). Creativity and the schizophrenia spectrum: More and more interesting. *Creativity Research Journal, 13*(1), 111–132.

Richards, R. (2001). A new aesthetic for environmental awareness: Chaos theory, the natural world, and our broader humanistic identity. *Journal of Humanistic Psychology, 41*(2), 59–95.

Richards, R. (2006). Frank Barron and the study of creativity: A voice that lives on. *Journal of Humanistic Psychology, 46*, 1–19.

Richards, R., Kinney, D. K., Benet, M., & Merzel, A. P. C. (1988). Assessing everyday creativity: Characteristics of the Lifetime Creativity Scales and validation with three large samples. *Journal of Personality and Social Psychology, 54*, 476–485.

Rolling Stones, The (2003, 17 November). *Four flicks*, Disk 1 [DVD recording]. Metropolis DVD.

Sass, L. A. (2000–2001). Schizophrenia, modernism, and the "creative imagination": On creativity and psychopathology. *Creativity Research Journal, 13*(1), 55–74.

Schuldberg, D. (1999). Chaos theory and creativity. In M. A. Runco & S. R. Pritzker (Eds.), *Encyclopedia of creativity* (Vol. 1; pp. 259–272). New York: Wiley.

Schuldberg, D. (2000–2001). Six subclinical "spectrum" traits in "normal creativity." *Creativity Research Journal, 13*(1), 5–16.

Schuldberg, D. (2002). Theoretical contributions of complex systems to positive psychology and health: A somewhat-complicated affair. *Nonlinear Dynamics, Psychology and Life Sciences, 6*, 335–350.

Schwartz, B. (2004). *The paradox of choice: Why more is less*. New York: Harper Collins.

Schwartz, B., Ward, A., Monterosso, J., Lyubomirsky, S., White, K., & Lehman, D. R. (2002). Maximizing versus satisficing: Happiness is a matter of choice. *Journal of Personality and Social Psychology, 83*, 1178–1197.

Seligman, M. E. P. (2002). *Authentic happiness: Using the new positive psychology to realize your potential for lasting fulfillment*. New York: Free Press.

Simon, H. A. (1979). *Models of thought*. New Haven, CT: Yale University Press.

Taylor, R. P., Micolich, A. P., & Jonas, D. (1999, June 3). Fractal analysis of Pollock's drip paintings. *Nature, 399*, 422.

Whitman, W. (1999). *Leaves of grass*. Retrieved March 7, 2007, from http://www.bartleby.com/142/14.html. (Original work published 1855)

Wittgenstein, L. (1953). *Philosophical investigations* (G. E. M. Anscombe, Trans.). New York: Macmillan.

Zausner, T. (1996). The creative chaos: Speculations on the connection between nonlinear dynamics and the creative process. In W. Sulis & A. Combs (Eds.), *Nonlinear dynamics in human behavior: Studies of nonlinear phenomena in life science* (Vol. 5, pp. 343–349). Singapore: World Scientific.

# 3

## ARTIST AND AUDIENCE: EVERYDAY CREATIVITY AND VISUAL ART

TOBI ZAUSNER

To live a creative life, we must lose our fear of being wrong.
—Joseph Chilton Pearce

Each of us has an enormous reservoir of creativity within ourselves. It is part of being human and provides a means of knowing ourselves and our world in new ways. Revealing inner depths we never imagined, it builds strength through resilience, helps us cope with problems, and allows us to more fully reach our potential. One way we express our creativity is through visual art. The benefits can come through making or viewing art and are available to us whether or not we are artists.

This chapter, which focuses on visual art, begins by highlighting our everyday creativity, a capacity that encompasses the wide range of original and meaningful activities in our lives (Richards, 1998). Although we may not be aware of it, we are constantly creative and this capacity is fundamental to our existence. We see how this extensive creative capacity can generate abilities in more than one domain by looking at artists with multiple talents in both Eastern and Western and traditions. This will show that everyday creativity can be a path to eminence. One way this occurs is through creative activity that begins or flourishes during illness. Starting as a distraction from pain, it turned from resilience to a career, and eventually led to fame for the French painter Henri Matisse, the American painter Albert Pinkham Ryder, and the Canadian painter Maud Lewis.

While the first part of this chapter concentrates on the making of art, the second part examines the experience of viewing art, because this too is a creative act. The associations we bring in response to looking at art come from the wellsprings of our creativity, the combined potential of our conscious and unconscious mind. We see that art is both a source of information and a method of communication. Finding meaning in a work of art allows us to participate in its process and become cocreators with the artist. Because art can affect us on a deep level, it has been used for centuries as a vehicle of influence and power. Part of this power resides in archetypes, which Carl Jung (1971, 1973) said are primordial ways of thinking that lie deep within us and are activated by viewing corresponding archetypal images in a work of art. We also see how realism and symbolism contribute to the power of art and that looking at art is an internal experience. To view a work of art is to incorporate it within ourselves. Finally, art is presented as a source of transformation and an integral part of our interconnected universe.

## CREATIVITY AS FUNDAMENTAL

We are all creative; it is fundamental to our nature (Richards, 2006). Every choice we make in life is a decision and that decision has a creative basis. It brings together a synthesis of all of our past experience in a new way as a direct response to a specific stimulus. No two people are exactly alike; even genetically identical twins have different lives. Because of this, no two people have exactly the same experience, thoughts, and desires. We summon all of these components in a unique way with every choice we make. Each person's reaction is a creative synthesis of who they are at that moment. Our response to life is our everyday creativity at its most basic level.

We are also more than we think we are, and have more ability than we realize. Our conscious minds are small relative to the vast capacity of the unconscious (Ellenberger, 1970). And, according to Jung (1962, 1973), our unconscious minds rest on an even larger structure, the collective unconscious, a universal substrate common to all humankind. All that we think and do comes from these depths because unconscious processes affect conscious thought (Jung, 1971). This vast reservoir of hidden strength and potential is activated through our inherent everyday creativity and manifested not only in the visual arts, but also throughout the multiple facets of daily living.

Richards (1997, 2004) says we use our everyday creativity whenever we improvise solutions or cope with the contingencies of daily living. She gives examples such as solving problems, raising children, cooking food, landscaping the yard, or doing any of the complex tasks that fill our lives. Like so many things, creativity has both positive and negative manifestations. Positive ways to use everyday creativity are activities such as gardening, building a house, decorating, wrapping gifts, farming, and dancing. However, everyday creativity can also be used in negative ways that bring injury. Examples of negative everyday creativity would be designing computer viruses, lying, manipulating other people, playing practical jokes, and creating waste. Everyday creativity is energy that can be used for good or ill. An inherent gift, it comes free with being human. Yet it is up to us and our free will to bring it into a positive or negative manifestation.

## MULTIFACETED CREATIVITY AND OUR ENORMOUS POTENTIAL

People have argued that creativity is limited to one area or domain (Kaufman & Baer, 2004), but evidence from the lives of visual artists demonstrates that this is not the case. Individuals may show greater accomplishments in one domain of creativity than another, but the capacity to be creative appears to be a general ability rather than a restricted one (Plucker & Beghetto, 2004). The reason may be because the everyday creativity that permeates our daily existence tends to find many opportunities for expression. That is why it is not surprising to hear of someone who is a software designer and also a good cook or of the novelist who likes to play the piano.

This multifaceted aspect of creativity is seen in the lives of visual artists who excel in more than one domain. The name that comes to mind first is usually the Italian Renaissance artist Leonardo da Vinci, who was a painter, inventor, engineer, musician, writer, and multifaceted scientist (da Vinci, ca. 1489–1519/1970; Vasari, 1568/1996). Many multitalented individuals also come from the United States: Samuel F. B. Morse was a painter, writer, politician, and the inventor of the telegraph (Kloss, 1988; Morse, 1826/1983); and Everett Shinn was a painter, playwright, and acrobat (Eliot, 1957). In Germany, Albrecht Dürer (1506–1528/1958, 1528/1972; Hutchinson, 1990) was a painter, printmaker, poet, writer, engineer, and naturalist, who investigated the geometry of human proportions. In the Netherlands, Carel Van Mander (1604/1936), who was the first Northern European art historian, was also a painter, poet, playwright, art theorist, and archaeologist. From his book *Dutch and Flemish Artists* (Van Mander, 1604/1936) we learn that Jan Van Eyck was a painter, alchemist, chemist, diplomat, and inventor of oil painting; Pieter Koeck was a painter and printmaker, who wrote books on building, geometry, perspective, and architecture, and was also a linguist, translator, and an observer of social customs; and Jooris Hoefnaghel was a painter, scholar, writer, poet, and naturalist.

The Eastern tradition also has artists who are accomplished in multiple domains (Binyon, 1969; Sickman & Soper, 1956). In China, Wang Wei was a painter, physician, writer, poet, naturalist, and court official; Huang Kung-Wang was a painter, scholar, musician, and poet; Chao Mêng-fu was a painter, calligrapher, scholar, and court official, who rose to be a minister; Wang Yüan-ch'i was a painter, government official, scholar, and editor; Liu Chüeh was a painter, high government official, and humanist scholar, who enjoyed gardening; and Li Lung-mien was a painter, scholar, writer, poet, and antiquarian. In Japan, Hishikawa Moronobu was an artist who was also the inventor of Japanese picture books of woodcut prints; and Koyetsu, a painter, ceramic artist, and art expert, was asked to authenticate works of art.

For the sake of brevity, the artists mentioned here are just a small sample of the enormous number of creative individuals with abilities that span domains. One of the reasons that artists are often multiply accomplished is that they allow themselves to create. We are all creative, but not all of us give ourselves the permission to express our creativity. When we do, we may find that creativity bubbles up from within and emerges in more than one part of our lives. Sometimes, seeing friends or family members making art can spark our creative process, or it may begin in the structured setting of a class. Creativity can also start during illness when our usual activities are not possible and there is a need to fill the empty hours of an extended convalescence (Zausner, 1998, 2007).

## CREATIVITY, ILLNESS, AND EMINENCE

During illness, everyday creativity can be a coping mechanism, a way to make an uncomfortable situation easier to bear (Rhodes, 1997). One of the reasons people find creativity helpful during illness is because it can divert the mind from pain (Camic, 1999). We usually concentrate on only one thing at a time, so fixing our attention on creative activity can be a way to block both physical and emotional distress. Some people become creative for the first time when they are sick. It takes courage to begin something new, but the strength that is born of despair may bring personal transformation and a better way of life.

Other individuals, who were creative before becoming sick, may deepen their commitment to art and work with an intensity that springs from the desire to escape physical discomfort. When children begin everyday creativity during illness, they need the support of a parent or other nurturing person to supply both encouragement and art supplies (Zausner, 2007). Art supplies are crucial to visual art; they are the means by which inspiration becomes manifest.

For some people, the everyday creativity that begins during poor health leads to fame and a professional career. However, they do not start out by making masterpieces; this comes with continued effort. In the lives of Henri

Matisse, Albert Pinkham Ryder, and Maud Lewis, everyday creativity became eminent creativity and they all turned to art during illness (Zausner, 1998, 2007).

## HENRI MATISSE

When he was young, the French painter Henri Matisse (1869–1954) had chronic intestinal problems that may have been caused by appendicitis, ulcerative colitis, or a hernia (Flam, 1986; Sandblom, 1996; Spurling, 1998). The exact source of Matisse's symptoms is unknown but as the oldest son, he was expected to run his father's grain and hardware business. Because of his continuing poor health, his parents instead chose his younger brother, August, to head the company. Matisse was told to study law because this way he could have a quieter life and still be useful to the family business. Acceding to parental pressure, Matisse studied law even though it held no interest for him. At that time in his life, art was so far from his mind that when he spent a year in Paris studying for a law exam, he never once visited the Louvre. The only creative activity ascribed to his youth was the negative everyday creativity of playing practical jokes. After Paris, Matisse returned to his hometown of Bohain in the north of France and began working as a law clerk. His job, which entailed copying long legal documents, made him both angry and unhappy. Although Matisse thought he would be trapped at the law office for life, in the winter of 1889 after about a year of work, he had an acute gastric attack.

Whether the attack was from appendicitis, ulcerative colitis, or a hernia, all of these conditions were inoperable in the late 19th century and extended rest was the only cure. As his convalescence dragged on, Matisse searched for something to end his boredom. Another patient in the hospital suggested he try doing some chromos, which were an early version of painting by numbers. Although he had never painted before, this type of everyday creativity appealed to the young man. His strict father disapproved, but his artistic mother bought him a box of paints with two small chromos. Just holding the art supplies in his hands transformed him. "I had the feeling that my life was there," he said (Flam, 1986, pp. 27–28). Matisse began to paint in every spare moment: before work in the morning, at his lunch break, and again in the evening. Eventually he convinced his parents to let him study art in Paris. The pastime that started as everyday creativity turned into a world famous career.

When he was 70 years old, illness changed Matisse's life again (Flam, 1986; Sandblom, 1996). An operation for intestinal cancer went poorly and the resulting complications left him an invalid for the rest of his life. Unable to stand for long periods of time, but determined to work, Matisse began making art from his wheelchair (Elderfield, 1978; Gilot & Lake, 1964; Jedlicka, 1955/1988). No longer capable of doing the large oil paintings that made him famous, he turned to a medium associated with everyday creativity: scissors and colored paper. Matisse cut brightly colored pieces of paper into different shapes and sizes and directed his assistants to place them on canvases, on sheets of white paper, or to attach them directly to the wall. These cutouts eventually became large works of art and included the series called *Jazz* and his designs for the chapel at Vence. Although Matisse was not expected to survive the operation, he lived another 13½ years and the paper cutouts he created during the last period of his life are some of his greatest work.

## ALBERT PINKHAM RYDER

The American artist Albert Pinkham Ryder (1847–1917) also focused on creativity during an early illness (Eliot, 1957; Zausner, 1998). Ryder, who grew up in the Massachusetts seaport town of New Bedford, liked art from early childhood. He was a quiet and gentle boy whose favorite everyday creativity was lying on the floor looking at picture books and drawing (Homer & Goodrich, 1989). One of the great treats of his childhood came from an older seafaring brother who brought home some art magazines with reproductions of pictures in the Louvre. Ryder was so taken with the images that he copied the artist's names into his notebook (Brown, 1989).

When he was a child, Ryder developed a severe response to a vaccination (Brown, 1989). The reaction settled in his eyes, leaving them chronically inflamed for the rest of his life. It was most likely the smallpox vaccine because that was the only kind available at the time (Zausner, 2007). The vaccination may have occurred in 1854 because there was a smallpox outbreak recorded in neighboring Vermont. As an active seaport, New Bedford was especially vulnerable to smallpox and had been promoting vaccines in response to outbreaks since 1840. Even today there is a risk of blindness from smallpox vaccinations but the possibility was higher in the 19th century when the vaccine quality was less uniform.

Ryder's father, who sold fuel on the New Bedford waterfront, was a compassionate man who wanted to help his son. Instead of focusing on the boy's diminished sight, he instead remembered his son's favorite everyday creativity and bought him art supplies. Like Matisse, Ryder had a moment of epiphany when he received them. Standing in front of the new white canvas on his easel, his father handing him a paint box and brushes, Ryder believed he could "create a masterpiece that would live throughout the coming ages," and insisted, "The great masters had no more" (Goodrich, 1959, p. 24). Because of poor eyesight, Ryder had difficulty discerning details

(Eliot, 1957). Instead, he painted with broad bands of color, giving his work greater intensity. Ryder experienced eye inflammations for the rest of his life (Goodrich, 1959), but his weakened vision empowered his art.

## MAUD LEWIS

Considered to be the Grandma Moses of Canada, Maud Lewis (1903–1970) is one of her country's most beloved folk artists (Riordan, personal communication, March 1999; Woolaver, 1996, 1997). Born Maud Dowley in South Ohio, Nova Scotia, Lewis started her career with everyday creativity in response to illness. For the first few years of her life, she enjoyed normal health, but then, sometime after the age of 4, Lewis developed early onset juvenile rheumatoid arthritis. The illness was severe. Her shoulders became hunched, her spine twisted, her chin pulled in toward her neck, and rheumatoid nodules impeded the use of her hands, the right hand more than the left hand. The condition also affected her growth and for the rest of her life, Lewis stayed the size of a child.

Even though Lewis was intelligent, she never completed her education (Woolaver, 1996). When the other children at school ridiculed her condition on the 20-minute walk home from class, Lewis was often reduced to tears. At times, too upset to complete the journey, she took refuge in the house of her aunt, a teacher, who lived closer to the school. After leaving school at 14 years of age, she stayed home with her mother, who gave her art lessons and together they made greeting cards. Lewis loved to paint and the hours she devoted to this everyday creativity laid the foundation for her future career (Zausner, 2000, 2007). By spending time at home alone making art in childhood, Lewis developed the ability to spend the necessary time alone painting in adulthood.

At the age of 34 she married Everett Lewis, a fish peddler, and moved into his house in Digby, Nova Scotia. There, Maud Lewis's life was filled with everyday creativity. She decorated their little 12½ × 13 foot home inside and out with the colorful flower, bird, and animal motifs found in her paintings. She painted the walls, floor, trays, canisters, stairs to their sleeping loft, and she even painted flowers on the window panes. To supplement her husband's small income, Lewis decorated shells and utilitarian objects such as dust pans, which she sold in addition to her paintings. Although Maud Lewis continued to experience painful and severe rheumatoid arthritis, her visual art shows only her joy. She never traveled far from home, but by the 1950s Lewis became known as a folk artist. In the 1960s she was on television and articles were written about her. As a result, there were many requests for her work including one from the White House. What started out as everyday creativity for Maud Lewis is now cherished and conserved as fine art (Hamilton, 2001). Her paintings, decorated objects, and little house are all in a museum as part of the permanent collection of the Art Gallery of Nova Scotia in Halifax.

## VIEWING ART IS CREATIVE

Making art is a creative activity, but viewing art is creative as well. Just as we activate our everyday creativity in response to life, we also activate it in response to art. Every time we look at a work of art, we become cocreators with the artist because it is our response to art that brings it to completion. Art is made to be seen: The artist makes the art and the audience completes the action by viewing it. Each viewing provides us with an opportunity to be creative. This is because whenever we see a work of art, we activate our everyday creativity through the myriad personal associations that comprise our response to a visual stimulus at that specific moment. These associations come from our great interior resource, the combined potential of our conscious and unconscious mind.

The numerous personal associations we bring forward in response to art alter as a result of our life at a specific moment and our life is always changing. As the ancient Greek philosopher Heraclitus says, you can never step into the same river twice (5th century BCE/1987). Like the flowing river, our lives are in a continual flux of becoming; we are constantly changing. Although we may not be aware of it, everyday creativity accelerates our rate of transformation by providing opportunities to confront and embrace new situations. This happens in both creating and viewing works of art. Both activities stimulate our everyday creativity through moments of doubt, surprise, and the confrontation of multiple possibilities. These chaotic moments of uncertainty can be modeled by chaos theory, a part of the science of nonlinear dynamics (Paar, 1993). In a time of uncertainty we have the opportunity to make a choice, and that creative choice gives us the possibility of changing ourselves and our world.

## ART AS INFORMATION AND COMMUNICATION

Viewing a work of art is an experience of communication, with the viewer completing the intention of the artist as the recipient of its information. Because artists create so actively from the unconscious (Neumann, 1959) they are often not aware of the full meaning of their work. This has repeatedly happened to me when people have pointed out meaning or symbolism in my art of which I had no conscious knowledge. I have been amazed and grateful for the interpretations that people offer in response to viewing my work. It is their creativity in response to mine that makes the work of art a more profound experience for both the artist and the viewer.

This is possible not only because the artist communicates through the artwork to the viewer but also because the viewer has an internal dialogue in response to the art. This internal dialogue is an exercise of everyday creativity. Each person receives the information from a work of art in a uniquely creative way and–just as no two people are exactly alike–no two people see a work of art in exactly the same manner. Every one of us brings up our own life experiences, both consciously and unconsciously, when viewing art and it is these life experiences combined with our everyday creativity that make enjoying art a creative and meaningful experience.

One of my most significant experiences with a work of art happened when I was a teenager and saw Rembrandt's (Rembrandt Harmenszoon van Rijn, Dutch, 1606–1669) self-portrait at the Frick Collection in New York. I had already decided to be an artist but my profound response to this painting deepened the commitment. At the time, I did not know Rembrandt's biography or that this life-sized self-image was completed in 1658, years after the deaths of his wife and three of his four children, after bankruptcy and the loss of his elegant house and much of his belongings to creditors (Marx, 1960). Although the painting shows a face ravaged by time, Rembrandt still looks at us with a steadfast gaze. He sits royally, dressed in a shining golden garment holding his mahl stick (a long wooden pole used to support the hand while painting) like a king holds his scepter. Problems would plague Rembrandt for the rest of his life, but he continued to make masterpieces. Triumphing over difficulties with his art, Rembrandt shows us the indomitable strength of a human being despite severe and ongoing hardships. That is what I responded to as a teenager not even knowing why I had such an emotional reaction. As an adult, I too paint images of perseverance. It is art's capacity to inspire a response, both conscious and unconscious, that is the source of its appreciation and the foundation for the important role that art has played across cultures and throughout time.

## THE USES AND POWER OF ART

From prehistory to the present, art occupies a special place in our world and serves a dual purpose. It is simultaneously an expression of visible beauty and also a vehicle for the invisible, a carrier of information, influence, and power. One way that power expresses itself is through images that act as archetypes (Edinger, 1968; Jung, 1973). Examples of archetypes are images that remind us of masculine or feminine parental figures, such as the Virgin Mary as a mother or the paternal Uncle Sam symbolizing the United States.

According to Jung (1971), archetypes are primordial organizing principles in our unconscious minds that manifest as images and symbols in dreams, mythology, and works of art. They touch the deepest part of our nature and responding to them with our all of our psychological associations is part of our everyday creativity.

Because of their enormous power, archetypes such as Uncle Sam are used to promote political goals or, like the Virgin Mary, they may be religious symbols. But they can also be tools for social cohesion as seen in Paleolithic cave art of 18,000 to 10,000 BP. The bison and other animals depicted in the caves of Altamira in Spain and Lascaux in France were not only exquisitely rendered objects of beauty (Beltram, 1999; The Cave of Lascaux, n.d.) and meant to be conveyors of great spiritual power (Clottes & Lewis-Williams, 1998, pp. 110–111) but also used as vehicles of social cohesion to assist in feeding the community.

These images are presumed to be part of shamanic rituals (Clottes & Lewis-Williams, 1998). We do not know the exact ceremonies that took place, but they probably incorporated ritually enacted hunts of animals like the bison, which were a vital food source. These accomplished works of art most likely sprang from the everyday creativity of people idly scratching in the sand with sticks or their fingers—what could be called prehistoric doodling. Over generations this was refined into the exquisite accomplishment of the wall paintings. In a ritualized hunt, it is important that the animal be depicted realistically to convince the hunter of its presence. Realism was so important that a Lascaux bison is shown molting his coat of black winter wool, so that his red summer fleece appears. The reality of the image is potentially a tool to increase the self-confidence of the hunter. Having been close to the painted bison, and remembering his successful ritualized hunt, the hunter will have less fear in approaching the actual animal while using his everyday creativity to strategize his moves.

Practicing a hunt through imagery and ritual in a cave is psychologically similar to our current practice of learning through simulated computer environments. Both provide a safe space to learn skills necessary for the real world. Today virtual images are used to teach a variety of abilities, from training astronauts to dispelling phobias. In all cases the digital experience is made to appear as realistic as possible. In computer environments and Paleolithic art the psychological power and influence of images comes from their realism.

## SYMBOLISM AND MULTIPLE WORLDS

In addition to conveying the realism of the actual world, art is also a carrier of religious symbolism and spiritual aspirations. As such, it is a cross-cultural and cross-temporal phenomenon that attempts to bring the miraculous into everyday reality. Examples are works of art that depict deities or miracles, such as Biblical illustrations, whose purpose is to make them look real and believable to the viewer. One explanation for the power of religious art derives from a theory of antiquity that is also central to the Neoplatonic humanism of the renaissance (Yates, 1979). It is the *theory of correspondences*, which states that like manifests like (Plotinus, 1991/250 CE, 328; Chastel, 1975, pp. 73–74). Presuming that a person exposed to transcendent images in art would experience a corresponding response of spiritual elevation, it also postulates that the power of a religious image comes from a nonphysical source. Like Platonic philosophy (Plato, 1950/4th century BCE), it speaks of another world whose structure defines our physical reality. Quantum physicist David Bohm (1983) gives a modern correlation to this principle by postulating implicit or hidden order that underlies and forms the visible or explicit order of our everyday existence.

This principle of correspondence is also active in Eastern images of deities, such as the many statues of Kwan Yin, the Chinese Goddess of Compassion, who is the feminine aspect of the Buddhist deity Avalokiteshavara (Blofeld, 1978). Kwan Yin, who symbolizes the transformation of distress into engaged compassion and the achievement of serenity despite sorrow, is meant to inspire these qualities in the viewer. She becomes a role model and the three-dimensionality of the statue emphasizes her psychological reality and enhances her influence. Although Kwan Yin symbolizes many beneficent qualities, there is still the gap between the idealized role model and the actual situation of the viewer. It is the everyday creativity of imagination that allows a person to bridge that gap and imagine those qualities to be attainable. Everyday imagination is the first step to achievement.


## AN INTERIOR EXPERIENCE THAT CONNECTS US ALL

One of the reasons art is both convincing and powerful is that it physically enters the body of the viewer. When we look at something in our visual field, photons excite the optic nerve and the image neurologically enters our brain. Because of this, we see the "real world" and a work of art in the same physiological way. The same neurons and optic nerve respond inside our brains. This internal response accounts for the success of visualization, a process whereby images are called up internally "in the mind's eye" to influence our life in the external world. For centuries, Tibetan Buddhism has used visualization to open the mind (Thurman, 1991). As part of this spiritual practice a meditator visualizes a deity and then merges with that deity in the hopes of obtaining greater insight, and ultimately enlightenment.

As a secular practice, visualization is used to improve our health, our emotions, and our immune system (Ornstein & Sobel, 1987). Visualization may also have originated from everyday creativity. In this case, it would be our imagination that allows us to see and react with images "in the mind's eye."

All religious works of art and many secular pieces as well are meant to transform the viewer. That is the greatest power of art—its ability to effect change in us and, through our actions, change the world. Art has this power because we feel multiple connections to it. From a psychological and social standpoint, we may feel connected because of a shared culture, physical proximity, or interest in the subject matter. As a spiritual experience, it may seem that we and the work of art are parts of a greater whole. This experience of oneness is a foundation of Buddhist philosophy which says that the entire universe is interconnected due to the "interbeing" of all things (Nhat Hanh, 1974, p. 41). And the Huna religion of Hawaii speaks of an interlocking web of *aka threads*, invisible filaments that link everything to anything with which it has ever been in contact (Berney, 2001). In current science the concept of a holographic universe also postulates extensive connections. It says everything is part of an enormous hologram in which we and all works of art share a common ground of being (Kaku, 2004; Talbot, 1991).

## CONCLUSION

In conclusion, the strength and potential involved in creating and viewing art appears to be part of a multifaceted phenomenon embedded in the very fabric of our psychology and our existence. We partake of this power when we activate our inherent everyday creativity and it gives us a new view of human nature. Using everyday creativity in creating and responding to art, we can acquire an innovative outlook on life, change ourselves, and even transform our world.

## REFERENCES

Beltram, A. (Ed.). (1999). *The cave of Altamira.* New York: Abrams.

Berney, C. (2001). *Fundamentals of Hawaiian mysticism.* Freedom, CA: The Crossing Press.

Binyon, L. (1969). *Painting in the far East.* New York: Dover.

Blofeld, J. (1978). *Bodhisattva of compassion: The Mystical tradition of Kwan Yin.* Boston: Shambhala.

Bohm, D. (1983). *Wholeness and the implicate order.* London: Ark Paperbacks.

Brown, E. (1989). *Albert Pinkham Ryder*. Washington, DC: Smithsonian Institution Press.

Camic, P. (1999). Expanding treatment possibilities for chronic pain through the expressive arts. In C. Malchioiti (Ed.), *Medical art therapy with adults* (pp. 43–61). London: Jessica Kingsley.

The Cave of Lascaux. (n.d.). Retrieved March 12, 2007, from http://www.culture.gouv.fr/culture/arcnat/lascaux/en/

Chastel, A. (1975). *Marsile Ficin et l'art* [Marcilio Ficino and art]. Geneva, Switzerland: Libraire Droz.

Clottes, J., & Lewis-Williams, D. (1998). *The shamans of prehistory: Trance and magic in the painted caves*. New York: Abrams.

da Vinci, L. (1970). *The notebooks of Leonardo da Vinci (Vols. I & II)*. (J. P. Richter, Ed. & Trans.). New York: Dover. (Original work written ca. 1489–1519)

Dürer, A. (1958). *The writings of Albrecht Dürer*. (W. M. Conway, Ed. &Trans.). New York: Philosophical Library. (Original work from 1506–1528)

Dürer, A. (1972). *The human figure by Albrecht Dürer*. (W. L. Strauss, Ed. & Trans.). New York: Dover. (Original work published 1528)

Edinger, E. F. (1968, Spring). An outline of analytical psychology. *Quadrant, 1*, 8–19.

Elderfield, J. (1978). *The cut-outs of Henri Matisse*. New York: Braziller.

Eliot, A. (1957). *Three hundred years of American painting*. New York: Time.

Ellenberger, H. (1970). *The discovery of the unconscious*. New York: Basic Books.

Flam, J. (1986). *Matisse: The man and his art*. Ithaca, NY: Cornell University Press.

Gilot, F., & Lake, C. (1964). *Life with Picasso*. New York: McGraw-Hill.

Goodrich, L. (1959). *Albert P. Ryder*. New York: Braziller.

Hamilton, L. (2001). *The painted house of Maud Lewis: Conserving a folk art treasure*. Halifax, NS: The Art Gallery of Nova Scotia.

Heraclitus. (1987). *Fragments: A text and translation*. (T. M. Robinson, Commentator). Toronto, Ontario, Canada: University of Toronto Press. (Original work from the 5th century BC)

Homer, W. I., & Goodrich, L. (1989). *Albert Pinkham Ryder: Painter of dreams*. New York: Harry N. Abrams.

Hutchinson, J. C. (1990). *Albrecht Dürer: A biography*. Princeton, NJ: Princeton University Press.

Jedlicka, G. (1988). Die Matisse kapelle in Vence [The Matisse chapel in Vence]. In J. Flam (Ed.), *Mattisse, a retrospective* (pp. 378–379). New York: Parklane. (Original work published in 1955)

Jung, C. G. (1962). *The secret of the golden flower*. (C. F. Baynes, Trans.). New York: Harcourt, Brace & World.

Jung, C. G. (1971). *On the nature of the psyche*. (R. F. C. Hull, Trans.). Princeton, NJ: Princeton University Press.

Jung, C. G. (1973). *Four archetypes* (R. F. C. Hull, Trans.). Princeton, NJ: Princeton University Press.

Kaku, M. (2004). *Parallel worlds: A journey through creation, higher dimensions, and the future of the cosmos*. New York: Doubleday.

Kaufman, J. C., & Baer, J. (2004). Hawking's haiku, Madonna's math: Why it is hard to be creative in every room of the house. In R. J. Sternberg, E. L. Grigorenko, & J. L. Singer (Eds.), *Creativity: From potential to realization* (pp. 3–19). Washington, DC: American Psychological Association.

Kloss, W. (1988). *Samuel F. B. Morse*. New York: Harry N. Abrams.

Marx, C. R. (1960). *Rembrandt*. (W. J. Strachan & P. Simmons, Trans.). Paris: Pierre Tisné Éditeur.

Morse, S. F. B. (1983). *Lectures on the affinity of painting with the other fine arts*. (N. Cikovksky Jr., Ed.). Columbia, MO: University of Missouri Press. (Original work published 1826)

Neumann, E. (1959). *Art and the creative unconscious*. (R. Mannheim, Trans.). Princeton, NJ: Princeton University Press.

Nhat Hanh, T. (1974). *Zen keys*. (P. Kapleau, Trans.). New York: Doubleday.

Ornstein, R., & Sobel, D. (1987). *The healing brain: Breakthrough discoveries about how the brain keeps us healthy*. New York: Simon & Schuster.

Paar, D. W. (1993). Introducing confusion to create change. *The Psychotherapy Patient, 8*(1–2), 93–105.

Plato. (1950). The Republic. *The Works of Plato* (Vol. II, pp. 1–416; B. Jowett, Trans.). New York: Tudor Publishing. (Original work written 4th century BC)

Plotinus. (1991). *The Enneads* (S. MacKenna, Trans.). London: Penguin Books. (Originally written 250 CE)

Plucker, J. A., & Beghetto, R. A. (2004). Why creativity is domain general, why it looks domain specific, and why the distinction does not matter. In R. J. Sternberg, E. L. Grigorenko, & J. L. Singer (Eds.), *Creativity: From potential to realization* (pp. 153–167). Washington, DC: American Psychological Association.

Rhodes, C. (1997). Growth from deficiency creativity to being creativity. In M. A. Runco & R. Richards (Eds.), *Eminent creativity, everyday creativity, and health* (pp. 247–263). Norwood, NJ: Ablex Publishing.

Richards, R. (1997). Everyday creators: Psychological problems and creativity. In M. A. Runco & R. Richards (Eds.), *Eminent creativity, everyday creativity, and health* (pp. 97–98). Norwood, NJ: Ablex Publishing.

Richards, R. (1998). Creativity, everyday. In H. S. Freeman (Ed.), *Encyclopedia of mental health* (Vol. I, pp. 619–633). San Diego, CA: Academic Press.

Richards, R. (2004, March). *The arts and self-expression in mental health*. An invited address at the Carter Center, Atlanta, GA.

Richards, R. (2006). Frank Barron and the study of creativity: A voice that lives on. *Journal of Humanistic Psychology, 46,* 352–370.

Sandblom, P. (1996). *Creativity and disease.* New York: Boyars.

Sickman, L., & Soper, A. (1956). *Art and architecture of China.* London: Penguin Books.

Spurling, H. (1998). *The unknown Matisse: A life of Henri Matisse: The early years, 1869–1908.* Berkeley, CA: University of California Press.

Talbot, M. (1991). *The holographic universe.* New York: HarperCollins.

Thurman, R. A. F. (1991). Tibet, its Buddhism and its art. In M. M. Rhie & R. A. F. Thurman, *Wisdom and compassion: The sacred art of Tibet* (pp. 20–38). New York: Abrams.

Van Mander, C. (1936). *Dutch and Flemish artists* (C. van de Wall, Trans.). New York: McFarlane, Warde, McFarlane. (Original work published in 1604)

Vasari, G. (1996). *The lives of the artists* (Vols. I & II; G. Du C. De Vere, Trans.). New York: Knopf. (Original work published in 1568)

Woolaver, L. (1996). *The illuminated life of Maud Lewis.* Halifax, Novia Scotia, Canada: Nimbus Publishing and Art Gallery of Nova Scotia.

Woolaver, L. (1997). *Christmas with Maud Lewis.* Fredericton, New Brunswick, Canada: Goose Lane Editions.

Yates, F. (1979). *Giordano Bruno and the hermetic tradition.* Chicago: University of Chicago Press.

Zausner, T. (1998). When walls become doorways: Creativity, chaos theory, and physical illness. *Creativity Research Journal: Interdisciplinary Studies of Psychology, the Arts, and the Humanities, 11*(1), 21.

Zausner, T. (2000, August). Wholeness and perfection: Special challenges, art, and creativity. Invited address to the 108th Annual Convention of the American Psychological Association, Washington, DC.

Zausner, T. (2007). *When walls become doorways: Creativity and the transforming illness.* New York: Harmony Books.

# 4

# TO UNDERSTAND IS TO CREATE: AN EPISTEMOLOGICAL PERSPECTIVE ON HUMAN NATURE AND PERSONAL CREATIVITY

MARK A. RUNCO

To understand is to invent.
—Jean Piaget

Constructivist epistemology has much to say about creativity and human nature. Its basic premise is that knowledge is created by the individual. Knowledge is literally a construction of understanding. Often the constructive process provides an original interpretation of experience. This process is a creative one, at least when the resulting interpretations are both original and effective. These are the two key criteria of creativity (Rothenberg & Hausman, 1976; Runco, 1988), though sometimes originality is labeled novelty instead of originality, and sometimes effectiveness is labeled utility, appropriateness, or "fit." Of course, some interpretations are original only for the individual (and not for larger groups), in which case they represent what has been called *personal creativity* (Runco, 1996, 2003b).

Importantly, this constructive (and potentially creative) process is used by each of us, in all domains of activity and performance. It is not a special capacity found only in an occasional "great man" or "great woman," but is instead universal and intrinsic to human nature. In addition to supplying interpretations of experiences, it is the process that allows each of us to cope with daily hassles, express our individuality, and, sometimes, change the world.

Personal creativity requires *discretion* (deciding when to construct original interpretations and when to conform instead) and *intentions* (which reflect the values that motivate creative efforts) as well as *the capacity to construct original interpretations of experience*. This chapter examines these three critical aspects of our creative potential, with implications for how we might become even more creative. I explore several issues in this chapter, including the question of when to construct original views and when to conform. The values that motivate our efforts are also described, as are distinctions between reactive adaptation and proactive creativity. There is discussion of the possibility that creativity is both personal and social. However, a claim is made that all creativity is personal (whatever its contextual origins), whereas only some creativity eventually has social impact. All of this adds up to a view of human nature as personally creative.

## CREATIVE POTENTIAL

Creativity is an enormously important part of human nature. Simply put, it is human nature to be creative. This implies that creative talents are widely shared, a position I explore and defend in this chapter. It also implies that the "great man–great woman" view of creative talent, which only recognizes eminent and productive individuals, is suspect—another position I defend herein. If only a select group of persons was creative, it would be inaccurate to describe creativity as a part of human nature.[1] The position here is that creative talents are shared among all of us, and thus creative potential is a part of human nature.

Not all definitions of creativity apply so broadly. Some definitions assume greatness or outstanding productivity. The definition that does apply broadly is a part of the theory of *personal creativity*. This theory not only describes creativity in terms that apply to every person but also bridges eminent and everyday creativity (Runco & Richards, 1998). As a matter of fact, this is one of the critical premises tying creativity to human nature.

---

[1] An alternative view is that there are great men and great women because greatness is possible within the spectrum of "human nature." But with that logic, we would also need to accept murder, waste, greed, and various other proclivities as part of human nature. They, too, sometimes occur. The assumption in this chapter is that human nature is clearest in universals. Personal creativity represents a universal tendency. Those other things reflect exceptionalities, proclivities that are possible but not common, necessary, nor indicative of what all people share. Any behavior that is already demonstrated is a possibility, and as such within human nature, but creative potential is universal, whereas murder and so on are not. Exceptionalities may occur for various reasons, including mutation and accident, and they are important for idiographical analyses (cf. Brower, 1999; McLaren, 1993).

Creativity is an everyday phenomenon. As noted earlier, it helps each person cope with hassles, express him- or herself, and adjust to changes. Not a day goes by, and perhaps not an hour, without the need for adjustment.

In a sense, everyday creativity is a domain within which we all perform (Runco & Richards, 1998). This concept must be underscored because creative talents cannot be understood without recognizing domain differences. Creativity is obviously expressed in different ways in different domains (e.g., music, mathematics, performing arts, science, language arts). If everyday creativity is recognized as a kind of domain, the universality of personal creativity is indubitable, as is its connection to human nature. It may be most accurate to view everyday creativity as a higher order- or metadomain. This is because many domains vary in terms of their symbol systems, neuroanatomical bases, and developmental prerequisites (Gardner, 1983). Everyday creativity, however, results from nomothetic rather than idiographic capacities. It is, again, something we all share. Yet it is distinct from artistic, mathematical, or other specialized expressions of originality.

## TO UNDERSTAND IS TO CREATE

The universality of personal creativity is strongly suggested by epistemology. Consider, for example, Piaget's (1976) theories of cognition. Piaget focused on cognitive development rather than creativity, yet as we shall see in this chapter there are a number of commonalities between his theory and the creative epistemology. What is most important at this juncture is that Piaget's epistemology—and his answer to the epistemological question "how do we obtain knowledge?"—was *adaptation*. For Piaget humans assimilate (changing information such that we can bring it into our cognitive systems) and then accommodate (changing our cognitive structures, and understanding, in response to that new information). By doing this we resolve any disequilibrium that develops when the individual's level of understanding does not match an experience. Piaget's theory describes new understandings as responses, or adaptations, to experience. These are "genetic" in various ways, and thus as you would expect, universal. (Piaget referred to his approach as a *genetic epistemology*.) Universals include the potential to adapt, but also the potential to develop four different kinds of thinking (apparent in different stages of development).

The genetic drive to resolve misunderstanding, what Piaget called *disequilibration*, is relevant to studies of creativity because it implies that we are intrinsically motivated to construct understandings (see also chap. 8, this volume). In this light Piaget offered an explanation for the commonly observed intrinsic motivation of creativity as well as a process by which understandings are created. Piaget preferred the word *"invention"* over "*creation*" or "*creativity*," as is implied by the title to his monograph, *To Understand Is to Invent*. It is my contention that the process he used to explain the invention of understanding applies directly to the construction of original and useful ideas and solutions; and if these are original and useful, we can call them creative and have a process explanation for creative efforts.

Admittedly, Piaget focused on adaptation, which is typically a reaction of some sort.[2] Creative thinking, in contrast, often allows humans to behave proactively (Heinzen, 1999; Richards, 1993) and not just reactively. We do not simply solve problems; we foresee them. We define and redefine them. And sometimes, we avoid them. True, humans sometimes behave in a maladaptive (rather than adaptive) manner (Runco, 1994a). This also distinguishes creativity from adaptation. Still, Piaget's work is very helpful—his definition of *invention* involves development of original and useful schemas. It may be best here to outline the theory of personal creativity and, while doing so, refer to Piaget's theory, as well as the implications for our understanding of human nature.

## PERSONAL CREATIVITY

There are three key features of personal creativity: interpretation, discretion, and intentionality. Interpretation occurs whenever an individual constructs meaning or develops an understanding of his or her experience. Note the involvement of the individual in this regard. An interpretation does not result from recall or any memory; it is not merely "reproductive" (Cofer, 1977). Interpretations are always individualistic. Every individual personally constructs them and can neither borrow them nor obtain them without mindful involvement and effortful processing of information. Because every individual constructs his or her own interpretations, they may differ from individual to individual, even if these persons have the same objective experience.

Our knowledge does not perfectly represent the environment, or even our own experience; it is instead a selective and biased view that is actively constructed as the individual processes information. Piaget described the selective process as *assimilation*. By including assimilation in the developmental process, Piaget was able to circumvent a paradox. After all, how can an individual think about something he or she does not understand? How can people process information about something before it is understood? How can individuals learn knew things? Learning is possible because individuals first assimilate and then accommodate. The individual assimilates by

---

[2] Piaget described *reflective abstraction* as a purely cognitive act and one that is not a reaction to the environment.

selecting parts of the new experience he or she can grasp, and by changing the rest so that it can be processed and considered. The experience is changed—at least it is in our conception of it. What is taken away from a new experience is information that is in some ways indicative of the experience but not necessarily all that accurate a picture of it. This allows the person to bring the new information into the cognitive system and accommodate to it. Accommodation is accomplished when the cognitive system changes (new structures are built or existing structured are differentiated) to take the new information into account. The most important part of this for personal creativity—and for our understanding of human nature—is that meaning is constructed. It is a personally creative act. This is the mechanism that allowed Einstein to conceive of relativity, in addition to being the process by which each of us learns during childhood about the world and ourselves.

Examples of assimilation and interpretation are easy to find. Piaget felt that imaginative play was the epitome of assimilation. A child using his or her imagination tends to ignore those parts of experience that are incompatible with the imagined world. Children may pretend that their friend is a monster, and they ignore the fact that the so-called monster (a) looks exactly like his or her own best friend, and (b) 1 minute earlier the monster was not a monster at all but was the person laughing during a very calm tea party. Similar personal constructions are apparent in each of our lives, though we certainly do not play enough as adults!

Consider the experience of stress. There are no stressors in the environment, no objects that guarantee that each of us will experience stress. (Well, other than the Internal Revenue Service.) Instead, we each react to certain things as stressful. This is why many of us calmly give lectures in front of large groups of students, but someone unaccustomed to teaching may experience stress when speaking in front of exactly the same group. The two people can have the same objective experiences but different subjective interpretations. The person who experienced stress speaking publicly might later decide to relax by visiting a theme park. Perhaps riding a rollercoaster is fun and relaxing to that person—but to the calm public speaker, a rollercoaster may elicit extreme stress. Each person interprets experiences in an idiosyncratic fashion. It is idiosyncratic because each individual is constructing his or her own interpretations of the event.

Creative thinking occurs when we use this same process to construct original interpretations. Reiterating, if those interpretations are effective as well as original, they qualify as everyday creativity. Creative things are original and effective (Rothenberg & Hausman, 1976; Runco, 1988). And if the original interpretations impress others, and perhaps change the way these other people think, they may be socially accepted creative achievements (Kasof, 1995). If hugely impressive, they may change a field and a domain, in which case the individual may be eminently creative (Csikszentmihalyi, 1990; Gardner, 1993). The process begins with the individual, however, and with some insight, idea, or solution—an original interpretation for them. In this sense interpretation plays a role in all creativity. And this is something for which each us has the capacity.

We do not and should not use this capacity all of the time. A child who is always imagining things will not fit in socially and may never learn the conventions that are necessary for maturity. An adult who only constructs original interpretations will probably be deemed a nonconformist or even psychotic. He or she will be out of touch with reality.

This is where discretion comes in. Discretion allows the individual to know when to be original and when to conform. Significantly, given that the interpretive process is shared by each of us, many individual differences in creative potentials and creative achievement reflect discretion and not more basic cognitive capacities. Both potential and actual achievement will differ because one way a person may exercise his or her discretion is in a decision to invest (or not invest) in his or her own creative potentials (Rubenson & Runco, 1992). Investments may involve practice, reading, taking classes, enrolling in workshops, and so on. Investments are necessary if the individual is to fulfill potentials. However, there are opportunity costs; investing in one thing keeps you from investing time in something else. For creativity, there are often risks. It can be quite risky to invest in creative potential when the resulting creative talents may or may not lead to socially accepted ends. (See also chaps. 1 & 7, this volume.)

Certainly motivation also plays a role in the relevant investment, and in creative achievements. As noted previously, that motivation may be mostly intrinsic. It is recognized in the theory of personal creativity, though subsumed under the label *intentions*. Intentions also include values, and values can dramatically influence creativity. People often exercise discretion by selecting what is valuable. They will invest in skills because they view those skills as valuable.[3] Parents and teachers will communicate values and the corresponding appropriate behaviors to children via socialization and even formal education (Runco, 2003b). Indeed, this is the part of personal creativity that explains cultural differences (Runco, 2004). Each of us has the potential to be creative, but there are differences between individuals (reflecting motivation and decision making) and between various groups, including cultures (reflecting values).

---

[3] These may be the domain-specific skills that are so frequently used to explain creative performances. Indeed, this may be where domain differences are most apparent and the best explanation for domain differences. After all, the interpretive process that is at the heart of personal creativity is essentially universal; all people construct interpretations of experience. That does not explain domain differences. These differences no doubt largely reflect the domain-specific skills that are acquired through experiences and selected investments.

## CREATIVE PRODUCTS, PROCESSES, PLACES, AND PEOPLE

The creativity literature can be organized using product, process, place, and people (or person) emphases (Richards, 1999; Runco, 2004). The product research examines inventions, publications, works of art, and so on. The idea is that these products can be counted and judged in an objective fashion. The process perspective examines cognitive (Runco & Chand, 1995; Wallas, 1926) or social process (Csikszentmihalyi, 1990; Kasof, 1995) which may lead to creative performance. The place (or press) research looks to environments which are conducive to creative work (Amabile, 1990; Witt & Beorkrem, 1989). The creative person or personality category identifies core characteristics, traits, or tendencies that are typical of creative people (Barron, 1995; Domino, 1994). Often the people involved in this last category of research are eminently creative.

The theory of personal creativity was initially a reaction to product theories and those theories which claim that creativity always involves a social judgment. I was particularly disturbed by the attributional theory of creativity (Kasof, 1995), because it not only suggested that creativity can only be judged after it is shared but also offered suggestions, such as *impression management* (the attempt to manipulate what others think of us), to improve one's creativity. I suggested that impression management was a displaced investment (Runco, 1995) and might actually undermine a person's creative potentials. Just as extrinsic motivations sometimes distract the creator, so too could worry about the impression one projects distract and misguide the individual. I suggested that all creativity starts on a personal level (with interpretation, discretion, and intentions) and only sometimes becomes a social affair.

## POSTCONVENTIONALITY AND CREATIVITY

Personal creativity can also be understood as a kind of *postconventional* behavior. Postconventionality was originally proposed by Kohlberg (1987) to describe the highest level of moral development, or at least the highest level of moral reasoning. The earlier stages are preconventional (the child does not have the cognitive capacity to grasp "rules," "morals," or "conventions" of any sort) and conventional (the individual blindly conforms to what others do and expect). I suggested that the conventional stage is apparent not only in moral reasoning but also in creative performances (Runco, 1993). It may help explain the fourth-grade slump (Torrance, 1968; Runco, 1999c), for example, as well as the literal stage of language (Gardner, 1980) and the loss of self-expression in children's representational art (Rosenblatt & Winner, 1988).

Postconventional reasoning characterizes the individual who under-stands conventions but still thinks for him- or herself. This is often a matter of taking immediate context into account. A person may need to bend the rules to play baseball, for example, if there are too few players or the field is imperfect. That is a kind of flexibility, which allows adaptability and creative solutions to problems. The terminology here is important: Post-conventional individuals take immediate context into account—which is another way of saying that they exercise some discretion. In a sense, then, creativity results from the capacity to construct original interpretations, combined with the postconventional discretion to explore and use those interpretations only when it is appropriate to do so.

## PERSONAL CREATIVITY, SELF-ACTUALIZATION, AND EGOSTRENGTH

One advantage of the theory of personal creativity is that it distin-guishes creativity from problem solving.[4] The postconventional thinking mentioned just previously, for instance, sometimes allows the individual to be proactive. That distinguishes creativity from problem solving because problem solving is always a kind of reaction. First there is a problem, then, with a bit of luck and skill, there is a solution. Proactive creativity sometimes allows the individual to identify, anticipate, or define a problem, although these actions are different from solving a problem.

Proactive creativity may be seen when an individual knows what is typical and accepted by everyone else, but thinks for him- or herself and realizes that the status quo is inadequate. You might say that this individual has either foreseen a problem, or that the individual has identified a problem that was hitherto unnoticed. Both of these behaviors are proactive, and both can be of great assistance to us when managing the world's resources and politics. Proactive thinking ties creativity to morals and ethics (Gruber, 1993; Richards, 1993). As Gruber (1993) put it, "can implies ought." A similar sentiment is suggested by the adage, "an ounce of prevention is worth a pound of cure," though the idea of postconventional thinking is more of an explanation than a recommendation.

Proactive thinking may well be limited to humans. We can now define human nature. Human nature should be defined in terms of characteristics

---

[4]Creative efforts are sometimes elicited by problems (Runco, 1994a, 1994b), and just as surely many enormously creative insights have in fact been solutions to problems. Then again, some creative inventions and insights have created problems! McLaren (1993) referred to the worst of this as the "dark side of creativity." Atomic weapons, certain environmentally disturbing synthetics, and overdemanding technologies all represent this dark side.

that are unique to humans. Otherwise we might be explaining "mammalian nature" or "animal nature" or something more general than human nature. Proactive thinking is probably limited to humans, and it is one of our most important capacities. Richards (1993) was absolutely correct when she suggested that these kinds of skills are of utmost importance and should be nurtured at every opportunity.

Creativity is clearly distinct from problem solving when the creator is expressing him- or herself. This could be a kind of problem solving if the person has the need to disclose something, or if the individual is exploring artistically in an attempt to refine technique or best capture a subject. Of course, even the self-expression of an artist may be, on some level, an attempt to solve a problem. It may be a personal problem, and the artist may not even consciously recognize it as such! It could be an issue from childhood (Csikszentmihalyi, 1988; Jones, Runco, Dorinan, & Freeland, 1997), or it could be a problem of technique and the best way to capture an idea or concept. Perhaps it is best to accept the fact that artistic creativity is sometimes a kind of problem solving, but also sometimes self-expression, exploration, experimentation, or some other activity that is not problem solving.

Apparently, self-expression comes naturally to the self-actualized person, which further separates creativity from problem solving. Self-expression is not necessarily a kind of problem solving. It is typically more spontaneous rather than reactive. This is especially clear in the creativity that is a part of self-actualization (Maslow, 1971; Rogers, 1961; Runco, 1999a). The association between self-actualization and creative self-expression is frequently overlooked. This may be because the disorders that sometimes characterize creative persons (e.g., bipolar disorders) are more salient and memorable. The disorders of creative people are sometimes even newsworthy, especially if they lead to suicide. But Maslow (1971) and Rogers (1961) both felt that creative expression was characteristic of self-actualized individuals. Rogers (1961) eventually concluded that creativity and self-actualization were inextricable.

Creative self-expression may not come naturally to everyone. In fact, difficulties with self-expression may represent the most common blocks or hurdles to the fulfillment of creative potential. After all, everyone has the cognitive potential to think in a creative fashion—at least as suggested by the theory of personal creativity—but we do not always use those skills, nor always develop them. We often fail to use them because we are conforming, or simply fitting in. It is much easier to fit in with a social group when you go along with convention and conform to expectation, but it is antithetical to the originality and individualism required by creative behavior. (See also chap. 7, this volume.)

No wonder Rogers (1961) described the creative process as a therapeutic process. Providing unconditional positive regard can support and thereby validate the individual as an individual. Similarly, it is no surprise that Harrington, Block, and Block (1983) found that parents who provide the same kind of environment (characterized by psychological safety and unconditional positive regard) best support the creativity of their children.

I take this one step further and suggest that it is ego strength that is particularly in need of support. An individual with mature and resilient ego strength is the most likely to stand up for his or her own perspective. It will not be a false contrarianism, a rebellion for the sake of rebellion, but will instead be a realistic expression of one's self, even if it is contrary to (unrealistic) expectations. In sum, it is ego strength, even more than cognitive skills, which should be the first priority in schools, homes, and organizations, if creative self-expression and the fulfillment of potential are desired.

## NATURE AND NURTURE

These ideas about supporting creativity assume that nurturance is extremely important. The possibility of enhancing creative potential does not, however, imply that "nature" and biology are unimportant. Certainly creativity depends on the interplay of nature and nurture. In fact, some of the most thrilling empirical research uses functional magnetic resonance imaging to uncover the sensitivity of the prefrontal lobes to conventions. This research is reviewed by Runco (2006b). There are individual differences, with some persons reacting (on a neurological level) to social pressures (e.g., advertisements) more than others. Creativity was not directly assessed in this research, but it is easy to tie creativity to low levels of sensitivity to convention. Recall here the connection explored earlier between creativity and postconventional thinking. The postconventional person thinks for him- or herself. That individual does not conform or give in to convention.

Adults are in special need of tactics for creative self-expression and not just egostrength. This is because of what might be called the trajectory of human nature. Children are unconventional by virtue of their preconventionality. They are spontaneous and uninhibited and free of the assumptions and routines that make creative thinking difficult as we get older. With maturity comes a mindless tendency (Langer, 1989; Moldoveanu & Langer, 1999). During adulthood there is a common tendency to become more rigid and to rely more and more on assumption and routine. Assumption and routine make us more efficient, but they also keep us from being spontaneous and creative.

Additional problems may result from long-term investments (Rubenson & Runco, 1992, 1995). Most problematic are investments in certain skills and patterns of thought. Similar to financial investments, the more the individual has at risk, the less open he or she will be to change and alternatives. If you invest a huge amount in, say, one scientific theory, one style of art, or one spouse, you may resist change—and the longer or more we invest, the more we have to lose and the more resistant we are likely to be. That is the psychoeconomic explanation for the cost of expertise. It only characterizes adults; children have not had the time to make these investments. This allows them to be flexible, and thereby creative.

Tactics can help adults compensate for these assumptions, inhibitions, routines, and long-term investments. In this context tactics are tricks, procedures, and shortcuts that can refresh our originality or help us to adopt an approach to problem solving that increases the likelihood of a creative result (Runco, 1999b). One of the most powerful tactics is that of shifting perspectives. A shift of perspective usually suggests different alternatives and forces the individual out of his or her routine. Perspectives can be shifted in many ways: talking to other people, moving to a different vantage point, changing the problem (by making it bigger, smaller, or altering the representation or medium), standing back, zooming in, turning the problem on its head, or putting it aside for a time, and so on.


## ACCOMMODATION AND CREATIVITY

Elsewhere I distinguished between assimilatory tactics and those that involve accommodation (Runco, 1999b). I mention this here for several reasons. First, the shifts of perspective just mentioned involve a change in the problem or context. This is, in a sense, assimilatory. The information changes when the problem or perspective changes. Such assimilatory tactics are consistent with the theory of personal creativity, given its emphasis on interpretation and the assimilatory process.

The other Piagetian process is, however, also useful for some kinds of shifts of perspective and for creative thinking. This is the process of accommodation, which I defined earlier as a change in the individual's understanding (and underlying cognitive structures). This kind of restructuring is often used to explain creative insights.

Insights appear to be quick and sudden; they give us the "ah-ha!" feeling. But actually they are protracted and develop over a period of time (Gruber, 1989; Wallace, 1991). They may feel sudden because the end result of spending a long time thinking about subject matter is a change in how the problem or the key information is represented in our cognitive systems. This is restructuring, or what Piaget called accommodation. Hence this part of the adaptive process, accommodation, can also participate in creative thinking, at least when the creativity is in the form of an insight. Tactics may depend on accommodation. Questioning one's assumptions, for example, is often useful and helps to uncover alternatives and avoid conceptual ruts.

## CONCLUSIONS

To be most accurate we should view the features of personal creativity—interpretive capacity, discretion, and intentionality—as constituting creative potential. If those potentials are fulfilled and applied, the individual may actually perform in an impressive and creative fashion, or perhaps achieve something. But again, unlike many social and product approaches to creativity, the theory of personal creativity focuses on potential. In this view, creativity is something we all have, a potential we share as humans, regardless of our social tendencies, our socially recognized achievements, and the impressions others may have of us.

The idea of potential is important for our understanding of human nature because we should not equate human nature with actual creative production and performance. Interpretive capacity, discretion, and intentions merely provide the potential to perform in a creative fashion, the potential to adapt and cope, and the potential for proactive creativity. Nothing is guaranteed. We need experience to fulfill potential. We also need to avoid certain (constraining) experiences. We need ego strength, for example, and we do not need to be overly conventional or conforming. Of course there are optimal levels of all things, ego strength and conventionality included (Runco, 2001).

I should back up slightly and modify one of my claims. I have defined personal creativity as asocial and individualistic. It is probably most accurate to say that interpretation, discretion, and intentions define an individual's creative potential, but that humans are social creatures. We are, in the words of Aronson (1980), a social animal. (Or in John Donne's words, "no man is an island.") It is our nature to be social, and in fact the potentials defined by personal creativity will not be fulfilled nor applied without particular social experiences. Family and education, for example, have significant influence over the fulfillment of potentials. Yet the potential is there even without these particular experiences.

Even the possibility of tactical creative problem solving tells us about human nature. It tells us that humans can modify their behavior, and do so intentionally, and thereby take control of themselves and to a certain degree their environments and experiences. I hope such intentional efforts will be done on a grand scale, across the population, and done so proactively to cure societal and environmental ailments.

Note that I am not dismissing eminent creativity. Indeed, one of the advantages of the theory of personal creativity is that it applies across the population, from the infant to the adult, from someone who "never produces anything original or useful" (Nicholls, 1972/1983) to the unambiguously creative superstar. All of them rely on the same processes and mechanisms for their creativity. The creativity is simply expressed in different ways in the various groups (and perhaps expressed more or less regularly among some of them). Personal creativity does not just describe the original interpretations of experience constructed by individuals in a workaday situation. Eminent creators also have their insights in part because they are using interpretive, assimilatory processes to construct their dramatic world-shaking insights (Runco, 2006a).

A definition of human nature should recognize the following:

1. Humans have creative potentials and may use these in extremely diverse ways.
2. Humans are both reactive (and adaptable) and potentially proactive. Some of our creativity is used to solve problems, but it is also apparent in our spontaneous self-expression.
3. Humans are not tightly governed by instinct, but genetics no doubt determines the range of potential.
4. Children have advantages in their spontaneity, lack of inhibition and convention, and lack of knowledge (assumption and routine). Adults have an advantage in their mindful capacity and their intentional adoption of tactics.
5. Potential can be fulfilled such that we work in moral and ethical directions (e.g., to humanity's benefit) or such that the dark side is manifested (e.g., in weapons).
6. Creativity is often unpredictable, and always original, and thus creative people are, in a manner of speaking, deviant. On societal and individual levels, what is needed, then, is a tolerance of individual differences and unconventional behavior.

## FINAL COMMENTS

People sometimes express themselves in a spontaneous and uninhibited fashion. This is apparently especially true of self-actualized individuals (Maslow, 1971; Rogers, 1961; Runco, 1999a). Some forms of self-expression are functionally related to physical health as well as psychological health (Pennebaker, Kiecolt-Glaser, & Glaser, 1997). Creativity may also be spontaneous (not reactive) when an individual is proactive (Heinzen, 1999; Richards, 1993) or working to improve something. The "thing" being improved may be a machine or other physical entity, a process, or just a perspective. If improvement was required, the creativity would be a kind of problem solving, but sometimes the improvement is not required, not necessary. The creator may just have an idea for improvement. This may reflect problem finding, problem identification, problem construction, or problem definition (Runco, 1994b). It is proactive rather than reactive. Of course creativity may be used to solve problems, including personal problems. It may be related to coping (Flach, 1990) and adaptability (Cohen, 1989; Runco, 1994a). Cohen (1989) presented a continuum of adaptive behaviors, covering the lifespan, each related to creative potential. Creativity may also be seen in imaginative play or humor (Koestler, 1965; O'Quin & Derks, 1998). Bruner's (1972) definition of creativity as effective surprise applies especially well here, for a joke's punch line has just that: It is unforeseen but fitting. The list of creative behaviors is long, but the point is that creativity takes many forms. It contributes greatly to the diversity of the human population. Another way of saying the same thing is that creative potential is universally shared and a critical aspect of human nature.

## REFERENCES

Amabile, T. M. (1990). Within you, without you: Towards a social psychology of creativity, and beyond. In M. A. Runco & R. S. Albert (Eds.), *Theories of creativity* (pp. 61–91). Newbury Park, CA: Sage.

Aronson, E. (1980). *The social animal* (3rd ed.). San Francisco: Freeman.

Barron, F. (1995). *No rootless flower*. Cresskill, NJ: Hampton Press.

Brower, R. (1999). Crime and creativity. In M. A. Runco & S. R. Pritzker (Eds.), *Encyclopedia of creativity* (Vol. 1, pp. 443–448). San Diego, CA: Academic Press.

Bruner, J. (1972). The conditions of creativity. In J. Bruner (Ed.), *On knowing: Essays for the left hand*. Cambridge, MA: Harvard University Press.

Cofer, C. N. (1977). Constructive processes in memory. I. L. Janis (Ed.), *Current trends in psychology: Readings from "American Scientist"* (pp. 166–172). Los Altos, CA: William Kaufman.

Cohen, L. M. (1989). A continuum of adaptive creative behaviors. *Creativity Research Journal, 2*, 169–183.

Csikszentmihalyi, M. (1988). The dangers of originality: Creativity and the artistic process. In M. M. Gedo (Ed.), *Psychoanalytic perspectives on art* (pp. 213–224). Hillsdale, NJ: Analytic Press.

Csikszentmihalyi, M. (1990). The domain of creativity. In M. A. Runco & R. S. Albert (Eds.), *Theories of creativity* (pp. 190–212). Newbury Park, CA: Sage.

Domino, G. (1994). Assessment of creativity with the Adjective Checklist: A comparison of four scales. *Creativity Research Journal, 7*, 21–23.

Flach, F. (1990). Disorders of the pathways involved in the creative process. *Creativity Research Journal, 3*, 158–165.

Gardner, H. (1980). *Artful scribbles: The significance of children's drawings*. New York: Basic Books.

Gardner, H. (1983). *Frames of mind: A theory of multiple intelligences*. New York: Basic Books.

Gardner, H. (1993). *Creating minds*. New York: Basic Books.

Gruber, H. E. (1981). *Darwin on man*. Chicago: University of Chicago Press.

Gruber, H. E. (1989). The evolving systems approach to creative work. *Creativity Research Journal, 1*, 27–51.

Gruber, H. E. (1993). Creativity in the moral domain: OUGHT implies CAN implies CREATE. *Creativity Research Journal, 6*, 3–16.

Harrington, D. M., Block, J., & Block, J. H. (1983). Predicting creativity in pre-adolescence from divergent thinking in early childhood. *Journal of Personality and Social Psychology, 45*, 609–623.

Heinzen, T. E. (1999). Proactive creativity. In M. A. Runco & S. R. Pritzker (Eds.), *Encyclopedia of creativity* (Vol. 2, pp. 429–431). San Diego, CA: Academic Press.

Jones, K., Runco, M. A., Dorinan, C., & Freeland, D. C. (1997). Influential factors in artists' lives and themes in their art work. *Creativity Research Journal, 10*, 221–228.

Kasof, J. (1995). Explaining creativity: The attributional perspective. *Creativity Research Journal, 8*, 311–366.

Koestler, A. (1965). *The act of creation*. New York: MacMillan.

Kohlberg, L. (1987). The development of moral judgment and moral action. In L. Kohlberg (Ed.), *Child psychology and childhood education: A cognitive developmental view*. New York: Longman.

Langer, E. (1989). *Mindfulness*. Reading, MA: Addison-Wesley.

Maslow, A. H. (1971). *The farther reaches of human nature*. New York: Viking Press.

McLaren, R. B. (1993). The dark side of creativity. In M. A. Runco & S. R. Pritzker (Eds.), *Encyclopedia of creativity* (Vol. 1, pp. 483–491). San Diego, CA: Academic Press.

Moldoveanu, M. C., & Langer, E. (1999). Mindfulness. In M. A. Runco & S. Pritzker (Eds.), Encyclopedia of creativity (Vol. 1, pp. 221–234). San Diego, CA: Academic Press.

Nicholls, J. C. (1983). Creativity in the person who will never produce anything original or useful. In R. S. Albert (Ed.), *Genius and eminence: A social psychology of exceptional achievement* (pp. 265–279). New York: Pergamon. (Original work published 1972)

O'Quin, K., & Derks, P. (1997). Humor and creativity: A review of the empirical literature. In M. A. Runco (Ed.), *Creativity research handbook* (Vol. 1, pp. 223–252). Cresskill, NJ: Hampton Press.

Pennebaker, J. W., Kiecolt-Glaser, J. K., & Glaser, R. (1997). Disclosure of traumas and immune function: Health implications for psychotherapy. In M. A. Runco

& R. Richards (Eds.), *Eminent creativity, everyday creativity, and health* (pp. 287–392). Norwood, NJ: Ablex Publishing.

Piaget, J. (1976). *To understand is to invent*. New York: Penguin.

Richards, R. (1993). Seeing beyond: Issues of creative awareness and social responsibility. *Creativity Research Journal, 6*, 165–183.

Richards, R. (1999). Four Ps of creativity. In M. A. Runco & S. R. Pritzker (Eds.), *Encyclopedia of creativity* (Vol. I, pp. 683–687). San Diego, CA: Academic Press.

Rogers, C. R. (1961). *On becoming a person*. Boston: Houghton Mifflin.

Rosenblatt, E., & Winner, E. (1988). The art of children's drawings. *Journal of Aesthetic Education, 22*, 3–15.

Rothenberg, A., & Hausman, C. (1976). *The creativity question*. Durham, NC: Duke University Press.

Rubenson, D. L., & Runco, M. A. (1992). The psychoeconomic approach to creativity. *New Ideas in Psychology, 10*, 131–147.

Rubenson, D. L., & Runco, M. A. (1995). The psychoeconomic view of creative work in groups and organizations. *Creativity and Innovation Management, 4*, 232–241.

Runco, M. A. (1988). Creativity research: Originality, utility, and integration. *Creativity Research Journal, 1*, 1–7.

Runco, M. A. (1993). *Creativity as an educational objective for disadvantaged students*. Storrs, CT: University of Connecticut.

Runco, M. A. (1994a). *Creativity and affect*. Norwood, NJ: Ablex Publishing.

Runco, M. A. (1994b). *Problem finding, problem solving, and creativity*. Norwood, NJ: Ablex Publishing.

Runco, M. A. (1995). Insight for creativity, expression for impact. *Creativity Research Journal, 8*, 377–390.

Runco, M. A. (1996). Personal creativity: Definition and developmental issues. *New Directions for Child Development, 72*, 3–30.

Runco, M. A. (1999a). Self-actualization and creativity. In M. A. Runco & S. R. Pritzker (Eds.), *Encyclopedia of creativity* (pp. 533–536). San Diego, CA: Academic Press.

Runco, M. A. (1999b). Tactics and strategies for creativity. In M. A. Runco & S. R. Pritzker (Eds.), *Encyclopedia of creativity* (pp. 611–615). San Diego, CA: Academic Press.

Runco, M. A. (1999c). The forth-grade slump. In M. A. Runco & S. Pritzker (Eds.), *Encyclopedia of creativity* (pp. 743–744). San Diego, CA: Academic Press.

Runco, M. A. (2001). Creativity as optimal human functioning. In M. Bloom (Ed.), *Promoting creativity across the lifespan* (pp. 17–44). Washington, DC: Child Welfare League of America.

Runco, M. A. (2003a). Creativity, cognition, and their educational implications. In J. C. Houtz (Ed.), *The educational psychology of creativity* (pp. 25–56). Cresskill, NJ: Hampton Press.

Runco, M. A. (2003b). Education for creative potential. *Scandinavian Journal of Education, 47,* 317–324.

Runco, M. A. (2004). Creativity. *Annual review of Psychology, 55,* 657–687.

Runco, M. A. (2004). Personal creativity and culture. In L. Sing, A. N. N. Hui, & G. C. Ng (Eds.), *Creativity: When East meets West* (pp. 9–21). Singapore: World Scientific Publishing.

Runco, M. A. (2006a). Creativity is always personal and only sometimes social. In J. A. Schaler (Ed.), *Howard Gardner under fire: The rebel psychologist faces his critics* (pp. 169–182). Chicago: Open Court.

Runco, M. A. (2006b). Reasoning and personal creativity. In J. C. Kaufman & J. Baer (Eds.), *Creativity and reason in cognitive development* (pp. 99–116). New York: Cambridge University Press.

Runco, M. A., & Chand, I. (1995). Cognition and creativity. *Educational Psychology Review, 7,* 243–267.

Runco, M. A, & Richards, R. (1998). *Eminent creativity, everyday creativity, and health.* Greenwich, CT: Ablex Publishing.

Torrance, E. P. (1968). A longitudinal examination of the fourth-grade slump in creativity. *Gifted Child Quarterly, 12,* 195–199.

Wallace, D. B. (1991). The genesis and microgenesis of sudden insight in the creation of literature. *Creativity Research Journal, 4,* 41–50.

Wallas, G. (1926). *The art of thought.* New York: Harcourt Brace.

Witt, L. A., & Beorkrem, M. (1989). Climate for creative productivity as a predictor of research usefulness and organizational effectiveness in an R&D organization. *Creativity Research Journal, 2,* 30–40.

# 5

# AUDIENCE FLOW: CREATIVITY IN TELEVISION WATCHING WITH APPLICATIONS TO TELETHERAPY

STEVEN R. PRITZKER

All of our knowledge has its origins in our perceptions.
—Leonardo da Vinci

Television viewing is the most popular use of free time, and its popularity is growing. According to A.C. Nielson, the time spent watching television in the average U.S. home "during the 2005–2006 television year was 8 hours and 14 minutes per day" (Nielson Media Research, 2006). Television viewing has often been criticized as a passive activity that can contribute to negative behavior and stunt cognitive growth. Here it is suggested that apparently passive viewers may at certain times be actively creating, especially when engrossed in a program that offers sufficient cognitive stimulation. This falls into the category of everyday creativity which is defined by Richards (1999) as the "originality of everyday life . . . vital for our flexible adaptation to life, and sense of personal well being" (p. 683). Psychologists could be more effectively involved in media literacy programs to make better use of this potential for creative growth.

The present chapter does not deny the potential negative effects of television viewing, but presents the new view that television, in some cases, can create a state of audience flow. *Flow* is a term coined by Csikszentmihalyi (1996), involving a highly focused and almost effortless state of consciousness, merging action and awareness around activities that are challenging, yet within a person's capacity, involving immediate feedback, some element of novelty, and which are self-sustaining and rewarding in themselves. *Audience flow* is defined as the experience of viewing a play, movie, dance work, television show, work of art, listening to music or poetry, reading a book, or other related activity, in an active and mentally engaged state that may allow insights and new perspectives to develop. As Csikszentmihalyi said of flow in general (1990, 1996), the experience will also strengthen concentration, involvement, enjoyment, and provide some degree of challenge well suited to the individual's capabilities (Csikzentmihalyi, 1990, 1996). The viewer brings his or her own life experience, taste, and expectations to the process so that no two members of the audience have exactly the same experience. A "conversation" develops between the viewer and the work that is so engaging that all sense of time is lost. This cognitive engagement means that being part of an audience can be enjoyable, educational, active, and creative.

This chapter begins with a review of the negative and positive effects of television viewing. The concept of active versus passive viewing is discussed along with suggestions of how to explore the phenomenon of positive audience flow in therapeutic situations. The new concept of teletherapy is introduced. Teletherapy is a method of healing using television shows with a potential similar to bibliotherapy and videotherapy. This assertion is based on the acknowledged importance of television as a means of learning and modeling. Specific dramatic and comedy shows are suggested. By helping clients look at situations applicable to their own lives, teletherapy can help create new options for behavior. Humor is, by its nature, creative and offers the opportunity to discuss real-life problems in a way that does not threaten the client. Episodes of dramatic shows can model ways of dealing with issues such as parental loss, alienation, and aging. Thus teletherapy can contribute to everyday creativity by helping clients engage in new behaviors.


## IS TELEVISION VIEWING A WASTE OF TIME?

Television watching has a bad reputation. The "boob tube" is disparaged by scores of intelligent people as a time-wasting, mind-numbing habit.

Many people do not want to admit they have moments when they are couch potatoes. I have met hundreds of people who proudly proclaim that they never watch television. There is an unspoken elitism in that assertion with implications of evenings spent reading the classics by a fireplace or having profound intellectual discussions filling any gap in incredibly busy schedules. However, I know that many of those puritanical nontelevision watchers are not telling the truth. I know this because I was a television writer and producer for many years, working on weekly situation comedies including *The Mary Tyler Moore Show* and *Room 222*. After people told me that they "never watched television," they asked me what shows I had worked on. I was always amazed that somehow many of them had seen these shows—often not just one episode, but many of them.

The stigma of being a television watcher is not attached to active hobbies, reading books, visiting art museums, attending concerts, or reading intellectual magazines, which are all considered to be valuable leisure time activities because they involve complexity and activity rather than passive activities. (Csikszentmihalyi, 1990; Schooler & Mulatu, 2001). Csikszentimihalyi (1990) notes, for example, the positive flow effects possible in listening to music, including being focused and engaged, and actively encountering the medium at several levels, perhaps at times with particular goals (e.g., how does the bass section from the Chicago Symphony compare to the Los Angeles Philharmonic?). Csikszentmihalyi (1990), at the same time, specifically disparages highly passive television watching saying that "TV can provide continuous and easily accessible information that will structure the viewer's attention, at a very low cost in terms of the psychic energy that needs to be invested" (p. 119).

Although not denying that television, as with some other forms of entertainment, could provide the "kind of goals and rules that are inherent in flow activities" (p. 120), Csikszentmihalyi (1990) charges a "tremendous leisure industry" (p. 162) with providing more passive fare for the population at large.

> We do not run risks acting on our beliefs, but occupy hours each day watching actors who pretend to have adventures, engaged in mock-meaningful action. . . . The flow experience that results from the use of skills leads to growth; passive entertainment leads nowhere. Collectively we are wasting each year the equivalent of millions of years of human consciousness. (pp. 163–164)

The question this chapter asks is whether this must always be so. When and how is television watching a creative act, and how can we increase its benefits?

## Effects of Watching Television

There have been thousands of studies measuring the effects of television viewing primarily focusing on children. The majority of these studies have shown negative effects, including physical aggression and bullying in boys and girls (Coyne & Archer, 2005; Manzo, 2005), increased adolescent alcohol use (van der Bulck & Buellens, 2005), less time studying resulting in lower academic achievement (Shin, 2004), misunderstanding of reality

(Low & Durkin, 2001), and obesity in 34 countries (Janssen et al., 2005). For those interested in an overview of the complex relationship between children and television, excellent summaries of the research are available in *The Handbook of Children and the Media* (Singer & Singer, 2001).

One of the major concerns for adults as well as for children is the amount of violence on television. Friedrich-Cofer and Huston (1986) stated that research until that point indicated that there was a direct link between viewing violence and aggressive behavior. However, Haridakis and Rubin (2003) pointed out that factors such as disinhibition and locus of control in the individual can influence the effect of viewing violence. Research on adults has indicated a preference for violent sports programming with a resulting lowering in positive mood (Raney & Depalma, 2006). Watching television for more than 2 hours per day was directly linked to obesity in female war veterans (Johnson, Nelson, & Bradley, 2006) Television viewing in adults was connected to increased posttraumatic stress disorder symptoms following 9/11 (Ahern, 2004).

Having acknowledged the many potential negative aspects of television viewing, let us examine how it can possibly be beneficial. A significant amount of research indicates that television shows such as *Sesame Street* use curricula that can help children attend, and actively and enjoyably learn (Fisch, 2000; Fisch, Truglio, & Cole, 1999; Graves, 1999). However, this view is controversial. Razel (2001) found in a meta-analysis of 1 million students that with "small amounts of viewing, achievement increased with viewing, but as viewing increased beyond a certain point, achievement decreased" (p. 371). The Children's Television Act of 1990 (Federal Communications Commission, 1996) was designed to help foster more educational and informational programming for children. Calvert et al. (2001) investigated children's programming by having 97 children post their reactions on the Internet to "4 educational or informational programs a week, primarily from Nickelodeon and PBS" (p. 103). They concluded "children are *learning* lessons of social and informational value from programs" (p. 103).

An interesting study by Charlton and O'Bey (1997) looked at the introduction of television in 1995 to the remote island of St. Helena in the South Atlantic Ocean. After 2 years, children were watching quite a bit of television, but some of their antisocial behaviors actually decreased. The authors suggested that television may be serving as a scapegoat for antisocial problems inherent in other aspects of society, an argument used frequently by commercial broadcasters.

In adults, television viewing has been shown to decrease stress in some individuals (Verghese, 2006). Watching presidential political debates can expand viewer knowledge and aid in decision making regarding the character of candidates, resulting in potential change in voting (Benoit, Hansen, & Verser, 2003). Other research seemed to indicate no positive effects from television viewing although some studies looking solely for negative effects failed to find any. Most studies were designed with the hypothesis that television viewing in adults is a negative attribute so the results were skewed in that direction.

One of the hallmarks of creativity is openness, so if you have developed a negative perception of television viewing based on all the studies you have read and your personal opinion, then I ask you keep your mind open to the contrarian ideas expressed in this chapter.

## Active Versus Passive Viewing

People watch television for many reasons, sometimes selecting a specific show, but at other times just wanting to relax and be entertained. Paul Klein, an NBC programmer, came up with the term "least objectionable program." Lindheim (1998) describes how Klein came up with this concept:

> Paul kept lecture audiences hysterical in guilty laughter as he explained how people switched from channel to channel, disliking everything, before determining to watch the least objectionable show in favor of other non-media pursuits like reading, sleeping and talking with other members of the family. (p. 14)

The average individual watches television 3 hours a day, so obviously there is a great deal of passive viewing. Videotapes of children and adults watching television revealed that 46% of the time people were doing other things at the same time (Schmitt, Woolf, & Anderson, 2003). Television viewing can become an escape from the real world—a seemingly safe place to hide from the reality of life, sometimes, ironically, by watching "reality" shows.

McIlwraith (1998) found that 24 of 237 adults aged 18 through 72 described themselves as television addicts. They were more neurotic, introverted, and easily bored than the rest of the sample, using television to distract themselves from unpleasant thoughts, regulate moods, and fill time (p. 371). In a similar vein, Henning and Vorderer, (2001) suggested that television watching may be a place some people go when they do not want to think.

I started thinking about this quality of television viewing while reflecting on my own experience as a television writer. My best writing occurred when I was in a flow state. Perry (1999) said "When you're in flow, you become so deeply immersed in your writing, or whatever activity you're doing that you forget yourself and your surroundings. . . . You feel challenged, stimulated, definitely not bored" (p. 1). Csikszentmihalyi (1999) stated the following:

> The concept describes a particular kind of experience that is so engrossing and enjoyable that it becomes autotelic, that is, worth doing for its

own sake even though it may have no consequence outside itself. Creative activities, music, sports, games, and religious rituals are typical sources for this kind of experience. (p. 826)

When I was writing in a flow state, the work came so easily that there were times when it felt as if I were watching a show played out in front of me and just needed to write down what the people were saying. Other writers and the audience sometimes saw jokes and subtleties that I did not even consciously construct. Occasionally these scenes provided me with insights into behavior that touched on basic psychological truths. In thinking about this, it was natural for me to question if the audience ever experienced a similar state of flow in which they somehow made new connections, and learned something about their life from watching a scene or an episode.

Zhu (2002) completed an interesting dissertation examining flow states in teachers versus flow states in students. The conclusion reached was that when teachers were experiencing flow, 25% more of the students in class were cognitively engaged than when teachers were not experiencing flow. The same may eventually prove true for writers, musicians, and artists, but that is yet to be determined.

I thought about my own movie and television watching and immediately recognized that I had experienced a flow state at times. This almost always occurred during active viewing when I was watching something that engaged me completely—a movie like *Chinatown* or a television series such as *Six Feet Under*. Though active television and movie viewing is entertainment, it can also provide insight into real behavior.

I believe several elements need to be present to inspire the kind of involvement that develops into a flow state. Attention and identification with at least one of the characters must be strong enough to lead to galvanizing emotion, and active response to the situations presented. Then there has to be a connection to an issue of personal or cosmic significance. An example from *Six Feet Under* is the return of the dead father who engages with his oldest son. This brought to mind the kinds of issues I would discuss with my own father if he were to appear in a similar manner. Thinking about our unfinished business led to reviewing some of the misunderstandings and differences I had with my father, as well as touching on the inevitably of death. This provided benefits similar to a creative flow state because I was able to garner insights into my past that had the potential to change my current attitude and behavior.

Thus there is a clear distinction between active viewing—specifically selecting a show to watch for a particular reason versus the passive act of watching television as a way of killing time. Csikszentmihalyi (1996) acknowledges both possibilities, saying that "television is a fantastic tool for increasing the range of what we can experience, but it can make us addicted to redundant information that appeals to the lowest common denominator of human interests" (p. 319).

Most people have moments when they are passive television viewers and moments when they are active. The decision to watch a specific show because the viewer is interested in the subject area or likes the characters is an active choice. Furthermore, there are clearly shows of high quality which most viewers, critics, and professionals acknowledge are at the very least well executed. Examples include *The Mary Tyler Moore Show, MASH, Frasier, Seinfeld,* and *Curb Your Enthusiasm.* (See also chaps. 1 & 3, this volume, for active observer involvement.)

## AUDIENCE FLOW

If there is audience flow that creates cognitive growth, what would be the factors that could make that happen? It is my contention that selective television viewing of specific high quality shows can produce positive flow experiences for some members of the audience through empathetic involvement, active inner response, and expanded awareness. Recognition of the potential for new creative perspectives from watching television is clear when we look at the dynamics of active television viewing. These include the acknowledged importance of television as a means of learning and the impact of storytelling as a learning device.

### Television as a Means of Learning

Television shows set examples that can have a great influence on audience behavior, as has been demonstrated by the many damaging results attributed to television viewing presented earlier (Coyne & Archer, 2005; Janssen et al., 2005; Low & Durkin, 2001; Manzo, 2005; Shin, 2004; Van der Bulck & Buellens, 2005). It is logical that anything that can have such a strong influence in a negative direction could also be a powerful force in positively influencing behavior.

Television has a special power to convince and persuade. Because it is viewed primarily in the home, it creates a unique sense of intimacy and inspires a level of trust not found elsewhere. Advertisers attest to the powerful influence of television when they pay premium rates to reach television audiences. Society indicates concern for what is on television by interest in how culture is represented there. I have found articles investigating the television portraiture of virtually every minority community in the country. There have been complaints about the way African Americans (Patton,

2001; Rome, 2004), Latinos (Rivadeneyra, 2006), Asians (Mok, 1998), Indians (Meek, 2006), gay men and lesbians (Hart, 2000), people who are overweight (Greenberg, Eastin, Hofschire, Lachlan, & Brownell, 2003), and other groups have been presented. Psychologists and psychiatrists are not immune from this fixation. Articles and dissertations have focused on how psychologists have been presented in a negative light in movies and on television (Haberman, 2003; Keith, 2005); one article probed the burning question of whether it was bad for the psychology business when Tony Soprano temporarily left his therapist in *The Sopranos.*

Television seems particularly effective at teaching social skills. Rosenkotter (1999) looked at whether moral lessons in *The Cosby Show* and *Full House* influenced prosocial behavior in children. He concluded that students in the first and third grades who could identify a moral lesson in these shows and watched more prosocial sitcoms demonstrated more prosocial behavior.

Some educators in psychology have used commercial television shows as an educational aid. Eaton and Uskul (2004) used clips from *The Simpsons* to illustrate key social psychology concepts:

> Students rated the clips favorably and reported that the clips helped them understand the material better and apply social psychological concepts to real-life situations. In addition, students' exam performance was significantly better on clip-related questions than nonclip-related questions. These findings suggest that television clips can facilitate the learning process. (p. 77)

Gilkey and Protinsky (1992) wrote an article about *The Andy Griffith Show* entitled "The Teaching Tales of Sheriff Taylor" in which they described scenes demonstrating Sheriff Taylor's tolerant listening style to "explore the value of accepting the symptom as presented by the client" (p. 27). *The Simpsons* was used as homework in a nonfamily counselor education program in which practicum students rated the behavior of the cartoon family using the Clinical Rating Scale. Mathis and Tanner (1991) reported that the students analyzing *The Simpsons* showed significant improvement in their systems thinking compared with a control group. College students who viewed 10 episodes of *Six Feet Under* indicated an increased fear of death and decreased concern about what happens to their body after they die, similar to the results recorded in death education classes (Schiappa, Gregg, & Hewes, 2004). Key factors in these examples include a specific desire to watch these television shows, leading to active viewer response in watching.

Many people believe much of what they see on television and that belief strongly influences how they think and behave. Van den Bulck and Vandebosch (2003) completed an interesting study in Belgium in which they found that first-time prisoners thought that their prison would be like those they had seen in U.S. television shows even if they were not aware from what show they had gotten their impressions. A number of studies have indicated that television viewing can directly influence viewers' perceptions of their quality of life and life choices, especially in the United States (Csikszentmihalyi, 1999; Sirgy et al., 1998). It would be valuable to study the ways in which viewers process certain material, even when their goal is to be passive and to relax.

The forensic investigation series *CSI: Crime Scene Investigation* and its spin-offs, *CSI: Miami* and *CSI: New York*, were highly rated programs in the 2005 through 2006 television season. The shows, which make forensic investigation look like glamorous work, have inspired a huge increase in applications to schools in forensic science. In addition, Stockwell (2005) reported that *CSI* has had the unintended consequence of making convictions harder to obtain:

> Prosecutors say jurors are telling them they expect forensic evidence in criminal cases, just like on their favorite television shows, including "CSI: Crime Scene Investigation." In real life, forensic evidence is not collected at every crime scene, either because criminals clean up after themselves or because of a shortage in resources. Yet, increasingly, jurors are reluctant to convict someone without it, a phenomenon the criminal justice community is calling the "CSI effect." (p. A1)

Television viewing has been linked directly to perceived quality of happiness, especially in the United States. If you are thinking "this doesn't apply to me," you may be demonstrating the third-person effect that Peiser and Peter (2000) found in Germany. This is the phenomenon in which "people tend to believe others are more susceptible to media influences than they are themselves" (p. 25), with more educated people feeling less influenced than individuals with a lower educational level. Salwen and Dupagne (1999) surveyed 721 U.S. adults with a median age of 42. They found significant evidence indicating that people will support restrictions on television content for specific issues such as violence or negative advertising based on the third-person effect (p. 523).

I will admit television has influenced my life. I made a decision to attempt a career as a comedy writer, at least partially from watching *The Dick Van Dyke Show*, which actually portrayed the life of a fictional comedy writer. I could see people using their senses of humor to make a living, which meant there was a place to use my former enjoyable occupation as class clown in a positive way. Furthermore, I wrote elsewhere (Pritzker, 2000) that television and movies helped create false impressions about the reality of love that led to a dramatic whirlwind romance and marriage.

## Media Literacy

When the enormous amount of time spent watching television is combined with its powerful effect on behavior, it becomes clear that psychologists have the potential to make a valuable contribution by becoming more active in the media literacy movement. Media literacy involves teaching individuals, especially children, how to become more critically aware of what they are watching so they can understand the difference between what is reasonably true and what is designed to persuade and mislead them (Yates, 1998). The American Psychological Association (APA) is to be commended for warning the public about the danger of children's viewing of violence in 1985. The Web site claimed that the average child watches 28 hours of television per week and sees as many as 8,000 murders by the age of 11 (APA, 2004). However, this same Web site also announced that in 2004, APA gave the Golden Psi award to *Law and Order: Special Victims Unit* for responsibly portraying mental health professionals. Although the purpose of this award was specific, one must wonder if some, nonetheless, might be receiving a mixed message, given that a show featuring violent murders and criminal actions is commended. This example comes close to home and suggests that professionals need always be mindful and creatively vigilant, whatever the context, to be responsibly active in media literacy (APA, 2004).

The "No Child Left Behind" Act of 2002 requires media literacy as part of children's education, so all 50 states have at least some initiative for media literacy. Educational psychologists' concerned with cognitive and affective development could make a much larger contribution to future conversations concerning how to teach children to cope in a manipulative environment that has the potential to cause serious harm. Active and critical viewing is necessary. There is also the potential to lead parents, teachers and children to an enriching use of television as a positive learning tool. The APA coalition for psychology in schools and education could be a helpful instrument to help schools develop media literacy programs.

Psychologists are in a position to help television improve and a few television shows may be able to help psychologists work more effectively. Some psychologists' clients will already have developed an interest in specific shows which may serve as a vehicle for discussion of creative ways in which behavior can be changed. These shows can be recommended, with particular objectives. Viewers develop intense relationships with characters in a television series. This involvement and these situations can be used as a framework in a similar tradition that therapists have used in working with books and movies. Teletherapy is a method based on the traditions of bibliotherapy and videotherapy, which make deliberate and active use of these two forms of communication.

## Bibliotherapy

The idea of recommending fictional and nonfictional literature for work in religious and moral education was first proposed in 1840 by Sir Walter Gait (Heston & Kottman, 1997). The term *bibliotherapy* dates back to 1916. It is defined as "a form of supportive psychotherapy in which carefully selected reading materials are used to assist a subject in solving personal problems or for other therapeutic purposes" (*American Heritage Dictionary*, 1992, p. 182).

Bibliotherapy is based on the principle that books can provide metaphors that help clients understand more about their own cognitive process. They can provide examples that can aid in developing a specific treatment plan by offering negative or positive narratives. As clients become engaged in stories, they can influence feelings that aid and add to the impact of cognitive insights. Books must be carefully selected—there is always the potential for harm.

Psychologists use the term bibliotherapy to describe working with clients in several ways. The simplest form of bibliotherapy in one-to-one therapy is suggesting books for clients to read for a particular purpose. These can include self-help books or works of fiction which are later discussed in sessions with the therapist. However, bibliotherapy can also be used as a stand-alone form of therapy in which clients read suggested books with no direct intervention by therapists.

*Bibliocounseling* is the use of suggested books by counselors in a school setting. Using specific books is especially helpful with adolescents who often avoid talking directly about sensitive issues. Selecting the right kind of book can offer information and insight about problems, offer new values and attitudes, show how others have dealt with similar problems, and provide potential solutions (Pardeck, 1994). Pardeck suggests some creative follow-up exercises for such clients, including writing a diary of a character or sending a letter from one character to another, drawing a map of story events adding imagined details, making a collage illustrating the book and role playing significant scenes. Bibliotherapy has been used in therapy with children who have problems resulting from parental divorce, parental loss, remarriage, adoption, foster care, and sexual abuse (Pardeck, 1994).

*Developmental bibliotherapy* is the process of assigning gifted students books that help encourage personal growth and development. In this case, there is not a clinical agenda. Because gifted and creative children in general tend to be more sensitive and emotional than average students, they often feel isolated. Discussions that are based on books offer the opportunity for gifted students to see that other students are experiencing similar feelings (Hebert & Kent, 2000). Developmental bibliotherapy has also been used to overcome problems such as math anxiety (Furner & Duffy, 2002) and to better understand cultural diversity.

Bibliotherapy is also used in clinical and counseling therapeutic situations. Interactive bibliotherapy has been used in conjunction with other techniques, such as play therapy, in the treatment of sexually abused children (Rasmussen & Cunningham, 1995), grieving children (Moody & Moody, 1991), depressed adults (Jamison & Scogin, 1995), cancer patients (Pardeck, 1992), individuals with eating disorders (Lewis, Blair, & Booth, 1992), individuals who abuse alcohol (Gallant, 1989), and individuals who experience panic disorders (Gould, Clum, & Shapiro, 1993; Lidren et al., 1994). Bibliotherapy has been used with a variety of developmental issues and concerns and may be the basis for direct introduction of these issues in the counseling environment.

Some published meta-analyses (Apodaca & Miller, 2003; Gregory, Canning, & Lee, 2004; Gregory, Schwer Canning, Lee, & Wise, 2004) concluded that bibliotherapy, combined with psychotherapy, was significantly successful in dealing with problems such as depression and alcoholism. Indications are also that bibliotherapy is effective with adolescents if candidates are carefully screened by skilled therapists.

## Cinematherapy

The concept of bibliotherapy evolved into *cinematherapy*, which uses movies in a similar fashion. Clients are asked to watch specific movies in between sessions and then the films are discussed with the therapist. Films can be used to discuss a general situation or specifically to present a metaphor that identifies a problem. Films are less often suggested without any subsequent discussion.

Films may provide vivid metaphors that open the door to discussing sensitive issues in a safe way. Sharp, Smith, and Cole (2002) asserted the following:

> Cinematherapy takes advantage of our ability to receive communication at two levels. When direct communication is too threatening and clients respond with resistance, therapists can speak to clients through indirect communication. Using metaphors and stories via movies allows therapists to communicate to a more receptive, less defensive part of our clients. This shared communication can bypass resistance and send a powerful message that can, among other benefits, suggest solutions to problems, plant seeds for growth, reframe problems and build rap-

port by providing a shared experience between client and therapist. (p. 273)

Seeing others struggle through and overcome the same issues that clients are dealing with may provide models that give clients hope, offer new forms of behavior, help reexamine values, inspire insights into problems, expand emotional range, bring up deeply buried feelings, offer information, encourage acceptance, and provide examples that can be used to develop new strategies (Hesley & Hesley, 1998; Lampropoulos, Kazantzis, & Deane, 2004). Use of films also may benefit the therapist by imparting new ways of approaching a situation with a client.

Cinematherapy is widely used. Lampropoulos, Kazantzis, and Deane (2004) received survey responses from 827 licensed practicing psychologists and found that 67% strongly agreed or agreed that "quality entertainment motion pictures that deal with psychological issues can be beneficial and could be used for therapeutic purposes (e.g., awareness raising, modeling behavior, and client inspiration)" (p. 537). Ninety percent of respondents had discussed a film with a client in therapy and 67% had recommended a film to a client.

Films have been used with a variety of clients who might resist traditional therapy, including older couples (Peake & Steep, 2005), men with performance anxiety (McCullough & Osborn, 2004), and adolescent girls (Bierman, Krieger, & Leifer, 2003). Dermer and Hutchings (2000) compiled a list of specific movies clinicians suggested using in therapy covering an extensive number of problems, including physical and sexual abuse, adolescence, adoption, affairs, aging and ageism, HIV/AIDS, conflict resolution and communication, chronic terminal illness, physical and mental challenges, divorce, eating disorders, family-of-origin and transgenerational issues, friendship, grieving and loss issues, intimacy issues and relationships, parenting and parent–child relations, posttraumatic stress disorder, power and control issues, religion, blended families, sexual assault, substance abuse, tolerance of differences, transition to adulthood as well as values and ethics.

Although there is anecdotal evidence from many therapists of its usefulness, cinematherapy needs serious comprehensive research to formally evaluate its effectiveness. There are no clear criteria other than the subjective evaluation of each therapist to recommend each film. Eventually some reliable evaluation methodology might improve the selection of films and the way they are used in a therapeutic context.

## Videotherapy

Videotaping has been explored in several ways in therapy. The term *videotherapy* has been used in the relatively sparse literature to date to describe both the use of videotaping sessions and having clients make their own creative videotapes. This can be confusing because these are two different approaches. Furthermore, the process of viewing a videotape is physically passive and making a videotape is physically active.

Videotaped replays of therapy sessions have been used to provide feedback in marital counseling and to provide training for parenting. Videotherapy is also used as the term for having children make their own tapes in a divorce situation. I suggest that a term such as *videomaking* be used for the process of making tapes versus watching them. The terminology is further muddled by the use of the term videotherapy to describe the process of watching movies or self-help tapes in a therapeutic context. Watching tapes of movies, informational, or self-help films should fall into the category of cinematherapy.

## TELETHERAPY

Despite the popularity of many shows, I did not find any mention of the use of television in the literature on bibliotherapy and videotherapy. The reason may be that until recently television shows were not available on demand. However, with the release of many television series and episodes on DVDs, it is practical to start considering television shows as a valuable tool. High-quality television shows provide an opportunity to work with a wide range of client issues.

Thus I am introducing the term *teletherapy*—the use of television shows as a method of healing. This method might prove especially effective when dealing with a less-literate population. Unfortunately, the percentage of people reading books continues to decline, but television viewing is ubiquitous. Homework, which is what reading a book may be perceived to be by many clients, may be a lot more palatable if it consists of watching an episode of a television show. Teletherapy may work well with adolescents who already presumably have a lot of reading they need to do for school.

### Use of Humor

Humor has been acknowledged as an important ingredient in relationships in psychology, dating back to Freud. Often situations can be presented and discussed in a humorous context that could not be handled nearly as well in a dramatic format. As Koestler (1964) pointed out, humor bridges two previously incongruous frames of reference. It is by nature creative, forges new links, and often brings to light material that was not fully conscious. Humor thus asks for awareness as well as creative learning and change in the viewer. By its nature, humor provides the opportunity to discuss and bring up serious problems that might not be addressed otherwise in a less-threatening manner.

A great example is the classic *Mary Tyler Moore Show* in which television personality Chuckles the Clown participates in a parade dressed in a peanut costume and then dies and an elephant tries to shell him. Mary's coworkers at the television station where she works cannot stop laughing about it; she tells them that making jokes about death is in poor taste and it is not funny. However, at Chuckles's funeral, Mary starts laughing and cannot stop. All of the anxiety surrounding the subject of death is beautifully presented in this show—and it is extremely funny.

In fact, television comedy series, especially if they are already familiar to the client, may offer the possibility of a deeper identification than movies. Viewers develop intense personal long-term relationships with the characters in series they watch regularly. Examples include Hawkeye Pierce in *MASH*, Frasier Crane in *Cheers* and *Frasier*, Candice Bergen as *Murphy Brown*, Larry David in *Curb Your Enthusiasm*, and the casts of *Seinfeld* and *Everybody Loves Raymond*.

Furthermore, domestic comedies can offer familiar situations in a non-threatening way. I have been researching creativity in television writing for 12 years and there is a simple truth that I have found to be the case in my own writing and that repeats itself in interviews with writers—the best episodes are based on incidents that happen in real life. Because episodes are short, they can effectively focus on one key conflict.

Let me give an example of an episode of *Everybody Loves Raymond* that could be used with a couple who are having difficulty with sexual satisfaction. The premise is that Ray's wife Debra loses her desire to sleep with him. Eventually, she reluctantly tells him that he rushes things. Ray finds this painful, but it is clear that the conversation is valuable to the couple's relationship. Admittedly, situation comedies often take complex problems and oversimplify them, but problem solving can still be modeled and discussed.

### Drama

Several series provide excellent examples of dealing with challenging situations. A number of episodes of *Six Feet Under* dealt specifically with issues concerning parental loss, grief, sibling rivalry, alienation, gay male and heterosexual relationships, aging, mental health, promiscuity, and adoption. *The Wire* dealt with issues of alcoholism. *Thirtysomething* included stories about marriage, friendships, and parenting issues (Hersch, 1988).

Therapists are encouraged to incorporate their own ideas and creativity into the use of television programs. Depending on the client, there may be opportunities to select dramatic television movies that deal with issues in a way that could be helpful to clients. Medical shows such as *E.R.* or *House* might have individual episodes which deal with conditions such as aging or cancer that could be useful to particular people. Finally there are the self-help shows such as *Dr. Phil* and *Oprah*. I have not watched these shows regularly, but on the basis of my viewing they sometimes do a disservice to the psychological profession by simplifying complex issues. Nevertheless, specific shows might prove helpful in triggering discussions for some clients.

## CONCLUSION

This chapter provides an introduction to the terms audience flow and teletherapy. These are exciting concepts because they extend the recognition of the power of the arts to provide creative inspiration and growth in the audience member. Paying more attention to the idea of encouraging audience flow may provide a useful way to help clients develop more creative solutions to life situations. Furthermore, the study of audience flow may prove useful in developing more creatively open resources in Western art, similar to Japanese art in which the artist deliberately leaves the picture incomplete with the expectation that the audience members will bring their own interpretation to the work so that the experience becomes a collaboration.

There is a great deal to be learned about the phenomena of audience flow. A few of the many possible questions include: What types of work and conditions inspire audience flow? What type of responses can be encouraged, and what cognitive changes occur as a result during audience flow? To what extent is flow in the creator reflected by flow in the audience?

Teletherapy opens the door to discussing a wide range of life experiences in a new way. Knowing the power that television has to influence cognition and to do harm as well as good, it is vital for psychologists to become more involved in media literacy programs. There is also the opportunity to be creative in finding new uses for television shows with both individuals and group therapy. So next time you watch the tube, consider opportunities to use television as a tool to help yourself and your clients become more flexible and creative.

## REFERENCES

Ahern, J. (2004). Television images and probable posttraumatic stress disorder after September 11: The role of background characteristics, event exposures, and perievent. *Journal of Nervous and Mental Disease, 192,* 217–226,

*American Heritage Dictionary of the English Language* (3rd ed.). (1992). Boston: Houghton Mifflin.

American Psychological Association (2004, February 19). *Violence in the media— psychologists help protect children from harmful effects.* Retrieved May 31, 2005, from http://www.psychologymatters.org/mediaviolence.html

Andison, F. S. (1977). TV Violence and viewer aggression: A cumulation of study results 1956–1976. *Public Opinion Quarterly, 41,* 314–332.

Apodaca, T., & Miller, W. R. (2003). A meta-analysis of the effectiveness of bibliotherapy for alcohol problems. *Journal of Clinical Psychology, 59,* 289–304.

Benoit, W. L., Hansen, G. J., & Verser, R. M. (2003). A meta-analysis of the effects of viewing U.S. presidential debates. *Communication Monographs, 70,* 335–350.

Bierman, J. S., Krieger, A., & Leifer, M. (2003). Group cinematherapy as a treatment modality for adolescent girls. *Residential Treatment for Children and Youth, 21*(1), 1–15.

Calvert, S. A., Kotler, J. A., Murray, W. F., Gonzales, E., Savoye, K., Hammack, S. W., et al. (2001). Children's online reports about educational and informational television programs. *Journal of Applied Developmental Psychology, 22*(1), 103–117.

Charlton, T., & O'Bey, S. (1997). Links between television and behaviour: Students' perceptions of TV's impact in St. Helena, South Atlantic. *Support for Learning, 12*(3), 130–136.

Coyne, S. M., & Archer, J. (2005). The relationship between indirect and physical aggression on television and real life. *Social Development, 14,* 324–338.

Csikszentmihalyi, M. (1990). *Flow: The psychology of optimal experience.* New York: Harper & Row.

Csikszentmihalyi, M. (1996). *Creativity: Flow and the psychology of discovery and invention.* New York: HarperPerennial.

Csikszentmihalyi, M. (1999). If we are so rich, why aren't we happy? *American Psychologist, 54,* 821–827.

Dermer, S. B., & Hutchings, J. B. (2000). Utilizing movies in family therapy: Applications for individuals, couples, and families. *American Journal of Family Therapy, 28*(2), 163–180.

Eaton, J., & Uskul, A. (2004). Using the Simpsons to teach social psychology. *Teaching of Psychology, 31,* 277–278.

Federal Communications Commission. (1996, August 8). *Children's educational television.* Retrieved March 15, 2007, from http://www.fcc.gov/mb/policy/kidstv.html

Fisch, S. M. (2000). *Children's learning from educational television: Sesame Street and beyond.* Mahwah, NJ: Erlbaum.

Fisch, S. M., Truglio, R. T., & Cole, C. F. (1999). The impact of Sesame Street on preschool children: A review and synthesis of 30 years' research. *Media Psychology, 1*(2), 165–190.

Friedrich-Cofer, L., & Huston, A. C. (1986). Television violence and aggression: The debate continues. *Psychological Bulletin, 100,* 364–371.

Furner, J. M., & Duffy, M. L. (2002). Equity for all students in the new millennium: Disabling math anxiety. *Intervention in School and Clinic, 38*(2), 67–74.

Gallant, D. M. (1989). How can alcoholism treatment be improved? *Alcohol Health and Research World, 13,* 328–333.

Gilkey, J., & Protinsky, H. (1992). The teaching tales of Sheriff Taylor. *Journal of Strategic and Systemic Therapies, 11*(1), 27–32.

Gould, R. A., Clum, G. A., & Shapiro, D. (1993). The use of bibiotherapy in the treatment of panic: A preliminary investigation. *Behavior Therapy, 24,* 241–252.

Graves, S. B. (1999). Television and prejudice reduction: When does television as a vicarious experience make a difference? *Journal of Social Issues, 55,* 707–727.

Greenberg, B. S., Eastin, M., Hofschire, L., Lachlan, K., & Brownell, K. D. (2003). Portrayals of overweight and obese individuals on commercial television. *American Journal of Public Health, 93,* 1342–1348.

Gregory, R. J., Canning, S. S., & Lee, T. W. (2004). Cognitive bibliotherapy for depression: A meta-analysis. *Professional Psychology: Research and Practice, 35,* 275–280.

Gregory, R. J., Schwer Canning, S., Lee, T. W., & Wise, J. C. (2004). Cognitive bibliotherapy for depression: A meta-analysis. *Professional Psychology: Research and Practice, 35,* 275–280.

Haberman, C. (2003, January 24). Analyzing the imagery off the couch. *The New York Times,* B1.

Haridakis, P., & Rubin, A. M. (2003). Motivation for watching television violence and viewer aggression. *Mass Communication and Society, 6*(1), 29–56.

Hart, K. R. (2000). Representing gay men on American television. *Journal of Men's Studies, 9*(1), 59–79.

Hebert, T. P., & Kent, R. (2000, April 1). Nurturing social and emotional development in gifted teenagers through young adult literature. *Roeper Review, 22*(3), 167–171.

Henning, B., & Vorderer, P. (2001). Psychological escapism: Predicting the amount of television viewing by need for cognition. *Journal of Communication, 51*(1), 100–121.

Hersch, P. (1988, October). Thirtysomethingtherapy: The hit TV show may be filled with "yuppie angst," but therapists are using it to help people. *Psychology Today, 22,* 62.

Hesley, J. W., & Hesley, J. G. (1998). *Rent two films and let's talk in the morning: Using popular movies in psychotherapy.* New York: Wiley.

Heston, M. L., & Kottman, T. (1997). Movies as metaphors: A counseling intervention. *Journal of Humanistic Education and Development, 36*(2), 92–99.

Jamison, C., & Scogin, F. (1995). The outcome of cognitive bibliotherapy with depressed adults. *Journal of Consulting and Clinical Psychology, 63,* 644–650.

Janssen, I., Katzmarzyk, P. T., Boyce, W. F., Vereecken, C., Mulvihill, C., Roberts, C., et al. (2005). Comparison of overweight and obesity prevalence in school-aged youth from 34 countries and their relationships with physical activity and dietary patterns. *Obesity Reviews, 6*(2), 123–132.

Johnson, K. M., Nelson, K. M., & Bradley, K. A. (2006). Television viewing practices and obesity among women veterans. *Journal of General Internal Medicine, 21,* S76–S81.

Keith, A. L. (2005). Psychology and media: The effects of media portrayals on attitudes and expectations of potential clients. *Dissertation Abstracts International, 66,* 9B. (ProQuest No. 3189056)

Koestler, A. (1964). *The act of creation.* London: Pan Books.

Lampropoulos, G. K., Kazantzis, N., & Deane, F. P. (2004). Psychologists' use of motion pictures in clinical practice. *Professional Psychology: Research and Practice, 35,* 535–541.

Lewis, V. J., Blair, A. J., & Booth, D. A. (1992). Outcome of group therapy for body-image emotionality and weight control self-efficacy. *Behavioural Psychotherapy, 20,* 155–165.

Lidren, D. M., Watkins, P. L., Gould, R. A., Clum, G. A., Asterino, M., & Tulloch, H. L. (1994). A comparison of bibliotherapy and group therapy in the treatment of panic disorder. *Journal of Consulting and Clinical Psychology, 62,* 865–869.

Lindheim, R. (1998). Paul Klein, irascible TV visionary. *Electronic Media, 17*(30), 14–15.

Low, J., & Durkin, K. (2001). Children's conceptualization of law enforcement on television and in real life. *Legal and Criminological Psychology, 6*(2), 197–214.

Manzo, K. K. (2005). Bullying behaviors. *Education Week, 24*(31), 20.

Mathis, R., & Tanner, Z. (1991). Clinical assessment of a TV cartoon family: Homework to encourage systemic thinking in counseling students. *Family Therapy, 18*(3), 245–254.

McCullough, L., & Osborn, K. A. (2004). Short term dynamic psychotherapy goes to Hollywood: The treatment of performance anxiety in cinema. *Journal of Clinical Psychology, 60,* 841–852.

McIlwraith, R. D. (1998). I'm addicted to television: The personality, imagination, and TV watching patterns of self-identified TV addicts. *Journal of Broadcasting & Electronic Media, 42,* 371–386.

Meek, B. A. (2006). And the Injun goes 'how!': Representations of American Indian English in white public space. *Language in Society, 35*(1), 93–128.

Mok, T. (1998). Getting the message: Media images and stereotypes and their effect on Asian Americans. *Cultural Diversity and Ethnic Minority Psychology, 4*(3), 185–202.

Moody, R. A., & Moody, C. P. (1991). A family perspective: Helping children acknowledge and express grief following the death of a parent. *Death Studies, 15,* 587–602.

Nielson Media Research (2006, September 16). *Nielsen Media Research reports television's popularity is still growing.* Retrieved October 26, 2006, from http://www.nielsenmedia.com/nc/portal/site/Public/menuitem.55dc65b4a7d5adff3f65936147a062a0/?allRmCB=on&newSearch=yes&vgnextoid=4156527aacccd010VgnVCM100000ac0a260aRCRD&searchBox=view

Pardeck, J. (1992). Using bibliotherapy in treatment with children in residential care. *Residential Treatment for Children and Youth, 9*(3), 73–89.

Pardeck, J. (1994), Using literature to help adolescents cope with problems. *Adolescence, 29*(114), 421–427.

Patton, T. O. (2001). Ally McBeal and her homies: The reification of white stereotypes of the other. *Journal of Black Studies, 32*(2), 229–260.

Peake, T. H., & Steep, A. E. (2005). Therapy with older couples: Love stories—the good, the bad, and the movies. In M. Harway (Ed.), *Handbook of couples therapy* (pp. 80–101). New York: Wiley.

Peiser, P., & Peter, J. (2000). Third-person perception of *television-viewing* behavior. *Journal of Communication, 50*(1), 25–45.

Perry, S. K. (1999). *Writing in flow: Keys to enhanced creativity.* Cincinnati, OH: Writers Digest Books.

Pritzker, S. (2000, January–February). Stupid Cupid. *Psychology Today, 33,* 88.

Raney, A. A., & Depalma, A. J. (2006). The effect of viewing varying levels and contexts of violent sports programming on enjoyment, mood, and perceived violence. *Mass Communication and Society, 9*(3), 321–338.

Rasmussen, L., & Cunningham, C. (1995). Focused play therapy and non-directed play therapy: Can they be integrated? *Journal of Child Sexual Abuse, 4,* 1–20.

Razel, M. (2001). The complex model of television viewing and educational achievement. *Journal of Educational Research, 94,* 371–379.

Richards, R. (1999). Everyday creativity. In M. A. Runco & S. R. Pritzker (Eds.), *The encyclopedia of creativity* (Vol. 1, pp. 683–687). San Diego, CA: Academic Press.

Rivadeneyra, R. (2006). Do you see what I see?: Latino adolescents' perceptions of the images on television. *Journal of Adolescent Research, 21,* 393–414.

Rome, D. (2004). *Black demons: The media's depiction of the African American male criminal stereotype.* Westport, CT: Praeger.

Rosenkotter, L. (1999). The television situation comedy and children's prosocial behavior. *Journal of Applied Social Psychology, 29,* 979–993.

Salwen, M. B., & Dupagne, M. (1999). The third-person effect. *Communication Research, 26,* 523–549.

Schiappa, E., Gregg, P. B., & Hewes, D. E. (2004). Can a television series change attitudes about death? A study of college students and Six Feet Under. *Death Studies, 28,* 459–475.

Schmitt, K. L., Woolf, K. D., & Anderson, D. R. (2003). Viewing the viewers: Viewing behaviors by children and adults during television programs and commercials. *Journal of Communication, 53*(2), 265–281.

Schooler, C., & Mulatu, S. M. (2001). The reciprocal effects of leisure time activities and intellectual functioning in older people: A longitudinal analysis. *Psychology and Aging, 16,* 466–482.

Sharp, C., Smith, J. V., & Cole, A. (2002). Cinematherapy: Metaphorically promoting therapeutic change. *Counselling Psychology Quarterly, 15*(3), 269–276.

Shin, N. (2004). Exploring pathways from television viewing to academic achievement in school age children. *Journal of Genetic Psychology, 165*(4), 367–381.

Singer, D. J., & Singer, J. L. (2001). *Handbook of children and the media.* Thousand Oaks, CA: Sage.

Sirgy, M., Lee, D., Kosenko, R., Meadow, H. L., Rahtz, D., Cicic, M., et al. (1998). Does television viewership play a role in the perception of quality of life? *Journal of Advertising, 27*(1), 125–142.

Stockwell, J. (2005, May 22). Defense, prosecution play to new 'CSI' savvy; Juries expecting TV-style forensics. *The Washington Post,* p. A1.

van den Bulck, J., & Buellens, K. (2005). Television and music video exposure and adolescent alcohol use while going out. *Alcohol and Alcoholism, 40*(3), 249–253.

van den Bulck, J., & Vandebosch, H. (2003). When the viewer goes to prison: Learning fact from watching fiction. A qualitative cultivation study. *Poetics, 31*(2), 10–117.

Verghese, J. (2006). To view or not to view: Television and mental health. *Southern Medical Journal, 99*(3), 202.

Yates, B. L. (1998). *Media literacy and the policymaking process: A framework for understanding influences on potential educational policy outputs.* Paper presented at the National Media Literacy and Media Citizenship Conference in Birmingham, AL. (ERIC Document Reproduction Service No. ED424602)

Zhu, N. Q. (2002). The effects of teachers' flow experiences on the cognitive engagement of students. *Dissertations Abstracts International, 62,* 10A. (ProQuest No. 726022241)

# 6

# STRUCTURES OF CONSCIOUSNESS AND CREATIVITY: OPENING THE DOORS OF PERCEPTION

ALLAN COMBS AND STANLEY KRIPPNER

This I shall do by printing in the infernal method by corrosives, which in Hell are salutary and medicinal, melting apparent surfaces away, and displaying the infinite which was hid.
—William Blake, *The Marriage of Heaven and Hell*

Few people imagine that our everyday human experience is dependent on "structures of consciousness." Whereas the play of unalloyed consciousness is said to be "pure creativity" (Guenther, 1989, p. 229), in ordinary life it is often profoundly more limited. Particular "structures" of consciousness act like colored lenses through which pure consciousness is inflected. Both psychological and historical evidence indicate that human consciousness has existed as a series of such structures that continue into the present as multiple aspects of contemporary experience. Each gives birth to unique forms of creative expression.

This chapter presents examples of such creativity as it arises spontaneously through the structures that unfold across individual development. A similar hypothetical landscape of unfolding structures characterizes the history of humankind.

## CREATIVITY AND THE EMPTY MIND

The term *creative* can be applied to any act, idea, or product that creates changes in an existing domain, or that transforms parts of an existing domain into a new one. A phenomenon is creative if it is novel and, in some manner, useful or appropriate for the situation in which it occurs (Krippner, 1999). Creativity flows naturally from the unfettered human spirit, that primal aspect of the psyche that resists cultural conditioning because of both its intense embodiment and its deep connection to transcendent inspiration and experience. Perhaps this is why those spiritual traditions, such as Zen Buddhism, that emphasize the cultivation of unconditioned mind–body systems are also associated with expressions of creativity through painting, poetry, flower arranging, and garden design, all of which emphasize both spontaneity and form.

Zen Buddhism is one of several traditions, both in the East and the West, that emphasizes the achievement of the open or "empty" mind, not troubled by delusions, passions, or projections that stand between reality and experience (Alexander, 1992; Fenner, 2002; Loy, 1988). This goal has also been explicitly expressed in Tibetan schools, particularly the *rDzogs-chen* (supercompleteness) teachings (Guenther, 1989), and in the Madhyamika tradition (Huntington, 1989), but is implicit in many other traditions, including certain Sufi orders (Shaw, 1994), and evidently the Christian Rhineland Mystics as well (Studsill, 2002). Similar views are found in Plato's (1892/1942) *Phaedo*, when Socrates observes that, at death, the soul of the true lover of knowledge

> will not ask philosophy to release her in order that when released she may deliver herself up again to the thraldom of pleasures and pains [of the world of the living], doing a work only to be undone again, weaving instead of unweaving her Penelope's web. But she will make herself a calm of passion and follow Reason, and dwell in her, beholding the true and divine (which is not a matter of opinion), and thence derive nourishment. Thus she seeks to live while she lives, and after death she hopes to go to her own kindred and to be freed from human ills. (p. 129)

Studies in transpersonal and developmental psychology suggest that such an unfettered state of mind can occur spontaneously to virtually anyone (Greeley & McCready, 1975; Spence, 1992). However, it is not achieved as a stable condition unless it is acquired through the successful mastery of a series of developmental stages (Combs & Krippner, 2003; Cox, 2005; Wilber, 1998a). This does not mean that there is no creativity to be found in consciousness unless one has achieved an advanced stage of personal growth. Indeed, it would seem that each stage carries its own implicit style of creativity. These styles emerge during the growth and maturation of the individual, and in an interesting twist on the theme of growth and development, are apparently mirrored in artistic expressions seen throughout the long history of human civilization. We will have more to say about both of these in the following pages, but first let us briefly review the developmental models on which our thinking is based. (See also chap. 9, this volume, on Eastern and Western models of creativity.)

## INDIVIDUAL GROWTH AND DEVELOPMENT

Developmental models of cognitive and emotional development can be traced back at least as far as turn-of-the-century American psychologist James Mark Baldwin (1906), but became highly influential in American psychology with the widespread introduction of the writings of Jean Piaget (e.g., 1923, 1928/1959) in the 1960s. Since then, psychological research has demonstrated the existence of more or less parallel lines of growth in cognitive development (e.g., Cook-Greuter, 1999; Fischer & Bidell, 1998), moral and emotional maturity (Gilligan, 1993; Kohlberg, 1981; Thompson, 1987), and artistic expression (e.g., Feldman, 2000; Gowan, 1974; Kellogg, 1969; Leman & Duveen, 1999; Milbrath, 1998).

Given this range of well-researched developmental lines it is not surprising to find, as Piaget (1929/1960) discovered, that expressions of creativity also change with maturation. Yet the topic of creativity and development would be of little interest if it amounted to nothing more than the observation that maturity makes one less childish and more adultlike, or even that one's creative expressions become more clever and intelligent as one grows up. What would be of real interest would be to find qualitative changes in forms of creative expression as children mature into adults, and as adults continue to grow both mentally and emotionally. There is, in fact, every reason to suspect that such changes are real and substantial.

## PIAGET'S DEVELOPMENTAL PERIODS

The general form of Piaget's (1923, 1959/1928, 1929/1960) original developmental model, although it has been substantially updated over the years (Gruber, 1999), has such wide application and undeniable verisimilitude that it has served as a guide for virtually all theories of development since. For example, it has been useful in understanding the changing sense of self during social development in children and adolescents (Kegan, 1982; Piaget & Inhelder, 1967) and, as noted earlier, the growth and maturation of moral judgment as well as transformations of artistic expressions of art in children. (See also chap. 4, this volume, on creative thinking and Piaget's theory.)

Piaget's basic notion was that children and adolescents grow through a series of more or less distinct stages, or periods, of development on their way to adulthood. Although the human organism is self-constructing, it functions in a biological framework that provides various constraints on development, thus guaranteeing that human mind–body systems "will share certain cognitive characteristics" (Gruber, 1999, p. 381). For Piaget, every developmental step opens the way to new possibilities, the expression of creativity being one of them.

Most of the readers of these pages will be familiar with Piaget's stages, or *periods* as they are usually designated in Piagetian terms, but a brief overview includes the following:

- A *sensorimotor period* during roughly the first 2 years of life is a time when children begin to master basic sensory and motor capacities, begin to understand and use language, and form the first internal representations of objects and other people.
- A *preoperational period*, extending to about 7 years of age, brings the first mastery of symbolic thought, still prelogical and expressed in terms of concrete objects. This is also an important play period for children, during which they practice complex social interactions.
- A *concrete operations* period, from roughly 6 or 7 to 11 or 12 years of age, sees the mastery of many cognitive skills that are basic to adult intelligence, including multiple classification, hierarchical and asymmetric relationships, and various forms of conservation.
- *Formal operations* or adult intelligence brings abstract concepts and hypotheticodeductive reasoning.

Theorists have both suggested and researched stages beyond formal operations, especially emphasizing systems thinking and the ability to abstract and appraise multiple systems of knowledge at once (Alexander & Langer, 1990; Combs & Krippner, 2003; Fischer & Bidell, 1998; Gowan, 1974; Kegan, 1982, 1994; Koplowitz, 1984; Wilber, 1998a). In this vein, Gowan's (1974) model of developmental stages paid special attention to creativity, which he considered "an emergent and characteristic outcome" of development (p. 10), providing a detailed analysis of postformal operations thinking and how such creativity is an "outcome of self-awareness" (p. 69). He also integrated material from Tibetan Buddhism into his model, noting a "remarkable . . . goodness of fit" between Western psychology and Eastern thought (p. 55).

Several researchers (Cook-Greuter, 1999; Erikson, 1963; Kegan, 1982, 1994; Miller & Cook-Greuter, 1994; Morton et al., 2000) have examined changes in the sense of self that accompany postformal operations thinking. It seems, in fact, that each stage of development is associated with a style of relating to others, a mode of moral judgment, and a particular sense of self. It is not surprising that each is also associated with a style of creativity as seen, for instance, in children's art. This will be discussed more later, but first it is important to note another interesting aspect of the overall picture, namely that the developmental stages described by Piaget (1929/1960), Kohlberg (1981), Gilligan (1993), Kegan (1982), and others, also seem to be associated with a broad series of historical epochs as evidenced in art, literature, and culture. As we will see, these epochs appear to be expressions of distinct forms of consciousness in which reality was experienced in particular ways.

Gruber (1999, p. 383) provides one provocative example. In one of Piaget's experiments, he discovered that adolescents could already construct an experiment about the period of a pendulum demonstrating that, among a number of other variables, only the length of the pendulum's cord made a difference. This form of consciousness is associated with formal operations thinking and, in particular, with rational thought and logic as the primary arbiter of consensual reality. In the history of science, it was only around 1600 CE that Galileo made his celebrated—and similar—observations about pendulum motion.

Finally, Feldman (2004) reconsidered and modified Piaget's stage construct by shifting stage transitions to the midpoint of each stage, adopting recursive transition processes from non-Piagetian models, expanding Piaget's consideration of the role consciousness plays in each of Piaget's stages, and emphasizing *decalage* (gaps and intervals) as a necessary aspect of the construct. As a result, Feldman proposes that Piaget's stages can still retain their place as general guides to cognitive development and as sources of the constraints and functions available to one's developing mind. Without these modifications, Feldman says, Piaget's stages remain an "unfinished symphony" (p. 175).

## HISTORICAL STRUCTURES OF CONSCIOUSNESS

Piaget was perhaps the first modern researcher to note that, at a certain stage, young children attempt to understand their world through "magical thinking," although Freud and other psychodynamic theorists also had insights along these lines. Piaget observed, for example, that if a 3-year-old child is asked why it rains in the spring, the child is likely to say, "so the flowers can grow." Later stages yield more mature answers, but not until the young person grows to master formal operations will the reply reflect adult Aristotelian-style logic. It is of interest to note that historians have tracked similar transformations in the history of art (Gablik, 1976; James, 2001; Richter, 1937/1982), imagination (Kearney, 1998), as well as the evolution of Judeo-Christian religious thought (Barnes, 2000). (Here we are forced to limit our discussion to Western sources, for the most part, because of space constraints.) Thus, it would seem that a case can be made for the extraordinary idea that ontogeny recapitulates phylogeny, at least in a developmental and cultural sense. In fact, there is considerable scholarship supporting such a notion (e.g., Combs, 2002; Feuerstein, 1987; Wilber, 1981, 2000).

Jean Gebser (1949/1986) was the first scholar in modern times to explore the idea that the long span of human cultural history has exhibited a series of "structures of consciousness" that reflect distinct ways of experiencing and understanding reality. The marked similarities between the structures of consciousness he described and the successive periods identified in the developmental psychology literature suggest the presence of a common map representing a progression of ways that human beings come to understand reality. Furthermore, this map reflects both individual and historical growth and transformation. Here it is useful to outline these structures, both historically and developmentally, considering them in terms of the kinds of creative expressions with which they are associated.

## Archaic Consciousness

The oldest and most primitive structure of consciousness, in Gebser's thinking (1949/1986), was the archaic structure. He viewed it as a transitional form of consciousness, emerging from the purely prehuman mammalian experience. Gebser had little to say about this structure, except that it set the stage for later forms of consciousness. It is of interest to note that the emergence of the human mind from that of the prehuman hominid has been a matter of considerable modern speculation (e.g., Donald, 1997; Mithen, 1999; Plotkin, 1988). For example, Donald emphasizes the development of prelinguistic communication in the form of mimicry and miming, an idea that seems commensurate with the recent discovery of "mirror cells" in the primate motor cortex (Gallese & Goldman, 1998).

Thus, although we know few of the details, it would seem that the roots of the human mind–body, and with them the roots of culture and language, are to be found in our long transition as a species from the mind–body of other primates to that of a human. It is apparent that with the advent of our appearance as human beings we were already the most creative of all creatures, using the definition of *creative* cited at the beginning of this chapter.

## Magical Consciousness

An interesting aspect about each of the structures of consciousness, as Gebser (1949/1986) conceived them, is that they stay with us, even in adulthood, and even in modern times. In other words, each structure of consciousness continues as an active agent in the psyche of the modern human adult. As an interesting comparison, creativity appears commonly to access diverse modes of thought from different developmental levels of origin, both conscious and less conscious, using "regression in the service of the ego" for access, while adapting material to the demands of the creative project (Kris, 1976; Richards, 1981).

As we have seen, during Piaget's preoperational period, children give magical explanations for the events they experience in the world around them. Evidently this is a reflection of a time, identified by Gebser (1949/ 1986), when magical explanations were the dominant form of thinking for adults as well. Meanwhile, later in life, a creative individual might use magical thinking by choice, to access creative material, within a broader developmental context of use.

Gebser (1949/1986) considered each structure of consciousness to be a legitimate and somewhat valid way of understanding reality. He did not consider indigenous people to be inferior or ignorant. Indeed, he felt that to live in a magical world is to experience magical possibilities such as putative synchronicity, telepathy, and clairvoyance, as a regular aspect of reality. We cannot speak for the world of young children, but it indeed seems the case that such experiences are not considered unusual among modern primary cultures in which magical explanations and magical thought are regarded as common fare. Taylor (2003) has taken this notion even further than Gebser, presenting evidence that discounts the claim that "primal people were less spiritually and socially developed" than modern humans (p. 61).

Ancient creative productions of this structure of consciousness include the remarkable paintings found in the great cave sanctuaries of southern Europe, such as Lascaux and Altamira (Lewis-Williams, 2004). Although they clearly represent a variety of contemporary animals, closer examination discloses that few of these are depicted with anatomical precision. As with children's art (Kellogg, 1969), it is evident to anyone who examines these paintings thoughtfully that anatomical precision is not what they are about. Some exhibit fantastic features, such as long forking antlers. (See also chap. 3, this volume, for art in ritual in various world cultures.)

Sometimes a small nodule becomes an animal's eye; at other times a natural swell of a rock face delineates the shoulder of a beast or an edge of a rock shelf becomes a creature's back (Clottes & Lewis-Williams, 1996/1998). Many modern scholars have made an excellent case for the idea that these are creatures inspired by shamanic and alternative states of consciousness (Krippner, 2000; Lewis-Williams, 2004; Ryan, 1999). Yet, other contemporary scholars (e.g., Berman, 2000) caution that the portrayals may reflect a simple desire to execute a naturalistic representation. Sometimes, grazing deer are simply grazing deer.

One aspect of these cave paintings that is easy to overlook unless one sees them in their original setting is that they were often drawn right over the top of each other in what appears to be a nearly random welter of images. This plethora of images is apparent not only in Spain and France but also in South Africa where the animals of Bomvu Ridge date back some 40,000 years. Gebser (1949/1986) points out that this disregard for space, as well as time, is characteristic of magical consciousness, in which events separated in space and even time can interact with each other, or even be experienced as a single occurrence. This, in fact, is the essence of magic: action that transgresses the boundaries of time and space.

This unawareness, as it were, of time and especially of space, seems to be one of the hallmarks of the magical structure of consciousness. It is, at least in part, what makes the practice of magic, for instance by shamanic practitioners, possible, and is also one of the most important features of the magical structure as it continues to dwell even in modern consciousness. For example, Shanon (1998) examined the content of participants' experiences in ayahuasca rituals, finding a preponderance of jungle cats, serpents, and birds in their reported visualizations, regardless of their background, their expectations, or the settings in which the drug was ingested.

Gebser (1949/1986) associated the magical structure particularly with musical expressions, which transport us, as Thomas Mann once said, to the land behind the music. Gebser believed that in ancient primary cultures music and rhythm such as drumming brought people together into a single experiential event. Contemporary music, whether in symphony halls, in rock "gigs," or at midnight "raves," does much the same.

Indeed, any experience that merges human experience into a unified event that transcends the isolation of the individual qualifies as a potential production of the magical structure. This includes all manner of shared experiences, and particularly the experience of love. Some scholars have recently made substantial arguments, based on controversial but well-designed scientific research, that we human beings are, or at least under certain circumstances can be, connected in intimate ways, through subtle, or submicroscopic, quantum patterning (Laszlo, 2003, 2004; Sheldrake, 1981). True or not, if feelings can be considered creative, then love and compassion obtain high marks.

## Mythic Consciousness

Gebser (1949/1986) associated mythic consciousness most prominently with the early horticultural and agricultural civilizations of the Mediterranean and Middle East. This mode of consciousness represented a shift from the magical world, in which living spirits and meaningful events were found everywhere in nature, to a world created and sustained by great gods and goddesses. Many forms of the great Mother, or Earth goddess, characterized a period from roughly 10,000 years CE until the rise of the great city-states of the Middle East. She was associated with nature, fertility (as well as menopause), the night, bison (and other totem animals, depending on the area), and the moon, with its monthly cycles. We know few details of these first major mythic spiritual traditions, but evidence of them is found widely throughout Europe and Asia in the form of small carved images of the goddess. The Minoan civilization seems to have been the last great home of the goddess.

The advent of the city-states in the Fertile Crescent, the pre-Trojan War Greek civilization, and concurrent changes in the Egyptian mythic pantheon, saw a shift of importance to powerful male gods. They included Marduke in Mesopotamia, Zeus in Greece, Horus in Egypt, and Jehovah in Israel, all associated with the sky and often linked with powerful birds such as eagles and hawks. Sky gods also can be found in West Africa and Mesoamerica, although in these locations they tended to coexist with Earth goddesses rather than supplant them.

The creative gift of the mythical structure of consciousness is humanity's ability to understand the world, and our place within it, through mythological stories and allegorical narratives. This structure is also associated with a historical efflorescence of the imagination. Although in Piagetian terms mythical consciousness is developmentally associated with concrete operational thinking, Gebser (1949/1986) considered it the fountain of all epic narratives in the history of the cosmos and the construction of meaning in life. In this aspect it is associated with poetry and epics, and is the source of all theistic religions, both ancient and modern. The mythic mind seeks answers to the great enigmas of life, questions such as where we come from and what our lives are about, and spins these explanations into epic stories. Thus, the great questions are addressed in the larger-than-life accounts of gods and goddesses.

Unlike magical consciousness, which can even seem open-minded and liberal to a modern person, mythical consciousness is prone to the construction of strong polarities, framing reality in terms of good and evil, light and dark, and so on. Thus, it is not surprising that so many wars and so much bloodshed has been associated with the mythic structure. Of course, mythology is rarely one-sided or simplistic; Levi-Strauss (1963) pointed out that enduring myths typically resolved polarities and combined dualities.

Nevertheless, it is this structure of consciousness that lends meaning to our everyday lives. For many people this meaning flows from religious narratives. However, aside from the majestic mythic epics, it is the personal stories we live and act out that make sense of the events of our day-to-day lives. Without such stories, without a feeling that each day we play a meaningful part in some narrative—no matter how small—life can seem vacuous, and personal problems can remain unresolved (Harvey & Weber, 2002).

One of the authors of this chapter has coauthored an entire book on the importance of personal myths, which has also given rise to a form of psychotherapy that explores life's meaning in terms of personal narratives (Feinstein & Krippner, 1988). A body of psychological research supports the notion that human beings construct personal and cultural myths to cope with their awareness that death is imminent, and to buffer this knowledge with belief systems and worldviews that infuse their existence with meaning (e.g., Greenberg, Porteus, Simon, Pyszczynski, & Solomon, 1995).

## Mental Consciousness

This form of consciousness is associated with formal operations thinking. In the Western world, it came into prominence with the Greek pre-Socratic philosophers such as Thales, Anaximander, Anaximenenes, Pythagoras, and Anaxagoras (de Quincey, 2002), and reached an early high water mark in Plato's dialogues. The rational approach to understanding the world experienced a setback during the Middle Ages, but returned in the Renaissance with an emphasis on perspectival art, and soon after with analytic thought. As a result of the Renaissance and its subsequent paradigms, human consciousness has come to experience the world as a kind of extended Cartesian space, and time as a linear Newtonian dimension.

This way of understanding the world has given us philosophy, mathematics, engineering, and Western science. It is, in fact, how modern humans interpret reality, although many people in the world today still give considerable credence to mythic beliefs, the so-called scientific creationists being one example. Alone, mental consciousness cannot impart meaning. Efforts to make it do so, such as secular humanism and Sartre's brand of existential philosophy, leave many people unfulfilled. It seems that the greatest creative productions of rational thought, which often reach full expression in the mythic structure of consciousness, are fired by human imagination. However, mental consciousness is equipped with the mental tools for logical problem solving, which, in combination with mythic imagination, can give rise to great works of engineering, science, art, literature, architecture, and so on. This brings us to the topic of integral consciousness.

## Integral Consciousness

Gebser (1949/1986) believed that a new structure, one that he termed *integral consciousness*, appeared on a wide scale at the end of the 19th century. It is characterized by a fluidity of thought and perception no longer limited to a single point of view, as in perspectival art and imagination, but experienced simultaneously from multiple perspectives. It is also marked by a more fluid sense of time and space. Both aspects are evident, for example, in Picasso's painting of the bombing of Guernica, in which we see bits and pieces of people, animals, and buildings flying about in a kind of cubist mélange in which everything is happening at once. Chagall presented a quite different artistic perspective, but one in which multiple events assault the viewer. His "Paris from a Window" presents flying, oddly-positioned, and two-headed people of various sizes and dimensions coexisting in a panorama of buildings, flowers, and vehicles that, oddly, produces a coherent and aesthetically satisfying order from what at first seems to be hopeless chaos.

It is impossible to locate the integral consciousness structure in any of Piaget's developmental stages because it clearly represents a mode of understanding that transcends formal operations. Even the models of intelligence offered by postformal operations theorists do not exactly match Gebser's description (1949/1986) of such a fluid sense of reality, which paradoxically is more concrete than any of its predecessors, and at the same time more spiritually illuminated. With all this in mind, perhaps the best way to understand what Gebser recognized as integral in *fin de siècle* art, literature, science, and so on, is to say that he was looking across a range of postformal developmental strata. They were evidenced in many such expressions, and Gebser concluded that they represented a single structure of consciousness. Indeed they do, from a cultural standpoint, because their introduction on a wide scale has done more to transform the Western world than anything since the previous great transformation of consciousness in the Renaissance (Anderson, 1995).

The defining feature of integral consciousness for Gebser (1949/1986) was that it releases the free play of all the structures of consciousness. In other words, the magic, mythic, and mental structures can all be active simultaneously. Late in his life, Gebser advised his readers to "live all the structures all the time" (p. 275). This was his formula for a rich life, and it releases an astonishing degree of creativity. One may recall that creative thought can draw readily from all developmental levels. Such richness is apparent in the profound transformations of philosophy, science, literature, music, and dance, all occurring within a few decades after the year 1900. This effervescence of creativity was nowhere more conspicuous than in the new visual arts. Painters such as Cézanne, Monet, and Picasso began to explore the world through the multifaceted and fluid lens of integral perception. This generation of artists, and those since, intentionally departed from the old tradition of art as representation of a Newtonian-like external reality, making a radical shift to art as conscious depiction of experience itself.

Comparable changes were taking place in dance; Serge Diaghilev, for example, persuaded gifted choreographers (e.g., Michael Folkine) to work with innovative dancers (e.g., Tamara Karasvina, Vaslav Nijinsky), musicians (e.g., Igor Stravinsky), and designers (e.g., Leon Bakst). Similar developments were taking place in music, literature, jurisprudence, and even in science and mathematics (Gebser, 1949/1986). The physicist Werner Heisenberg (1952/1979) wrote an essay on "the new idealism," in which he pointed out that, at bottom, the material world is no longer comprised of Aristotelian "matter." Rather, it is the stuff of probabilities and wave functions (in other words, a form of mathematics), themselves creations of the human mind. Beyond this, we need only be reminded of how fluid and elusive time and space have become in the new physics, invented around the turn of the century as well.

In the 20th century the nimble and multifaceted capabilities of integral consciousness released a wealth of creativity and invention that would take whole encyclopedias to catalog. It is worth noting that the agile and many-sided intelligence of integral consciousness can be creative and constructive, as seen in much contemporary art, but it can also be lyrical, trickster-like, and even destructive. The epitome of destruction in the 20th and 21st centuries has been the unparalleled devastation wrought by religious, ethnic, and political wars (Krippner & McIntyre, 2003). Many of these wars reflect the frustration of zealots caught in the grips of mythic consciousness, fighting adversaries who reflect mental consciousness, which is seen as a threat to everything the militants consider sacred and holy. Integral consciousness is rarely seen as an alternative by either side in the struggle.

More benign are the so-called various deconstructionist perspectives in literature and art (e.g., Derrida, 1995), which take advantage of the manifold perception of integral consciousness to dissect works of art and philosophy, as well as individual characters, like plucking legs off a fly. Such "ironic" activity may be satisfying to the intellect, but often deprives the mythic and magical sensibilities that lend meaning and excitement to objects as well as ideas, people, and situations.

However, one branch of postmodernism has not been content to deconstruct works of art, but has reconstructed them in new and novel ways, fostering the self-reflection that is characteristic of integral consciousness (e.g., Misra & Gergen, 1993). This trend is especially apparent in the eclecticism of postmodern architecture. In commenting on Venturi's post-modern wing to London's National Gallery, Butler (2002) stated, "Architects like Venturi thought that the form-following-function language of modernist architecture was far too puritanical and should allow for the vitality, and no doubt the provocation to be gained from disunity and contradiction. Work like this happily deconstructs itself" (pp. 90–91). Glass and Wilson's opera "Einstein on the Beach" contains no coherent narrative line but is, nonetheless, fascinating and captivating for a growing number of enthusiasts. Another postmodern opera, Adams's "Nixon in China," has a narrative line but a minimalist orchestral score often termed "retro-postmodern" (Butler, 2002, p. 85). Crimp's "stolen" photography, Morley's "super-realistic" canvases, and Madonna's continually reinvented stage persona all are examples of postmodernism's irony, antiauthoritarianism, and resurrection of the repressed. It is suggested that creativity in the 21st century will verify or refute what we propose is a perennial need for myth and magic, as part of a bigger picture, however it may be culturally constructed.

## TRANSPARENCY, SPIRITUALITY, AND CREATIVITY

Gebser (1949/1986) spoke of the diaphanous quality to integral consciousness, meaning that it exhibits an open and translucent quality through which reality is experienced in a clear and less conditioned way. In this sense it may indeed be on the path to the nondual and unconditioned consciousness described in many traditions, as noted at the beginning of this chapter. Although far from a full realization, instances of such clarity are reported widely, and are evidently experienced by many creative individuals from time to time. Here may be found a directed absorption, as in Franck's meditation-in-action in art, or what Zen Master Sekida has called "positive samadhi," a "total involvement with some object or activity" (Richards, 1999, p. 212). The state of "flow" described by Csikszentimihalyi (1990) is related, and highly gifted artists, poets, musicians, and mathematicians often seem to be able to achieve such a state during their work (Barušs, 2004; Combs & Krippner, 2003; Csikszentmihalyi, 1990; Wilber, 1998b), although they may otherwise live quite ordinary lives.

The task, it would seem, includes clearing one's mind of the myriad elements that distract our attention and distort our perceptions. As taught in many spiritual traditions, these include emotions such as hatred, greed, resentment, envy as well as negative attitudes, thoughts, and speech of any kind. In Buddhism, one speaks of the "three poisons": greed, hatred, and ignorance. Together such features are often referred to as dirt or contaminants of the mind, in that they cloud our experience, condition our awareness, and stifle our creativity. It is well known that many highly creative people are able to put various distractions aside during their creative work. Csikszentmihalyi (1990) refers to this as one condition of flow, but it is more than absorption in the task at hand. It is also a clearing of conscious awareness so as to allow creative ideas and impulses to emerge freshly and without effort.

The extent to which we are able to avail ourselves of this clear mind state in our work or play is the extent to which we open ourselves to the optimal creativity of the integral structure of consciousness. The extent to which we can avail ourselves of this condition in our daily lives is the extent to which we open our entire lives toward unconditional creativity. It involves openness to what can be learned from other paradigms, other worldviews, and other cultures. This is a much more challenging goal, but in terms of creativity, as well as quality of life, it is the pearl beyond price.

How can we achieve this state? There is no easy answer to this question, or perhaps we should say, rather, that there is no easy path to its solution. Understanding, however, that integral consciousness, and the creativity that flows from it, may share features found on the path to spiritual awareness, we need only look to the advice of the spiritual and philosophical traditions that aspire to this path. Here one finds clues as to how to proceed (e.g., Combs & Krippner, 2003; Wilber, Engler, & Brown, 1986). Such advice fills volumes, but boils down to a few basic goals: the achievement of a quiet and settled mind, along with a sense of detachment from the turmoils of everyday life, paradoxically combined with the ability to engage in it completely. Psychological research, as well as the insights of traditions, both ancient and contemporary, both Eastern and Western, suggest that the most effective way to move us in this direction is to practice some form of regular meditation or contemplation, especially what is often called "mindfulness meditation" (Nhat Hanh, 1998). To delineate these methods more fully would require another essay. For the moment, however, let us labor to live more fully in all the structures of consciousness at our disposal, embracing the world and the life we are given.

## REFERENCES

Alexander, C. N. (1992). Peaceful body, peaceful mind, peaceful world [Special issue]. *Modern science and Vedic science*, 5(1–2). Retrieved December 26, 2002, from http://www.mum.edu/m_effect/alexander/

Alexander, C. N., & Langer, E. (1990). *Higher stages of human development*. Cambridge: Oxford University Press.

Anderson, W. T. (1995). Introduction: What's going on here? In W. T. Anderson (Ed.), *The truth about the truth: De-confusing and re-constructing the postmodern world* (pp. 1–11). New York: Tarcher/Putnam.

Baldwin, J. M. (1906). *Mental development in the child and the race, methods and processes.* New York: Macmillan.

Barnes, H. B. (2000). *Stages of thought: The co-evolution of religious thought and science.* New York: Oxford University Press.

Baruss, I. (2004). Transition to transcendence: Franklin Merrell-Wolff's mathematical yoga. *Journal of Conscious Evolution, 1.* Retrieved February 1, 2005, from http://www.cejournal.org/index.html

Berman, M. (2000). *Wandering god: A study in nomadic spirituality.* Albany, NY: SUNY Press.

Butler, C. (2002). *Postmodernism: A very short introduction.* New York: Oxford University Press.

Clottes, J., & Lewis-Williams, D. (1998). *The shamans of prehistory: Trance and magic in the painted caves* (S. Hawkes, Trans.). New York: Abrams. (Original work published 1996)

Combs, A. (2002). *The radiance of being: Understanding the grand integral vision; Living the integral life* (2nd ed.). St Paul, MN: Paragon House.

Combs, A., & Krippner, S. (2003). Process, structure, and form: An evolutionary transpersonal psychology of consciousness. *International Journal of Transpersonal Studies, 22,* 47–60.

Cook-Greuter, S. (1999). *Postautonomous ego development: A study of its nature and measurement.* (Doctoral dissertation, Harvard University, 1999). *Dissertation Abstracts International-B, 60–06,* 3000.

Cox, R. H. (2005). A proposed paradigm for the developmental stages of spirituality. In R. H. Cox, B. Ervin Cox, & L. Hoffman (Eds.), *Spirituality and psychological health* (pp. 33–56). Colorado Springs, CO: Colorado School of Professional Psychology Press.

Csikszentmihalyi, M. (1990). *Flow: The psychology of optimal experience.* New York: Harper & Row.

de Quincey, C. (2002). *Radical nature: Rediscovering the soul of matter.* Montpelier, VT: Invisible Cities Press.

Derrida, J. (1995). The play of substitution. In W. T. Anderson (Ed.), *The truth about the truth: De-confusing and re-constructing the postmodern world* (pp. 86–91). New York: Tarcher/Putnam.

Donald, M. (1997). *Origins of the modern mind: Three stages in the evolution of culture and cognition.* Cambridge, MA: Harvard University Press.

Erikson, E. (1963). *Childhood and society.* New York: Norton.

Feinstein, D., & Krippner, S. (1988). *Personal mythology: The psychology of your evolving self.* Los Angeles: Tarcher.

Feldman, D. H. (2000). Figurative and operative processes in the development of artistic talent. *Human Development, 43,* 60–64. (DOI: 10.1159/000022659)

Feldman, D. H. (2004). Piaget's stages: The unfinished symphony of cognitive development. *New Ideas in Psychology, 22,* 175–231.

Fenner, P. (2002). *Edge of certainty: Dilemmas on the Buddhist path.* Berwick, ME: Nicolas-Hays.

Feuerstein, G. (1987). *Structures of consciousness: The genius of Jean Gebser.* Lower Lake, CA: Integral Publishing.

Fischer, K. W., & Bidell, T. R. (1998). Dynamic development of psychological structures in action and thought. In W. Damon & R. M. Lerner (Eds.), *Handbook of child psychology: Vol. 1. Theoretical models of human development* (5th ed., pp. 467–561). New York: Wiley.

Gablik, S. (1976). *Progress in art.* New York: Rizzoli.

Gallese, V., & Goldman, A. (1998). Mirror neurons and the simulation theory of mind-reading. *Trends in Cognitive Neuroscience, 2,* 493–501.

Gebser, J. (1986). *The ever-present origin.* (N. Barstad & A. Mickunas, Trans.). Athens, OH: Ohio University Press. (Original work published 1949)

Gilligan, C. (1993). *In a different voice: Psychological theory and women's development.* Cambridge, MA: Harvard University Press.

Gowan, J. C. (1974). *Development of the psychedelic individual.* Buffalo, NY: Creative Education Foundation.

Greeley, A., & McCready, W. (1975). Are we a nation of mystics? In D. Goleman & R. J. Davidson (Eds.), *Consciousness, brain, states of awareness, and mysticism* (pp. 175–183). New York: Harper & Row.

Greenberg, J., Porteus, J., Simon, L., Pyszczynski, T., & Solomon, S. (1995). Evidence of a terror management function of cultural icons: The effects of mortality salience on reactions to the inappropriate use of culturally valued objects. *Personality and Social Psychology Bulletin, 21,* 1221–1228.

Gruber, H. E. (1999). Jean Piaget. In M. A. Runco & S. R. Pritzker (Eds.), *Encyclopedia of creativity* (Vol. 2, pp. 381–385). San Diego, CA: Academic Press.

Guenther, H. V. (1989). *From reductionism to creativity: rDzogs-chen and the new sciences of mind.* Boston: Shambhala.

Harvey, J. H., & Weber, A. L. (2002). *Odyssey of the heart: Close relationships in the 21st century.* Mahwah, NJ: Erlbaum.

Heisenberg, W. (1979). *Philosophical problems of quantum physics.* Woodbridge, CT: OxBow Press. (Original work published 1952)

Huntington, C. W. (1989). *The emptiness of emptiness: An introduction to early Indian Madhyamika.* Honolulu: University of Hawaii Press.

James, V. (2001). *Spirit and art: Pictures of the transformation of consciousness.* Great Barrington, MA: Anthroposophist Press.

Kearney, R. (1998). *The wake of imagination.* New York: Routledge.

Kegan, R. (1982). *The evolving self: Problem and process in human development.* Cambridge, MA: Harvard University Press.

Kegan, R. (1994). *In over our heads: The mental demands of modern life.* Cambridge, MA: Harvard University Press.

Kellogg, R. (1969). *Analyzing children's art.* Palo Alto, CA: National Press Books.

Kohlberg, L. (1981). *Essays on moral development* (Vol.1). San Francisco: Harper & Row.

Koplowitz, H. (1984). *A projection beyond Piaget's formal-operations stage: A general system stage and a unitary stage.* In M. L. Commons, F. A. Richards, & C. Armon (Eds.), *Beyond formal operations: Late adolescent and adult cognitive development* (pp. 272–296). New York: Praeger Publishers.

Krippner, S. (1999). Altered and transitional states. In M. A. Runco & S. R. Pritzker (Eds.), *Encyclopedia of creativity* (Vol. 1, pp. 59–70). San Diego, CA: Academic Press.

Krippner, S. (2000). The epistemology and technologies of shamanic states of consciousness. *Journal of Consciousness Studies, 7,* 93–118.

Krippner, S., & McIntyre, T. M. (2003). Overview: In the wake of war. In S. Krippner & T. M. McIntyre (Eds.), *The psychological impact of war trauma on civilians: An international perspective* (pp. 1–14). Westport, CT: Praeger Publishers.

Kris, E. (1976). On preconscious mental processes. In A. Rothenberg & C. Hausman (Eds.). *The creativity question* (pp. 135–143). Durham, NC: Duke University Press.

Laszlo, E. (2003). *The connectivity hypothesis: Foundations of an integral science of quantum, cosmos, life, and consciousness.* Albany: State University of New York Press.

Laszlo, E. (2004). *Science and the Akashic field: An integral theory of everything.* Rochester, VT: Inner Traditions.

Leman, P. J., & Duveen, G. (1999). Representations of authority and children's moral reasoning. *European Journal of Social Psychology, 29,* 557–575.

Levi-Strauss, C. (1963). *Structural anthropology.* London: Thames & Hudson.

Lewis-Williams, D. (2004). *The mind in the cave: Consciousness and the origins of art.* New York: Thames & Hudson.

Loy, D. (1988). *Nonduality: A study in comparative philosophy.* Amherst, NY: Humanity Books.

Milbrath, C. (1998). *Patterns of artistic development in children: Comparative studies of talent.* New York: Cambridge University Press.

Miller, M. E., & Cook-Greuter, S. R. (1994). *Transcendence and mature thought in adulthood: The further reaches of adult development.* Lanham, MD: Rowman & Littlefield.

Misra, G., & Gergen, K. G. (1993). Beyond scientific colonialism: A reply to Poortinga and Triandis. *International Journal of Psychology, 28,* 251–254.

Mithen, S. (1999). *The prehistory of the mind: The cognitive origins of art, religion and science.* New York: Thames & Hudson.

Morton, K. R., Worthley, J. S., Nitch, S. R, Lamberton, H. H, Loo, L. K., & Testerman, J. K. (2000). Integration of cognition and emotion: A post-formal operations model of physician-patient interaction. *Journal of Adult Development, 7,* 151–160.

Nhat Hanh, T. (1998). *The heart of the Buddha's teachings*. Berkeley, CA: Parallax Press.

Piaget, J. (1923). *The language and thought of the child*. Cleveland, OH: Meridian.

Piaget, J. (1959). *Judgment and reasoning in the child*. Totowa, NJ: Littlefield, Adams. (Original work published 1928)

Piaget, J. (1960). *The child's conception of the world*. Paterson, NJ: Littlefield, Adams. (Original work published 1929)

Piaget, J., & Inhelder, B. (1967). *The child's conception of space*. New York: Norton.

Plato. (1942). *Five great dialogues. Apology, Crito, Phaedo, Symposium, Republic* (B. Jowett, Trans.). Roslyn, NY: Black. (Original work published 1892)

Plotkin, H. (1988). An evolutionary epistemological approach to the evolution of intelligence. In H. J. Jerison & J. Jerison (Eds.), *Intelligence and evolutionary biology* (pp. 73–91). New York: Springer-Verlag.

Richards, R. (1981). Relationships between creativity and psychopathology. *Genetic Psychology Monographs, 103*, 261–324.

Richards, R. (1999). The subtle attraction: Beauty as a force in awareness, creativity, and survival. In S. Russ (Ed.). *Affect, creative experience, and psychological adjustment* (pp. 195–219). Philadelphia: Brunner/Mazel.

Richter, G. (1982). *Art and human consciousness*. Edinburgh: Floris Books. (Original work published 1937)

Ryan, R. (1999). *The strong eye of shamanism*. Rochester, VT: Inner Traditions.

Shanon, B. (1998). Ideas and reflections associated with ayahuasca visions. *Newsletter of the Multidisciplinary Association for Psychedelic Studies, 8*(3), 18–21.

Shaw, I. (1994). *The commanding self*. London: Octagon Press.

Sheldrake, R. (1981). *A new science of life*. London: Blond & Briggs.

Spence, J. (1992). *Hear our voices: A phenomenological study of the transpersonal (spiritual) emergent experienced in American culture, its effects, helps and hindrances, and implications*. Unpublished doctoral dissertation. Cincinnati, OH: Union Institute.

Studsill, R. (2002). *Systems theory and unity of mystical traditions: A comparative analysis of rDzogs-chen and Rhineland mystics*. Unpublished doctoral dissertation. Berkeley, CA: Graduate Theological Union.

Taylor, S. (2003). Primal spirituality and the onto/phylo fallacy: A critique of the claim that primal peoples were/are less spiritual and socially developed than modern humans. *International Journal of Transpersonal Studies, 22*, 61–76.

Thompson, R. A. (1987). The development of children's inferences of the emotions of others. *Developmental Psychology, 23*, 124–131.

Wilber, K. (1981). *Up from Eden*. New York: Doubleday/Anchor.

Wilber, K. (1998a). *Integral psychology*. Boston: Shambhala.

Wilber, K. (1998b). *The marriage of sense and soul.* New York: Random House.

Wilber, K. (2000). *Sex, ecology, spirituality: The spirit of evolution* (2nd ed.). Boston: Shambhala.

Wilber, K., Engler, J., & Brown, D. P. (1986). *Transformation of consciousness: Conventional and contemplative perspectives on consciousness.* Boston: Shambhala.

# II
## CREATIVITY AND SOCIETY

# 7

# TELLING THE NEW STORY: DARWIN, EVOLUTION, AND CREATIVITY VERSUS CONFORMITY IN SCIENCE

DAVID LOYE

Important as the struggle for existence has been and even still is, yet as far as the highest part of our nature is concerned there are other agencies more important. For the moral qualities are advanced either directly or indirectly much more through the effects of habit, by our reasoning powers, by instruction, by religion, etc., than through natural selection.
—Charles Darwin, *The Descent of Man*, Conclusions, p. 404

For a century, many of psychology's great founders and innovators, in keeping with Darwin's long-ignored full theory of evolution (Loye, 2004)—of which we will say much more here—have struggled to build a humanistic, moral, and action-oriented theory of evolution. Beyond the prevailing constraints for their field, it can now be seen that they were seeking an alternative to the prevailing paradigm accepted by biologists, Neo-Darwinians, and the so-called "man in the street" of "survival of the fittest" and selfishness as prime drivers for human, as well as prehuman, evolution. Darwin not only had much more to say about evolutionary motivation at the human level but also, unknown to them, had earlier stated what became the driving ethos for scores of creative psychologists. This is a story much in need of telling.

This chapter explores this pivotal but little known chunk of our history as a case Writ Large of creativity against conformity—that is, of forces supporting open and innovative inquiry versus those promoting falling in line with dominant views. What now adds urgency to the story is that in the conflict of paradigms that shape science, society, and the lives of every one of us, it is becoming evident to many of us that conformity to the "old" Darwinian paradigm of "survival of the fittest" and "selfishness above all" is relentlessly driving our species toward destruction (Loye, 2004).

Among the highly creative pioneers for what might be called a "second Darwinian revolution," we will look at Darwin's disciple George Romanes, along with Freud, Fluegel, Morgan, Baldwin, James, Mead, Dewey, Piaget, Lewin, Fromm, Tomkins, Kohlberg, Gilligan, Maslow, and Assagioli, and in more recent times, Csikszentmihalyi, Wilber, Combs, Krippner, Ornstein, Wilson, de Waal, Damon, and others. With threats to the well-being of our species steadily mounting, we will close with a look at the new Darwin Project and prospects for an alliance of psychologists along with evolutionary systems scientists to more effectively and swiftly shift from old to new.

If we move out beyond psychology's usual focus on the individual and the small group (e.g., family, workplace, or organization) to look at the increasingly troubled situation of our species, a large problem affecting us at all levels becomes apparent: We face immense challenges in the 21st century, calling for new views of human nature (Loye, 2004) and a vast increase in everyday creativity (R. Richards, 1999). Yet both are still radically constricted through a tragic triumph of conformity over creativity.

The specific problem is that we have arrived at what the great body of science as a whole agrees is a pivotal juncture in human evolution without a fundamental source for guidance, namely an adequate theory and story of evolution to provide a reasonably sure sense of the path for humanity from past and present into the future. The theory we have is based almost entirely on the study of the past and the prehuman and the subhuman.

The tragedy is that the creativity of the founders and innovators of the field of psychology as well as all of social science, who set out to give us precisely what was needed, again and again fell victim to the age-old pressures and dynamics of conformity that Barron (1969), Crutchfield (1964), Csikzentmihalyi (1996), R. Richards (chaps. 1 & 13, this volume), and scores of other psychologists have revealed. To appreciate what is at stake, we need to bring back into the discourse shaping psychology and social science as a whole, the minds and voices of all those whose works we can now see are still of prime relevance to the development of a fully human theory and story of evolution.

By "fully human" what is meant is this: 20th-century science did a remarkable job of making both the theory and story of cosmic evolution come to life for us via physics. It also gave us an impressive theory and story of biological evolution via chemistry and biology. But when it came to dealing with the explosion out of nature of higher brain, mind, and consciousness, which characterizes the emergence of our species and our impact on this planet, and constitutes the subject matter for the field of psychology, it fell tragically short of what was needed.

Why tragic? As that great innovator in the study of creativity Silvan Tomkins (1962–1992) made evident with his pioneering development of script theory (Carlson, 1995), we live by story. Yet what about the unsettling demonstration of Tomkins's insight that the newspapers now force on us almost daily? We live by story, and the story we live by is driving our species to extinction (e.g., see Laszlo, 1994; Elgin, 2000).

What can we do about it? The studies in this chapter reveal that within our heritage as psychologists lies the powerful answer the great founders and innovators kept trying to advance. The idea, which lies at the core of our whole field, is that if we change the theory, we can change the story. The hope rising from this demonstrable fact is that by changing the "old" theory and the "old" story for evolution, we can bypass the road to extinction and move on to build the better world. (Also see chaps. 10, 11, & 12, this volume, for varied views on paradigm shifts.)

Another source for the same answer is a discipline of increasing interest to many psychologists, in which Kurt Lewin (1951) was a major contributor, the field of systems science. Driving psychology in this direction has been the growing interest in nonlinear dynamical systems, or "chaos," theory (see chap. 2, this volume). During the 4 decades of my own involvement in the past and present for both fields as well as involvement with evolutionary and futures studies and chaos theory (Loye, 1977, 1978, 1984, 1998, 2000a, 2004), I have come to see that if we are to achieve the fully human theory of evolution that the future for our species requires, it calls for a new working partnership between these two, psychology and systems science, with thereafter the widening involvement of the other fields of social science as well as natural science and the humanities.

We first look at the heritage of psychology's past, including Darwin's "lost theory," bearing on our chance for the better future, then at the same for systems science, and last at how the two are beginning to come together in projects that, with widening scientific and educational involvement, could be large enough to have a significant impact on our lives throughout the rest of the 21st century and beyond.

## CREATIVITY VERSUS CONFORMITY IN THE EVOLUTION THEORY AND STORY

Another psychologist noted for creativity studies, Howard Gruber, in his study of the creative thrust for the theory and story of evolution, was the first to uncover the startling degree to which Darwin's underreported work originally anticipated the development of modern cognitive, social, and humanistic psychology (Gruber & Barrett, 1974/1981). The pioneering interest Darwin displayed in psychology in *The Expression of Emotions in Man and Animals* (Darwin, 1872) has long been noted. Yet after a lengthy probe of the early notebooks as well as *The Descent of Man* (Darwin, 1871), what Gruber (1974/1981) reported in his award-winning *Darwin on Man* was that for his far-ranging insights, Darwin deserves far more credit as a founder of modern psychology in addition to evolution theory than had been realized.

On digging further into this neglected side of Darwin in a major study of the relation of psychology to evolution theory, University of Chicago psychologist and historian of science Robert J. Richards (1987) discovered an aspect of this relationship that is of central importance both in the reclamation of the "other" Darwin and in the meaning for our future. This is the fact that along with such well-known early psychologists as J. M. Baldwin and William James, in a way almost wholly unsuspected, Darwin was a major moral theorist.

Digging still further, by applying rigorous content as well as hermeneutical analysis from an advanced systems scientific perspective, I uncovered the rest of a startling picture wholly at odds with the prevailing stereotype.

Driven by neo-Darwinian science—including, most forcefully, the claims of evolutionary psychology and sociobiology today—for over a century, as noted earlier, the prevailing paradigm has locked onto "survival of the fittest" and selfishness as the prime Darwinian drives for the evolution of ours as well as all other species. Working, however, with the advantage of a computerized version (Goldie & Ghiselin, 1997) of the book in which Darwin specifically tells us he will focus on human evolution, *The Descent of Man*, I found this frankly astounding twist to the lost story of Darwin and all the great psychologists who, without knowing it, were his heirs in the uphill drive to launch a "second Darwinian revolution."

My instrument was nothing more than the computer "find" procedure that today any computer-literate 8-year-old can use. Despite all the years of development by psychologists and other social scientists of the use of word count as one of the most powerful tools of the methodology of content analysis, so automatically and routinely accepted was the "old" prevailing Darwinian paradigm that no one had bothered to apply it to either of Darwin's supposedly sacred basic texts on evolution for the primary theory underlying psychology and all the other sciences of living systems.

I first tried the "find" button to look for how many times Darwin wrote about the central concepts for the prevailing paradigm. In 898 pages of very fine print in *The Descent of Man*, I found that Darwin wrote only twice about "survival of the fittest," once to actually apologize for ever using the term! And what of the other obvious concepts? Only 12 times for selfishness, and 9 times for competition. I then tried the other set of concepts which, throughout the century, one great psychologist after another, from Baldwin and Piaget to Maslow, has tried to establish as being of paramount importance in our development, reaching what might call the apogee with the development of humanistic, transpersonal, and positive psychology.

In the sharpest possible contrast to "survival of the fittest"—in this book in which he specifically tells us he will move on from the evolution theory of *Origin of Species* to what mainly drives evolution at our species' level—Darwin writes of love 95 times. He writes of moral sensitivity 92 times. He writes of sympathy 61 times. And he writes of mutuality or mutual aid (the terms they used for cooperation in those days) 24 times. Furthermore, in keeping with the expanding portrait of Darwin the psychologist, of the thrust of creativity that was to distinguish 20th century psychology at its best, he writes of mind 90 times, intellectual qualities and powers 75 times, reason 53 times, imagination 25 times, learning 18 times, consciousness 15 times, curiosity 14 times, and instruction 10 times. Darwin further writes, in regard to what became a primary area for James (1890/1950), Hull (1952), Skinner (1965), and the whole field of educational psychology, 108 times of habit, and bearing on the neuropsychology of the 20th and 21st centuries, 110 times of the brain including his prescient interest in the frontal brain.

If we consider the fact that Darwin's has long been considered the single most important theory underlying not only psychology but all fields of science concerned with living systems, is it too much to suggest that we are looking at the most colossal case of the triumph of scientific conformity over scientific creativity now on record?

What emerges in the text behind these astounding word counts (Loye, 1994, 1998, 1999, 2000, 2001, 2002b, 2007a) is a clear picture of the structural relation of *The Origin of Species* to *The Descent of Man*. This is of major bearing on the challenge to us to break the shell of conformity to the old paradigm for evolution and give not just peace but creativity a chance. In the first book, Darwin lays down the biological foundation, or "first half" on which both science and society fixated. Yet in the second book, he outlines the psychological superstructure, prefiguring the development of cognitive, social, developmental, humanistic, transpersonal, and positive psychology in our time. Of the most neglected urgency, it is in this second book that he provides the basic sketch for a moral and action-oriented second or completing half for his theory of evolution that psychology, as well as the rest of science, has only barely begun to build (Loye, 1994; Rachels, 1998).

This is important to keep in mind because it indicates where Darwin was headed in the development of his theory of evolution. We are also looking at how he clearly hoped to see this development proceed after his death.

# THE LOST STORY OF WHAT MIGHT HAVE BEEN:
## SELF-ORGANIZING PROCESSES

From this point on we are looking at the lost story of what might have been. On Darwin's death he left all his papers on psychology to his worshipful young disciple George Romanes (R. J. Richards, 1987), who went on not only to become a leading British psychologist but also the first to lament what was repeatedly to block any chance for psychology to advance evolution theory in Darwin's intended direction. The problem was the progressively more fierce possession of evolution theory by biology and its adroit exclusion of the perspective and creativity of other fields. Only 10 years after Darwin's death, there was a move afoot by biologists to "hide certain parts of Darwin's teaching, and give undue prominence to others," Romanes (1897, p. 9) states in *Darwin and After Darwin*. Posthumously published after Romanes died of a brain tumor, Romanes had left this book to his student Lloyd Morgan to finish.

Whether "the misrepresentation be due to any unfavourable bias against one side of his teaching, or to sheer carelessness in the reading of his books" (Romanes, 1897, p. 9), it was inexcusable that the "neo-Darwinians"—for it was Romanes in this book who first coined the phrase—should "positively reverse" Darwin's teachings. The new breed of self-proclaimed Darwinians were "unjustifiably throwing over their own opinions the authority of Darwin's name," Romanes charged (1897, pp. 9–10). "I myself believe that Darwin's judgment with regard to all these points will eventually prove more sound and accurate than that of any of the recent would-be improvers upon his system," Romanes predicted (1897, pp. 9–10).

The next attempt to advance evolution theory in Darwin's intended direction came with no less a founding father for humanistic and many other fields of psychology than William James, although the ill-fated James, Mark Baldwin, and by now Romanes's student and disciple, the British neuropsychologist Lloyd Morgan, were more heavily involved (R. J. Richards, 1987). Perceiving the need for a new concept to account for evolution at the level of human emergence, Baldwin, Morgan, James, and the anthropologist Henry Osborn proposed the idea of *"organic selection"* as the higher developmental alternative to natural selection (Baldwin, 1896). Despite difficulties in explaining the idea for Baldwin et al.—and their functionally forgotten successors in psychology, as we see later in this chapter—the core idea was actually quickly conveyed by the wording. In radical contrast to "natural selection" as the basic explanation for how evolution shapes all organisms by the selection of "winners" by overriding external forces, the core idea for "organic selection" is of how the organism (e.g., ourselves) shape evolution by our selection of who or what we want to become.

In other words—astounding how at the time and thereafter this was so seldom clearly perceived—this was the basic heresy for the departure of psychology from all previous scientific fields. For here was the first statement for a perspective that could have brought the psychology of learning, experience, and choice by both group and individual into a theory of evolution that might then seamlessly segue from biological into cultural evolution.

However, fate intervened to further consolidate the monopoly of evolution theory by biology. As a result of R. J. Richards's (1987) detective work, more has now come to light of how what happened to Baldwin may have changed the course of history. In pursuit of the most important ignored emphasis for Darwin's "higher" theory, Baldwin was the first of a long line of psychologists pioneering not only the heretical psychology of "organic selection," but even more so of moral development. Then in 1908 he was discovered in a Black brothel in Baltimore by a newspaper reporter. The scandal not only forced Baldwin to flee to France but also seemed to help slam the door on the whole field of psychology through guilt by association.

It also seems to have so effectively scuttled the disruptive insight of "organic selection" as the higher level counterpart to "natural selection," that it took much of a century for the idea to fight its way back into mainstream scientific consciousness. This was the core idea for psychologist Gordon Allport's concept of "functional autonomy" in the 1950s (Allport, 1964); again for Jean Piaget in the 1970s (Piaget, 1980). Then in another touch of the irony that overlays the tragedy of this story, the advance for psychology that had been shut out of evolution theory by the monopoly of physics and biology by the end of this effectively "lost" century, now spread like wildfire throughout physics and biology. This was the evolutionary relevance (also known as "the Baldwin effect" or "organic selection") of what through a variety of radically advancing new concepts out of chaos and complexity theory is now known as "self-organizing processes" (Csanyi, 1989; Depew, 2000; Depew & Weber, 1996; Jantsch, 1980; Kauffman, 1996; Maturana & Varela, 1987; Prigogine & Stengers, 1984; Salthe, 1993).

## THE LOST STORY OF WHAT MIGHT HAVE BEEN: MORAL DEVELOPMENT AND MORAL EVOLUTION

The other closely allied, and in his pioneering for science as well as evolution theory for Darwin, and the most important factor in "higher level" evolution, was the drive of moral development and moral evolution. Here, once again, the originating creativity of a handful of great psychologists was blocked and sidelined by the conformity of social as well as natural science—and the social, economic, political, and educational systems legitimized by this truncated science—to a neo-Darwinian biological paradigm of "survival of the fittest" and "selfishness above all." Particularly interesting is the fact that the chief "lost" moral concern for Darwin, which was dropped by his successors in biology for much of a century, was also central to the work of Sigmund Freud and his disciples J. C. Fluegel, George Herbert Mead, John Dewey, Jean Piaget again as well as Baldwin.

Generally forgotten today is the hit or miss interest in evolution that Freud (1989) displayed in *Civilization and Its Discontents*. Among his greatest contributions was his extensive definition of the nature and operation of the superego and the ego ideal in relation to the ego as the basis for our moral development (Freud, 1990)—a position elaborated and greatly extended by Fluegel (1945). Although identified mainly as a sociologist today, George Herbert Mead (1934) is considered to be one of the fathers of social psychology. Again, in works almost wholly neglected today, can be found an intensive exploration of both evolution and moral directionality. The same is true of Mead's much better known friend and occasional mentor, the most widely influential American psychologist of his time, John Dewey (1922). As for Piaget (1965), uniquely equipped as a biologist as well as a psychologist through his studies of the moral as well as more general mind of the child, his was quite possibly the 20th century's greatest contribution to our understanding of moral as well as cognitive development and its tremendous importance to cultural evolution.

However, with the worldwide lionizing of Freud by psychotherapy and of Dewey and Piaget by the fields of education as well as the demands of other broad-gauged interests that took all of them elsewhere, their attempt to expand and update evolution theory was again easily deflected by the biologists. The biologists came to the monopoly of evolution theory equipped with the seemingly safe, familiar, and systems-popularized theory and the tale of the neo-Darwinian paradigm. From grade school through graduate studies they were also always there—by now entrenched in the textbooks for all levels of education throughout the Western world seemingly beyond all contesting.

Another pivotal figure in the vital stream of creativity is the psychologist most likely headed for a major revival of interest in the 21st century. If we look at his work again today, it can be seen that Kurt Lewin (1951; Loye, 1971) was not just another so-called father of social psychology and group dynamics. It becomes apparent that along with his pioneering of a clearly morally oriented action research—to solve, for example, the problems of racism, socialization of street gangs, design of better cities, equality of employment, the dynamics of democratic versus totalitarian governance— Lewin was also the precursor genius within psychology for the chaos and complexity theories prefiguring the needed wedding of evolutionary systems science with psychology (Abraham, 1997; Loye & Eisler, 1987).

We are now into the 1930s and 1940s and the Great Depression, the cataclysmic impact of Hitler, World War II, and the shock and implications of the explosion of the atom bomb and the devastation of Hiroshima and Nagasaki. Out of this profound stirring of the pot of concern emerged the new creativity of the moral evolutionary studies of psychologists Erich Fromm, Lawrence Kohlberg, and Carol Gilligan.

Stemming from his roots in Freud and Marx, in the remarkable *Man for Himself: An Inquiry Into the Psychology of Ethics*, Fromm (1947) wrote what still remains one of the most stirring arguments for the development of humanistic psychology in this direction. He also laid out the criteria for establishing a Global Ethic, first most widely and effectively answered by theologian Hans Kung (Kung & Kuschel, 1993 and then, from the perspective of evolutionary systems science as well as psychology, more recently by myself (Loye, 1999, 2006b). Building on the prior work of Baldwin and Piaget, Kohlberg (1984) launched the first major study of moral evolution to be sustained by the kind of institutional infrastructure that is needed to provide our species with what the challenge of the 21st century requires. Then came the jolt that unsettled Kohlberg as well as the male domination of science more generally as, in 1982, Gilligan—along with psychologist Jean Baker Miller (1976), sociologist Jessie Bernard (1981), and cultural evolution theorist Riane Eisler (1987)—finally managed to bring the neglected perspective of half the species into the moral evolutionary discourse.

## THE CREATIVE BREAKOUT FOR HUMANISTIC PSYCHOLOGY

Despite the firm continuing hold by biology and physics on practically everything taught throughout Western society at all levels of education as evolution theory, by the second half of the 20th century, there was a widening consciousness of the need for the "higher" or more advanced form of evolution theory that Darwin prefigured as it affected humans. Out of by now 50 years of attempts bearing on the updating and expanding of evolution theory came the rise of humanistic psychology and the contribution of Abraham Maslow and others such as Roberto Assagioli (1965) and Kazimierz Dabrowski (1964).

Historically, Maslow (1968) most effectively stated both the initial and long range creative vision for humanistic psychology as well as transpersonal psychology and most recently the challenge of positive psychology. In the end what do we seek? Again the emphasis was on moral evolution, but with an increasingly urgent edge to go beyond just studying it, to direct intervention by the human agent in shaping human evolution. Said Maslow

(1971), the goal for the most critical challenge for human creativity is to develop the Good Person and the Good Society.

In other words, our evolutionary goal is not to bypass or transcend ourselves, as it might be said were the goals for behaviorism or a wholly otherworldly religion. Nor, contrary to the prevailing rhetoric for conventional theory is it merely to "adapt" to whatever comes our way. Through the ultimate outreach for creativity, our goal is to fulfill ourselves.

In so doing, as is generally well-known by now, in Maslow's (1968, 1971) needs hierarchy, one fulfills "deficiency needs" and continues on to "being needs." These include "self-actualization" which has, as one aspect, a "self-actualizing creativity" that operates in everyday creativity, a construct it helped inspire (R. Richards, 1999). In keeping with Darwin's original vision of the higher level of growth and health to which the individual can aspire—which culture can either nurture and advance or warp and block—for Maslow (1971) the self-actualizing person is relatively more aware, spontaneous, free, expressive, concerned with "being values" such as truth, goodness, beauty, wholeness, dichotomy-transcendence, aliveness, and justice.

Further intensifying the emphasis and the urgency of this message were two survivors of the Nazi devastation of Europe and the global threat of fascism, Assagioli and Dabrowski. "Superficiality, vulgarity, absence of inner conflict, quick forgetting of grave experiences, became something repugnant to me," Dabrowski wrote in proclaiming a heroic stance both for humanistic psychology and for the wedding of psychology with evolution theory (Piechowski, 1975, p. 234). "I searched for people and attitudes of a different kind, those that were authentically ideal, saturated with immutable values, those who represented 'what ought to be' against 'what is'" (p. 234).

Since those days, as the *Handbook of Humanistic Psychology* (Schneider, Bugental, & Pierson, 2001), *Handbook of Positive Psychology* (Snyder & Lopez, 2001), and sources for transpersonal psychology such as *Paths Beyond Ego* (Walsh & Vaughan, 1993) make apparent, there have been advances. Along the path we are pursuing here, Ken Wilber (1993), Allan Combs (1997), Stanley Krippner (1980), and Robert Ornstein (1991) have explored the evolution of consciousness. From Darwin's long-ignored concept of moral action as a central driver of our evolutionary level, Mihaly Csikszentmihalyi (1993), Frans de Waal (1996), David Sloan Wilson (Sober & Wilson, 1998), and Piagetian William Damon (1995) have brought this perspective back into the picture for evolution-relevant psychology. Yet after a whole century, the effort is still scattered and sporadic, with little more assurance of relating to or helping to build a body of theory in common—or of any significant recognition by society at large, rather than only by a special subgroup—than existed at the beginning for Baldwin, Piaget, Fromm, Kohlberg, Gilligan, or most of the rest of the earlier figures.

This takes us to what increasingly looms as a pivotal question for both psychology and evolution theory today: What happened to Maslow's vision of the Good Person and the Good Society?

## THE COUNTERREVOLUTION OF EVOLUTIONARY PSYCHOLOGY

One could say that into the quasi-vacuum once filled with the humanistic aspiration that earlier prevailed in psychology, out of neo-Darwinian biology, there moved a particularly hard-edged new attempt to reassert its ownership of evolution theory with a biologized sociology and a biologized psychology. Another perspective would be that, in reaction to what is in effect a "second Darwinian revolution" I have been describing, came the counterrevolution of a backward shift toward the celebration of selfishness and "survival of the fittest" in both science and society. In other words, as decried by scientists and other scholars in a number of fields, in tandem with the dynamics of a radical rightward shift in national politics, first sociobiology and then evolutionary psychology emerged to close out the century with a bang (Rose & Rose, 2000).

Under fire by critics, evolutionary psychology has been evolving toward a less abrasive and more culturally sensitive approach. At the outset, however, to those of us old enough to have known and treasured the history of psychology as more than something to flip through in a textbook, not since the early days of American behaviorism has a new school of psychology trashed the views of its predecessors with such arrogance, vituperation, and ignorance. The introduction to the handbook for the new field, Barkow, Cosmides, and Tooby's (1992) *The Adapted Mind*, offers what are by now classic examples. Within this book, however, and behind the off-putting glitter of the new field's best-selling trade books, can be found something of enduring importance. In the quieter work of some of those attracted to evolutionary psychology by its popularity but leery of its excesses (e.g., Allott, 1991; Axelrod, 1984), can be found a critique of the status quo importantly bearing not just on the future for psychology, or of science, but possibly also of our species.

It could be said of humanistic psychology that it became too much a matter of catering to the needs of the comparatively well-off upper middle and upper class for therapy and self-absorbed work on personal development. By contrast, in keeping with the earlier emphasis for Kurt Lewin, the brash new field of evolutionary psychology focused anew on the problems of the lower class (e.g., urban decay and violence) threatening to tear society apart (see relevant papers in Barkow et al., 1992).

It could be said of transpersonal psychology that, with notable exceptions (May, Krippner, & Doyle, 1994), it suffered from a tendency within so-called New Age spirituality to celebrate a spiritual evolution devoid of the age-old essential link for spirituality with moral evolution applied to conflicts in our real world. By contrast, in keeping with the basic concern for Assagioli and Dabrowski as well as Darwin originally, in its focus on the nature and dynamics of altruism—as powerfully articulated by sociobiology founder E. O. Wilson (1975)—the brash new field focused on what drives and shapes morality as a bedrock concern for a society in which corruption and amorality threaten to shut off hope for any better future.

Most important, recognizing this as the central structural weakness for the social science of the 20th century, evolutionary psychology, at its best, focused on trying to link and bind together the sprawl of social science to evolution theory from which, ironically, biology had excluded psychology for more than a century. This is the powerfully expressed and historically vital central point for the otherwise problematic introduction to *The Adapted Mind* (Barkow et al., 1992).

However, with the arrival of the 21st century and the shock of events that have deepened awareness of the grim nature and true size of the challenges our species faces, again the excesses threaten to outweigh the advances for evolutionary psychology. Whereas some within or otherwise attached to the field strive creatively to join others in the search for a liberating new moral paradigm, many others still remain entrenched in what, despite all disavowals, essentially remains the old "selfishness uber alles" and "survival of the fittest" Darwinian paradigm (Loye, 2006b).

What seems to be happening is this: Rather than leading to an inviting new vision, and an inclusive outreach that might enlist science, education, and the necessary part of leadership for our society in a new effort to meet the true size of challenges facing us—as humanistic psychology and the human potentials movement so memorably promised earlier—evolutionary psychology has led to the kind of time-wasting squabbles that only the trade book publishers eager for best-sellers and regressive politicians eager for votes can enjoy.

Instead of humanistic psychology's earlier heralded "dawning of the age of Aquarius," where all might live together peaceably, we have a society scientifically and socially split apart. Socially, still after a century of billions spent on educating Americans, we are mired in the "Darwin Wars" pitting the creationists against the evolutionists. Scientifically, we are similarly mired in questions and issues that were either long ago resolved in philosophy or science (e.g., the "straw man" of the "blank slate"), or transcended by advanced evolution researchers using chaos, complexity, second-order cybernetics, synergetics, and comparable theories (Depew & Weber, 1996; Knyazeva, 2003; Salthe, 1993).

The heading for a book review in *Science* (Bateson, 2002) of Steven Pinker's (2002) best-selling paean to evolutionary psychology *The Blank Slate* seems to capture a reaction that is widening not just among psychologists but also in the higher levels of scholarship more generally: "the corpse of a wearisome debate."

## THE CASE FOR EVOLUTIONARY SYSTEMS SCIENCE

Thus we have this brief history of the triumph of conformity over creativity in the case of a need to update and expand both the theory and the story of evolution. We have glimpsed the fact that beyond this, what is at stake is the survival of the outcome over millennia of the thrust and glory of human creativity at its best. So have we come to a dead end? Or can we find something new that can offer a mutually respectful new home for creativity in science as well as creativity in spirituality, to take us beyond being mired in the study and the rituals of our species' dismal past and present something useful for shaping our way into a better future?

In 1949 out of the scientific outback in which he had been relegated by mainstream biology and mainstream psychology, the renegade biologist Ludwig von Bertalanffy (1976) announced an idea for a potentially disruptive new field. As happened with all other fields of science within the 20th century, biology and psychology had become accustomed to living comfortably separated from one another with the guiding rule that one did not stray into the other's territory. The potentially disastrous consequences of this separation were also accentuated by the proliferation of ever more tiny subfields or disciplinary baronies wherein the holistic outreach of creativity was smothered by the constraints of subfield conformity. So the new idea did not catch on at first. However, von Bertalanffy was not to be stopped in his insistence on the importance for science of a new field that might transcend the dynamics of disciplinary and subfield conformities to liberate the new collective creativity of the "general systems theory" he was developing with Russian physicist, Nicolaus Rashevsky.

As von Bertalanffy had gained fame in the field of biology for, among other things, his development of a new method of diagnosing cancer, he could not be easily dismissed by biologists. Thus, when in 1960 he established an Advanced Center for Theoretical Psychology in Canada—which for 30 years thereafter was in the forefront of the evolutionary study of cognitive psychology—the wedding he envisaged between not only biology and psychology but also all the disparate fields of science became an ever more troublesome issue for traditional (i.e., conformist) science.

But while mainstream science found endless difficulties with the notion, it was seized with great enthusiasm along the creative periphery. To join in the founding of this new scientific alignment, which they decided to call "systems science," out of economics came the evolution theorist and peace activist Kenneth Boulding (1978). Out of anthropology came Margaret Mead (1955). As his own work both foreshadowed and laid important groundwork for this development, out of the field of psychology Kurt Lewin would logically have joined them, but at the age of 56 he died in 1947.

From this amorphous newcomer to science then emerged the new core alignment that by now seems best designated as *evolutionary systems science*. Here, as celebrated and explained by Erich Jantsch (1980) in *The Self-Organizing Universe*, were the innovators of a variety of theories that became popularly clumped together as chaos theory. These included the Belgian thermodynamist Ilya Prigogine (Prigogine & Stengers, 1984) with a self-directive concept of autocatalysis and the Chilean biologists Humberto Maturana and Francisco Varela (1987) with autopoesis.

The base for chaos theory was in mathematics and natural science. However, soon, as I was among the first to point out in pioneering papers (Loye, 1990; Loye & Eisler, 1987), through the liberative thrust of the core idea of self-organizing processes, a revolutionary potential for the application of chaos theory to all of social science became apparent. It was during this time that a former Director of Research for the United Nations, general systems philosopher Ervin Laszlo, entered the picture with his formation of the General Evolution Research Group (or GERG, as it became known), in which I was involved as one of two psychologists along with two biologists and a physicist among its cofounders. Drawing together scientists of a variety of disciplines from ten nations, Laszlo launched what increasingly seems to me was one of the great creative visions out of the often radically diminished horizon for the social, humanistic, and moral science of the 20th century.

The world was still shuddering under the threat of potential nuclear holocaust when, in 1984, toward the close of the cold war, those of us who later formed GERG were called by Laszlo to a clandestine meeting in Budapest, then still under Russian control. The question he raised was to see if we thought it might be possible to use the then-rising popularity of chaos theory to build his vision of an action-oriented theory of general evolution that might be used by humanity to end the endemic insanity into which our species has fallen.

Long range, it was the vision of an evolution theory that might go beyond the scientific stalemate of the conformist fixation on biology and the past to incorporate the vast creative advances in social, systems, and futures science that for much of a century had been almost wholly excluded from the development of mainstream evolution theory. It was the vision of an evolution theory with ourselves—we humans, our species—at the leading edge, equipped to focus on gaining a better future for this earth and all living systems.

However pressing this might have been, the following situation was of greater immediacy and urgency. With scientists there from both sides of the iron curtain—seven of us from the West and three from Russia and Hungary—we were meeting in a Hungary still then ringed with a double wall of barbed wire and armed Russian guards, and in the background the thousands of tons in nuclear overkill for both sides of the Cold War.

What rather quickly gripped us was the vision of a theory that might be used not merely to understand, but to save our own and all other species. With chaos theory then coming into vogue, in getting underway Laszlo enlisted Prigogine, Varela, the Hungarian biologist Vilmos Csanyi (with a comparable theory of the evolutionary action of autogenesis), and American mathematician and chaos theorist Ralph Abraham.

The expanding idea was immense in difficulties but basically simple in goal: Why not use chaos theory to find a way of guiding our species through the social, political, and economic chaos we faced to an evolutionary stage of a higher and better order? In other words, why not find funding for and get underway with the development of a theory of evolution that might at last realize the cumulating vision from Darwin on, that is, of a creative theory that might be used by the thinking people of this earth and an enlightened social leadership to guide our species through the time of escalating and indeed species-threatening troubles now facing us to reach the higher plateau for humanity—long the dream of the great spiritual and philosophic as well as scientific visionaries?

## THE GREAT ADVENTURE

Nudging at prevailing paradigms for psychology, forcing new thought, this was a time of maximal ferment for chaos theory, cybernetics, brain research, and systems science. In the midst of all these currents for thinking about evolution and the challenge lying ahead for our species, in 1985, along with three of his students, psychologist Stanley Krippner published a paper that, in retrospect, became of historic importance (Krippner, Rutenber, Engelman, & Granger, 1985). Although Krippner was at the time a former president of the Association for Humanistic Psychology (or HP) and a founding member of the HP-launched Saybrook Graduate School, the paper escaped the notice of all but a handful of us in the emergent field of evolutionary systems science. By now within the GERG membership, besides myself there was an authority on the evolution of consciousness, Saybrook and University of North Carolina psychologist Allan Combs (1997).

"At present, HP lacks a commonly-understood scientific paradigm to provide a theoretical framework with which to develop and evaluate models, methods, research, theories and therapies," Krippner and colleagues (1985) wrote in the article, "Toward the Application of General Systems Theory in Humanistic Psychology." "We believe that GST [general systems theory] can perform just such a service to HP" (p. 113).

In raising the need for a new working partnership between psychology and systems science, this paper pointed toward the wedding between psychology and evolution theory that, despite the difficulties, seemed to be seeking to emerge. By the end of the 20th century, however, so little discernible progress was being made toward fleshing out a theory in keeping with the vision that originally animated GERG that I decided on a frontal attack. As in the old tale of the blind men trying to describe an elephant by feel—where one feels a leg and reports it is a tree, one feels the tail and reports it is a rope, and so on—it seemed to me that, along with other multidisciplinary systems scientists, for 14 years we GERGians had been meeting around the world in symposia for ever more ingenious reports on the "tree," the "rope," and so on. Increasingly, however, the message of events was that time was running out—if not for our species then most certainly for any chance of affecting anyone's vision of a better world. Why not then force the issue by bypassing leg, and trunk, and tail, and go directly for the elephant as a whole?

To probe new directions for science at the beginning of the 3rd millennium, the International Society for Systems Sciences, with GERG and 19 other organizations as cosponsors, had organized a World Congress of the Systems Sciences to draw scientists from all around the world to Toronto in 2000. Restating our goal as specifically the building of a "full spectrum, action-oriented," or fully human theory of evolution, and drafting a Toronto Manifesto to hopefully mark the occasion historically, from our GERG membership I pulled together two panels and a general discussion to focus not on something exotic, but rather, in the spirit of Lewin's action research, first to discuss "What should it look like?" and then "How do we build it?"

All too often science seems to move at less than a snail's pace in relation to the problems confronting our species. However, since then, with surprising rapidity, a promising prospect for both the long sought wedding of fields and the "full spectrum, action-oriented" theory has emerged.

Along the vital publications route, our Toronto papers first became a special issue for the main journal providing an international gathering place for evolutionary systems scientists, *World Futures: The Journal of General Evolution* (Loye, 2002a). More recently an update has been published as a book by the State University Press of New York with the title *The Great Adventure: Toward a Fully Human Theory of Evolution* (Loye, 2004).

With a foreword by the well-known explorer of creativity and cofounder of positive psychology Mihaly Csikszentmihalyi, including the publication of my reconstruction of what now appears to be the psychologically oriented completion for Darwin's theory of evolution, *The Great Adventure* covers the "full spectrum" from natural through social science. Beginning with the foundational spectrum from physics through biology, GERG members Ervin Laszlo, biologist Stanley Salthe, cultural evolution theorist Riane Eisler, sociologist Raymond Bradley, psychotherapist (and past president of the Society for the Study of Chaos Theory in Psychology and the Life Sciences) Sally Goerner, systems scientists Ken Bausch and Aleco Christakis (a Club of Rome cofounder and past president of the International Society for the Systems Sciences), and systems scientist Alfonso Montuori of the California Institute for Integral Studies along with psychologists Allan Combs and Ruth Richards of Saybrook and Harvard Medical School fleshed out the prospects for the long scattered, divisive, and excluded superstructure, for example, the cultural base in the brain and the psychology and the higher reaches of creativity and consciousness. I provide a summary identifying 17 foundations and 10 guidelines in these chapters for what the fully human theory should look like, then in the last chapter a plan for building the theory as well as the new, more hopeful story of human evolution.

"Where is the new covenant going to emerge from?" Csikszentmihalyi asks in his foreword. The themes we have sought to bring back as well as newly introduce in *The Great Adventure*, he suggests, "are likely to be among the central ones of any new worldview," among them

> a new faith . . . of human beings about human beings. Not the traditionally taught evolutionary scenario dominated by competition and selfishness, but an understanding closer to the original Darwinian one that sees cooperation and transcendence of the self as the most exciting parts of the story. (Csikszentmihalyi, 2004, p. xii)

It is a heady prospect. A Darwin Project, with a council of over 50 distinguished American, European, and Asian scientists, educators, and media activists, has been formed to establish a strong educational base in new evolution studies to serve as a foundation for building the "fully human" theory of evolution. Already the Web site outlining our goals, with projection for distance learning courses and functioning library and book store (http://www.thedarwinproject.com), has been visited by over 400,000 presumably interested people in the United Kingdom, Germany, France, Italy, Switzerland, the Netherlands, Spain, Canada, Brazil, Mexico, Australia, Japan, as well as the United States.

Will creativity at last prevail over conformity?

We shall see, we shall see.

# REFERENCES

Abraham, F. D. (1997). An holistic thread in the dynamical fabric of psychology. In *The dynamics of evolution: Essays in honor of David Loye*, Montuori, A., (Ed.), *World Futures: The Journal of General Evolution*, 49(1–2), 159–201.

Allott, R. (1991). Objective morality. *Journal of Social and Biological Structures*, 14, 455–471.

Allport, G. (1964). *Pattern and growth in personality*. New York: Holt, Rinehart & Winston.

Assagioli, R. (1965). *Psychosynthesis: A manual of principles and techniques*. New York: Viking Press.

Axelrod, R. (1984). *The evolution of cooperation*. New York: Basic Books.

Baldwin, J. M. (1896). A new factor in evolution. *The American Naturalist*, 30, 441–481, 536–553.

Barkow, J. H., Cosmides, L., & Tooby, J. (Eds.). (1992). *The adapted mind: Evolutionary psychology and the generation of culture*. New York: Oxford University Press.

Barron, F. (1969). *Creative person and creative process*. New York: Holt, Rinehart & Winston.

Bateson, P. (2002, September 27). The corpse of a wearisome debate. *Science*, 297, 2212–2213.

Bernard, J. (1981). *The female world*. New York: Free Press.

Boulding, K. E. (1978). *Ecodynamics: A new theory of societal evolution*. Beverly Hills, CA: Sage.

Carlson, R. (1995). Silvan Tomkins's legacy: A grand theory of personality. In V. Demos (Ed.), *Exploring affect: The selected writings of Silvan S. Tomkins* (pp. 295–414). Cambridge, England: Cambridge University Press.

Combs, A. (1997). *The radiance of being: Complexity, chaos, and the evolution of consciousness*. St. Paul, MN: Paragon House.

Crutchfield, R. S. (1964). Conformity and creative thinking. In H. E. Gruber, G. Terrell, & M. Wertheimer (Eds.), *Contemporary approaches to creative thinking* (pp. 120–140). New York: Atherton Press.

Csanyi, V. (1989). *Evolutionary systems and society*. Durham, NC: Duke University Press.

Csikzsentmihalyi, M. (1993). *The evolving self: A psychology for the third millennium*. New York: Harper.

Csikszentmihalyi, M. (1996). *Creativity: Flow and the psychology of discovery and invention*. New York: HarperCollins.

Csikszentmihalyi, M. (2004). Foreword. In D. Loye (Ed.), *The great adventure: Toward a fully human theory of evolution* (pp. xi–xiii). Albany, NY: SUNY Press.

Dabrowski, K. (1964). *Positive disintegration*. Boston: Little, Brown.

Damon, W. (1995). *Greater expectations: Overcoming the culture of indulgence in our homes and schools*. New York: Free Press.

Darwin, C. (1871). *The descent of man.* London: John Murray.

Darwin, C. (1872). *The expression of the emotions in man and animals.* London: John Murray.

Depew, D. (2000). The Baldwin effect: An archeology. *Cybernetics and Human Knowing, 7*(1), 7–20.

Depew, D., & Weber, B. (1996). *Darwinism evolving.* Cambridge, MA: MIT Press.

de Waal, F. (1996). *Good natured: The origins of right and wrong in humans and other animals.* Cambridge, MA: Harvard University Press.

Dewey, J. (1922). *Human nature and conduct.* New York: Henry Holt.

Eisler, R. (1987). *The chalice and the blade: Our history, our future.* San Francisco: Harper & Row.

Elgin, D. (2000). *Promise ahead: A vision of hope and action for humanity's future.* New York: Morrow.

Fluegel, J. C. (1945). *Man, morals, and society.* New York: International University Press.

Freud, S. (1989). *Civilization and its discontents.* New York: Norton.

Freud, S. (1990). *New introductory lectures on psychoanalysis.* New York: Norton.

Fromm, E. (1947). *Man for himself: An inquiry into the psychology of ethics.* New York: Holt, Rinehart & Winston.

Gilligan, C. (1982). *In a different voice.* Boston: Harvard University Press.

Goldie, P., & Ghiselin, M. (1997). *Darwin* (2nd ed.) [CD-ROM]. Available from Lightbinders, Inc., 2325 Third St., Suite 324, San Francisco, CA 94107.

Gruber, H. E., & Barrett, P. H. (1981). *Darwin on man: A psychological study of scientific creativity* (2nd ed.). Chicago: University of Chicago Press. (Original work published 1974)

Hull, C. L. (1952). *A behavior system.* New Haven, CT: Yale University Press.

James, W. (1950). *Principles of psychology* (Vol. 1). New York: Dover. (Original work published 1890)

Jantsch, E. (1980). *The self-organizing universe.* New York: Pergamon Press.

Kauffman, S. A. (1996). *At home in the universe.* New York: Oxford University Press.

Knyazeva, H. (2003). Self-reflective synergetics. *Systems Research and Behavioral Science, 20*(1), 53–64.

Kohlberg, L. (1984). *The psychology of moral development.* San Francisco: Harper & Row.

Krippner, S. (1980). *Human possibilities.* New York: Anchor Books.

Krippner, S. (1985). Psychedelic drugs and creativity. *Journal of Psychoactive Drugs, 17*(4), 235–245.

Krippner, S., Rutenber, A. J., Engelman, S. R., & Granger, D. L. (1985). Toward the application of general systems theory in humanistic psychology. *Systems Research, 2*(2), 105–115.

Kung, H., & Kuschel, K. J. (Eds). (1993). *A global ethic: The declaration of The Parliament of the World's Religions*. London: SCM Press.

Laszlo, E. (1994). *The choice: Oblivion or evolution*. Los Angeles: Tarcher.

Lewin, K. (1951). *Field theory in social science*. New York: Harper & Row.

Loye, D. (1971). *The healing of a nation*. New York: Norton.

Loye, D. (1977). *The leadership passion: A psychology of ideology*. San Francisco: Jossey-Bass.

Loye, D. (1978). *The knowable future: A psychology of forecasting and prophecy*. New York: Wiley.

Loye, D. (1984). *The sphinx and the rainbow: Brain, mind, and future vision*. New York: Bantam.

Loye, D. (1990). Chaos and transformation: Implications of non-equilibrium theory for social science and society. In E. Laszlo (Ed.), *The New Evolutionary Paradigm* (pp. 339–372). New York: Gordon & Breach Science.

Loye, D. (1994). Charles Darwin, Paul MacLean, and the lost origins of 'the moral sense': Some implications for general evolution theory. *World Futures: The Journal of General Evolution, 40*, 187–196.

Loye, D. (1998). The general evolution research group: A brief history. In D. Loye (Ed.), *The evolutionary outrider: The impact of the human agent on evolution* (pp. 29–37). Westport, CT: Praeger Publishers.

Loye, D. (1999). Can science help construct a new global ethic? The development and implications of moral transformation theory. *Zygon, 34*(3), 221–235.

Loye, D. (2000a). *An arrow through chaos*. Rochester, VT: Park Street Press.

Loye, D. (2000b). Darwin's lost theory and its implications for the 21st century. *World Futures: The Journal of General Evolution, 55*(3), 201–226.

Loye, D. (2001). Rethinking Darwin: A vision for the 21st century. *Journal of Future Studies, 6*(1), 121–136.

Loye, D. (Ed.). (2002a). The third force: Toward a humanistic theory of evolution [Special issue]. *World Futures: The Journal of General Evolution, 58*(2–3).

Loye, D. (2002b). The moral brain. *Brain and Mind, 3*, 133–150.

Loye, D. (Ed.). (2004). *The great adventure: Toward a fully human theory of evolution*. Albany, NY: SUNY Press.

Loye, D. (2007a). *Darwin's lost theory*. Carmel, CA: Benjamin Franklin Press.

Loye, D. (2007b). *The glacier and the flame I: Rediscovering goodness*. Carmel, CA: Benjamin Franklin Press.

Loye, D., & Eisler, R. (1987). Chaos and transformation: The implications of natural scientific nonequilibrium theory for social science and society. *Behavioral Science, 32*(1), 53–65.

Maslow, A. (1968). *Toward a psychology of being*. Princeton, NJ: Van Nostrand.

Maslow, A. (1971). *The farther reaches of human nature*. New York: Viking.

Maturana, H., & Varela, F. (1987). *The tree of knowledge*. Boston: New Science Library.

May, R., Krippner, S., & Doyle, J. L. (1994). The role of transpersonal psychology in psychology as a whole: A discussion. In F. Wertz (Ed.), *The Humanistic movement: Recovering the person in psychology* (pp. 192–201). Lake Worth, FL: Gardner Press.

Mead, G. H. (1934). *Mind, self, and society.* Chicago: University of Chicago Press.

Mead, M. (1955). *Sex and temperament in three primitive societies.* New York: Mentor.

Miller, J. B. (1976). *Toward a new psychology of women.* Boston: Beacon Press.

Ornstein, R. (1991). *The evolution of consciousness.* Englewood Cliffs, NJ: Prentice Hall.

Piaget, J. (1965). *The moral judgment of the child.* New York: Free Press.

Piaget, J. (1980). *Adaptation and intelligence.* Chicago: University of Chicago Press.

Piechowski, M. M. (1975). A theoretical and empirical approach to the study of development. *Genetic Psychology Monographs, 92,* 231–297.

Pinker, S. (2002). *The blank slate: The denial of human nature.* New York: Penguin.

Prigogine, I., & Stengers, I. (1984). *Order out of chaos.* New York: Bantam.

Rachels, J. (1998). *Created from animals: The moral implications of Darwinism.* New York: Oxford University Press.

Richards, R. (1999). Everyday creativity. In M. A. Runco & S. R. Pritzker (Eds.), *Encyclopedia of creativity* (Vol. I, pp. 683–687). San Diego, CA: Academic Press.

Richards, R. J. (1987). *Darwin and the emergence of evolutionary theories of mind and behavior.* Chicago: University of Chicago Press.

Romanes, G. (1897). *Darwin and after Darwin.* Chicago: Open Court.

Rose, H., & Rose, S. (Eds). (2000). *Alas, poor Darwin: Arguments against evolutionary psychology.* New York: Harmony Books.

Salthe, S. (1993). *Development and evolution: Complexity and change in biology.* Cambridge, MA: MIT Press.

Schneider, K. J., Bugental, J. F. T., & Pierson, J. F. (Eds.). (2001). *The handbook of humanistic psychology.* Thousand Oaks, CA: Sage Publications.

Skinner, B. F. (1965). *Science and human behavior.* New York: Free Press.

Snyder, C. R., & Lopez, S. J. (Eds.). (2001). *Handbook of positive psychology.* New York: Oxford University Press.

Sober, E. R., & Wilson, D. S. (1998). *Unto others: The evolution and psychology of unselfish behavior.* Cambridge, MA: Harvard University Press.

Tomkins, S. (1962–1992). *Affect, imagery, consciousness* (Vols. 1–4). New York: Springer Publishing Company.

von Bertalanffy, L. (1976). *General systems theory.* New York: Brazilier.

Walsh, R., & Vaughan, F. (Eds.). (1993). *Paths beyond ego: The transpersonal vision.* Los Angeles: Tarcher.

Wilber, K. (1993). *The spectrum of consciousness.* Wheaton, IL: Quest.

Wilson, E. O. (1975). *Sociobiology: The new synthesis.* Cambridge, MA: Harvard University Press.

# 8

## STANDING UP FOR HUMANITY: UPRIGHT BODY, CREATIVE INSTABILITY, AND SPIRITUAL BALANCE

MIKE ARONS

Our body is not in space like things, it inhabits and haunts space.
—Maurice Merleau-Ponty

When he is up, I knock him down. When he is down, I boast of him,
Until he realizes he's an incomprehensible animal.
—Blaise Pascal

The term *originality* implicates two opposing yet paradoxically related vectors: to the origins and to the new and unique. Perhaps one new view of human nature and its transformative creative spirit comes from reflection on our species' oldest distinguishing mark: the biped upright body posture. Can attention directed to this lived high-rise platform provide new insights into human being and potential?

This chapter explores a postulated linkage of human creative capacity, values, and aspirations, with tensions inherent in the lived upright body posture. It considers evolved organic–anatomic links to an upright posture

I would like to thank Dr. Howard Whitehouse for insightful dialogue and general assistance with this paper.

(e.g., cognitive, vocal, manual capacities) as well as value-implicating expressions (e.g., "upstanding citizen," "down to earth"), which appear conditional to the lived experience of a physically challenging upright stance. These organic–anatomical inquiries are then viewed in light of traits and dynamics implicating both creative and spiritual endeavor. The chapter concludes by suggesting that human creative capacity may be both expression and mediator of the physical instability and disharmony inherent in the upright stance—fostering both survival and spiritual needs, and implicating human strivings for balance and harmony.

## BACKGROUND

### Revived Interest in Creativity, Consciousness, Values and Body

In the mid-20th century, psychology found itself refocusing on creativity, consciousness, and other specifically human capacities and qualities, including meaning and values. These qualities were largely being ignored by many mainstream psychologists, or else treated as epiphenomenal, or sidelined for methodological reasons (Arons, 1994; Arons & Richards, 2001). At about this same time—even if only at its perimeter—psychology's interest in the body and somatic experience was also resuscitated, sparked by interest in such Western writings as those of Wilhelm Reich and Maurice Merleau-Ponty, and by a newly born interest in Eastern, shamanic, and other esoteric psychological–spiritual traditions. However, with few exceptions, such as Erwin Straus (1966) and Stanley Keleman (1981), the habitual human biped upright body posture remained mainly a concern of the evolutionary sciences, not of psychology.

Creativity can be defined broadly as encompassing originality and meaningfulness (Barron, 1969). This casts creativity as a human quality, potentially found in everyone, whether taking the form of eminent, talent-centered, self-actualizing, inventive, or everyday creativity (Arons & Richards, 2001). However, much early research into creativity narrowly emphasized elite examples. For instance, Roe (1951) studied living scientists and (Maslow, 1959, 1962) studied self-actualizing individuals described as exhibiting heightened states of awareness, "being" values, and having notable creative capacity. The issue remained whether eminent individuals are exceptions or represent everyone to an outstanding degree. Are creative capacity, self-actualizing values, and enlightened consciousness the potentials of all humans? The answer, when postulated in the affirmative, came to foster interest in *everyday creativity* (Richards, Kinney, Benet, & Merzel, 1988) and a universalized model of self-actualization.

Whether one subscribes to the elitist queen-bee and drone or universal model of creative capacity, scholars of evolution and creationist theologians likely concur on at least one point: *Homo sapiens* is specially endowed, among species, with a highly developed and self-reflective consciousness, and an extraordinary creative and inventive capacity. What might be the relationships between these consciousness-creative capacities and the unique human upright body posture?

## UNSTEADY PLATFORM AND ORGANIC–ANATOMICAL LINKS

Why we stand upright is a question not yet answered definitively by the evolutionary sciences or Christian theology. There is no specific reference in the scriptures, for example, to this unique human body architecture. Some evolutionary theories date the biped upright posture to a human ancestor called Toumai, as far back as 7 million years ago. There is a range of explanations for the postural rise, including changing environmental conditions that required appropriate adaptation, including the "down from the trees out to the savanna" theory. None of these views is without contemporary critics (Stanford, 2001). Nearer to our times and present human form, science tells us that *homo habilus*, found at the boundary between early and modern humans, prospered between 2.3 and 1.3 million years ago, marked by an increasingly upright stance, use of tools, and more cooperative living. There was also a remarkable increase in brain size. *Homo habilus* was followed by *homo erectus* (upright human) with further and marked increase in brain size—before either organized society or the advent of language (Ornstein, 1991).

Despite the evolving distinctions between human and ape, recent DNA evidence draws a close genetic relationship between them, notably with the chimpanzee. This intimate genetic tie is all the more surprising given the observably radical distinctions in endowment and achievement that apparently separate the two species. This conundrum has inspired a renewed line of research (e.g., Goodall, 1986; Stanford, 2001; Steeves, 1999). On one side, it focuses on overlaps, postulating that behavioral, sentimental, and cognitive-related similarities between human and ape are far more pronounced than the common stereotype, and previous research, indicate. On the other side, another line of research—including this inquiry—seeks to understand the definite differences and their bases that at least comparatively, if not absolutely, distinguish and define human nature.

One marked, if still overlapping, distinction between modern man and ape is the upright body posture. For humans, unlike apes, the biped upright posture is habitual. Much that is organic and anatomical has developed in concert with this habitual human stance. Likewise, although researchers of what we might call the "overlap" school are coming to discover intimations of "creative" thinking in apes (e.g., symbol manipulation, meaningful gestures and utterances, tool making), all this, incontestably, has developed to a far more advanced level in humans.

To what degree can the incongruity of close DNA kinship and vastly distinguishing creative output between chimp and human be attributed to difference in habitual stance and walk? To start with a puzzle: How has *Homo sapiens* survived and thrived encased in a vertical anatomical architecture that challenges gravity and other natural forces? It is a puzzle, because this stance is tenuously balanced and is not in apparent harmony with the laws of nature. Would one buy a two-legged stool?

Look at the human body! We typically link consciousness and creative capacity to the large, complex brain, to our wide-ranging verbal capacities, to a rapport between freed-up hands and the invention of tools. However, all of these handy, brainy, and talky human features are organically linked from an evolutionary perspective to the biped upright body posture. The biped walk frees the arms and hands. A raised body expands the perceptual horizon. And, the complex brain nestled in its large cavity replaces the massive front-loaded muzzle structure. Moreover, a combination of this diminished muzzle and a gravity-stretched vocal tract—both related to skeletal rise—helps explain human verbal agility (Straus, 1966). The large, well-developed human brain has a history of how it evolved. Of that history, it is important to note that living the world from a vertical rather than horizontal platform is not the same experience. As Straus (1966) points out, "Men and mice have not the same environment even if they share the same room" (p. 139). Thus, it is not too daring a thought to suggest that the human brain learned, and, by at least one mechanism, genotype-environment interaction, structurally incorporated much from its lived world(s) of experience afforded by that vertical platform.

**The Shape of Things**

We look at some of these posture-related lived worlds presently. First, consider that standing biped—upright in a world in which gravity has a strong pull—is a remarkable accomplishment. Again, would one buy a two-legged stool? It is remarkable to the degree of provoking the question of why our ancestors did this at all. It is an achievement as puzzling as it is remarkable: This vertical human stance is an aberration and, in ways, an apparently costly one. Look around! Nearly all unrooted objects and creatures are horizontal. This horizontality, presumably, is not only a matter of complying with gravity's demands but also the best design to accommodate other of nature's elements. As with birds or planes, horizontality is better suited to navigate the air, roam the earth, or, like fish or submarines, to ply the waters.

Moreover, the top-heavy vertical stance of the human posture is not the only factor that sets it at odds with gravity. As artists will verify, the human body's anatomical shape consists of three inverted modified pyramids, set tenuously one atop the other. It is hard to imagine a less stable structure. When a pyramid is stood upright, broad bottom down, fine pinnacle up, it is a mythical symbol of balance and harmony, as used by Abraham Maslow (1962), for example, to symbolize his needs hierarchy, a matter we return to at the end of this chapter.

Erwin Straus (1966) enumerates some current costs to humans associated with the upright posture, beyond the lengthy evolutionary span required for developing adept balancing mechanisms. These costs, as the Riddle of the Sphinx (Sophocles, 1982) mythologizes, include the extraordinarily long developmental time required for a human infant to stand and walk; this is why we celebrate "the first step," and the consequent lengthy period of childhood dependency. There is also, later in life, the need for third-leg support. Across the life cycle there is a stature-linked proneness to a number of breakdowns (e.g., back problems, hernias, and even flat feet; Weidenreich, cited in Straus, 1966). Overall, human life is exceptionally challenged to stay upright and balanced. This is while reharmonizing—on its own resourceful terms—with the lawful natural world. Think of the technological break-through of the Segway scooter, and its dynamic stability. For human or machine, this is a feat. Have we not signs of a defiant posture?

What is defying nature compared with defying God, as Judeo-Christian-Islamic theology would have it? Might one speak, in both the corporeal and divine worlds, of a general species proclivity toward rebellion, or at least an assertion of achieving balance and harmony on human terms? (See chap. 11, this volume, for a chaos theory perspective on instability.)

## Uplifting Spirit, Embedded Values

Keleman (1981) makes a powerful observation that links posture to consciousness and spirit. The human body, already physically unstable, is not even held up by its legs. Consider that while the supporting columns of a disintegrating ancient temple may well continue to stand firmly erect, human legs may become shaky and crumble with the body, for example, when consciousness wanes or the mood gets too dispirited.

Put this way, the human body, legs included, is held up by its consciousness and spirit. All this suggests that if we did not recognize it in the evolutionary effort to stand upright, that *up* may carry a positive value for humans as indicated in such *up*lifting common expressions as an "*up*standing individual."

Indeed, Lakoff (1987) addressed this example in his "spatialization of form hypothesis." This involves "a metaphorical mapping from physical space into a 'conceptual space'" (p. 283). Hierarchical structure, for instance, can be understood in terms of *up–down* schemas, and foreground–background structure in terms of *front–back* schemas. Lakoff does not go further, however, in suggesting reasons for these particular spatial mappings and the values they may carry.

Here, however, I continue this argument. Let us note that *up* comes to stand for positive longings (strong desires) and longings can be linked to values and ideals. Powerful longings can be linked to deeply embedded value dispositions (positive, for example, progressively upward and negative, for example, avoiding one's downfall). Embedded in what? When some feeling is deeply embedded, one may say "I feel it in my bones," which is a figurative English expression. Perhaps, though, our bones do have something to do with values in terms of anatomical architecture and spatial mappings through and from which we experience and live the world.

## TWO PSYCHOLOGICAL MODELS OF
## BALANCE AND HARMONY

### Constancy Model

A great human longing is for balance and harmony. This paired duo reveals itself as such across a range of spheres, whether expressed in Platonic idealism, or in the wholesome aims of Tai Chi, diet, psychology, politics, investment, aesthetics, or ecology. This merged value of balance and harmony was recognized by an earlier psychology under the related term *homeostasis*, a model it borrowed from biology, emphasizing restoration of a state of constancy from a state of psychological instability. This state is achieved by reducing destabilizing tension or anxiety (Arons, 1994). Taken in its most mechanistic sense, this is a model following the principle of inertia, or an indisposition to motion, exertion, or change, that is, *stasis*. Homeostasis offered the psychology of the mid-20th century a coherent model for conceptualizing pathology and psychological health. (Let us also note here that in practical terms, inertia and gravity have much in common.)

### Emerging Model of Complexity and Paradox

However, as humanistic and creativity research critics came to point out, the homeostatic model did not well accommodate the far more complex and dynamic—and often tension engendering, even destabilizing—picture emerging from their own inquiries of the creative individual (Arons &

Richards, 2001; Krippner, 1994). In fact, they were notably disposed to motion, exertion, and openness to change, and prone to the toying with constancy and order in the interest of gleaning new and higher unities, a heuristic dynamic that also applied to those engaged in self-exploration. The creative individual would be best described in paradoxical terms— including more complex indices of health and pathology—as exemplified in Barron's (1963) famous description of the creative genius in his book *Creativity and Psychological Health,* "He is both more primitive and more cultured, more destructive and more constructive, occasionally crazier and yet adamantly saner than the average person" (p. 234).

The emerging model in psychology is not a full rejection of the old homeostatic balance. With the advent of complex dynamical systems (and chaos theory) in psychology, however, a precarious balance may be found instead "far from equilibrium"—one which at times can change in an instant, and with little provocation, to find new balance (Arons & Richards, 2001; Krippner, 1994). One example of this is the so-called butterfly effect. Hence the present model adds an expanded and, especially with regard to creativity, tensional, less predictable, more open-ended, and more paradoxical dimension to it. This includes an interplay of opposites that relate to the new model itself (e.g., tension-reducing–tension-inducing), as well as an interplay of what Maslow (1962) called "basic" and "being" needs and values. When basic needs are satisfied, only then is there a personal opening to as yet unrealized self-actualizing needs. At this point, the earlier and relative place of the basic needs is seen, against the larger scheme of optimally lived human possibilities. (See also chaps. 1, 4, and 12, this volume, on Maslow.)

## HIGH WIRE HUMAN CONDITION AND THE BALANCING ACT

### Eschatological, Existential, and Postural Finitude

This more complex vision of psychological health joins the adventurous to the quiescent, as it does the chaotic to the previous order. Here are coconstituting and, hence, covalued determiners of human balance and harmony. The creative genius at the moment of illumination and the spiritual seeker who attains a deeper meditative state shares with the rest of the species a human condition. That condition, taken from theology or philosophy, is one of finitude. A finitude that is shared not only universally but also of which human beings—uniquely perhaps—are potentially conscious: an awareness of life's impermanence, and a sense of the underlying profound interconnection of all that exists. Yet, so much is unknown, unseen, and likely also unsuspected. The expanded perceptual horizon from upright posture might have abetted this finite–infinite consciousness. Yet, given the awe-inspiring, fear-inducing, open-endedness of this horizon, conscious humans stand homeless between the open-ended mysteries of earth and the heavens, amidst an infinite surround, betwixt their source and destiny. The term *originality* implies homage to this intermediate state in the vital interplay of its double vectors: to the origins and to the new and unique. (See also chap. 9, this volume, and the poles of Eastern and Western views of creativity.)

This eschatological alienation from origins and destiny, both ends grasped for through religion, meditation, philosophy, art, and science, led existentialists to speak of the *void*, in Sartre's (1943/1948) term, the "noth-ingness" out of which we are "condemned to choose." For some existential-ists, this condition is experienced as angst. Yet, there is a condition, lived consciously and fully, that can lead to what Watts (1951), speaking for some Eastern traditions, called the *wisdom of insecurity*. Could the conditions of our tenuous existential state prompting such wisdom as how to best live it be incarnated in the upright body posture, both as the condition's symptom and symbol? Could that condition, as well, heuristically in forms of explora-tion, discovery, invention, and creativity serve both to satisfy survival needs and foster eschatological inquiry?


## TALKING THE WALK

### A Lived Orientation Geometry via Posture-Value Expression

It seems possible that the evolutionary process of standing upright has left impressions on the modern human psyche, especially considering the energy expended over many millions of years developing the organic balanc-ing mechanisms. Are there meanings and values of these impressions revealed in the psyche's expressions? Using some common expressions and the values they imply, let us see if we can discern what might be called an orientation-value geometry of the lived upright body posture.

Our terms *up* and *down* are linguistic indicators of opposite lived spatial directions in a vertical orientation, having solely the earth as a solid reference. This is a fundamental point: Only the vertical up and down plane or direction has such a solid unequivocal reference as earth, *terra firma*. For *front* and *back*, on the horizontal, one can turn in any direction. There is a plane of infinite orientations. Let us call this the *all-around*. Experienced directions are referenced to the body with face and visual senses concentrated *up front*. Front is wherever the body is facing and back is its opposite. The sides and all-around lived spaces, similar to front and back, have no direct, fixed, and firm earthly equivalent. Rather, there are diverse reference points related to objects (including the body). Thus, to indicate an object horizontally tangential to the body, rather than saying "up or down, back or in front there" we say, for example "It's over there, next to the mirror and above the sink." Hence, the lived world(s) of the lateral all-around directions are both more other-dependent and relative to context. In sum, the up and down axis has an absolute quality to it (earth referenced), whereas the front and back orientation is referenced to the infinity of possible front-faced postures. Are there meanings and values embedded in these orientations and experiences?

One can compare these directional indicators to commonly expressed Western values: In one sense, *up* joins *forward* almost synonymously, whereas *down* becomes a near-synonym of *back*. We value prosperity. Therefore, it is good for the stock market to be *up*, to move *forward*. Our financial prospects are *up*, we are moving *forward*, that is, progressing. Compatibly, our spiritual fortunes are *up*, in the heavens, (we hope), not *down, below*. Intellectually, psychologically, socially, politically, we *progress*, we hope, not *regress* or *retrogress, return,* or *go back down*: that is, *back down* religiously to original sin, intellectually to ignorance, culturally to the savage, epigenetically to the child, phylogenetically *back* to the animal; microgenetically to the realm of the unconscious.

Even when our banker or friend says they will *back* us they mean back us *up* (the back being more vulnerable than the front), or *support* our good credit *standing*. For, we are *upstanding* citizens. Let us hope they will not let us *down*. To be honest is to be *straightforward*; to be frank is to be *up-front*. Whereas, our worst fears and character weaknesses have to do with the *back* and *down*. For example, betrayal is characterized as being stabbed in the *back*. We cover our *rear*. Inability to sustain religious devotion is called *back*sliding. We are cautious about our tentative many-sided (lateral) worlds: the conditional worlds of "this depending on that," or, for other matters, expressed as "a *side* issue," or "be*side* the point." We describe pathology (unbalanced) and criminality (crooked) as deviance from norms, and "normal" folks as *straights*, implying also balanced and forward moving. Finally, we are also suspicious of politicians who speak from the *sides* of their mouths and we disdain hypocrites who speak out of both *sides* of their mouths.

## Melded Space–Time Directionality and Ambiguities of the Lived Body

Let us pinpoint an observation so far bracketed, that is, put a*side*. The spatial posture-value links between *up* or *forward* and *down* or *backward* meld into the temporal. Now, *up* or *forward* in space becomes *up* or *ahead* in time. "What's *up?*" is the semantic equivalent of "What's *new?*" *Forward* signifies ahead in time as well as in space; for example, "I am looking *forward to* meeting you." We physically progress along a footpath as we psychospiritually progress in our lives. Progress is *forward* and *up* while regress is, *backwards* and *down*. Many of the opposites of the positives *up* and *forward* are in the temporal dimension *down* and *back*. "Our earnings are down because we are *behind* (schedule) in our work." Even when we speak nostalgically of the "good ol' days", we think *back* to them, to those many opportunities left behind. Sadly, they cannot be recaptured, as they now belong to the past. The only solution to our current dismay is to get *back up* (once again) on our feet, and move on (*forward*) with our lives. Physically, to do this we reach for a branch or any solidly grounded object around, spiritually and psychologically, for a pastor or therapist or a healing practice.

Having suggested that lived body architecture can resonate with certain values, let us now consider, as did Merleau-Ponty (1962), some of the ambiguities and tensions such posture-linked values bring to the foreground. *Up* and *forward* often attach themselves to positives, yet too much of a good thing can be just that: too much. Being too *up* front, in 60s slang, can also be a *downer*. Nobody likes a person who is *up*pity. Thus, it is not "more is better." In moving forward, the right balance is again sought.

Conversely, we laud certain individuals for being "*down* to earth" (solid, stable, grounded) and for kneeling prayerfully. Certain cultural groups, such as the Scandinavians (perhaps as a reaction to their Viking ancestors who got too *high* and mighty) seem to value a *lower* profile and socially-attuned, or spread-*out*, consciousness. Or consider the message God sent to those overreaching constructors of the Tower of Babel as he leveled, spread out, and divided humanity using mutually incomprehensible languages.

### Life's Ins and Outs

Let us look at another, the *in* and *out* plane of lived experience. Consider the role of proximity in the notion of objectivity. To take mainstream scientific inquiry as a case in point, there is a tension implicated along this *in* and *out* lived value plane. To make positive advances in science, a distance is needed to avoid subjectivity, that is, the body's needs and desires may obscure, confuse, and therefore distort an unbiased view of what is observed. From this perspective, the body—taken as unreliable interiority—is seen as a negative for inquiry.

However, our touch with the objective "real" world is often expanded and enhanced by *in*sights. Here the subject–object distance is decreased, and may even momentarily disappear. Intuition has its place in all phases of *in*quiry. Many scientists, including Einstein (1934), have insisted that intuition is at the heart of all science in process (Runco & Pritzker, 1999). One might also add the following "*ins*" to the creative heuristic disposition required for science's advances: *in*terest, *in*trospection and *in*spiration. Also, if our thesis about the upright posture's *in*herent relationship to the value world is valid, let us certainly consider *in*cluding a skeletally evolved *in*stinct.

And these are distinct from the often related terms such as *outlook, outcome, output, outflow, outwit, outstanding,* and so forth.

These posture-related metaphors and value-tensions, I suggest, manifest themselves in diverse forms and phases of human inquiry and, in fact, are implicated in the supreme values of balance and harmony toward which human inquiry ultimately strives.

## COLLECTIVE INQUIRY, BALANCE AND HARMONY, AND THE HUMAN CONDITION

### Creativity at the Intellectual Macro Level: Tensions and Balance

Contemporary scholarship is often involved in a balancing act of debate, for example when a relativistic postmodernist takes on modern rationalism, with its *up*ward bent toward unifying truths. This modern–postmodern dialog reflects tensions that, in a variety of forms, have repeatedly expressed themselves throughout the history of Western inquiry: under such polar terms as *idealism* versus *empiricism, realism* versus *nominalism,* and *the One* versus *the Many.* Are such intellectual balancing acts extrapolations of the anatomically disposed value orientations?

Such debates draw out tensions between the high and the low, the vertical and the horizontal, the far and the near, the in and the out. Are there universal truths that can be grasped by the human mind, or can we trust only the relative givens of our bodily senses? Or, as nominalists claim, can we trust only the diverse signs assigned to designate bits of reality? Theologically, is there, as Judeo-Christian-Islamic faiths hold, one absolute God *up* in the Heavens, a single *high* Creator of the infinite diversity or, as some pagan traditions hold, a multiplicity of earthly deities?

As to our means of inquiry, we find similar tensions. Do we trust the *in*nards of *in*dividual *in*tuition, or only that which is collectively testable by detached methods of experimentation? Are detached facts our touch with reality? Or must these be grounded for logical and theoretical coherence and even more *in*timate *under*standing, for example, by means of a hermeneutic exegesis that, in its spiraling interplay of interpretations, brings the distant and multiple *in*tuitively home: an *in*ner grasp; an *in*timate joining of the objective and subjective, *multiple* and *singular, distant* and *near, up* and *down.*

### In, Out, and All-Around Pathways of Progress

These posture-related value tensions are expressed in virtually all inquiry traditions. Each has their ins and outs, as do the variations of history. Like China, who offered us the introspections of Lao Tze in one period and the engineering marvel of the Great Wall in another, the West has had its *introverted* periods of soul-searching and *extroverted* periods of science and technology, seen as a whole, as aspiring to both the more immediately practical and more distant eschatological ends. All this marks the unique progression of humankind.

Even the notion of progress—taken figuratively as an upward and advancing trip—takes on a different sense relative to inquiry spheres. Technological inquiry marks its advances by clear criteria. Hence, model TX-2 (say of an airplane) is a progressive advance over the previous (*backward*) model, TX-1, according to, say, the criteria of greater speed, shorter landing distance, and greater fuel efficiency. Whereas, in the inquiry worlds of art, poetry, and much of philosophy—or the meditative traditions of the East— it is far more difficult to speak of progress in this vertical–linear sense. Is Surrealism a *forward* advance over, say, Impressionism, and Impressionism over cave art? (Technique-wise this may be true, but as an art form, perhaps not.) Here progress may be marked laterally in revealing a wide range of ways in which humans experience and interpret their worlds.

Yet, art can also reflect the advancing progress of deepening and unifying consciousness, just as science can move between the two modes of progress, expanding (spreading) and lifting (raising) human consciousness. All these creative vehicles, as an ensemble, like the double vectors of the word *originality*, stretch our consciousness *back* toward discovery of our mysterious origins, while stretching consciousness *forward* toward realization of an equally mysterious destiny.


## CREATIVE INDIVIDUAL, PROCESS, AND PRODUCT

What can be said about those individuals who create advances across domains and disciplines? Are they involved in some sort of balancing act? Of such eminent creative people, Csikszentmihalyi (1996) wrote, "If I had to express in one word what makes their personalities different from others, it would be complexity" (p. 57).

Csikszentmihalyi (1996), although specifying a range of paradoxical personality traits, like Rogers (1959) and others studying the creative in-dividual, also adds the trait "openness to experience," the opposite of psychological defensiveness. That is, openness, in the sense of presence— engagement, awareness, and sensitivity. In addition—and this relates to presence—what these people bring of themselves to any sphere, domain, or discipline is what Csikszentmihalyi calls a *multitude,* or an entire range of human possibilities within themselves. Hence, for example, they bring to any creative engagement or everyday life not only their adult qualities—

for example, seriousness, realism, logic, skill, knowledge, and responsibility—but also their childlike (not childish) qualities, of naivety, imagination, awe, wonderment, playfulness, and even a disposition for irresponsibility. All these dispositions are available to them as resources to call on in the interest of a dynamic heuristic interplay with life events or specific creative projects.

The creative process itself can be a dance of apparent opposites, such as "detached-engagement" (moving *out–in*), or as in Kris's (1952) neo-Freudian characterization of "regression in the service of ego," where there is a *backing down* to what the ego put *aside* (i.e., to preconscious resources); all this is in the interest of deepening (*in*) and expanding (*all-around*) ego's grasp of reality. Phases of the process may call for opposing states of mind or ongoing tension of both, in particular, of divergent–convergent processing (Richards, 2000–2001). An embracing of complexity engenders an emergent result that Skolimowski (1984) refers to as a "higher order simplicity" (p. 47): a new form of unity that contains the earlier multiplicity, such as one finds in the elegant solution to a complex problem.

### Creativity and Psychological Health

Pathologies of many kinds are found among eminently creative individuals who, themselves, are not cast in a single mould (Runco & Richards, 1998). Consider the bizarre life of Dali or the state of depression Darwin experienced for decades. Yet, even these pathologies can take on a different, healthy meaning when viewed broadly in the light of the larger creative context and, specifically, in the light of our thesis. Paradoxically, imbalance, stress, and disruption, in the right holding context, can idiosyncratically serve the larger creative balancing and harmonizing act. In creative context, imbalances such as obsessive traits and hyperemotionality may serve both to ground and free the mind.

The very factors creative individuals tend to have in common, including openness and preference for complexity (Barron, 1969), foster the paradox of accepting, even thriving on, imbalance in the interest of ultimately greater balance and harmony. Drawn by life and project, possessing multiple resources, they can create a kind of overall, albeit flexuous, safety zone of balance. For instance, the childlike imagination that belongs to the same creative dynamic as the adult reality checks such as logic and caution can be permitted to expand all the more freely and playfully. Here are potential examples of divergent and convergent types of processing. One can be reassured by these reality checks that the creator will not eventually be carried overboard into insanity or wild and consuming fantasy. Similarly, focus and perseverance can be exercised more freely without changing into the uncontrollably obsessive. Some anxiety and ambiguity can be tolerated without these degrading into debilitating neurotic vacillation or procrastination. Consider the letting go experience, for example, the need to put aside a heated creative engagement for a time, which might even result in depression. In this *fluid center* (Schneider, 2004) resides such a strong *inner* sense of confidence that even such phases of let*down* have their place in the creative process. At times, the process may be somewhat like pregnancy, where pain and malaise may be (even joyously) endurable because they are inherent to a necessary period of *incubation*. The creative process, similar to pregnancy, has its own phase of *incubation*, and ultimately engenders something meaningfully new and unique, as well as being a fulfillment and extension of one's self.

This openness to experience combined with complexity represents, in the condition of open presence and engaged multitude, and despite some delays and false starts, an overall balancing and harmonizing act. At the product level, whether in the arts, sciences, or everyday life, a new human–world unity can be produced. At the individual level, a new and *intimate* connection is established between self and external reality as well as between self-as-known and its own expanding horizons of possibility. The creative process may be a portal to yet deeper and wider potentials of *innovation* and expression as well as a portal to self-understanding and expanding states of consciousness.

Considering this dynamic, it is perhaps understandable that certain creative individuals also report what Maslow (1962) called peak experiences, ecstatic, rapturous moments that can transform one's experience of self or world. These experiences can be accompanied by a profound feeling of satisfaction, and may sometimes include a sacred sense of being, seemingly aided by a force beyond self, as in a gift of illumination, or a "guided hand" recognition that "the painting painted itself." The experience may be accompanied by a dual sense of humility and fulfillment: having more than realized one's personal talents and calling, while being at that moment in a supreme state of balance and harmony. The creator's life as well as receptive humanity may meaningfully be advanced. Here are moments to feast on, but also—if the creative individual or humanity should succumb to achievement-incited hubris—moments prone to get *up*pity.

## Spiritual Paths to Balance and Harmony

Let us conclude our inquiry with a snapshot tour of some of the world's great spiritual traditions, and take a speculative look at our directional themes. Spiritual traditions vary greatly but typically hold that "reality is not limited to the material, sensory world . . . [there is] a spiritual reality . . . be it belief in a supreme being or order, life after physical death, an ultimate reality, or supernatural beings like angels or demons" (Miller & Thoresen, 1999, pp. 5–6). In our worldly sphere, practitioners are in search of how to live in balance and harmony and toward a greater goal.

Let us begin with the notion of *up*pity, or when events, directionally, go too far. This might be magnified to eschatological proportions. Original sin marks, for Christians, the rupture with divine unity and harmony. Christ comes down, in body, from the heavens to save the multitude of souls otherwise doomed by their base and earthly ways, which averts the fate of hell *below* as well. The moment of grace (i.e., my cup runneth over) is one of sublime reunion with God, and leads to a new, balanced, and more harmonious way of living the mortal life. One may see aspects of a creative detached engagement by being in but not of the world.

Other spiritual traditions also begin with rupture from a harmonious origin. In the Judaic tradition of Kabbalah, during the process of incarnation from the unity realm, of which all are a part, into the separate ego and world of diversity, one is wounded—one's vessel (individual and the world) "becomes cracked." Once individuals are capable of negotiating the many challenges posed by this world of multiplicity, they are able to return to the unity realm in order to bring back (down) healing energy, the divine sparks, which can be used to repair or heal the cracks in the vessel. This process of return from peak to base in order to repair or heal, to reestablish harmony and unity in the world of complexity and contradiction, is called *tikkun* (Cooper, 1997; Hoffman, 1985; Matt, 1997).

A spiritual voyage that encompasses up and down, in and out, back and forward and the multiplicity of the all-around, in the interest of balance and harmony, expresses itself in different ways in other traditions. In the varied practices of shamanism (Harner, 1990; Heinze, 1991), shamans, acting on behalf of their communities and its members, are able to access altered states of consciousness so they can mediate between the sacred and profane. This includes ability to travel between the lower, upper, and middle worlds to obtain information necessary for healing individuals and their communities. Whether through the use of drumming, the ingestion of powerful psycho-active substances, or other means, activities disrupt practitioners' ordinary consciousness and open them to the liminal realm, which becomes a portal for many possibilities, including magical cures, visions of an extraordinary nature, and visits with ancestral spirits (Matt, 1997).

In the multiple traditions of yoga—"to bind together, hold fast, or yoke" (Eliade, 1969, p. 4)—students are guided in the process of refocusing their reactive, habit-bound, states of consciousness through the use of a variety of somatic and meditative practices. The ultimate goal of liberation presupposes a preliminary breaking of bonds, to transcend the world of suffering, for ultimate knowledge and self-mastery. Among many diverse practices, there are energetic techniques for moving energy (evolution, expansion, involution), upward, outward, and downward, to further harmony and balance within the individual and the greater cosmos (Chaudhuri, 1965, 1977).

In Western psychology, Maslow (1962) chose the ancient symbol of the pyramid to depict elegantly the process he calls *self-actualizing*, at the peak of his hierarchy of needs. There is movement *up*ward from the array of *down*-pulling basic needs, such as physiological and safety needs; most of these shared with other animals. When satisfied, one ascends through middle level (belonging and self-esteem) needs—those more uniquely human, such as belongingness and love. One then ascends to a pinnacle of *being* needs, developing fully to one's capacity. Attainment of this may be accompanied by *peak experiences*, moments of unity and deep insight; of experiencing the sacred in the mundane, the all in the particular.

The form of the pyramid expresses the need for groundedness before ascent. The four corners of this grounded base all join to the pinnacle. This is the point from which insights may be brought, geometrically and communicatively, down to the world of the base as a transcendent and prophetic message. The goal is to provide benefit, but not to get stuck (hung-*up*) *down* there. In pointing to Maslow's symbolic pyramid, we might also take note that one who meditates in the lotus position has formed his or her body into the shape of a pyramid.

## CONCLUSIONS

The human creative capacity may be viewed as a mediator between body and psyche, and body and spirit. Also, as the double-vectored term originality implies, the creative process may represent a kind of revolving doorway between our mysterious human origins and equally open destiny. Resourcefully, this creative capacity converts tensions, some anatomically associated with the upright posture's lived values, toward individual survival and the remarkable achievements of the species as well as the farther reaches of human possibility.

Seen in this light, the answer to our earlier question of whether creativity capacity and the potential for spiritual development are reserved for the elite, or are the birthright of everybody, shifts in favor of the latter. Both appear embedded and embodied in humanity. One may then ask why some people do not exercise these human capacities more fully. Just as the world of upright posture may be taken for granted, perhaps we are not adequately recognizing potential for creativity and spiritual growth that are embedded in the activities of everyday life.

The nexus I propose between upright posture, creativity, and supreme values of balance and harmony helps us better understand how inspiring dancers or acrobats, stretching to their body limits in performance, can fall under the same creative label as the *insight*-producing artist, and can evoke awe. Similarly, the architect or paradigm-shifting scientist can amaze us, drawing us to new heights of order and balance.

This raises a question for scholars of evolution, the sort psychologists have raised when their observations took them beyond the constancy hypothesis. Why did any of the earliest ancestors of *Homo sapiens* stand upright? How and why did this begin? The outcomes would seem to impose this question. For, given this creature's unique and remarkable accomplishments, not least among these is coming to relative harmony with nature on its own terms, and thriving, to boot—all this given the vulnerabilities of the human posture—one wonders if whatever set that transformation in motion can be explained in survival terms alone.

## REFERENCES

Arons, M. (1994). Creativity, humanistic psychology, and the American zeitgeist. In F. Wertz (Ed.), *The humanistic movement* (pp. 45–61). Lake Worth, FL: Gardner.

Arons, M., & Richards, R. (2001). Two noble insurgencies: Creativity and humanistic psychology. In K. Schneider, J. Bugental, & J. Pierson (Eds.), *The handbook of humanistic psychology* (pp. 127–142). Thousand Oaks, CA: Sage.

Barron, F. X. (1963). *Creativity and psychological health*. Princeton, NJ: Van Nostrand.

Barron, F. X. (1969). *Creative person and creative process*. New York: Holt, Rinehart & Winston.

Chaudhuri, H. (1965). *Integral yoga: A concept of harmonious and creative living*. Wheaton, IL: Theological Publishing House.

Chaudhuri, H. (1977). *The evolution of internal consciousness*. Wheaton, IL: Theological Publishing House.

Cooper, D. (1997). *God is a verb: Kabbalah and the practice of mystical Judaism*. New York: Riverhead Press.

Csikszentmihalyi, M. (1996). *Creativity*. New York: HarperCollins.

Einstein, A. (1934). *Essays in science*. New York: The Philosophical Library.

Eliade, M. (1969). *Yoga: Immortality and freedom* (2nd ed.). Princeton, NJ: Princeton University Press.

Goodall, J. (1986). *The chimpanzees of Gombe: Patterns of behavior*. Cambridge, MA: Harvard University Press.

Harner, M. (1990). *The way of the shaman: A guide to power healing*. New York: Harper & Row.

Heinze, R. I. (1991). *Shamans of the 20th century*. New York: Irvington Publishers.

Hoffman, E. (1985). *The heavenly ladder: Kabbalistic techniques for inner growth*. New York: Harper & Row.

Keleman, S. (1981). *Your body speaks its mind*. Berkeley, CA: Center Press.

Krippner, S. (1994). Humanistic psychology and chaos theory: The third revolution and the third force. *Journal of Humanistic Psychology, 34*(3), 48–61.

Kris, E. (1952). *Psychoanalytic explorations in art*. New York: International Universities Press.

Lakoff, G. (1987). *Women, fire, and other dangerous things: What categories reveal about the mind*. Chicago: University of Chicago Press.

Maslow, A. H. (1959). Creativity in self actualizing people. In H. H. Anderson (Ed.), *Creativity and its cultivation* (pp. 51–56). New York: Harper.

Maslow, A. H. (1962). *Towards a psychology of being*. Princeton, NJ: Van Nostrand.

Matt, D. C. (1997). *The essential Kabbalah: The heart of Jewish mysticism*. Edison, NJ: Castle Books.

Merleau-Ponty, M. (1962). *Phenomenology of perception*. (C. Smith, Trans.). London: Routledge & Kegan.

Miller, W. R., & Thoresen, C. E. (1999). Spirituality and health. In W. R. Miller (Ed.), *Integrating spirituality into treatment: Resources for practitioners* (pp. 3–18). Washington, DC: American Psychological Association.

Ornstein, R. (1991). *Evolution of consciousness: Darwin, Freud and cranial fire—The origins of the way we think*. New York: Prentice Hall.

Richards, R. (2000–2001). Millennium as opportunity: Chaos, creativity, and J. P. Guilford's Structure-of-Intellect Model. *Creativity Research Journal, 13* (3 & 4), 249–265.

Richards, R., Kinney, D., Benet, M., & Merzel, A. (1988). Assessing everyday creativity: Characteristics of the Lifetime Creativity Scales and validation with three large samples. *Journal of Personality and Social Psychology, 54*, 476–485.

Roe, A. (1951). A psychological study of eminent biologists. *Psychological Monographs, 64*(14), 1–68.

Rogers, C. R. (1959). Towards a theory of creativity. In H. H. Anderson (Ed.), *Creativity and its cultivation* (pp. 69–82). New York: Harper.

Runco, M. A, & Pritzker, S. R. (1999). *Encyclopedia of creativity* (Vols. 1–2). San Diego, CA: Academic Press.

Runco, M. A., & Richards, R. (Eds.). (1998). *Eminent creativity, everyday creativity, and health*. Greenwich, CT: Ablex Publishing.

Sartre, J. P. (1948). *Being and nothingness*. (H. E. Barnes, Trans.). New York: Philosophical Library. (Original work published 1943)

Schneider, K. (2004). *Rediscovery of awe: Splendor, mystery, and the fluid center of life*. St. Paul, MN: Paragon House.

Skolimowski, H. (1984). *The theatre of the mind: Evolution in the sensitive cosmos*. Wheaton, IL: Theosophical Publishing House.

Sophocles. (1982). *Oedipus Rex*. New York: Cambridge University Press.

Stanford, G. (2001). *Significant others: The ape continuum and the quest for human nature*. New York: Basic Books.

Steeves, H. P. (1999). *Animal others: On ethics, ontology and animal life*. New York: State University of New York Press.

Straus, E. (1966). The upright posture. In E. Eng (Trans.), *Phenomenological psychology* (pp. 137–165). New York: Basic Books.

Watts, A. W. (1951). *The wisdom of insecurity: A message for the age of anxiety*. London: Vintage Books.

# 9

# CREATIVITY IN THE EVERYDAY: CULTURE, SELF, AND EMOTIONS

LOUISE SUNDARARAJAN AND JAMES R. AVERILL

> Art is the education of nature. . . . The human body is an instrument for the production of art in the life of the human soul.
> —Alfred North Whitehead

Nothing is more everyday than emotion, and nothing seemingly less creative. Yet, creativity in the domain of emotion, both eminent and everyday, is the topic of this chapter. As in other domains of creativity, a creative response must be effective in meeting some challenge or standard of excellence. Two other criteria for creativity are novelty and authenticity. Novelty requires that the response be unique to the individual or group, and authenticity requires that the response originates in the self, as opposed to being an imitation or copy. (As here conceived, the "self" can extend beyond the boundaries of the individual person.) The exact weight given to the criteria of novelty and authenticity may vary from one person to another, from one domain of creativity to another, and, most important for our present concerns, from one culture to another.

A second major concern of this chapter is the way cultures differ in the criteria for assessing creativity. Western cultures are often characterized as individualistic, and Eastern cultures as collectivist. These cultural orientations, we suggest, reflect dimensions along which a person's intra- and interpersonal transactions may vary, namely through (a) differentiation and (b) involvement. Through literary examples—John Keats from the West and Ssu-k'ung T'u from the East—we illustrate how differentiation and involvement relate to novelty and authenticity.

A third area of our investigation is how cultural differences can translate into individual differences in creativity. As in other domains, people differ in their ability to be emotionally creative. We relate such differences to self-construals that reflect the collectivism–individualism cultural divide and, more specifically, to the way elements of novelty and authenticity are differentially blended in the cognitive life-space of the person.

Last, we reflect on the difference and continuity between the eminent and the everyday in emotional creativity. Needless to say, emotions expressed in literature are not the same as emotions expressed in everyday life: The former may be considered eminent and the latter everyday; moreover, the former are manifested in words and images, whereas the latter may also involve bodily reactions. However, to the extent that, at their creative best, emotions are made an embodied art (cf. the epigram by Whitehead); the ideals of eminent and everyday creativity may converge in the emotional life. This continuity between life and art is emphasized in the Chinese tradition.

## EMOTIONAL CREATIVITY, FROM THE EMINENT TO THE EVERYDAY

At first blush, the juxtaposition of "emotion" with "creativity" might seem like an oxymoron. Consider, for example, the following observations by Robert Zajonc (1998), writing in the authoritative *Handbook of Social Psychology*:

> At the basic level we share emotions with lower animals. Except for trivial features, cognitions are probably uniquely human. . . . There are 'cognitive virtuosos'—mathematical prodigies, mnemonists, geniuses— but there are no 'emotional prodigies.' We can speak of an 'intellectual giant' but an 'emotional giant' is an absurdity. (p. 597)

We can only guess why the idea of an "emotional giant" seemed absurd to Zajonc. Human beings are not only the most intelligent of species but also the most emotional: Simple observation indicated that humans experience a greater variety of emotions than do chimpanzees; chimpanzees, greater than dogs; dogs, greater than mice; and so on down the "great chain of being." Stated differently, emotional and intellectual capacities have evolved together. This fact alone might suggest that the idea of emotional creativity is not an absurdity. William James, for one, did not think it absurd: "When a person has an inborn genius for certain emotions, his life differs strangely from that of ordinary people" (1902/1961, p. 215).

In the passage cited earlier, Zajonc (1998) mentioned two eminent mathematicians, Gauss and Pascal, as examples of cognitive virtuosos.

Applying James's observation to geniuses such as these, we might say that the world of mathematics also differs strangely from that of ordinary people. Yet, is it any less strange than the world of Augustine, say, or Dante, both of whom might be considered emotional geniuses? Genius in any domain is, by definition, rare and hence in some sense strange—but not thereby absurd.

If we turn from the eminent to the everyday, the idea of emotional creativity is as old as Aristotle, albeit under a different name—*catharsis*. We do not mean catharsis in the sense of purgation, which is only one possible translation of the original Greek. Aristotle's meaning is better captured by the notion of perfecting the emotions: By viewing drama or tragedy, the ordinary person learns to respond emotionally in new and presumably better ways (Oatley, 1999; Averill, 2001).

Also relevant to emotional creativity is the ancient Stoic distinction between first and second movements. The Stoics disagreed with Aristotle that emotions could be perfected. For the Stoics, the emotions were literally pathologies (*pathē*), and hence were to be expurgated completely. An obvious objection to this Stoic thesis is that we often respond in immediate and adaptive ways to painful and pleasurable events. Are we to deny that such reactions are emotions? Yes, according to the Stoics. Such reactions are only "first movements," automatic responses, such as turning pale at a frightening event, that are preliminary to the real emotion, which is a "second movement" that requires an additional assessment about what to do.

Some contemporary theories make a distinction similar to that made by the Stoics, but they make the opposite identification. That is, the *real* emotion is identified with an immediate reaction that may last for only moments; subsequent cognitive assessments are dismissed as secondary elaborations. Which conception is correct: Are emotions limited to first movements only, or do they also include second movements? The answer is both: The concept of emotion is sufficiently broad to encompass first and second movements. If we had to choose, however, we believe the Stoics had the better argument, provided we ignore their insistence that anything done out of emotion could be better done following rational deliberation (cf. Nussbaum, 1994).

We call attention to the Stoic position because it helps to clarify the limits of emotional creativity. The person who is suddenly confronted by the proverbial bear in the woods does not have time to be creative. His emotional response, at least immediately, comprises mainly "first movements." However, most emotional episodes are not like this, and they allow ample opportunity for innovation and change during the "second movement."

Some of the best evidence for emotional creativity comes from cultural differences in emotional syndromes; for example, aggression and related emotions may be unheard of in one culture (e.g., the Utku, described by

Briggs, 1970), but considered fundamental in another (e.g., the Yanomamö, described by Chagnon, 1992). Although such variations in emotional syndromes are well documented, the tendency has been to interpret them as a mere patina on more "basic" (biologically primitive) emotions. That tendency is itself a cultural prejudice, one deeply ingrained in Western intellectual history (Averill, 1974). We take a different view.

Given that emotions differ across cultures, the question arises: How did such variations come to be? The answer, we believe, is to be found in the emotional creativity of individuals, from the eminent to the everyday. At the level of eminent creativity, a genius with a new vision for emotions finds a niche for the new development. Augustine (1948) was such a person, a man of many and strong emotions: "Man is a great deep, Lord. You number his very hairs and they are not lost in your sight: but the hairs of his head are easier to number than his affections and the movements of his heart" (p. 14). Contrary to the Stoic notion of emotions as inherently pathological, Augustine's vision of human nature gave centrality to emotions: "In the *Confessions* for the first time in history is the analysis of the wellsprings of anxieties and frustrations of the modern soul" (Sheen, 1949, p. xi). Similarly, Confucius in China made refinement of emotions central to the self-cultivation of all Chinese who consider themselves "civilized" (Frijda & Sundararajan, in press; Sundararajan, 2002a).

At an intermediate level of creativity, practices emblematic of the new emotional order are needed. Legions of innovators—artists, poets, spiritual and political leaders—produce works that provide templates for everyday living. Continuing with Augustine as an exemplar in the West, his notion of the self as having a hidden dimension that is seething with emotional energy, and privy only to God or self-introspection, has been propagated through mystics in the medieval times and Freud and other thinkers in modern times. Similarly, great poets in China, such as Tu Fu and countless others elaborated on and made popular the Confucian vision of refined emotions (Sundararajan, 1998, 2002a).

At the level of everyday creativity, ordinary people live the vision of the trendsetters, often with variations that, if proven viable, percolate upward through the society. Thus, in addition to a top-down progression, from the eminent to the everyday, emotional creativity proceeds in a bottom-up direction, from the everyday to the eminent. The latter, in fact, is undoubtedly the more common mode of progression, although it is less easy to demonstrate because of its commonness and diffuseness. We will have more to say about everyday emotional creativity in a later section. For now, suffice it to note that social evolution, like biological evolution, typically proceeds in small increments, the cumulative effect of which is only solidified and made apparent through such "emotional geniuses" as Augustine and Confucius.

Emotional creativity is not ancient history. Carl Rogers provides a contemporary example. Born into a fundamentalist Christian family, Rogers was shy as a youth and married his childhood sweetheart—hardly the background for a "hidden genius of emotion" (Magai & Haviland-Jones, 2002). Yet, Rogers had a vision for a particular kind of emotional attunement that is therapeutic, and subsequently found a niche for this practice in client-centered therapy. At the next level in the top-down progression, client-centered therapists made Rogerian theory and techniques available to a wide audience. Finally, at the level of everyday creativity, a multitude of people innovated on the vision of Rogers in encounter groups and other countercultural movements of the 1960s.

The stage is now set for exploring emotional creativity in the cultural contexts of Eastern and Western societies. (By "Eastern," we mean the East Asian societies of China, Korea, and Japan; by "Western," we mean any country within the European cultural tradition, regardless of geographical location.)

## CRITERIA FOR CREATIVITY IN CULTURAL CONTEXT

How do we determine whether an emotional response is creative? There are three criteria. The first is effectiveness. For a response to be considered creative, it must be effective in meeting some challenge, for example, aesthetically in the case of art, commercially in the case of business, theoretically in the case of science, and, we suggest, interpersonally in the case of emotion. Needless to say, what counts as effective may vary from one domain to another, but also from one culture to another. Yet, regardless of domain or culture, no response will be considered creative unless it is of value.

Next to effectiveness, the most commonly mentioned criterion for creativity is novelty; that is, the creative response should be unique or different in some respect. As Arnheim (1966) has emphasized, however, novelty can be—indeed, typically has been—overemphasized. Difference for difference' sake, even when effective, may be a sign of eccentricity rather than creativity. Therefore, a third criterion must be added, namely, authenticity. Authenticity is a complex concept, but as we are using it here, it captures what Arnheim had in mind when he spoke of the "pregnant sight of reality" as a hallmark of creativity. The creative response must reflect the person's own vision of reality, whether novel or not.

Cultures differ not only in the emotions they recognize as standard, as the earlier examples of the Utku and Yanomamö illustrate, but they also differ in the extent to which they encourage or tolerate emotional creativity. This is particularly true with reference to the criteria of novelty and authenticity. In particular, Eastern societies place greater emphasis on authenticity than on novelty, whereas Western societies have the reverse emphasis (Averill, Chon, & Hahn, 2001; Sundararajan, 2002a). This point becomes clear in a dimensional analysis of culture. (See chaps. 3 & 8, this volume, for movement toward the more Eastern configuration in spiritual "balance" or healing.)

### Dimensions of Culture

Authenticity and novelty differ in directions of cognitive attention—inward toward the self versus outward toward the world, orientations that help shape the nature and content of our emotional experiences, as discussed, for example, by Marcel and colleagues (Lambie & Marcel, 2002). To elaborate on the difference in cognitive attention between authenticity and novelty, we propose two universal dimensions along which a person's intra- and interpersonal transactions may vary, namely, (a) differentiation and (b) degree of involvement. These dimensions are illustrated in Figure 9.1.

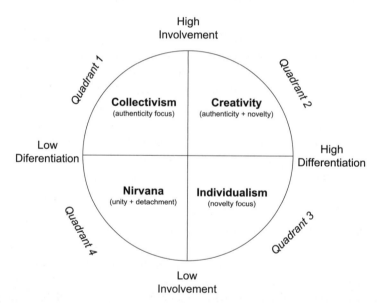

*Figure 9.1.* Two dimensions—differentiation and involvement—along which intrapersonal (self-to-self) and interpersonal (self-to-other) relations may vary. An authenticity focus, whether on the individual (interdependent) or cultural (collectivist) level, reflects high involvement and low differentiation (*Quadrant 1*), and conversely for a novelty focus (*Quadrant 3*). Creativity in its everyday sense (*Quadrant 2*) reflects a "blended space" that incorporates both the criteria of authenticity and novelty. A "blended space" of low involvement (detachment) and low differentiation (unity) can also be creative, but in a more esoteric sense, for example, as illustrated by the Buddhist concept of Nirvana (*Quadrant 4*).

The meaning of these dimensions is easiest to illustrate in the context of interpersonal relationships.

*Differentiation*, the horizontal axis in Figure 9.1, is anchored at the high end by perceived differences and at the low end by perceived similarities. That is, highly differentiated persons perceive themselves as unique and different from others.

*Involvement*, the vertical axis in Figure 9.1, is anchored at the high end by a sense of solidarity or integration and at the low end by a sense of separateness. People who perceive themselves as unique (highly differentiated) may still be highly involved in the lives of others; conversely, people who perceive themselves as similar to others (low differentiation) can nevertheless be socially disengaged or uninvolved. Hence, the two axes are depicted as orthogonal in Figure 9.1.

As noted earlier, the dimensions of Differentiation and Involvement can be interpreted on the intrapersonal (subjective) as well as interpersonal levels of analysis. This is because the way we relate to ourselves is a reflection of how we relate to others, says Vygotsky (1978) and others; the other way around is also true, says the philosopher Charles Peirce (Sundararajan & Schubert, 2005). How Differentiation and Involvement play out in the intrapersonal dimension is of particular relevance to creativity, as we shall see.

As illustrated in Figure 9.1, Authenticity (Quadrant 1) is characterized by high involvement (participation, solidarity, integration, etc.) and low differentiation (similarity, redundancy, etc.). These themes are best articulated by an inward orientation, a self-to-self relationship in which the partners of the transaction are the most similar "other." By contrast, Novelty (Quadrant 3) is characterized by low involvement (psychological distance, instrumentality, objectivity, etc.), and high differentiation (difference, uniqueness, etc.). These themes are best articulated by an outward orientation, a self-to-nonself relationship in which the partners of the transaction are dissimilar. This is the self-to-world transaction in which instrumentality and objectivity become important mental sets. Cast in the cross-cultural context, Eastern cultures show an intrapersonal orientation that privileges self-transformation and self-integration, whereas Western cultures value actions that change the world.

Creative people and societies, we chapter authors contend, inhabit the "blended space" (Turner, 1996) of Quadrant 2, which combines selective elements of novelty and authenticity (Averill & Sundararajan, 2005). This leaves Quadrant 4, characterized by low involvement and low differentiation. This condition is undoubtedly unstable, for most people cannot remain indifferent (low involvement), especially to those they perceive as similar (low differentiation). Furthermore, they cannot remain indifferent to themselves. However, there can be a positive side to this quadrant, particularly on the intrapersonal (self-reflexive) level. We have in mind the Buddhist notion of Nirvana, which reduces everything to the ground state of nonbeing, and all passion to detachment.

## Collectivism Versus Individualism

Eastern societies are often described as collectivist and Western societies as individualistic (Triandis, 1995). *Collectivist* cultures are characterized by high involvement and low differentiation. That is also the space represented by Quadrant 1 (Figure 9.1). Similarly, *individualistic* cultures are characterized by low involvement and high differentiation and hence occupy the space represented by Quadrant 3. With regard to the criteria for creativity, we thus propose a relation between Authenticity and Collectivism, on the one hand, and Novelty and Individualism, on the other. Since the emphasis on these criteria is relative, not exclusive, we may state the proposed relations as follows: Expressions of authenticity for people in individualistic cultures will have a novelty slant, whereas expressions of novelty in collectivist cultures will have an authenticity slant.

To demonstrate the proposed relations, we draw on two sources. First, we contrast the works of two poets, John Keats (English, 1795–1821) and Ssu-k'ung T'u (pronounced ss-coon-too; Chinese, 837–908), to illustrate cultural differences in conceptions of creativity and the self; second, we present empirical data to show how self-reports of authenticity and novelty correlate with measures of collectivism and individualism.


## SIMULATIONS OF EMOTIONAL CREATIVITY IN POETRY

Wordsworth (1805/1952) famously described poetry as "the spontaneous overflow of powerful feelings: it takes its origin from emotion recollected in tranquility ... the tranquility gradually disappears, and an emotion, kindred to that which was before the subject of contemplation, is gradually produced, and does itself actually exist in the mind" (p. 84). Couched in terms of modern computer science, Oatley (1999) has made a similar point, namely, that works of literature are ways of simulating emotions. Just as computer simulations give us a useful model of the weather, simulations of emotions through literature provide models of creativity.

## Models of Creativity, East and West

For the Western notion of creativity, we examine John Keats's poem "To Autumn," in which the potency of nature becomes the metaphor for the power to create. The following lines are particularly pertinent:

Conspiring with him [the sun] how to load and bless
With fruit the vines that round the thatch-eves run;
To bend with apples the moss'd cottage-trees,
And fill all fruit with ripeness to the core;
To swell the gourd, and plump the hazel shells,
With a sweet kernel . . . (cited in Fish, 1980, p. 263)

Consistent with our proposed novelty-focus cultures, Keats's "To Autumn" is a model of creativity with high differentiation and low involvement. Highly differentiated is the creator's role: It is on a different order of being from the created. Corresponding to the dichotomy between the creator and the created are binary oppositions between subject and object; action and passion. The creator—autumn—is the one who acts; the created—fruits, nuts, and vegetation—is the object being acted on. Coupled with this discontinuity in being is instrumental rationality that guides action. Donald Freeman (1978) in his nuanced analysis of this poem noted a plethora of verbs—loads, blesses, bends, fills, swells, and plumps—and instrumental phrases: "with fruit," with apples," with ripeness," and "with a sweet kernel." This observation led Fish (1980) to the conclusion that "The overriding agency of Autumn, by making everything her object, makes everything her instrument, even the sun" (p. 264).

In sharp contrast is the Chinese notion of creativity. Not having a creator myth, the Chinese notion of nature becomes necessarily self-referential: Nature is self-generating and self-renewing. In fact, the Chinese term for nature is *ziran* which means literally "self-so-ing" (Hall & Ames, 1995, p. 231). As can be expected, the Chinese notion of creativity is high in involvement and low in differentiation. A case in point is Ssu-k'ung T'u's poem on chaos—the primordial principle of creativity—entitled "*Hsiung-hun*":

Great power manifested without,
The genuine form is inwardly full;
Return to the void, enter the All
Gathering vigor it becomes potent.
Containing a myriad phenomena,
It extends across the great void,
Pale and billowing rain clouds,
Long winds in the empty vastness.
Leap beyond images and appearances
To reach the circle's center—
Hold it without coercion,
It will come without end. (Adapted from Yu, 1978, p. 93)

This poem, like many others by Ssu-k'ung T'u, shares with computer simulations a two-tiered structure of simulation per se, on the one hand, and instructions about how to conduct the simulation on the other (Oatley,

1999). Lines 1 through 9 are mental simulations of the Tao as primordial Chaos; the coda (Lines 10–12) gives instructions as to how best to appropriate this primordial source of energy and creativity. The title "*Hsiung-Hun*" literally means "potent, undifferentiated" (Owen, 1992, p. 303). The "undifferentiated" (*hun*) is "the primordial state of chaos," in which "all emergent shapes are constantly changing and blurring into all others" (p. 305). Ssu-k'ung T'u's imagery for this potent and primordial state is the flowing clouds: "The clouds are an appropriate sensuous form for *hun* [undifferentiated], while the steady gale that drives them will be associated with *hsiung* [potent]" (Owen, 1992, p. 305). This poem shares with Keats's "To Autumn" an emphasis on the energy and dynamism of the creative process.

In her exquisite analysis of this poem on chaos, Pauline Yu noted that "The interaction between inner and outer in lines 1–2 and 9–10, along with the active verbs *fan* [return], *ju* [enter], *heng* [extend], *chüeh* [(cutting) across], *yu* [flowing/billowing], *ch'ao* [leap beyond], all create a sense of movement" (1978, p. 94). Likewise, Owen (1992) claims that this poem celebrated "ceaseless activity" flowing from "pure potentiality" (p. 305). He explains that since "'potent, undifferentiated' (in Ssu-k'ung T'u's version) is not a truly determinate quality in its own right, but rather a capacity to produce all determinate qualities, it can be manifest only in the impression of energy, in an ability constantly to produce new forms and transformations of old ones" (p. 306). Yet, the activities of the Tao in its primordial state of chaos differ drastically from those of autumn as envisioned by Keats.

Whereas the transitive verbs of Keats's autumn accentuate mastery over the world, actions of the primordial chaos are mostly couched in terms of intransitive verbs such as returning, billowing, leaping—activities which render the doer "at once the desert, the traveler, and the camel," to borrow a felicitous phrase from Flaubert (cited in Blanchot, 1981, p. 127). Indeed, forceful action is explicitly forbidden in the coda of this poem: "Hold it [the creative force] without coercion,/It will come without end." What creativity of the Tao exemplifies is not mastery without, but integration within. The Chinese notions of authenticity and self-integration are frequently articulated by the binary opposition of inner and outer (Sundararajan, 2002a). The inner and outer dichotomy is underlined at the outset of this poem on chaos: "Great power manifested without,/The genuine form is inwardly full" (Lines 1–2). The exact relationship between the inner and the outer is open to multiple interpretations, of which Owen (1992) sampled a few from various commentaries: "the outward is an extension of the inner . . . or the outward transforms while the inner stays the same, or the outward must 'wither away' so that the inward can be nurtured" (p. 305). Whatever the case may be, the emphasis is on the integration of the inner and the outer, as the next line has it: "Return to the void, enter the All." The term *return* marks the reflexive movement of self-integration, thereby the creative force that engages itself in the world of forms and actions is able to replenish itself periodically by returning to the source, the void, or what is later referred to as the *circle's center* (Line 10)—"the empty space around which a wheel turns"—where the "still unrealized power for transformation" resides (Owen, 1992, p. 304).

Thus far, we have used poetry to simulate models of creativity in general. We turn now to creativity as it relates more specifically to emotional experiences. For consistency, we draw on the life and work of the same two poets, John Keats and Ssu-k'ung T'u.

## John Keats on Negative Capability

The contours of a person's self are outlined in emotion: Our hopes and fears, joys and sorrows, loves and hates—these and the myriad of other emotions experienced in everyday life are markers of who we are. Any fundamental change in emotion thus involves a change in the self, and vice versa.

An innovative notion of the self is expressed by Keats in his theory of "negative capability," which consists of a twofold capacity: (a) "to efface the self through sympathetic identification with others," and (b) to remain in "uncertainties, Mysteries, doubts without any irritable reaching after fact and reason," as Keats put it (Kucich, 2001, p. 193). The submergence of the self in the nonself is a salient theme in the works of Keats. Barnard points out that behind Keats's pursuit of sensations lies a deeper yearning, namely for "Being [to be] taken up into sensation, into something deeply other to the self" (1990, p. 63). Mellor notes that Keats's "camelion [sic]" self is a self that is "permeable, continually overflowing its boundaries, melting into another, and being filled by another" (2001, p. 216). Clubbe and Lovell, Jr. make the similar observation: "Such a poet quite literally lives not in the limited self but in other selves" (1990, p. 135). Commenting on the confession of Keats that "In a room with People . . . then not myself goes home to myself: but the identity of every one in the room begins to press upon me that, I am in a very little time an[ni]hilated" (cited by Clubbe & Lovell, Jr., 1990, p. 135), the authors conclude that "This is the expansionist urge to move outside the self, to unite with that which is the not-self" (1990, p. 135).

The theme of self-effacement through identification with the larger whole is an expression of self-transcendence. Counterintuitive as this may sound, self-transcendence is an expression of authenticity for the following reasons: (a) the "selfless" poet does in fact have a self, albeit an expanded, all-inclusive one; (b) self-transcendence capitalizes on one important theme of authenticity—low differentiation or high similarity (the self's identification or merge with the nonself). However, Keats's version of authenticity may be considered authenticity with a novelty slant. The novelty theme is salient in Keats's celebration of multiplicity and experience: "If a Sparrow come before my Window I take part in its existence [sic] and peck about the Gravel," wrote Keats (cited in Clubbe & Lovell, Jr., 1990, p. 135). Clubbe and Lovell, Jr. point out that the chameleon–poet of "no identity" is "a being of immense variety and breadth, delighting in every level of existence, unconfined by puritanical or rationalistic restraints" (1990, p. 134). At a deeper level, Keats's ever so changeable chameleon self that capitalizes on multiplicity rather than identity, is part and parcel of his agenda to amass experiences: "O for a Life of Sensations rather than of Thoughts!" as he puts it (cited in Stillinger, 2001, p. 257). Faint echoes of this theme can be found in the modern West, where the "passionate quest for experience" (Florida, 2002, p. 166) seems to be characteristic of the successful business person as well as the successful poet. In the eloquent words of Florida, the aspiration is to "'live the life'—a creative life packed full of intense, high-quality, multidimensional experiences" (p. 166).

Florida's (2002) investigation indicates that the novelty orientation goes hand-in-hand with affluent societies. What about societies with limited resources? How do members of such a community manage to maximize their experiences? For the answer to this question, we turn to Ssu-k'ung T'u.

## Ssu-k'ung T'u on the Art of Savoring

If Keats is like a kid who manages to taste as many lollipops as possible by vicariously filling in the shoes of other lollipop-possessing kids, we may think of Ssu-k'ung T'u as a kid who possesses only one lollipop, but manages to savor that one in all its nuances. Savoring is a strategy that capitalizes on redundancy rather than difference—to multiply one's experience is to double back, to reexperience an experience. It is novelty with an authenticity slant. Ssu-k'ung T'u's theory of savoring is cast in the framework of "flavor beyond flavor," the gist of which can be found in the following statements he made in a letter to a certain Mr. Li:

> [I]n my opinion we can adequately speak of poetry only in terms of making distinctions in flavors. In everything that suits the palate in the region south of Chiang-ling, if it is a pickled dish, then it is indeed sour—but it is nothing more than sour. If it is a briny dish, then it is quite salty—but nothing more than salty. The reason people from the north, when eating such food, simply satisfy their hunger and then stop eating is that they recognize it somehow falls short of perfect excellence

and lacks something beyond the distinction between "the merely sour" and "the merely salty." (Owen, 1992, p. 351)

The ideal poet, according to Ssu-k'ung T'u, is able to make subtle discriminations beyond the emotional equivalent of saltiness or sourness. Owen explains: "The opposition is between gross categories that have names, and fine judgments for which there are no names. Furthermore, those finer gradations are learned by experience: One who knows only the gross categories can apprehend only the gross categories; to be able to recognize the finer distinctions requires the education of a sensibility" (1992, p. 352). "Exactly this kind of sensitivity lies at the root of creativity" (p. 90) says Gelernter (1994) in reference to subtle discrimination of emotional nuances. The novelty dimension of savoring has to do with what Gelernter (1994) refers to as *emotional acuity*, which is defined in terms of the following sensibilities: (a) that you are able to register subtle or nuanced emotions—to experience subtle emotional reactions—when less acute people would have no emotional reaction at all; and (b) that you are able to distinguish many elements in a subtle emotional palette, when a less acute person would distinguish the emotional equivalent of red, green, blue.

The second component of savoring is to reexperience an experience—not vicariously someone else's, but one's own. Self-reflexivity is definitive of savoring to the extent that one cannot savor the taste or experience of someone else. This self-reflexive dimension of savoring entails what is known as second-order awareness (Sundararajan, 2001, 2002b, 2004a). In contrast to the first-order awareness of tasting the flavors in food, savoring capitalizes on the second-order awareness of knowing that one knows the flavors so as to manipulate the experience by prolonging it, making fine discriminations of it, and so forth. In the final analysis, savoring is a redundancy game. It is not fortuitous that Ssu-k'ung T'u used the term *flavor* twice in his "flavor beyond flavor." The redundancy reiterates the idea that savoring is a second-order awareness of the first-order taste—the "merely" sour or salty, or perhaps the equivalent of "basic" emotions in contemporary psychology. Likewise in common parlance, savoring is called *hui-wei* (resavoring), where the prefix *hui* means "again" or "twice," as in "twice-cooked pork," *hui-guorou*.

The Chinese notion of savoring is broader in scope than the contemporary Western formulation of the same (Bryant & Veroff, 2007), which is confined to that of positive experiences only. The Chinese notion of savoring, by contrast, refers to the ability to appreciate and derive aesthetic pleasure from negative events as well as positive ones (Sundararajan, 2004a, in press), and as such is characteristic of emotionally creative individuals (for clinical application of savoring, see Sundararajan, 2001, in press). Furthermore, this self-reflexive dimension is missing in the contemporary formulation of savoring (Bryant, 1989), which centers on the ability to amplify or prolong enjoyment of positive events without taking into consideration the role of second-order awareness. The Chinese notion of savoring, by contrast, is broader in scope. Whereas in Bryant's formulation savoring is confined to that of positive experiences, the Chinese notion of savoring refers to the ability to appreciate and derive aesthetic pleasure from negative events as well as positive ones (Sundararajan, 2004a, in press), and as such is characteristic of emotionally creative individuals (for clinical application of savoring, see Sundararajan, 2001). Whereas the Western notion of savoring entails basically the sense of relishing an experience in the here and now, the Chinese notion of savoring focuses not on the stimulus in situ so much as on its poststimulus persistence. Thus Owen states that "Chinese theorists tended not to speak of disjunctive acts of reflection on the 'meaning' of a text, but rather of the 'continuation' of the text in the mind after reading is over, a time in which the significance of the text gradually unfolds" (1992, pp. 593–594). The same is true with "*hui-wei*" (retasting), which refers to "a recollection in the mind of a previously encountered flavor" (Eoyang, 1993, p. 230). In the final analysis, self-referentiality is an indispensable dimension to savoring—what is experienced in savoring is not simply the stimuli, but the self as well. Savoring is an affirmation of the self as point of reference of all its experiences—an integrated self with its taste, values, and memories as the sole measure of what is worth savoring.


## EMOTIONAL CREATIVITY IN THE EVERYDAY

The use of eminent poets, such as Keats and Ssu-k'ung T'u, to model everyday emotional creativity involves a contradiction: The eminent is not the everyday. In this section, therefore, the chapter authors extend our analysis to include individual differences in the ability to be emotionally creative, and how such differences relate to independent and interdependent self-construals, reflective of individualist and collectivist cultural orientations, respectively. As before, our major focus is on novelty and authenticity as criteria for creativity.

### Assessing Everyday Emotional Creativity

Creativity occurs in stages, from initial preparation to verification and diffusion of the final product. The criteria for creativity mentioned earlier (novelty, authenticity, effectiveness) pertain to the stage of verification; that is, they represent standards for evaluating a response as creative. The best predictor of future behavior is past performance. Therefore, the application of these criteria to past and current emotions provides one way to assess

## TABLE 9.1
### Sample Items From the Emotional Creativity Inventory

| Category | Item |
|---|---|
| Preparation (7 items total) | I think about and try to understand my emotional reactions. I pay attention to other peoples' emotions so that I can better understand my own. |
| Novelty (14 items total) | My emotional reactions are different and unique. I have felt combinations of emotions that other people probably have never experienced. I sometimes experience feelings and emotions that cannot be easily described in ordinary language. |
| Effectiveness/Authenticity (9 items total) | My emotions help me achieve my goals in life. I try to be honest about my emotional reactions, even when it causes me problems. My outward emotional reactions accurately reflect my inner feelings. |

individual differences in emotional creativity. The initial stage of the creative process—preparation—provides another way. Some people consider emotions important to their lives; thus, they think about and try to understand their emotions, and they are sensitive to the emotions of others. We may assume that, on average, such people are better prepared emotionally than are their more indifferent (but not necessarily less reactive) counterparts.

On the basis of this rationale, a 30-item Emotional Creativity Inventory (ECI) has been constructed (Averill, 1999). Seven of the items refer to emotional preparation, 14 to the novelty of emotional experiences, 5 to effectiveness, and 4 to authenticity. Sample items from each category are presented in Table 9.1.

Although basically unidimensional, factor analyses suggest that the ECI can be broken down into three more homogeneous facets. The first facet represents emotional preparedness; the second facet, novelty; and the third facet a combination of effectiveness and authenticity. Using self-report measures, it has proved difficult to distinguish the perceived effectiveness of a response from its authenticity; people tend to judge their own emotions effective to the extent that they are authentic, and vice versa.

People who score high on the ECI are rated by their peers as emotionally more creative than are low scorers, and they are better able to express unusual emotions symbolically in stories and pictures (Averill, 1999; Averill & Thomas-Knowles, 1991; Gutbezhal & Averill, 1996). People who score high on the ECI are also better able than low scorers to benefit from solitude, a condition that traditionally has been associated with creative pursuits in a variety of fields (Long, Seburn, Averill, & More, 2003).

In terms of the "Big Five" personality factors (Costa & McCrae, 1985), the ECI is most closely related to Openness and Experience, but it is independent of Extraversion and Neuroticism, two traits closely related to positive and negative emotionality, respectively. The ECI is also modestly correlated with agreeableness (another of the Big Five), self-esteem, and an antiauthoritarian attitude (Averill, 1999). In short, the ECI seems to have reasonable construct validity, using both performance and self-report measures.

With regard to discriminant validity, total scores on the ECI are unrelated to general intelligence, as measured by SAT scores (Averill, 1999), or to emotional intelligence, as measured by the Mayer-Salovey-Caruso Emotional Intelligence Test (MSCEIT), a performance-based measure of emotional abilities (Ivcevic, Brackett, & Mayer, 2007).

## Novelty and Authenticity in Relation to Collectivism and Individualism

As discussed earlier with reference to Figure 9.1, collectivist cultures are characterized by high involvement and low differentiation (Quadrant 1), and hence occupy the same space as Authenticity; by contrast, individualistic cultures are characterized by low involvement and high differentiation (Quadrant 3), and hence occupy the same space as Novelty. It is thus reasonable to infer that collectivist cultures will have an authenticity focus and individualistic cultures a novelty focus (Averill et al., 2001). Nicole Giglio (2002) explored this possibility as part of her senior honors thesis.

Not all individualist and collectivist societies are organized in the same manner; for instance, some are hierarchically organized whereas others have an egalitarian structure. This has led to a fourfold distinction between *vertical* and *horizontal* varieties of individualism and collectivism, with self-report scales to match (Singeles, Triandis, Bhawuk, & Gelfand, 1995). In a sample of 199 (35 male, 162 female, 2 unspecified) American university students, Giglio (2002) found no relation between total scores on the ECI and either of the vertical individualism or vertical collectivism scales ($r = .11$, and $-.03$, respectively). This is not surprising since, as noted earlier, persons who score high on ECI tend to be nonauthoritarian. However, the ECI was highly correlated with horizontal individualism ($r [197] = .47$, $p < .001$), and somewhat less so with horizontal collectivism ($r [197] = .22$, $p < .01$).

The main concern of Giglio's thesis was not with emotional creativity as a whole; rather, it was with the relation between novelty and authenticity, on the one hand, and individualism and collectivism, on the other. Two scales were formed for this purpose: One scale consisted of the original 14 novelty items from the ECI (coefficient alpha = .84); the other consisted of the four authenticity items, to which 10 more similar items were added

**TABLE 9.2**
Correlations Between Self-Reports of the Authenticity and Novelty of
One's Emotional Responses and the Cultural Dimensions of
Horizontal Collectivism and Individualism

| Creativity dimensions | Cultural dimensions | |
|---|---|---|
| | Collectivism | Individualism |
| Authenticity | $.28_a$ | $.26_a$ |
| Novelty | $.05_b$ | $.36_a$ |

*Note.* Values having the same subscript (a or b) are not significantly different from one another.

(coefficient alpha for the 14 items = .78). The correlation between the two scales was nonsignificant ($r$ [197] = .11). This last result is consistent with the theoretical analysis presented earlier, in which creativity represents a blended space of both novelty and authenticity, assuming equal effectiveness (see Figure 9.1).

Horizontal Collectivism and Horizontal Individualism were assessed by scales developed by Singelis et al. (1995). Table 9.2 presents the correlations between the four scales: Novelty, Authenticity, Horizontal Collectivism, and Horizontal Individualism.

The relations are in the predicted direction. That is, authenticity, but not novelty, was correlated with collectivism; the difference between these two correlations (.28 vs. .05, respectively) was statistically significant ($t$ [196] = 2.39, $p < .05$). Also as predicted, novelty was more highly correlated with individualism (.36) than was authenticity (.26); in this case, however, the difference did not reach statistical significance.

The correlation between authenticity and individualism (.26) deserves brief comment, for it is larger than might be expected on theoretical grounds. One possible explanation is the fact that in individualistic (e.g., Western) cultures, in which the self is often distinguished from others, the criteria of novelty and authenticity collapse into a single dimension; that is, the person is authentic by being different. Indeed, there is in contemporary Western societies what has sometimes been called "a cult of authenticity"—but it is an authenticity that is almost indistinguishable from novelty. That is, a person is considered authentic to the extent that he or she is different from others, unique in style or appearance, answering only to self-interests. This kind of authenticity is different from that found in more collectivist (e.g., Eastern) societies, where the self is not so differentiated from others, and in which a person's own interests are consistent with group norms (involvement).

In short, authenticity does not mean the same when embedded in different cultural contexts, a fact that was also found in this chapter's earlier comparison of the "negative capability" of John Keats and the "savoring" of Ssu-k'ung T'u. Furthermore, as Ssu-k'ung T'u's poetics suggests, even in Collectivistic societies, it is the intrapersonal version of authenticity (self-reflexivity, self-integration, etc.) rather than the interpersonal version of the same (group affiliation, sociality) that plays an important role in creativity. When measuring authenticity in future studies, it would be helpful to tease apart empirically these two variants of authenticity by devising items in which a self-referential (self-to-self) orientation (e.g., "I feel good when I can express my emotions fully and adequately in verbal communications") is pitted against a social (self-to-other) orientation (e.g., "I feel good when I cooperate with my coworkers").

## DISCUSSION

This chapter has focused on emotions as potential objects of creativity. The analysis, however, has implications beyond the emotions—to art and literature, especially poetry, on the one hand, and to the self, culture, and human nature, on the other. These implications deserve brief additional discussion. The chapter began with the gap sometimes observed between the eminent creativity of great poets, as exemplified, for example, by Keats and Ssu-k'ung T'u, and the everyday experience of emotion. The authors then considered the bidirectional relation between emotion and culture, and how each helps to fashion the other. Finally, we concluded the chapter with a few observations on the triadic relation between emotions, culture, and human nature.

### The Gap Between Eminent and Everyday Creativity, in Poetry and in Life

Let us return for a moment to Wordsworth's (1805/1952) description of poetry as "the spontaneous overflow of powerful feelings . . . recollected in tranquility." The phrase highlights the close relation between poetry and everyday emotional experiences, but it is also misleading. In poetry, emotions are not so much recollected as imagined. It is one thing for a poet to recollect or imagine an emotion in novel and particularly effective ways; it is another thing to enact that emotion in everyday life. The person who is good at one need not be good at the other. To a certain extent, the two may even be incompatible. Poetry is primarily cognitive; emotions are "embodied" and cannot be abstracted, without distortion, from the whole person and from the rest of life (Sundararajan, 2005).

Domains of eminent creativity, such as arts and sciences, may be compared to clearings in a forest. To the extent that the clearings are well maintained, there will be discontinuity or gaps between the eminent product and the rest of life, just as the clearing is distinct from the rest of the woods (Sundararajan, 2002c). The arena for everyday creativity, in contrast, is the woods, or life itself. To the extent that life approximates the dense woods with an overgrowth of conventions, creativity in the everyday may be more difficult than eminent creativity.

It is not surprising, then, that creative poets in both the East and the West have not always fared well in real life. One who dances well in the clearing may stumble in the woods. The area of creativity needs to be expanded to encompass life itself—the everyday. This is the claim of the Chinese traditions, from Confucianism to Taoism and Zen. Literature and the arts may be viewed, as in Confucian poetics, as opportunities for one to rehearse more refined versions of emotions (Frijda & Sundararajan, in press) to make it in the "real" world (Sundararajan, 2002a). The gap between art and life is further narrowed in traditional China as the Confucian gentlemen attempted to shape their lives according to what they modeled in poetry (Sundararajan, 2002a).

These considerations raise a further issue, namely, the relation between emotions, creativity, and culture.

## Emotions and Creativity in Cultural Perspective

The claim of Zajonc (1998) that there are no "emotional giants" is understandable if by "giant" he means conspicuousness. Emotional geniuses are not as conspicuous as their cognitive counterparts. Emotion is diffused in life like salt in water—too much conspicuousness may be even pathological. There are, however, cultural differences concerning this matter: Emotional geniuses in the West, Byron being a classic example, are much more conspicuous in their emotional presentations than are most traditional Chinese poets, whose emotional lives may approximate the proverbial miso soup, the excellence of which is judged by the extent to which it loses its bean pasty taste in the mellow blend (Sundararajan, 2004b). Thus, emotional creativity is much more embedded in culture than cognitive creativity: It makes little sense to consider the formula of Einstein as being particularly "Jewish," but it is meaningful to refer to the poetry of Tu Fu as being characteristically Chinese. For a closer examination of the culture and emotion interface, the interested reader may consult a cross-cultural study of theories of emotion (Averill & Sundararajan, 2006).

The everydayness of emotion may seem nondescript and commonplace enough to warrant the claim of universality espoused by many psychologists. On closer examination, however, life in the everyday reminds one of the proverbial island that rests on an infinite regress of ontological and epistemological turtles, which may differ from culture to culture. To illustrate this point, we have shown in this chapter how commonplace notions such as creativity imply different assumptions about the self and agency across cultures. We have also shown how the yardstick of judging a work to be creative differs across cultures, with the West privileging novelty and the East authenticity. Furthermore, our dimensional analysis suggests that cultural and individual differences in emotional creativity are both variations along certain universal dimensions.

This translation from cultural to individual differences is supported by empirical studies. The first line of evidence comes from cognitive psychology (Lambie & Marcel, 2002) which has delineated a difference in cognition attention—self-to-self versus self-to-world—that shapes the content and modality of emotions. The divide of internal versus external focus has also been found to have a neurological basis (Lane et al., 1997; Gusnard et al., 2001). The possibility of a direct translation from cultural to individual differences is further supported by experimental studies that replicate the hypothetical individualistic versus collectivistic differences in the lab (Gardner, Gabriel, & Lee, 1999). The application of ECI to differences in self-construals, independent versus interdependent, adds convergent evidence.

The pervasive influence of culture, however, does not necessarily spell social and historical determinism. Our model of creativity as inhabiting a blended space implies that creativity necessarily goes beyond, although not without due influence by, cultural orientations such as a novelty or authenticity focus. In the final analysis, the relationship between culture and creativity is dialectic. On the one hand, culture serves as the meme pool for creativity; on the other hand, the creative individual often breaks free of local cultures. To the extent that culture serves as meme pool for emotional creativity, the technique of method acting, where aspiring actors practice experiencing as well as expressing emotions, is pertinent. To a certain extent, we are all method actors. Our training is not formal, of course, but as children and later as adults, we learn from parents, teachers, peers, and even gossips (Rimé et al., 1998) how to be emotional in accordance to the beliefs and rules of society. Popular culture (e.g., as manifested in stories and songs) is also an important means of emotional training. To be creative, however, one needs to go beyond the popular and the stereotypical (for a Chinese perspective, see Sundararajan, 2004a).

A Chinese proverb says: "In addition to burying himself in volumes of books, a consummate scholar frees himself by traveling great distances and meeting various people" (cited in Smith & Smith, 2005, p. 9). This recommendation has been taken seriously by all writers and artists in the Chinese tradition, and apparently even today (see Smith & Smith, 2005), for a good reason. The Chinese proverb names two ways to break free of the local meme pool—extensive reading and traveling. The creative individual is like a whale that needs to swim in the ocean, not the local pond, of memes. The Chinese philosopher Chuang Tzu told the following parable:

> In Sung there was a man who was skilled at making a salve to prevent chapped hands, and generation after generation his family made a living by bleaching silk in water. A *traveler* heard about the salve and offered to buy the prescription for a hundred measures of gold. The man called everyone to a family council. "For generations we've been bleaching silk and we've never made more than a few measures of gold," he said. "Now, if we sell our secret, we can make a hundred measures in one morning. Let's let him have it!" The *traveler* got the salve and introduced it to the king of Wu, who was having trouble with the state of Yüeh. The king put the man in charge of his troops, and that winter they fought a naval battle with the men of Yüeh and gave them a bad beating. [Because the salve, by preventing the solders' hands from chapping, made it easier for them to handle their weapons.] A portion of the conquered territory was awarded to the man as a fief. The salve had the power to prevent chapped hands in either case; but one man used it to get a fief, while the other one never got beyond silk bleaching—because they used it in different ways. (Watson, 1964, pp. 28–29, italics added)

Although this story captures nicely the economic principle of creativity referred to by Sternberg as "buy low sell high" (Sternberg & Lubart, 1991), it also brings to light another important factor, namely that one who is an outsider to the local group stands a better chance of making creative use of its meme pool. Yet a total stranger would not do. The best position to be in, as predicted by our model of creativity as inhabiting the blended space of novelty–difference and authenticity–solidarity, would be as an outsider with understanding. Thus reading (to increase one's knowledge base and understanding) and traveling have to go hand-in-hand for the aspiring poet and artist, according to traditional Chinese poetics. We hope this chapter on emotional creativity across cultures serves a similar purpose for those who consider themselves travelers in the global village of the 21st century.

## CONCLUDING OBSERVATIONS

The intimate relation between emotions and culture is bidirectional: Culture helps determine emotions, as discussed earlier, and in turn, emotions help define a culture. For example, a person, an anthropologist, say, does not participate fully as a member of another culture until he or she is able to participate in its emotional life, no matter how well he or she understands the culture on an intellectual level. Yet that is not all: Even more than culture, emotions help define human nature. We are not referring here to emotions as biological givens; on the contrary, we assume that all but the simplest emotions (e.g., sudden fright) are social constructions. If that were not the case, emotional creativity would have limited applicability. Throughout history, people have tended to assume that what is fundamental to their own culture (emotions being a prime example), is fundamental to humans everywhere. One manifestation of this assumption has been the unfortunate treatment of people from other cultures as somehow less than human.

Even scholars who unequivocally reject ethnocentrism may adhere uncritically to emotional fundamentalism. We started this chapter with a quote from Zajonc (1998) to the effect that the idea of an emotional genius is absurd. One reason for this seeming absurdity is the notion that emotions are fundamental to human nature: Change the emotions, and you change human nature. That conclusion, we agree is a *reductio ad absurdum*. The solution, however, lies not in denying the possibility of emotional creativity; rather, the solution is to recognize that the emotions are as much products of our cultural as our biological heritage. What is needed is not a change in human nature, but a change in our view of that nature, as the subtitle of this volume suggests.

## REFERENCES

Arnheim, R. (1966). *Toward a psychology of art*. Berkeley: University of California Press.

Augustine. (1948). *Confessions* (J. G. Pilkington, Trans.). In J. W. Oates (Ed.), *Basic writings of Saint Augustine* (Vol. 1). New York: Random House.

Averill, J. R. (1974). An analysis of psychophysiological symbolism and its influence on theories of emotion. *Journal for the Theory of Social Behavior, 4*, 147–190.

Averill, J. R. (1999). Individual differences in emotional creativity: Structure and correlates. *Journal of Personality, 67*, 331–371.

Averill, J. R. (2001). The rhetoric of emotion, with a note on what makes great literature great. *Empirical Studies of the Arts, 19*, 5–26.

Averill, J. R. (2005). Emotions as mediators and as products of creative activity. In J. C. Kaufman & J. Baer (Eds.), *Creativity across domains: Faces of the muse* (pp. 225–243). Mahwah, NJ: Erlbaum.

Averill, J. R., Chon, K. K., & Hahn, D. W. (2001). Emotions and creativity, East and West. *Asian Journal of Social Psychology, 4*, 165–183.

Averill, J. R., & Nunley, E. P. (1992). *Voyages of the heart: Living an emotionally creative life*. New York: The Free Press.

Averill, J. R., & Sundararajan, L. (2005). Hope as rhetoric: Cultural narratives of wishing and coping. In J. Eliott (Ed.), *Interdisciplinary perspectives on hope* (pp. 133–165). New York: Nova Science.

Averill, J. R., & Sundararajan, L. (2006). Passion and *Qing*: Intellectual Histories of Emotion, West and East. In K. Pawlik & G. d'Ydewalle (Eds.), *Psychological concepts: An international historical perspective* (pp. 101–139). Hove, England: Psychology Press.

Averill, J. R., & Thomas-Knowles, C. (1991). Emotional creativity. In K. T. Strongman (Ed.), *International review of studies on emotion* (Vol. 1, pp. 269–299). London: Wiley.

Barnard, J. (1990). *Endymion*: "Pretty Paganism" and "Purgatory Blind." In H. de Almeida (Ed.), *Critical essays on John Keats* (pp. 47–67). Boston: G. K. Hall.

Blanchot, M. (1981). *The gaze of Orpheus and other literary essays* (L. Davis, Trans.). Barryton, NY: Station Hill.

Briggs, J. L. (1970). *Never in anger: Portrait of an Eskimo family*. Cambridge, MA: Harvard University Press.

Bryant, F. B. (1989). A four-factor model of perceived control: Avoiding, coping, obtaining, and savoring. *Journal of Personality, 57,* 773–797.

Bryant, F. B., & Veroff, J. (2007). *Savoring: A new model of positive experience.* Mahwah, NJ: Erlbaum.

Chagnon, N. A. (1992). *Yanomamö: The last days of Eden.* New York, NY: Harcourt Brace Jovanovich.

Clubbe, J., & Lovell, Jr., E. J. (1990). Keats the humanist. In H. de Almeida (Ed.), *Critical essays on John Keats* (pp. 129–142). Boston: G. K. Hall.

Costa, P. T., Jr., & McCrae, R. R. (1985). *The NEO Personality Inventory manual.* Odessa, FL: Psychological Assessment Resources.

Eoyang, E. C. (1993). *The transparent eye.* Honolulu: University of Hawaii.

Fish, S. (1980). *Is there a text in this class?* Cambridge, MA: Harvard University Press.

Florida, R. (2002). *The rise of the creative class.* New York: Basic Books.

Freeman, D. (1978). Keats's "To Autumn": Poetry as process and pattern. *Language and Style, 11,* 3–17.

Frijda, N. H., & Sundararajan, L. (in press). Emotion refinement: A theory inspired by Chinese poetics. *Perspectives on Psychological Science.*

Gardner, W. L., Gabriel, S., & Lee, A. Y. (1999). "I" value freedom, but "we" value relationships: Self-construal priming mirrors cultural differences in judgment. *Psychological Science, 10,* 321–326.

Gelernter, D. (1994). *The muse in the machine.* New York: Macmillan.

Giglio, N. J. (2002). *Difference in evaluating creativity based on the culture, social orientation, and political beliefs of the evaluator, and the relationship between traumatic experiences and artistic creative behavior.* Unpublished senior honors thesis, University of Massachusetts, Amherst.

Gusnard, D. A., Akbudak, E., Shulman, G. L., & Raichle, M. E. (2001). Medial prefrontal cortex and self-referential mental activity: Relation to a default mode of brain function. *Proceedings of the National Academy of Sciences, 98,* 4259–4264.

Gutbezahl, J., & Averill, J. R. (1996). Individual differences in emotional creativity as manifested in words and pictures. *Creativity Research Journal, 9,* 327–337.

Hall, D. L., & Ames, R. T. (1995). *Anticipating China: Thinking through the narratives of Chinese and Western culture.* Albany: State University of New York Press.

Ivcevic, Z., Brackett, M. A., & Mayer, J. D. (2007). Emotional intelligence and emotional creativity. *Journal of Personality, 75,* 199–235.

James, W. (1961). *Varieties of religious experience.* New York: Collier Books. (Original work published 1902)

Kucich, G. (2001). Keats and English poetry. In S. J. Wolfson (Ed.), *The Cambridge companion to Keats* (pp. 186–202). Cambridge, England: Cambridge University.

Lambie, J., & Marcel, A. (2002). Consciousness and emotion experience: A theoretical framework. *Psychological Review, 109,* 219–259.

Lane, R. D., Fink, G. R., Chau, P. M. L., & Dolan, R. J. (1997). Neural activation during selective attention to subjective emotional responses. *NeuroReport, 8,* 3969–3972.

Long, C. R., Seburn, M., Averill, J. R., & More, T. A. (2003). Solitude experiences: Varieties, settings, and individual differences. *Personality and Social Psychology Bulletin, 29,* 578–583.

Magai, C., & Haviland-Jones, J. (2002). *The hidden genius of emotion: Life span transformations of personality.* New York: Cambridge University Press.

Mellor, A. K. (2001). Keats and the complexities of gender. In S. J. Wolfson (Ed.), *The Cambridge companion to Keats* (pp. 214–229). Cambridge, England: Cambridge University.

Nussbaum, M. C. (1994). *The therapy of desire: Theory and practice in Hellenistic ethics.* Princeton, NJ: Princeton University Press.

Oatley, K. (1999). Fiction as cognitive and emotional simulation. *Review of General Psychology, 3,* 101–117.

Owen, S. (1992). *Readings in Chinese literary thought.* Cambridge, MA: Harvard University.

Rimé, B., Finkenauer, C., Luminet, O., Zech, E., & Philippot, P. (1998). Social sharing of emotion: New evidence and new questions. In W. Stroebe and M. Hewstone (Eds.), *European Review of Social Psychology* (Vol. 9, pp. 145–189). Chichester, England: Wiley.

Sheen, F. J. (1949). Introduction. In *The Confessions of Saint Augustine* (E. B. Pusey, Trans.) (pp. vii–xiv). New York: Random House.

Singelis, T. M., Triandis, H. C., Bhawuk, D. P. S., & Gelfand, M. J. (1995). Horizontal and vertical dimensions of collectivism: A theoretical and measurement refinement. *Cross-Cultural Research, 29,* 240–275.

Smith, J., & Smith, L. (2005). Interview with artist Zhenmin Ji. *Bulletin of Psychology and the Arts, 5,* 5–10.

Sternberg, R. J., & Lubart, T. I. (1991). An investment theory of creativity and its development. *Human Development, 34,* 1–31.

Stillinger, J. (2001). The "story" of Keats. In S. J. Wolfson (Ed.), *The Cambridge companion to Keats* (pp. 246–260). Cambridge, England: Cambridge University.

Sundararajan, L. (1998). Reveries of well-being in the Shih-p'in: From psychology to ontology. In A-T. Tymieniecka (Ed.), *Analecta Husserliana,* (Vol. LVI, pp. 57–70). Norwell, MA: Kluwer.

Sundararajan, L. (2001). Alexithymia and the reflexive self: Implications of congruence theory for treatment of the emotionally impaired. *The Humanistic Psychologist, 29,* 223–248.

Sundararajan, L. (2002a). The veil and veracity of passion in Chinese poetics. *Consciousness and Emotion, 3,* 197–228.

Sundararajan, L. (2002b). Religious awe: Potential contributions of negative theology to psychology, "positive" or otherwise. *Journal of Theoretical and Philosophical Psychology, 22*(2), 174–197.

Sundararajan, L. (2002c). Humanistic psychotherapy and the scientist-practitioner debate: An "embodied" perspective. *Journal of Humanistic Psychology, 42,* 34–47.

Sundararajan, L. (2004a). Twenty-four poetic moods: Poetry and personality in Chinese aesthetics. *Creativity Research Journal, 16,* 201–214.

Sundararajan, L. (2004b). Ssu-k'ung T'u's vision of ultimate reality: A quantum mechanical interpretation. *Ultimate Reality and Meaning, 27,* 254–264.

Sundararajan, L. (2005). Happiness donut: A Confucian critique of positive psychology. *Journal of Theoretical and Philosophical Psychology, 25,* 35–60.

Sundararajan, L. (in press). *Kong* (Emptiness): A Chinese Buddhist emotion and it's therapeutic implications. In J. D. Pappas, W. Smythe, & A. Baydala (Eds.), *Cultural healing and belief systems.* Calgary, AB, Canada: Detselig Enterprises.

Sundararajan, L., & Schubert, L. K. (2005). Verbal expressions of self and emotions: A taxonomy with implications for alexithymia and related disorders. In R. D. Ellis & N. Newton (Eds.), *Consciousness & emotion: Agency, conscious choice, and selective perception* (pp. 243–284). Amsterdam: John Benjamins.

Triandis, H. C. (1995). *Individualism and collectivism.* Boulder, CO: Westview Press.

Turner, M. (1996). *The literary mind/The origins of thought and language.* Oxford: Oxford University.

Vygotsky, L. S. (1978). *Mind in society: The development of higher psychological processes.* Cambridge, MA: Harvard University Press.

Watson, B. (1964). *Chuang Tzu/Basic writings.* New York: Columbia University Press.

Whitehead, A. N. (1933). *Adventures of ideas.* New York: Mentor Books.

Wordsworth, W. (1952). Preface to second edition of lyrical ballads. In B. Ghiselin (Ed.), *The creative process* (pp. 83–84). Berkeley: University of California Press. (Original work published 1805)

Yu, P. R. (1978). Ssu-k'ung T'u's *Shih-p'in*: poetic theory in poetic form. In Ronald C. Miao (Ed.), *Chinese poetry and poetics* (Vol. 1, pp. 81–103). San Francisco: Chinese Materials Center.

Zajonc, R. B. (1998). Emotions. In D. T. Gilbert, S. T. Fiske, & G. Lindzey, *Handbook of social psychology* (Vol. 1, pp. 591–632). Boston, MA: McGraw-Hill.

# 10

# A "KNOWLEDGE ECOLOGY" VIEW OF CREATIVITY: HOW INTEGRAL SCIENCE RECASTS COLLECTIVE CREATIVITY AS A BASIS OF LARGE-SCALE LEARNING

S. J. GOERNER

That which created us designed us to create back.

—Josephine S. May

Western civilization is reinventing itself. The traditional modern mechanistic, imperialistic approach to life is failing and a new, collaborative learning, "ecosystem" vision of humanity and Global Integral Civilization is rising to take its place (Goerner, 1999; Ray & Anderson, 2000). This process of rethinking and rebirth will eventually recast every endeavor from business, education and politics to health, spirituality and science. An integration of *individual creativity*, *collective creativity*, and more effective *collaborative learning* seems crucial to achieving this next stage of civilization. The Integral science which accompanies the emerging Integral society provides a new backdrop in which individual and collective creativity are seen as subsets of an ongoing, large-scale learning process that allows human "knowledge ecologies" (defined later) to achieve new stages of development. Here, "creativity" means both "effective novelty" (e.g., Cropley, 1999) and also a natural, individual, and collective process that generates the necessary diversity of thought needed to develop better ways for the collective societal "mind."

## CRUMBLING AND LEARNING

Imagine that, thanks to the advent of computers, a new scientific vision of "how the world works" is emerging from new abilities to gather, calculate, display, integrate, and identify unseen patterns in vast quantities of information. As the advent of Chaos, Complexity, and Gaia attests, this new stage of scientific ability, which I will call the *Integral Science*, is forcing many scientists to revise their traditional views on human nature and on how civilization works (see Robertson & Combs, 1995). In *After the Clockwork Universe* (Goerner, 1999), I show how the result is an empirically grounded, scientific understanding that is as different from the standard modern theories as medieval beliefs were from modern ones. The result is a kind of perceptual flip that mirrors that which took place some 400 years ago.

For example, before the last scientific revolution in the year 1500, all the best minds "knew" that the earth was at the center of the universe because great thinkers like Aristotle had said so and because even ordinary observers could see the sun circle overhead during the day and the stars do the same at night. Many People were so sure Aristotle's view of a perfect, unchanging universe with humanity at its center was indisputable that they extended its logic to every facet of society, portraying feudalism, for example, as the final perfect system of society and claiming that people were as immutably fixed in their social stations as the stars were fixed in their orbits (Burke, 1985). Yet, over the next 200 years a raft of questioning minds aided by improved scientific tools overturned the earth-centered view and cemented a new, more effective perception in its place. Now modern people view the once illustrious, earth-centered view as unimaginably primitive and naïve.

The same kind of social and scientific perceptual switch seems to be happening today, only this time it is orthodox, modern views on (a) neo-Darwinian evolution; (b) selfish, combative human nature; and (c) civilization as an empire-building project, that will be reversed—and it won't take 200 years to complete. (See chaps. 7 and 12, both this volume, on related issues.)

Ironically, the Integral scientific understanding (hereafter called the *Integral Framework*) sheds new light on these kinds of cultural and scientific gestalt switches. For example, in the emerging view, human beings are not the selfish, genetically predetermined beasts of neo-Darwinian theory, but a more emotionally complex, *collaborative learning species* whose primary survival strategy is to improve collective understanding and then change collective behavior in line with better views. Groups learn as a whole by pooling information, dialoguing and integrating information, testing out new premises by trying out new behaviors, forging a better map of "how the world works," and then using the improved map to navigate reality better than before. Societies, in turn, constitute a kind of "knowledge ecology," an information-processing ecosystem in which diverse types of individuals and subgroups play different roles in an interdependent, information- and resource-processing network. Furthermore, groups are driven to change their mental maps under exactly the kinds of conditions we now face; that is, when their current pattern of living is not working well and the troubles caused by shortfalls become massive and pressing. In this perspective, therefore, societies facing the kind of massive, interwoven crises before us now are undergoing an evolutionary learning test with a single, multiple-choice question: "learn or die?" As the last scientific revolution and the Enlightenment that followed demonstrate, surviving this test by learning successfully can produce a new stage of development with new powers, abilities, perspectives, and understandings.

We are facing the same "learn or die" challenge today. For example, as the growing literature on "sustainability" attests, an increasing number of observers now believe that Western civilization is broken along the lines shown in Figure 1. If one then asks why the richest democracy on earth supported by the most sophisticated science of all-time is barreling into social, economic, political, and environmental disaster, it quickly becomes obvious that the root problem lies not in a single arena, but in an interconnected web of institutional crises and failures. From education, medicine, and toxic food to energy, media, and democracy, every field is in trouble. As Francis Moore Lappé (Lappé & Lappé, 2003) notes, the common denominator among these breakdowns appears to be a set of late modern beliefs that, "are now creating a world that we do not want and do not think of as our own." Indeed, in the *State of the World 2004*, the World Watch Institute (2004) suggests that the magnitude of today's intertwined disasters threaten the life and livelihood of global civilization itself. Yet, the situation seems hopeless because a host of experts in using apparently irrefutable scientific theories (e.g., Friedman, 2002, with neoliberal economics and Dawkins, 1990, with neo-Darwinian evolution) say that the socioeconomic system we have is "the end of history" (Fukuyama, 1993), the way things have to be. Yet, since most of these beliefs are only a century or so old, the more likely explanation is a failure to think outside the usual institutional boxes in order to learn our way out of today's dangerous morass.

What does any of this have to do with creativity? Creativity—particularly mass "collective creativity"—is crucial to collective learning. As the Enlightenment demonstrates, developing a more effective map of how the world works is a group project that requires many minds with

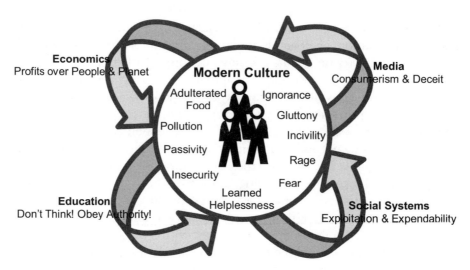

*Figure 10.1.* Toxic modern beliefs that are killing us.

diverse perspectives working not only to think outside the box of current orthodoxy, but also to find more effective solutions to pressing issues. At first, collective creativity may proceed piecemeal, in the form of individual creativity working across the spectrum of endeavors. Eventually, however, some individuals begin to realize that many fragments of solution connect to form a comprehensive new picture. Their creative contribution is integration, the fusing of diverse solutions into a single, commonsense framework. This framework then acts like a lens that shows everyday people a clear, coherent, new picture with simple connective logic that they can then use to rethink their lives. Together, the combination of individual solutions and a unifying framework can help determine whether the society survives and prospers at a more advanced stage of development or clings to outmoded ways until the system crumbles under its feet.

The good news is, in our case, that millions of people all over the world have been exercising individual creativity in every endeavor imaginable for decades already. Thanks to their efforts we are swimming in a sea of better alternatives that, taken together, constitute a better alternative to modern culture as a whole. Unfortunately, right now solutions that could save us lie about like so many disconnected dots in a child's drawing book. Until they come together in a coherent, pragmatically compelling, commonsense system, the troubles shown in Figure 10.1 will keep building until modern society collapses under the weight of problems caused largely by its own modes of living. After 15 years of traveling the world talking to reformers in fields from education and economics, to medicine and sustainability, I am now convinced that most of the solutions we need already exist. In

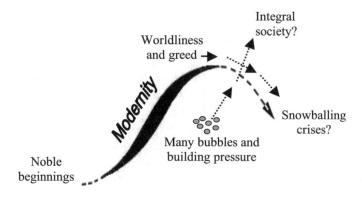

*Figure 10.2.* Crumbling and learning: The S-curve of great change.

my view, today's key challenge lies in the integration, clarification, and mobilization phase. The Integral scientific framework helps address this challenge by improving our understanding of the larger collaborative learning process, which collective creativity serves. In the rest of this article I attempt to clarify today's collaborative learning process by (a) illustrating the standard cycle of social learning, (b) outlining the basics of the Integral scientific view and how it changes our view of human nature and the nature of civilization, and (c) discussing how the new understanding of evolution gives new insights into how to fuse collective creativity into collective learning.

## COLLECTIVE CREATIVITY AND THE CYCLES OF CIVILIZATION

To understand collective learning, first realize that Western civilization has undergone massive societal change before this, always following a similar pattern (see Figure 10.2). In the Integral scientific view, this process represents both a learning struggle and a developmental passage from one system of societal organization to a new, more effective one. It unfolds roughly as follows. Over time, a once noble culture becomes corrupt and infirm. Individuals respond to this crisis by searching for better ways in the field that concerns them most: science, business, or education for some, spirituality (religion), or politics for others. Eventually, the combination of mounting frustration and a critical mass of better ways can fuse into a new cultural system organized around a new metaphor of life.

Yet, contrary to modern expectations, this process is not a "revolution" that starts over from scratch, but a learning process that must preserve important cultural lessons of the past while transcending current limitations and distortions. The result is a cultural metamorphosis much like that of a butterfly. In order to survive, the society looks within, slowly restructures essential systems and ideas, adds insights from new times, and then breaks out into a much-expanded way of being. Cherished life lessons of the past—about values, family, community, democracy, reason, free enterprise, spirituality, etc.—burst forth again, now at a whole new level of function and beauty. Like a snake shedding its skin, there is an adjustment to be made, but people lose the suffocating constraints of the old cocoon and the blinders of the old vision. Still, if the society fails to learn in a timely, effective manner, the old constraints cause suffering and, eventually, death.

Because the human brain uses metaphor to link ideas together, each new cultural system organizes itself a root metaphor about "how the world (and society) works" (Pepper, 1946). For example, Rome, built on the icon of "Empire," clung to its failing ways until its governmental infrastructure collapsed outright. Medieval European society rose from the rubble promising to build a healthier society around the metaphor of God's Design, a hidden, organizing, master plan underlying all things and largely beyond human ken. Rejecting the worldliness and greed that had killed Rome, medieval society (approximately 500–1500 AD) fused chivalry, common-cause, and faith into a powerful, practical, organic feudal whole that survived the barbarians and eventually moved out to conquer other parts of the world. Yet, by the late medieval period, chivalric lords and the faithful Catholic Church had become horribly corrupt and the medieval design began crumbling under the weight of its own worldliness and greed.

The cycle then repeated itself in the rise of modern society. From the Reformation to the Enlightenment (approximately 1550–1750), a growing number of thinkers began calling for a new, less corrupt social system based on freedom of religion, freedom of thought, and freedom of enterprise. These ideas and efforts arose first in the pressure cooker of Europe, but they made progress most easily in the freer air of the New World. Over time, generations of huddled masses made America the "Land of the Free" and the "Home of the Enlightenment Dream." Unfortunately, after a mere 200 years of modern culture, many believe that the Land of the Free is also now staggering under the weight of a new round of worldliness and greed. Now pressure is building again—and not just in America. A pandemic of 20th century calamities—world wars, depressions, genocide, plagues, and environmental ruin—started a worldwide rethinking that is now reaching critical mass. Modern corruption has become acute. Not only does environmental destruction, bio- and nuclear terrorism, and adulteration of food threaten human existence worldwide but also, the infrastructure of civilization itself is failing.

Omnipresent pressure is driving western civilization toward a new *Integral Society*, forming around the root metaphor of an "ecosystem" or "web." So, where modern, machine-age thinkers envisioned a clockwork universe of separable, streamlined parts, now integral thinkers are pointing out that we actually live in a web world, one planet in which all things are inseparably linked. Pondering the ecological nature of all things means that integral citizens realize the necessity of stewardship, meaning living in a way that sustains family, community, civilization, and environment even while making money. Socially, the integral age is working toward a networked-partnership culture linking a newly global civilization. Economically, it is bringing the Internet, the Information Age and, with them, a tremendous leap in collective, planetary intelligence.

Scanning current events through web-colored glasses makes it easy to see that today's collective creativity and learning is already well underway. Environmentalists started the ball rolling with the concept of ecology, meaning the web of life, but now the image has spread. It is now fashionable, for example, to reflect on how computers connect us, and how world civilization is becoming a single "global village." Web imagery is also seen in holistic alternatives in health, a global economy that binds us together, and a renewed commitment to community building.

Though less obvious, a similar rethinking is also sweeping through every field of science, from the Gaia Hypothesis, Complexity Theory and Systems Theory to Ecological Economics, Dynamic Evolution, and Quantum Mechanics. *Integral Science* represents the union of these and other "web-based" scientific insights, now fused into a logical, working whole.

Scanning the cycles of Western civilization, then, gives one a new appreciation for the pervasiveness and power of both individual and collective creativity. During great change, individuals in every endeavor from education and medicine to politics and science reinvent their fields in thousands of generative acts of "effective novelty." More curiously, somehow these shards of solution fit like pieces in a larger puzzle whose picture only becomes clear over time. The collective result is a better cultural roadmap that brings the society through critical times.

Seeing creativity in the context of societal learning cycles also reveals the importance of other factors, including widespread social pressure, naturally occurring diversity, artificially maintained orthodoxies, and abuse of power. Thus, at the end of each cycle of civilization—Roman, medieval, and modern—pressures caused by inadequacies in the dominant belief system appear to have fueled a wave of creativity in many facets of the society. Institutional failures popping up from government and environment to health and business push thousands, even millions of people in all walks of life to search for better ways, often at great risk to status, livelihood, and life. In the Reformation the agents of change were called heretics and in the Enlightenment they were called *philosophes*. Sociologists Paul Ray and Sherry Anderson (2000) call today's potential agents, "cultural creatives" (although they have yet to unite fully as an interest group). The authors show that they already constitute at least 25% of the adult U.S. population.

Some of these agents of cultural change become famous, but most do not. All of them make a difference, but timing, pressure, and context determine whether their effects are slow and cumulative or rapid and transformative. In normal times, most individual creativity has a slow, incremental effect, usually of limited scope. At such time, those who think outside the orthodox box seem crazy at best. However, during high pressure even small "effective novelties" can create a ripple effect whose energy, amplified by need and frustrations felt by others, gradually builds into great waves capable of sweeping away seemingly impregnable monoliths of power and belief. But, beware: High-pressure times are also like an accident waiting to happen. Because change happens rapidly with little time to integrate or test, there is no guarantee that the novelty that gets amplified will make things better. If the blocks to collaborative cultural learning remain too long, therefore, the society is more likely to die from taking an apparently promising but actually poisonous cure for the ills that ail it.

This well-known tendency to block effective collaborative learning until the eleventh hour is a dangerous potential feature of a societal system that has been around for about 5000 years, namely, the *imperialist* or *oligarchic* version of hierarchical society. In imperialist hierarchies, cadres of elites jockey for power. Achieving such power requires golden rationales that convince a critical mass of elites and peasants alike that those in power are the rightful rulers and that their system is necessary, inevitable, and/or good. To remain successful, however, the reigns of public power may end up being used to advance the power, position, and wealth of the cadre's supporters in the oligarchy. This invariably involves favoritism/cronyism and usually uses some form of "empire-building" (military, economic, political, etc.) that increases supporter wealth while passing most costs in blood, taxes, cruelty, and injustice to the broader society. Since the broader society eventually begins to notice the mismatch between those who benefit and those who are exploited, maintaining power also usually requires hiding detrimental information, suppressing alternative voices, manipulating emotions (e.g., hate and fear-mongering), and usurping cultural icons (e.g., flag-waving). These actions, of course, block effective novelty and thwart cultural learning.

In imperialist hierarchies, therefore, the root cause of social calamity is often the same. A culture of "worldliness and greed" insinuates itself around the machinery of public power and then tries to block all learning that does not serve oligarchic interests. Machiavelli's rationale, "the end justifies the means," can be used to justify maintaining cadre power using deceit, suppression, and manipulation of the society's core cherished icons. For example, where the original missionaries used the theory of God's Design to promote chivalry, community, and protection of the weak, late medieval clerics and aristocrats used God to justify multiple wars with effects including expansion of elite power while bleeding the lower- and middle-classes. Similarly, where the original Enlightenment philosophers saw free enterprise as "self-interest rightly understood" (i.e., that served community as well), today's oligarchs may end up destroying America's economic ecosystem by allowing unbridled, crony capitalism (think Enron and Haliburton) as "free enterprise." Here, it might seem that the "end" of corporate power justifies the "means" of policy favoritism and economic injustice.

Since we are still using imperialistic, hierarchical culture and concepts to run many major institutions, our collective learning is still limited by the whims and interests of the oligarchy and whichever cadre is in power. If Integral Society succeeds, however, this situation will change.

## HOW INTEGRAL SCIENCE CHANGES OUR PICTURE OF HUMANITY, CIVILIZATION AND EVOLUTION

Despite mounting pressure and a vast array of effective reforms, the integral age is barely a blip on modern civilization's radar screen. I suggest that we need three ingredients to unify and mobilize the movement to a Global Integral Civilization: (a) a unified, scientifically sound worldview that has (b) emotional relevance, direct links to deeply felt aspirations and also common sense; and (c) practical utility, enough practical detail to turn heartfelt dreams into well-functioning realities by providing effective solutions to pressing problems.

Integral science provides all three. It does so by changing our scientific picture of humanity, civilization, and evolution in a well-grounded and retrospectively obvious way. Today, as in the past, the science that emerges alongside a major cultural shift creates a kind of "perceptual flip." Like an optical illusion, the same observable facts are seen to fit a totally new arrangement. In the Integral synthesis, for example, the following ideas make perfect, empirical sense:

- *Science* centers itself on energy and interdependence, not matter and reductionism.
- *Evolution* is a self-organizing energy process, not random mutations acting on selfish genes.
- *Life* is a naturally integrated, mind–body, learning system, not an unfathomable accident.
- *Humanity* is a collaborative learning species, not a set of selfish, combative economic beasts.
- *Civilization* is a collaborative learning ecosystem that adapts by changing its collective mind, not an empire-building system seeking ever-new conquests.

## Science

Integral Science is merely a new stage of the same quest for the stable, empirical, mathematically precise understandings that have always marked science. The current picture of the facts, however, undergoes a radical rearrangement as a result of vastly improved scientific tools and a few small shifts in assumptions about energy, connectivity, and order. Thus, where modern mechanists centered their science on matter, simple causality, and a kind of pervasive randomness thought to riddle the world, Integral Science centers itself on energy, complex causality, and a growing awareness of pervasive order woven throughout the fabric of the cosmos (Goerner & Combs, 1998). Here we discover that there is order in chaos, structure within complexity, and a quiet set of universal patterns and principles that govern the evolution of all things in the cosmos, from the origins of matter to the latest cycles of civilizations.

## Evolution

Thanks to the new understandings of energy developed by Nobel laureate Ilya Prigogine (1980) and researchers such as Eric Chaisson of Tufts (2001), scientists are re-conceptualizing evolution as a universal, "self-organizing," energy flow process that gave rise to everything from matter and galaxies to life and civilization. Because energy follows certain universal patterns and principles that repeat at each level, the basic story of evolution can be seen in extremely simple systems. Figure 10.3 uses the process of boiling water to shows how the universal *S-curve cycle* of growth leads to increasing "intricacy" (complexity) and repeating, self-similar, "fractal" development in which new stages rise on top of old.

According to Self-Organization Theory (Jantsch, 1980; Prigogine, 1980), evolution has proceeded through a series of punctuated stages in which energy pressures drive a new level of organization into being by aligning smaller bits into a new pattern of flow. During the big bang, for instance, energy condensed into the first subatomic particles that, in turn, aligned into atoms and then molecules, gas, dust, and galaxies. Molten stars then accreted hot chunks called planets. On earth then, self-organizing chemical networks brewed in the fiery chemical soup, fused into the physical strands of life—metabolism, membranes, amino acids (Csanyi, 1989). Living cells, in turn, joined into complex, multicellular organisms that eventually grouped into families, herds, and societies. This process of forging increasingly complex wholes out of smaller bits that are still embedded in larger flows still continues today in the slow fusing of nation-states into a global civilization.

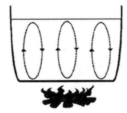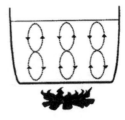

*Figure 10.3.* Self-organization and intricacy. Self-organization is an energy process in which pressure triggers diversity to create a new, faster flowing pattern of organization. For example, when you turn up the heat under a pot of water, the molecules begin colliding faster until they literally cannot go any faster. The system becomes unstable as heat (energy pressure) pushes for more speed. Little pockets of relatively hot molecules (naturally occurring diversity) begin to float upward because they are lighter and more buoyant than their surroundings and eventually one rises all the way to the top, loses its heat, and sinks back down, pulling other molecules in its wake. The entire region erupts into a coherent, circular motion that moves energy faster. If the fire is still on, the whole process repeats. The new circular motion pulls in energy, grows bigger, and accelerates to its limit. Diversity seeds a new, faster, more "intricate" pattern, something like a figure 8. "Intricate" patterns are faster and stronger because they link small, tight circles together.

## Life

In the integral view, "mind" and "body" are physically integrated because energy forms the basis for information, motion, and physical organization all at the same time. Thus, as mentioned, heat drove chemical dynamics to link into such bodily features as amino acids, cell membranes, metabolism, etc. Yet, the most significant difference between living and nonliving systems is that living cells search for food (i.e., a new energy source) by responding appropriately to incoming information about where food might be. For simple cells "information" comes in the form of an energy trail, a photon of light or a chemical gradient such as what we call "smell." Appropriate responses to energy-based information no doubt began accidentally, perhaps as a fortuitous forward movement after swallowing a photon of light. But, "functional" responses would have evolved rapidly because natural selection heavily favored every advance (Goerner & Combs, 1998).

Hence, energy makes it easy to see how mind and body—that is, information processing and appropriate bodily response—have been integrated physically from the first cell. Growth pressures (that is, getting bigger) then pushed mind–body systems to coevolve along standard patterns. Single-celled organisms process information alone, but multicellular organisms have specialist cells—such as lungs, heart, and legs—that must send signals to

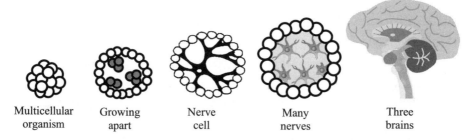

| Multicellular organism | Growing apart | Nerve cell | Many nerves | Three brains |

*Figure 10.4.* Growth pressure drives the development of nerves and brains.

each other to stay in sync. Cellular communication (chemical or electrical) works easily in small organisms because cells are either touching or in close proximity. But, as bodies got bigger, internal communication began to breakdown as cells began to grow apart. Because failure to communicate properly inside leads to death just as fast as failure to perceive what is going on outside, evolutionary pressure grew. Many organisms died out and others stopped growing. Yet, eventually, through some quirk of diversity, some organisms developed a new type of cell whose job was to maintain collaborative connection by carrying signals between distant groups. We call them nerves. (See Figure 10.4.)

The pattern then repeated. In simple forms of life, such as the giant sea slug, a single nerve cell suffices, but as organisms became bigger nerve cells multiplied. At some point, multiplying signals created a Tower of Babel. In some organisms the need for coordination drove a new kind of cell into being. Positioned atop crossroads with information pouring in from many directions, brain cells began responding to extremely subtle patterns in complex streams of information, eventually allowing their owners to recognize complex patterns and chose paths through complex contexts. The brain's ability to coordinate complex responses involving all parts of the body eventually brought life out of the ooze and into complex motion propelled with legs and fins. Freed from knee-jerk responses, animals with brains began to explore the world, learning new lessons that were stored, not in genes, but in the brain of the beholder, in neural circuits etched by experience. Storing lessons in the brain allowed organisms to learn faster and to learn without having to die. Mindlike behaviors also began to take the forms we associate with intelligence today—contexts, choices, and complex meaning.

Still, the brain did not become the sole arbiter of intelligence and controller of everything underneath. Instead, nature builds mind–body communities on a fractal principle of groups working within groups working within groups (Freeman, 1995). New levels of intelligence and organization stand on the shoulders of older levels that still operate within. Everything is connected; communication and commitment to common cause are crucial; and intelligence and empowerment are *distributed fractally* all the way down to the cellular level. Thus, information is processed and responses triggered at numerous stages and everything works on a *subsidiarity* principle similar to that used by the medieval church: Decisions are made at the lowest level possible. Without this kind of distributed intelligence and empowerment, life would respond too slowly to survive.

Increasing intelligence then moved to the herd level. Brains created a huge leap in intelligence but, when the individual who owned the brain died, the lessons it learned were lost. The next stage, therefore, grew from passing information and lessons between individuals and across generations using signaling and modeling. Animals began to congregate and communicate in families and herds because individuals survive better by working together as, for example, when a deer flicks its tail to signal the approach of a predator. Useful responses gleaned from years of experience were then passed to others and across generations by modeling and mimicking. This process created a kind of basic "cultural evolution" in which lessons life lessons accumulated in a kind of evolving, collective memory.

## Humanity

In human societies the process of pooling information and preserving collective memory blossomed into awesome new forms. We communicate by speaking and preserve lessons by writing. We collect information from billions of human beings over tremendous stretches of time. We build massive mental maps—called culture, worldviews, religious beliefs, and scientific theories—and we use them to navigate reality. We are, in short, the most powerful collaborative learning species on the planet. We are not swift of feet, sharp of tooth, or clever in niche finding. Rather, *as a collective*, we gather, digest, and apply information to help us survive and prosper like no other species. We bet our survival on flexibility and the pursuit of better pictures and, in the process, we gained dominance of the earth. To this day, our social health depends upon our ability to rethink our collective understandings in the face of our own growth pressures as well as lessons coming from an ever-changing world.

## Civilization

Similarly, in the integral view, civilization is an organic learning ecosystem, built of billions of cooperating, communicating, interdependent human beings that adapt by changing their collective mind. The new scientific lens helps us see that social evolution also follows in the same patterns and principles described earlier for energy-flow systems in general. For instance,

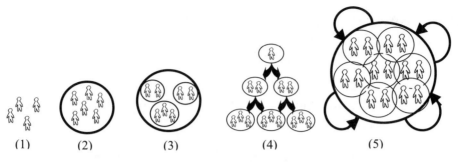

*Figure 10.5.* The major stages of socioeconomic development. 1 = Loose, foraging pods (~2 million BC). 2 = Organized hunting/gatherer bands (~100,000 BC). 3 = Partnership agrarian villages (~18,000 BC). 4 = War-based, hierarchical civilization (~3,000 BC). 5 = Networked learning civilization (emerging).

because societies are comprehensively connected, all their facets tend to coevolve in slow, sloshing S-curve steps, punctuated by periodic crescendos. Social structures, religious beliefs, political systems, and mainstay economic patterns are all entwined. Major new stages stand on the shoulders of older ones that recede, but never fully go away. In this way, human systems become more complex while at the same time preserving the main lessons of earlier ages. Over the eons, this developmental process has pushed human groups through four major organizational stages. It is now poised for a fifth. (See Figure 10.5.)

Every stage of development contains both lessons to preserve and immature habits to be outgrown. In today's case, we must preserve the lessons of hierarchical coordination and focused use of power, while outgrowing our addiction to war and eliminating beliefs such as "might makes right," "power means privilege," and "those on top should tell those on the bottom what to do." The necessary elements of the former and self-destructive aspects of the latter are easy to see.

Human hierarchy—say a king with an efficient bureaucracy—exists because it plays the same role as a brain and nervous system: It helps a large group act as a highly coordinated, farseeing, powerful whole. It even emerged for similar growth reasons. Once partnership villages reached about 350 people, they became easy pickings for raiders because no one was firmly in charge. One man making decisions and using an efficient chain of command allowed societies to mobilize rapidly for defense. Sitting atop a hierarchy with information flowing from all sides also helped elites build a broader picture. Ordinary people honored these leaders because kings such as the Egyptian Pharaohs served as godlike guardians who kept them safe from harm.

Yet, the culture that emerged with these warrior hierarchies was eventually turned to other ends. Hierarchies are designed to concentrate social, political, military, and monetary power in the hands of a few people so that they can *take care of the whole*. This is their evolutionary purpose. But, *imperialist* culture encourages people at the top to use that power to maintain their personal status, privilege, and power *at the expense of the whole*. If a new idea threatens the old power structure then it is suppressed. If oppressed groups want rights or workers want decent wages or voters want fair elections, then a vast network of money, muscle, spin, and insider connections goes to work. Yet, if elite supporters can get rich from favoritism or war, then community resources are poured into promoting it.

This process has been similar for 3,500 years. Unfortunately, over time such practices can destroy trust, dissolve community tissue, drain grassroots economies, distort information, and suppress learning. Because hierarchies are powerful, they can overrun smaller, less organized groups but, because societies become what they believe, imperialist/oligarchic cultures can invariably destroy themselves. As a result, imperialist civilization's reign is littered with glittering rises followed by calamitous falls. We are now facing its final collapse.

## IMPLICATIONS FOR OUR TIME

Global civilization is now aligning into a vast "society of mind," a budding planetary brain, but that mind is still clouded by imperialist beliefs. All over the world and in every field imaginable, cultural creatives have developed diverse and "effective novelties" useful to build the next stage of civilization. In the sustainability movement, for example, one sees improved alternative forms of energy (e.g., biodiesel, solar), new forms of construction (e.g., green building), innovative approaches to urban planning and business (e.g., Business Alliance for Local Living Economies), and forms of financing (e.g., micro-loans, grameen bank), as well as increasingly available forms of complementary and alternative healthcare (e.g., acupuncture, homeopathy, herbal medicine).

Yet, everywhere one looks, modern culture still pits people against people in war: right vs. left, black vs. white, men vs. women, Christianity vs. Islam, the powerful vs. the powerless. What we need now is a collaborative learning culture to release and harness the blocked energies and latent learning that already abounds. Achieving this will require major changes to both our organizational and cultural systems.

Organizationally, global civilization seems to be moving from hierarchy to *heterarchy*. Heterarchy is a blend of (a) hierarchy needed for coordination, speed, and concentration of public resources for public good and (b) sufficient *intricacy*, enough fine-grained, connective tissue to make sure energy, information and resources flow robustly to all corners of the whole. Culturally, we need to replace oligarchy with servant/guardian leadership. At the same

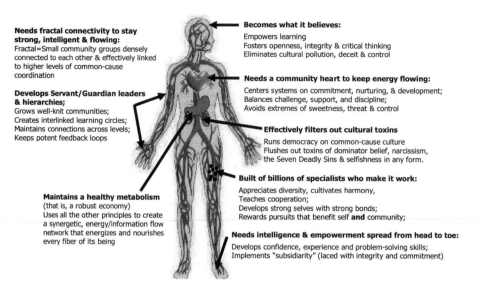

**Needs fractal connectivity to stay strong, intelligent & flowing:**
Fractal=Small community groups densely connected to each other & effectively linked to higher levels of common-cause coordination

**Develops Servant/Guardian leaders & hierarchies;**
Grows well-knit communities;
Creates interlinked learning circles;
Maintains connections across levels;
Keeps potent feedback loops

**Maintains a healthy metabolism**
(that is, a robust economy)
Uses all the other principles to create a synergetic, energy/information flow network that energizes and nourishes every fiber of its being

**Becomes what it believes:**
Empowers learning
Fosters openness, integrity & critical thinking
Eliminates cultural pollution, deceit & control

**Needs a community heart to keep energy flowing:**
Centers systems on commitment, nurturing, & development;
Balances challenge, support, and discipline;
Avoids extremes of sweetness, threat & control

**Effectively filters out cultural toxins**
Runs democracy on common-cause culture
Flushes out toxins of dominator belief, narcissism, the Seven Deadly Sins & selfishness in any form.

**Built of billions of specialists who make it work:**
Appreciates diversity, cultivates harmony,
Teaches cooperation;
Develops strong selves with strong bonds;
Rewards pursuits that benefit self **and** community;

**Needs intelligence & empowerment spread from head to toe:**
Develops confidence, experience and problem-solving skills;
Implements "subsidiarity" (laced with integrity and commitment)

*Figure 10.6.* Rules of an organic learning civilization.

time we must also develop a *knowledge ecology* mentality that (a) appreciates and develops diversity; (b) makes decisions at the lowest, most immediate level possible (subsidiarity); and (c) breeds commitment, integrity, and trust by emphasizing two-way bonds of contribution, fairness, and belonging. Figure 10.6 summarizes the proposed integral rules for building a healthy *Organic Learning Civilization*.

If you look closely, you will see that most of these rules support the original Enlightenment dream of democracy based on liberty, equality, fraternity, reason, and "self-interest rightly understood." These approaches, therefore, should also improve a civilization's collective creativity:

- *Democracy: The end goal of an intelligent society must be government of, by, and for all,* one that uses the commonwealth and the intelligence and perspectives of all its members to create a system that serves the whole, not merely oligarchic self-interest.
- *Liberty, Equality, and Fraternity*: Every member of the society must be free—intellectually, economically, politically, religiously, and even socially—because diversity is what leads to social improvements. "Equality" of rights and opportunities and the stronger position of "fraternity" including justice and fairness is necessary to keep natural diversity committed to serving the whole society as well as themselves.

- *"Self-interest rightly understood"*: As economists from Adam Smith to John Nash have documented (Kuhn & Nasar, 2002), societies and economies only work well when individuals do what is best for themselves *and* the society at the same time. How does one get from our current system of selfishness to a functional system of self *and* other? In the end, a human ecosystem is like a family in which everyone supports one another because they realize they are part of the same supportive, deeply connected whole. Proper familial treatment begets commitment, integrity, and reciprocation in kind.
- *Education:* Since social intelligence and speed depend on subsidiarity (that is, decisions being made at the lowest level possible), we need to prepare every child to be empowered, creative, problem-solving citizens, instead of insecure, obedient, patriotic drones.
- *Reason:* In most fields, developing more *effective* novelty requires a broad grounding in facts, a solid understanding of the patterns people have already discerned, a lot of personal, hands-on experience, open-mindedness, and a critical thinking mind. This is the essence of reason in its original Enlightenment sense. Integral Science adds awareness that reason too is a collective process, not merely an individual one.

To aid creativity, the integral framework suggests the following crucial elements:

### Appreciative Inquiry and Positive Psychology

In an Integral view, nature endows human beings with diverse talents and traits because the human ecosystems need all the diversity they can get. The best way to bring an individual's creativity forth is to help individuals appreciate themselves, that is, to see the positive contribution their unique traits bring to the larger ecosystem. Unlike traditional psychology, "appreciative inquiry" (Cooperrider & Whitney, 2000) encourages the positive exploration of individual differences in order to help everyone harness their intrinsic motivation in service to a larger society.

### Collaborative Culture and Skills

Human groups survive by building shared mental maps. Since forging better patterns of life is a collaborative affair we must also develop collaborative skills running from "please and thank you" and showing up on time, to the subtle skills of integrity, give-and-take, and dissent and assent "for the sake of the task."

## SUMMARY

Human beings survive by learning, that is, by communicating, pooling insights, preserving the lessons of the past, and creatively transcending current limits. Yet, sometimes we mistake our dominant mental map for the terrain of reality. Those societies that enforce old ways after they have proven faulty or inadequate eventually face regression or collapse. The best way to avoid the periodic calamities that pockmark human history is to instill an abiding commitment to collective creativity and ongoing learning at the heart of civilization. Integral principles can help us do just that.

## REFERENCES

Burke, J. (1985). *The day the universe changed.* Boston: Little, Brown.

Chaisson, E. (2001). *Cosmic evolution.* New York: Atlantic Monthly Press.

Cooperrider, D., & Whitney, D. (2000). *Collaborating for a change: Appreciative inquiry.* New York: Berrett-Koehler.

Cropley, A. J. (1999). Creativity and cognition: Producing effective novelty. *Roeper Review, 21,* 253–265.

Csanyi, V. (1989). *Evolutionary systems and society: A general theory of life, mind, and culture.* Durham, NC: Duke University Press.

Dawkins, R. (1990). *The selfish gene.* London: Oxford University Press.

Freeman, W. J. (1995). *Societies of brains.* Hillsdale, NJ: Erlbaum.

Friedman, M. (2002). *Capitalism and freedom: Fortieth anniversary edition.* Chicago, IL: University of Chicago Press.

Fukuyama, F. (1993). *The end of history and the last man.* New York: Perennial.

Goerner, S. (1999). *After the clockwork universe: The emerging science and culture of integral society.* Edinburgh, Scotland: Floris.

Goerner, S., & Combs, A. (1998). Consciousness as a self-organizing process: An ecological perspective. *BioSystems, 46,* 123–127.

Jantsch, E. (1980). *The self-organizing universe.* New York: Pergamon Press.

Kuhn, H. W., & Nasar, S. (Eds.). (2002). *The essential John Nash.* Princeton, NJ: Princeton University Press.

Lappé, F. M., & Lappé, A. (2003). *Hope's edge: The next diet for a small planet.* New York: Tarcher.

Pepper, S. (1946). *World hypotheses: Prolegomena to systematic philosophy and a complete survey of metaphysics.* Berkeley: University of California Press.

Prigogine, I. (1980). *From being to becoming*. New York: Freeman.

Ray, P., & Anderson, S. R. (2000). *The cultural creatives: How 50 million people are changing the world*. Three Rivers, MI: Three Rivers Press.

Robertson, R., & Combs, A. (Eds.). (1995). *Chaos theory in psychology and the life sciences*. Mahwah, NJ: Erlbaum.

World Watch Institute. (2004). *The state of the world 2004*. New York: Norton.

# 11

# CYBORGS, CYBERSPACE, CYBERSEXUALITY: THE EVOLUTION OF EVERYDAY CREATIVITY

FREDERICK DAVID ABRAHAM

> Improvisation is acceptance, in a single breath, of both transience and eternity.
>
> —S. Nachmanovich

Everyday creativity lives at the fractal interface of the individual and culture. Modern modes of communication, technology, and globalization are increasing the complexity of that interface and the pace of its evolution. It could prove important to evaluate the implications some trends and possibilities within that interface have for the evolution of human nature and everyday creativity.

Advances in science and technology drive much of this evolution. Some of these advances are in computer systems (cyberspace); some are in the hybridization of the human body with robotics (cyborgs); and some are in communications, artificial intelligence, cloning, genetic manipulation, stem cell ontogenetic manipulation (which can now make it possible to eliminate the male from reproductive participation), pharmaceutical and molecular manipulation, nanotechnology, and so on. This evolution of society and self influences the programs of emancipation suggested by post-modern social theory and philosophical hermeneutics. Cybersexuality—a philosophical, literary, and scientific genre inspired in part by new visions from science fiction—provides some prime examples.

This evolution also brings up some fundamental human motivations, for example, the desire to optimize knowledge and stability, to know our sources and destinies, our meaning, our ontological-existential quests. The quests for truth and for stability are at once two sides of the same tapestry, sometimes in conflict with each other, and sometimes synergistic, but always interactive, playing in the same conceptual attractors. Creativity lies in exploring where and how to weave within these fractal imbrications, and these involve tensions of stability and change. Creativity, or the generation of novelty (Montuori, Combs, & Richards, 2004) requires instability. How does the tension between the need for stability and instability resolve itself? Or put another way, why does stability require instability? (See chap. 8, this volume.)

One may wonder about the purpose of raising deep philosophical issues when addressing everyday creativity (the originality of everyday life). There are several reasons. One's basic existential position affects all aspects of our personality, and is represented in our everyday thinking more than we realize. Especially with respect to basic decision making, from selecting what tires to put on one's car, to what cable channel to turn to, what to write one's local paper or say on a local radio show about any issue from economics to global violence, to gay marriage, and so on, to planning one's day to minimize waste of time and energy, and to finding to what extent one is able to accept instability and risk, in order to make decisions, decisions that require creative elements. Furthermore, existential and religious ideas concern many people, and there are few areas in which independent thinking and creativity are more important, and are exercised with greater independence from social norms. One sees that the evolution of human nature interacts with ontological issues. In fact, everyday creativity itself may be an increasingly important factor in this evolution.

This chapter begins with commentary on this evolution of human nature within the context of a thread of literary and philosophical work that Jenny Wolmark (1999) calls *Cybersexualities*. The discussion begins with the relationships between life and information technology, turns back to whence human beings, through evolution, have come, and then ahead to postmodern envisioning of our potential future. In this context, I review human evolution to the present. The chapter goes on to consider potential changes in human nature based on trends in modern technology, and their implications for what it means to be human, and especially whether human freedoms for everyday creativity will be liberated or constrained.

*Cybersexualities* is the title of a book of readings edited and with commentary by Jenny Wolmark (1999). She subtitles the book "A reader on feminist theory, cyborgs and cyberspace." The topic arises from the confluence of postmodern cultural theory, feminist theory, and recent trends in science fiction and extrapolations from the fields related to artificial intelligence, which are largely due to advances in technology. That is, the gap between science fiction and reality seems to be shrinking due to advances in technology. There is much to consider.

Postmodern cultural theory arises, in turn, partly from the synthesis of Marxist theory, psychoanalytic theory, and existentialism (Poster, 1989). But at the same time, postmodern (and postanalytic, and hermeneutic) theory has challenged these and other traditional views in many ways. Consequently, each of these, Marxist, psychoanalytic, and existential theories, has undergone a transformation while being conflated into the whole. For example, Lacan's psychoanalytic concepts became more socially and less biologically founded. These confluences were heavily influenced, at least for Wolmark, by two principal texts, which found high favor in certain tech-savvy subpopulations: Donna Haraway's *A Manifesto for Cyborgs* (1985), and William Gibson's cyberpunk novel, *Neuromancer* (Gibson, 1984).

In Haraway's *Manifesto* (1985), Haraway says of the cyborg,

> A cyborg is a cybernetic organism, a hybrid of machine and organism, a creature of social reality as well as a creature of fiction. Social reality is . . . our most important political construction . . . The international women's movements have constructed 'women's experience', as well as uncovered or discovered this crucial collective object . . . Liberation rests on the construction of the consciousness, the imaginative apprehension of oppression, and so of possibility. The cyborg is a matter of fiction and lived experience that changes what counts as women's experience . . . This is a struggle over life and death, but the boundary between science fiction and social reality is an optical illusion. (p. 1)

Wolmark (1999) explains that the *Manifesto*

> employs the metaphor [of the cyborg] in order to argue, firstly, for a reconsideration of Marxist and feminist analyses of the social relations of science and technology which rely on a received model of domination and subordination and, secondly, for the development of an innovative socialist-feminist political strategy that is not dependent on totalizing theories and in which the formation of new and unexpected alliances and coalitions are prioritized. (p. 2)

In *Neuromancer*, Gibson (1984) states the following:

'The matrix has its roots in primitive arcade games,' said the voice-over, 'in early graphics programs and military experimentation with cranial jacks. . . . Cyberspace. A consensual hallucination experienced daily by billions of legitimate operators, in every nation, by children being taught mathematical concepts. . . . A graphic representation of data abstracted from the banks of every computer in the human system. Unthinkable complexity. Lines of light ranged in the nonspace of the mind, clusters and constellations of data. Like city lights, receding.' (p. 51)

Wolmark (1999), from an interview with Gibson, said that he

coined the term [cyberspace] to describe the 'consensual hallucination'. . . . 'Everyone I know who works with computers seems to develop a belief that there's some kind of actual space behind the screen, some-place that you can't see but you know is there.' (p. 3)

Wolmark continued as follows:

In my view, this is the real significance of the metaphors of the cyborg and cyberspace—not only did they embody the lived experience of information technology, but they also offered a means of reconceptualis-ing that experience in potentially non-hierarchical and non-binary terms. (p. 3)

Notice that these two metaphoric terms, *cyborg* and *cyberspace* emphasize nature and nurture. The cyborg emphasizes the innate nature, the biological foundations of beings. Cyberspace emphasizes the importance of environ-mental and learning contributions to being and becoming. The nature–nurture distinction is claimed mainly on the basis that the cyborg places a priority on replacing some of the biological aspects of being when human and machinery merge, while cyberspace changes the individual by replacing some of the environment with its virtual setting. This distinction is somewhat artificial. In the first place, nature and nurture never exist independently of each other. They interact and change in the process, a dynamical system. They do not exist independently of their mutual attractor, which one might call the abstraction of their dynamical process. In the second place, biological systems obviously can learn from their environment just as cyborgs do. And in the third place, cyberspace has its own nature, including fixed structural elements. Nonetheless, the nature–nurture, cyborg–cyberspace distinction can be useful.

# EXCURSUS ON THE EVOLUTION OF THE HOMINID BRAIN

Humans share the same basic anatomical plan, including that of the brain, which is found in all mammals (Livingston, 1967; Magoun, 1963) and even in amphibians and reptiles (Herrick, 1948, 1956; MacLean, 1958). Hominid evolution retains those basic features and overlays some important additions and elaborations. The first *Homidae*, *Australopithecus*, during the period of 5.5 to 7.7 million years ago (MYA), diverged from the *Panidae* which was facilitated by a rift and ecological isolation in East Africa (Coppens, 1982, 1996). The new ecological conditions favored the evolution of posture and locomotion, diet and dentition, culture and the use of tools, and encephalization and cortical reorganization. Endocasts of A. *afarensis* (species status remains unresolved) show an expansion of parietal cortex at the expense of primary visual cortex, at least by A. *africanus* at 3 to 4 MYA, suggesting shifts favoring intellectual capacity.

A. *africanus*, in fact, shows a small allometric increase in brain size (Holloway, 1996). Note that *allometry* measures the relationship between sizes of different body parts, showing if they have changed proportionately, or if one increases more rapidly than another. Of interest here is whether brain size increases more rapidly than body size, which Jerison (1973, 1991) has formalized as the encephalization quotient (EQ). For *Australopithecus*, this theory of cortical organization and increased brain size is denied by Tobias (1996) and others, but entertained as plausible by Coppens (1996).

Two to three MYA, further climatic changes took place in this region of eastern and southern Africa, with a concomitant rapid and dramatic evolution of hominids. Such rapid evolution usually requires geographic isolation and a relatively small gene pool, that is, a relatively small population (Gould & Eldridge, 1977). Here, the result was the appearance of *Homo* and two species of robust *Australopithecines*, of which the latter became extinct. *Homo* was more successful, and H. *habilis*, the first *Homo*, was, according to Coppens (1996), the "size of a chimpanzee, exceptionally intelligent, imaginative, inventive, creative, talkative, emotional, and social . . . and had a larger brain (640 cubic centimeters vs. 400 cubic centimeters for A. *africanus*), a more exclusive bipedalism, a new diet, and an improving culture" (pp. 108–109). (Cultural sophistication was usually witnessed by the nature of stone tools, in this case, the most crude, Oldovan, roundish with few faces. Regarding bipedalism, or upright stance, also see chap. 8, this volume.)

During the quarter million year reign of H. *habilis*, endocranial capacity increased considerably (up to about the 900 cc for entry-level H. *erectus*). Allometrically, these relative enlargements were even greater. In frontal and parietal areas of the cortex, there were increases in size and gyral details and in asymmetries. Especially, there was in a prominence at the position of Broca's area, well known for its importance in speech. Several factors suggest social communicative competence beyond any chimpanzee, according to Holloway (1996), including (a) the stronger communicative proclivities of yet higher primates; (b) the formation of a true *Homo*-like Broca's area in a small-brained hominid (*H. erectus*); (c) strong cortical asymmetry; and (d) the presence of stone tools all made to a standardized pattern. There is also greater venous cranial drainage, important for improvements in locomotion, cognition, spatio-temporal coordination, and increase in brain size. Thus while the change from chimpanzee to *A. africanus* was gradual, the evolution to *H. habilis* was rapid. It showed rapidly increasing brain size, organization, and the likelihood of speech in this upright early ancestor.

About 1.5 MYA, over a period of about a half million years, *H. erectus* appeared and migrated widely from East Africa to Africa, Europe, and the Far East. The Leakeys elucidated its unique Acheulian tool culture at the Olduvai Gorge in Tanzania (Leakey & Lewin, 1977). *H. erectus* was also the first to use fire. Beyond increase in brain size, there were other telling signs of sophistication, including (a) continued cortical lateralization, (b) reorganization of posterior parietal cortex for multimodal processing and for the integration important for natural selection via social pressures for increased communication, (c) visuospatial integration needed for tool use and hunting, and (d) memory of spatial location of self, others, and environment (Holloway, 1996). Increases in meningeal vascularization also support these postulated advances (Saban, 1996).

It should be noted that there was an earlier migration from Africa about 1.75–1.8 MYA by Dmanisi (Republic of Georgia) hominids, somewhat *habilis*-like but now tentatively designated as *H. erectus* (Dmanisi) by most anthropaleontologists. This early *H. erectus* was small, with smaller brain volume, had primitive Oldovan stone tools, but developed new stone tools (Balter & Gibbons, 2002; Gabounia, de Lumley, Vekua, Lordkipanidze, & de Lumley, 2002), and possessed empathy and speech (Meyer, Lordkipanidze, & Vekua, 2006). Prior to this finding, the later, more evolved *H. erectus* was assumed to be the first to migrate. This suggests more competence to the smaller brain than was previously appreciated, as well as also considerable evolutionary biological, cultural, and behavioral creativity.

Next, out of the radiation from Africa of *H. erectus*, there was apparently a gradual evolution of our *Neanderthal* ancestors, *Homo sapiens neandertalis* (500,000–120,000 years ago). There was a corresponding gradual increase of several skeletal features, in brain size and meningeal vascularization, and changes in tool culture. Coppens (1996) makes the point that there was more biological than technological evolution going on from *Homo erectus to Homo sapiens neandertalis*, based on a measure of the length of cutting edge per kilogram of stone tools. Yet subsequently, *Homo sapiens* showed greater technological evolution than biological. He conjectures, "It appears that 'instinct' was more important than knowledge during initial evolution, but that the volume of data to be learnt was becoming more important than 'instinct' 100 000 or 200 000 years ago" (p. 110). Here then was a significant shift in brain priorities. One may be alert for such shifts as the story continues.

The most dominant thrust of evolution of hominid brain seems to be on neocortex, which appears most responsible for cognitive development and control over the basic mammalian limbic-emotional system. However, there was also some evolution of the limbic system itself. The evidence is based on the comparison of living primates and their relationship to evolutionary history. Within the limbic system, the hippocampus, especially parts involved with memory and cognition are greater in humans than in apes. In the amygdala, the septum and cortico-basolateral parts increased relative to the centromedial nuclei. Thus "it can be concluded that in the limbic system, evolution tended to enhance those components related to pleasurable and enjoyable experience, while the components related to aggression and rage remained underdeveloped" (Eccles, 1989, p. 106). Stated more simply, processing of pleasure and positive emotions increased compared with aggression and negative emotions.

To approach this shift a different way, consider first that the basic limbic-emotional organization of the brain is ancient, evolutionarily speaking. And that, beyond this, the degree of expansion of neocortex with its layered and columnar organization and its multiple cortical sensory and motor mapping at first increased gradually. However, it potentially passed a critical bifurcation parameter, hastened by genetic isolation, yielding jumps in evolution called *punctuated equilibrium* (Gould & Eldridge, 1977). These developments changed the evolution of human culture from a more biological or instinctual basis to a more learning and cognitive basis. At the same time it increased the role of cooperation and altruism.

Why have I included this excursus on hominid evolution? Briefly, for at least four reasons: (a) Hominid evolution depended on the everyday acts of our predecessors, for example, flaking a stone tool in a new way was performed under the pressures of the need for food, clothing, and defense; (b) it produced a brain increasingly capable of information processing, creative thinking, and the everyday creativity we exhibit today; (c) this in turn fed back into the evolutionary process, a process which is itself inherently creative; and finally (d) it gives us a sense of our place in the universe, in history, as well as a clue to our destiny, and a sense of awe, hope, curiosity, and anxiety. (See chaps. 8 and 12, this volume, for other perspectives on brain and evolution.)

The potential for what one calls creativity, involving the innovative generation and combination of information, could increase, both for individuals and collaborative groups. Indeed, some of the evolutionary pressures generating biological evolution could now be turned to enhance cognitive functioning. Biology thus offers new potentialities for creativity, as well as placing limitations upon it. Turning to our present and possible futures, cybersexual discourse explores some of the possible next steps in the evolution of those potentialities and limitations, and the possibilities of their contribution toward emancipation—our personal freedom, social liberation, and creativity.

## EXCURSUS ON POSTMODERNISM AND GENDER

Postmodern literature, despite its great diversity, has a major theme of establishing the process of discourse, rather than one fixed ideology, as a means for providing a continuing flow of society toward equal opportunity and freedom from tyranny and discrimination. Wolmark's (1999) commentary, which sets the theme of her book, seems to place science fiction literature as sharing some communality with this postmodern discourse. (This is cryptically buried in her terms, "non-hierarchical and non-binary," quoted in the introduction earlier.)

Such communalities can coexist along with some differences. For example, Hutcheon (1989) has noted the communality of the theme of social liberation that is shared by feminist and postmodern agendas. This communality exists despite the differences that feminism has: an agenda and an ideology, while postmodernism avoids such ideologies in favor of establishing societies based on open forum discussion. (One might argue, perhaps, that postmodernism itself could be considered some sort of generic or nonspecific ideology, but it is at least an ongoing and flexible process that allows for alternative viewpoints toward complex and nonbinary resolutions.)

I think Wolmark inherits this language of nonhierarchical and nonbinary from French feminist, philosopher, playwright, and poet Hélène Cixous (Cixous & Clement, 1986). For Cixous, as for Jacques Derrida, oppositions (binaries) can be dangerous, a source of oppression. For those of us involved (and many who are not so involved) in dynamical systems theory (see chap. 2, this volume), we have a great deal of admiration for the Heraclitean model of oppositions as creating a process that produces a new dynamic of greater complexity (an *attractor*—a pattern of activity created by mutually interactive agents) that surpasses each component of the binary (Bird, 2003; Sabelli, 1989).

At the same time, we have to understand that the dynamical process may produce maladaptive or harmful cultural attractors, as well as desirable ones. This can happen especially when the relative strength of the influence of each part of the binary is asymmetrical. "A" clearly dominates "B." This is the meaning of Cixous's term, *hierarchical*. A healthy social process should minimize the asymmetry of the binary to produce possibilities beneficial to all participants in the binary opposition. It is probably no coincidence that creative thought also goes beyond polarities and favors the complex thinker who can tolerate ambiguity (Montuori, Combs, & Richards, 2004).

It is of interest that some of these hierarchical binaries include culture versus nature, form versus matter, speaking versus writing (to which I might add, conscious vs. unconscious, and logical vs. emotional). These binaries can also be related to the opposition between man and woman; and all have one element of the binary as privileged over the other (Sarup, 1993). Creative thought also supports individuals who are comparatively free of gender stereotyping, a tendency which has been called *androgynous* (Montuori, Combs, & Richards, 2004), and which is syntonic with the writings of Cixous:

> [Cixous] argues for the possibility of sustaining a bisexuality: not as a denial of sexual difference, but as a lived recognition of plurality, of the simultaneous presence of masculinity and femininity within an individual subject. For Cixous, writing is a privileged space for the exploration of such nonhierarchically arranged bisexuality. . . . she favors texts that are excessive in some ways, texts that undermine fixed categories. (Sarup, 1993, p. 111)

If two or more agents in a network are more symmetrically coupled, then instead of one winning over the other, a complex dialogue ensues, a linguistic strange attractor. (See also chap. 12, this volume, on gender and "partnership.")

Instabilities play a role, and these in turn can open the door to social change, a paradigm shift, a bifurcation, a "road not taken." Of note is creativity in the context of social constraints, resisted by great innovators. In my class on the psychology of creativity at Silliman University in the Philippines, one of our projects was to investigate politically oppressed people, principally, individuals incarcerated or executed by governments, such as Martin Luther King, Benigno Aquino, Nelson Mandela, Jesus, Galileo Galilei, Giordano Bruno, and others whose creativity is unquestionable, as well as their bravery. This project was prompted by Rollo May's (1975) discussion of Alexander Solzhenitsyn, and also his noting that creativity "involves potential conflict with those in power, be they gods or parents" (May, 1953, p. 159).

To permit such a dialogue surely requires Tillich's "Courage to Be" (Abraham, 1996; May, 1975; Tillich, 1952). It can also further enhance creativity.

# NOW, SOME INCURSIONS INTO CYBERSEXUALITY

The word *topoi* (Crucius, 1991) refers to a sense of community and home, of belonging and meaning from both the point of view of our place in the universe and from the point of view of our place within various contemporary communities in which we live. One source of such meaning in our lives derives from being a participant in the long evolutionary development of our species. This is the evolution of our cultures over numerous generations of *Homo sapiens*.

In science fiction, many authors examine disruptions in the role of reproduction and parenting. By doing so, they force a reexamination of those roles and their implications, both for understanding our human nature, and for providing guidance in the emancipation from some of the psychosocial aspects of those roles that have become repressive. This flexible understanding can help, as well, to nurture creativity in our own everyday lives, and this creativity is greatly needed. Science fiction is by no means the only literary genre dealing with these issues, yet the advances of modern science and technology has made many of these fictional disruptions a reality, giving them added urgency.

Mary Ann Doane (1999) states, "[for] some contemporary science-fiction writers—particularly feminist authors—technology makes possible the destabilization of sexual identity" (p. 20). As an example, she discusses *L'Ève Future* (*Tomorrow's Eve*) by Villiers de L'Isle-Adam (1886/1982) in which a mechanical Eve, a perfect (but sterile) replica of a woman, reveals the dissociation of sexual desire from reproductive capability and motherhood. *L'Eve* also exhibits the "compatibility of technology and desire," themes which have been repeated in much science fiction since then, for example, in the films *The Stepford Wives* (Forbes, 1975), *Alien* (Scott, 1979), *Aliens* (Cameron, 1986), and *Blade Runner* (Scott, 1982). According to Huyssen (1986), in Fritz Lang's film, *Metropolis* (1927) the replication engenders fear rather than desire: "The fears and perpetual anxieties emanating from ever more powerful machines are recast and reconstructed in terms of the male fear of female sexuality" (p. 36). Huyssen also claims that the ultimate technological fantasy is creation without the mother.

In some science fiction, empathy/sympathy for the other gender is, instead, promoted. In Ursula Le Guin's *Left Hand of Darkness* (1969) sexual partners undergo, occasional, sequential, synchronous, gender reversals. Thus knowledge and empathy with the partner is greatly enhanced compared to the human experience. Empathy can also be appreciated in the pair of *Alien(s)* movies in which there is stereotypic gender role reversal seen in the strength of the character of the female protagonist, and in the amplified violence of the human male giving "birth" to monstrous alien creatures.

As dynamical systems theory suggests, large changes occur when there is large instability. Doane's discussion of destabilization of sexual identity, the sexual transformations of Le Guin's *Left Hand of Darkness*, and "births" in the movie sequence, represent such instabilities. "Reproduction is diabolical in its nature, it makes something fundamental vacillate" (Baudrillard, 1981/1983). Doane (1999) pushes this concern one step further: "What makes it vacillate are the very concepts of identity, origin, and the original" (p. 31) a là Benjamin (1969).

In *Blade Runner*, the android, Rachel, tries to prove her authenticity as a human to Rick, a human. This raises the issue of the difference between an android and a human. What is the critical significance of the difference when so many human traits are encompassed in the android? The movie is based (with many themes left out), on Philip K. Dick's novel, *Do Androids Dream of Electric Sheep?* (1968) to which we now turn. This novel could be construed as skeptical of human nature, in presenting a society where religion is overly commercial, and pets overly important, and most importantly, when androids are becoming more exact replicas of humans, including their everyday creativity, as well as desires for self-preservation, love, etc. While the novel questions many aspects of human nature, it can also be taken as an affirmation of those human qualities, even when exported to machines.

Let us set the stage for the main theme. Androids are produced by the Rosen Association for export from a radioactive postapocalyptic earth (in year 2021), to be used as slaves in extraterrestrial colonies. Many of them do not like the bleak conditions there and sneak back to earth, where they are persona non grata, to be hunted and destroyed. There are psychological scales to discriminate between real humans and androids, employing psychophysiological measures (facial capillary and muscle reactions). Continual improvements of androids are made up to the current model, the Nexus-6, and a continual evolution of the sophistication of androids attempts to defeat the tests used to detect them. To complicate matters, the issue of false positive identification of a human as android could lead to the destruction of innocent humans. Some androids are running around northern California and Rick, the protagonist, a bounty hunter for the San Francisco Police Department, inherits the task of finding and destroying them. His predecessor had been shot by one of them, a very smart android. Rick heads for the Rosen factory in Seattle to check the adequacy of the test discriminating between some Nexus-6 androids and humans.

The critical difference, to which the test is directed, is that androids only lack one human trait, empathy. The test detects this by finding a "flattening of affect" to empathic questions. Schizophrenics fail the test, but are housed in mental institutions where they would not be tested for being android. If the android fails its test at Rosen Associates, the production of the Nexus-6 will have to be stopped. Rachel Rosen, presented as niece of the president of the corporation, meets Rick. The Rosen factory has an android group and a control group waiting for testing, but as Rick is about to start, Rachel says "Give me the test."

Rachel fails the test and Rick concludes she is android. Eldon (the president) counters that she is actually human, and the test has failed (yielded a false positive). He claims she has lived on a spaceship most of her life, the appropriate affect has not developed, and she has missed police checks by staying in the factory. She is one of the noninstitutionalized schizoids. Eldon charges that the results with Rachel show that the use of the tests is unethical, as they probably have made false identifications before. In addition, the Rosens had tried to influence Rick with the gift of a "real" owl. If the test is bad, he is temporarily out of bounty income until better tests can be created. Actually, like Rachel, the owl is a fake, being palmed off as real. The overimportance of pets, real and artificial, is an important subtheme of the book that also raises other important issues on the meaning of humanity, and humanity's desperation and contortion in a postapocalyptic world. Rachel refers to the owl as "it" and Rick gets suspicious. He puts the apparatus on her again and asks one question while referring to his briefcase as being made of human babyhide. She reacts emotionally to babyhide, which Rick's test detects and the test is exonerated. Rick says to Eldon, "Does she know?" (False memories in the past failed to defeat the test.) Eldon replies "No. We programmed her completely. But I think toward the end she suspected." Then, to Rachel he says "You guessed when he asked for one more try" (Dick, 1968, p. 59). Rachel nods affirmatively.

To summarize, not only is the meaning of being human tied up with the history and future of the human-android-pet relationships (where religion, incidentally, is yet another subtheme of the novel in the struggle between Buster Friendly, a mindless continual TV show and Mercerism, a mindless religion based on an over inflated empathy via mind-meld empathy boxes). There is also a lot of everyday creativity as the protagonists spar around these issues in this narrative, with the chance to expand their vision of human identity and possibility, in this nexus between everyday life and ontology. Indeed, these issues go beyond shedding gender or other specific features of body and psyche. Hiroshi Ishiguro, a leader in the use of cognitive, behavioral, and neuroscientific work in Japanese android science, also has stressed the implications of androids for understanding the meaning of human nature (Hornyak, 2006a, 2006b; Ishiguro, 2005).

Claudia Springer (1999) observes that much of cyberpunk popular literature, including comic books, has cyborgs or individuals entering the matrix (cyberspace) seeking to get rid of the "meat", the organic body, to become pure consciousness. That change should eliminate gender differences. She mentions Haraway's (1985) optimism that this situation makes the cyborg a "potentially liberating concept that could release women from their inequality under patriarchy" (Springer, 1999, p. 41).

However, Springer also points out that, paradoxically, gender becomes stereotyped and exaggerated in the popular cyberpunk literature, despite its transformation from organic to mechanical imagery, for example, with Robocop, and with Topo and Neon Rose in the comic book, *Cyberpunk* (Rockwell, 1989). Or as Anne Balsamo (1999) puts it, "Cyborg images reproduce limiting, not liberating, gender stereotypes" (p. 153).

However, Hans Moravec (1988), a leading robotics expert at Carnegie Mellon, envisions downloading human consciousness into computer networks. Here is disembodied consciousness. Lyotard (1988–1989) poses the related question, "Can thought go on without a body?" (p. 85). To which he replies that "the most complex and transcendent thought is made possible by the force of desire, and therefore 'thinking machines will have to be nourished not just on radiation but on irremediable gender difference'" (p. 85). Baudrillard (1988) "sees the collapse of clear boundaries between humans and machine as part of the same postmodern move toward uncertainty that characterizes the collapse of difference between genders: 'science has anticipated this panic-like situation of uncertainty by making a principle of it'" (p. 16).

Cyborgs epitomize the oppositions of immortality and death, an opposition that implies uncertainty, a theme Springer (1999) goes on to explore, saying "not even death is a certainty" (p. 52):

> William Gibson (e.g., 1984) and Rudy Rucker (1982, 1988) have made immortality a central theme in their books, raising questions about whether nonphysical existence—which can continue vastly longer than physical existence, or even indefinitely—constitutes life. Especially in Gibson's novels the question arises whether capitalism would allow only the extremely wealthy class to attain immortality. (p. 52)

Cyberpunk fiction is not without recognition of the paradoxes and dangers of immortality; "characters who become immortal are usually surrounded by a tragic aura of loneliness and decay." (p. 52)

> Even Topo, in the comic book *Cyberpunk*, rejects the idea of leaving his meat behind and remaining permanently in the Playing Field when he is offered the opportunity (Rockwell, 1990). What he rejects is immortality. But the comic book also reveals that the loss of his human body would be tantamount to death. Still, in this experience for Topo, something remains which may be relevant to evolution. [Nonetheless, Topo says,] 'after all, I'm only a data construct myself, now. Nothing equivocal about it. We live. We are forms of life, based on electrical

impulses. Instead of carbon or other physical matter, we are the next step.' (Springer, 1999, p. 52)

"These examples," according to Springer (1999), "show that cyborg imagery revolves around the opposition between creation and destruction of life, expressing ambivalence about the future of human existence" (p. 52).

Thus, we see (a) that human nature may come to share some qualities with (or adopt them from) the cyborg and our environment with cyberspace; (b) that this may call into question previously unchallenged assumptions about what makes us male or female, or, for that matter, even human, or alive, and science fiction can help us envision these questions; (c) that such advances in scientific technology offer us new chances for freedom and redefinition of who we are; while (d) at the same time manifesting a process of evolution, from hominid brain into the cyberworld, in which deliberate innovation and creativity play a growing role, where one (e) can manifest higher creative possibilities through a nonhierarchical nonbinary and multi-perspectival orientation. The resultant ability to produce higher level creative truth also fits well with phenomena in nonlinear dynamical systems and complexity theory—notably, bifurcation, emergence, and self-organization. Thus, (f) it behooves us to consider broader views of humanity and human nature as human nature becomes increasingly intertwined with the cyber-world of the future.


EPILOGUE

There have been opposite approaches in Western philosophy to the search for truth. One seeks absolute knowledge (the Eleatics, Plato, Confucius). The other seeks diversity and change (Heraclitus, Gorgias, Protagoras). These approaches have been involved in almost every philosophical inquiry from the Greek cosmologists to contemporary postmodern and gender-oriented literature. An early stage for this distinction was really set by "Heraclitus of Ephesus (c. 544–484 BC) [who] argued that the entire substance of the world is in a ceaseless process of change, while the Eleatic philosopher Parmenides (c. 540–470 BC) held to the opposing theory that the ultimate substance (Being) is unchanging and unchangeable, permanent" (Sahakian, 1968, p. 6).

Could the distinction be partly true and partly false, or even both fully true, as the Zen master says (Nhat Hanh, 1998). Many have tried to reconcile them. Xenophanes, made it an early attempt, viewing them as problems of being and becoming, and of rest and motion (Sahakian, 1968, p. 6). Due to my interest in nonlinear dynamics, I have viewed them as aspects of stability and instability (change).

In dynamical systems theory, patterns emerge in time and space from the interplay of one to many variables, each stretched out between oppositions, or ends of a continuum. When the interplay is complex, the patterns of potential interaction form "strange" or "chaotic" attractors (chap. 2, this volume), such as the well-known Lorenz attractor from a model of atmospheric activity (Lorenz, 1963; see Abraham, Abraham, & Shaw, 1990, pp. ii–71–75) or those conjectured for creativity (Abraham, 1996). While usually described by deterministic equations, the trajectories of these patterns are often characterized as uncertain. From a given starting position, trajectories can diverge from each other in the short term, due to the impossibility of getting infinite resolution in time and space for the starting coordinates. Thus, what is deterministic in theory may become predictable only in a probabilistic, not an exact, sense. Systems that possess this "strangeness" of "attractors" (pattern of activity to which a system settles down) exhibit two interesting characteristics: (a) this characteristic uncertainty, and more importantly, (b) large dramatic changes in their behavior with small changes in environmental or control conditions, a feature called "bifurcation."

Of great interest is the fact that change, from one stable attractor to another requires, initially, the creation of instability in the system. Hence, change, and creativity, whether in cosmological evolution, biological evolution, cognitive, or cultural evolution, and whether on a massive scale or in the details of "everyday" creativity, involve both uncertainty and instability (Abraham, 1996; Abraham et al., 1990; Sabelli, 2005).

Postmodernism and critical theory are heavily concerned with the relationship between emancipation and theory (Marçöl & Dennard, 2000; Poster, 1989) as follows:

> [Foucault, Derrida, and Lyotard claim] that the quest for certain truth and the claim of having attained it are the greater dangers. The logocentric philosophical tradition, with its strong assertions about truth, is complicit, for them, in the disasters and abominations of the 20th century Western history. On this difficult, even tragic issue of the relation of politics to truth, poststructuralists in general strive for a cosmopolitan position that makes every effort to recognize differences, even uncomfortable or disagreeable ones, and for a theory of truth that is wary of patriarchal and ethnocentric tendencies that hide behind a defense of reason as certain, closed, totalized. Above all, poststructuralists want to avoid forms of political oppression that are legitimized by resorts to reason, as this kind of legitimation has been, in their view, one of the paradoxical and lamentable developments of recent history. (Poster, 1989, p. 16)

Systems theory suggests that change and choice are dependent on having a certain amount of instability, of abandoning rigid ways of thinking and being. It thus, at least metaphorically, supports a Heraclitean and postmodern social theoretical view of the inherent importance of change, and thus, the ability to think flexibly and creatively and make choices. The discourse of change is an essential part of emancipation, of establishing an open society. But the essential source of change comes from within (self-organization, in systems language, including options for creative change). These conditions of flexibility best flourish with a great deal of personal courage in the face of our existential–cyborgian anxiety, and often despite conditions of inequality and oppression in a society. "Speaking of courage as the key to the interpretation of being-itself, one could say that this key, when it open the door to being, finds, at the same time, being and the negation of being and their unity" (Tillich, 1952, p. 32).

## REFERENCES

Abraham, F. D. (1996). The dynamics of creativity and the courage to be. In W. Sulis & A. Combs (Eds.), *Nonlinear dynamics in human behavior* (pp. 364–400). Singapore: World Scientific.

Abraham, F. D., Abraham, R. H., & Shaw, C. D. (1990). *A visual introduction to dynamical systems theory for psychology*. Santa Cruz, CA: Aerial.

Balsamo, A. (1999). Reading cyborgs writing feminism. In Wolmark, J. (Ed.), *Cybersexualities* (pp. 145–156). Edinburgh, Scotland: Edinburgh University Press.

Balter, M., & Gibbons, A. (2002). Were 'little people' the first to venture out of Africa? *Science, 297*, 26–27.

Baudrillard, J. (1983). *Simulations* (P. Foss, P. Patton, & P. Beitchman, Trans.). New York: Semiotest(e). (Original work published 1981)

Baudrillard, J. (1988). *Xerox and infinity.* (Agitac, Trans.). Paris: Touchepas.

Benjamin, W. (1969). *The work of art in the age of mechanical reproduction. Illuminations* (H. Zohn, Trans.). New York: Schocken.

Bird, R. J. (2003). *Chaos and life.* New York: Columbia University Press.

Cameron, J. (Director). (1986). *Aliens* [Motion picture]. United States: Twentieth Century Fox Film Corp.

Cixous, H., & Clément, C. (1986). Sorties. In B. Wing (Trans.), *The newly born woman* (p. 63). Manchester, England: Manchester University Press.

Coppens, Y. (1982). Qui fit quoi? Les plus anciennes industries préhistoriques et leurs artisans [Who did what? Oldest prehistoric industries and their craftsmen]. *Bulletin de la Société Préhistorique Française, 79*, 163–165.

Coppens, Y. (1996). Brain, locomotion, diet, and culture: How a primate, by chance, became a man. In J.-P. Changeux & J. Chavaillon (Eds.), *Origins of the human brain* (pp. 104–112). Oxford, England: Clarendon.

Crucius, T. W. (1991). *A teacher's introduction to philosophical hermeneutics*. Urbana, IL: National Council of Teachers of English.

Dick, P. K. (1968). *Do androids dream of electric sheep?* New York: Ballantine Books.

Doane, M. A. (1999). Technophilia. In Wolmark, J. (Ed.), *Cybersexualities* (pp. 20–33). Edinburgh, Scotland: Edinburgh University Press

Eccles, J. C. (1989). *Evolution of the brain: Creation of the self.* New York: Routledge.

Forbes, D. (Director). (1975). *The stepford wives* [Motion picture]. United States: Columbia Pictures.

Gabounia, L., de Lumley, M.-A., Vekua, A., Lordkipanidze, D., & de Lumley, H. (2002). Decouverte d'un nouvel hominide a Dmanissi (Transcaucasie, Georgie) [Discovery of a new hominid at Dmanisi (Transcaucasia, Georgia)]. *Comptes Rendus Palevol, 1*, 243–253.

Gibson, W. (1984). *Neuromancer.* New York: Ace.

Gould, S. J., & Eldridge, N. (1977). Punctuated equilibria. *Paleobiology, 3*, 115–151.

Haraway, D. (1985). A manifesto for cyborgs: Science, technology and socialist feminism in the 1980's. *Socialist Review, 80*, 65–107.

Herrick, C. J. (1948). *The brain of the tiger salamander.* Chicago: University of Chicago Press.

Herrick, C. J. (1956). *The evolution of human nature.* Austin: University of Texas Press.

Holloway, R. L. (1996). Toward a synthetic theory of human brain evolution. In J.-P. Changeux, & J. Chavaillon (Eds.), *Origins of the human brain* (pp. 42–54). Oxford, England: Clarendon.

Hornyak, T. (2006a, May). Android science. *Scientific American*, 32–34.

Hornyak, T. (2006b). *Loving the machine: The art and science of Japanese robots.* New York: Kodansha International.

Hutcheon, L. (1989). *The politics of postmodernism.* London: Methuen.

Huyssen, A. (1986). *After the great divide: Modernism, mass culture, postmodernism.* Bloomington: Indiana University.

Ishiguro, H. (2005). Interactive humanoids and androids as ideal interfaces for humans. *Proceedings of the 7th International Conference on Multimodal Interfaces, Italy, 137.* Retrieved March 19, 2007, from http://portal.acm.org/citation.cfm?doid=1088463.1088465

Jerison, H. J. (1973). *Evolution of the brain and intelligence.* New York: Academic Press.

Jerison, H. J. (1991). *Brain size and the evolution of mind.* Fifty-ninth James Arthur lecture on the evolution of the human brain. New York: American Museum of Natural History.

Lang, F. (Director). (1927). *Metropolis* [Motion picture]. Germany: Universum Film (UFA).

Leakey, R. E., & Lewin, R. (1977). *Origins.* New York: Dutton.

Le Guin, U. K. (1969). *The left hand of darkness.* New York: Walker.

Livingston, R. B. (1967). Introduction: Brain circuitry relating to complex behavior. In G. C. Quarton, T. Melnechuk, & F. O. Schmitt (Eds.), *The neurosciences: A study program* (pp. 499–515). New York: Rockefeller University Press.

Lorenz, E. N. (1963). Deterministic nonperiodic flow. *Journal of Atmospheric Sciences,* *20,* 130–141.

Lyotard, J.-F. (1988–1989). Can thought go on without a body? *Discourse, 11,* 74–87.

Magoun, H. (1963). *The waking brain* (2nd Ed.). Springfield, IL: Charles C Thomas.

MacLean, P. D. (1958). Contrasting functions of limbic and neocortical systems of the brain and their relevance to psychophysiological aspects of medicine. *American Journal of Medicine, 25,* 611–626.

Marçöl, G., & Dennard, L. F. (Eds.). (2000). *New sciences for public administration and policy: Connections and reflections.* Burke, VA: Chatelaine.

May, R. (1953). *Man's search for himself.* New York: Norton.

May, R. (1975). *The courage to create.* New York: Norton.

Meyer, M., Lordkipanidze, D., & Vekua, A. (2006). *Language and empathy in Homo erectus: Behaviors suggested by a modern spinal cord from Dmanisi, but not Nariokotome.* Paper presented at the annual meeting of the Paleoanthroplogy Society, San Juan, Puerto Rico.

Moravec, H. (1988). *Mind children: The future of robot and human intelligence.* Cambridge, MA: Harvard.

Montuori, A., Combs, A., & Richards, R. (2004). Creativity, consciousness, and the direction for human development. In D. Loye (Ed.), *The great adventure: Toward a fully human theory of evolution* (pp. 197–236). Albany: State University of New York Press.

Nachmanovich, S. (1990). *Free play: Improvisation in life and art.* Los Angeles: Tarcher.

Nhat Hanh, T. (1998). *The heart of the Buddha's teaching: Transforming suffering into peace, joy, and liberation.* Berkeley, CA: Parallax Press.

Poster, M. (1989). *Critical theory and poststructuralism.* Ithaca, NY: Cornell University Press.

Rockwell, S. (1989). *Cyberpunk. Book one, 1 (1).* Wheeling, WV: Innovative.

Rockwell, S. (1990). *Cyberpunk. Book two, 1 (1).* Wheeling, WV: Innovative.

Rucker, R. (1982). *Software.* New York: Avon Books.

Rucker, R. (1988). *Hardware.* New York: Avon Books.

Saban, R. (1996). Image of the human fossil brain: Endocranial casts and meningeal vessels in young and adult subjects. In J.-P. Changeux, & J. Chavaillon (Eds.), *Origins of the human brain* (pp. 11–38). Oxford, England: Clarendon.

Sabelli, H. C. (1989). *Union of opposites. A comprehensive theory of natural and human processes.* Lawrenceville, GA: Brunswick.

Sabelli, H. (2005). *Bios: A study of creation.* Singapore: World Scientific.

Sahakian, W. S. (1968). *History of philosophy.* New York: HarperCollins.

Sarup, M. (1993). *An introductory guide to post-structuralism and postmodernism* (2nd ed.). Athens: University of Georgia Press.

Scott, R. (Director). (1979). *Alien* [Motion picture]. United States: Twentieth Century Fox Film Corp.

Scott, R. (Director). (1982). *Blade runner* [Motion picture]. United States: Warner Bros. Pictures.

Springer, C. (1999). Pleasure of the interface. In Wolmark, J. (Ed.), *Cybersexualities* (pp. 34–54). Edinburgh, Scotland: Edinburgh University Press.

Tillich, P. (1952). *The courage to be.* New Haven, CT: Yale University Press.

Tobias, P. V. (1996). The brain of the first hominids. In J.-P. Changeux & J. Chavaillon (Eds.), *Origins of the human brain* (pp. 61–81). Oxford, England: Clarendon.

Villiers de L'Isle-Adam, A. (1982). *Tomorrow's eve* (R. M. Adams, Trans.). Champaign: University of Illinois Press. (Original work published 1886)

Wolmark, J. (1999). *Cybersexualities.* Edinburgh, Scotland: Edinburgh University Press.

# 12

## OUR GREAT CREATIVE CHALLENGE: RETHINKING HUMAN NATURE— AND RECREATING SOCIETY

RIANE EISLER

It is better to light a candle than curse the darkness.

—Eleanor Roosevelt

Our most urgent creative challenge is building a sustainable future. Not a utopia, not a perfect world. But a world where peace is more than just an interval between wars, where dire poverty, brutal oppression, insensitivity, cruelty, and despair are no longer "just the way things are."

For millennia, we humans have imagined a world of peace, beauty, and love. Sometimes we have imagined this world in an afterlife. But more and more in the last centuries we have imagined it here on Earth. Now, with terrorism, weapons proliferation, escalating wars and poverty, and human rights abuses, there is a new urgency to realizing our common wish for a sane, humane world.

All over the world, millions of people and thousands of grassroots organizations are using their creativity to help build cultures that are more equitable, sustainable, and peaceful. At the same time, the majority of people still doubt we are capable of leaving behind habits of cruelty, oppression, and violence.

Stories of an innately flawed humanity doomed by its "original sin" or by "evolutionary imperatives" persist. These narratives are obstacles to creating a better world, as we humans do not work for change that we think is impossible, change that goes against "human nature."

Clearly cruelty and insensitivity are human possibilities. But, as we see all around us, by the grace of evolution we also have enormous capacities for caring and consciousness. These capacities are integral to human nature—as is our enormous capacity for innovative, creative thought and action. Our enormous capacities for caring, consciousness, and creativity are our most distinctive human traits. And our most important creations are our cultures.

It is our cultural rather than natural environments that today most decisively affect what aspects of our large biological repertoire—our capacities for destructiveness, cruelty, and violence or for creativity, caring, and peace—will be inhibited or expressed. The cultures we create will largely determine whether we continue to kill one another and destroy nature's life-support systems, or build a humane and sustainable world.

Cultures that encourage "everyday creativity," which is to say, creativity in all people and in all areas (Richards, 1999) are essential at this critical time. We can choose to be passive. Or we can use our creativity to create cultures that are in synch with today's requirements for human survival and with the direction of evolution toward ever greater consciousness, caring, and creativity.

I realize that saying there is direction in evolution raises hackles. One objection is that direction implies a divine plan or intelligent design. Yet that is not the case: We do not have any way of knowing what lies behind evolution—and this is so whether we think evolution is directionless or not. Another objection is that to say there is direction implies that our species, as one of the latest to emerge, is the apex of evolution, and thus entitled to lord it over every other life form. This notion goes back to religious stories claiming that since "man" was created in God's image he is to have "dominion" over all other creatures (Genesis 1:16). I would instead argue that having unprecedented biological capacities means that it is our evolutionary responsibility to use these gifts in positive rather than negative ways—and that this is particularly urgent now that we possess technologies that impact all life on our planet.

Still, speaking of a direction in evolution is today considered a kind of scientific heresy. At best, it is acceptable to say there is evolutionary movement toward greater complexity and variability (e.g., Csikszentmihalyi, 1993). This is true. But, as Darwin himself noted, the movements in evolution go beyond complexity and variability to the emergence of needs, capacities, motivations, and possibilities of a different order than those present in earlier life forms (Loye, 2000, 2004).

If we look at biological evolution from this perspective, we see movement toward learning, consciousness, creativity, planning, and choice. We see an evolutionary movement toward the caring feelings, motivations, and behaviors we call love. And we see that, while they are not unique to us, these capacities are most highly developed in our species.

This chapter reexamines human nature and human culture from this larger perspective. The first part, Rethinking Human Nature, proposes a new perspective on evolution that takes into account the evolution of creativity, consciousness, and love. The second part, Recreating Society, then looks at a number of critical questions for our future: What kinds of cultures support or inhibit the expression of our human capacities for caring, consciousness, and creativity? Alternately, what kinds of cultures support our capacities for cruelty, insensitivity, and destructiveness? And what can help us create the conditions for our positive capacities to develop and flourish?

## RETHINKING HUMAN NATURE

In 1953, a teenage monkey called Imo attracted worldwide attention. Japanese scientists had been provisioning Imo's troupe of macaque monkeys with yams to lure them out of the dense forest where they lived. The troupe would come to the beach where the yams were placed, brush off the sand, and eat them. Until one day when something unexpected happened. On that day Imo dipped the yams in water and washed the sand off before eating.

Later, when scientists put out wheat grains on the beach, Imo was again creative. She discovered that wheat grains floated and sand grains sank. So she began to separate wheat grains from sand by dropping them in the water (Calvin, 1983; Kawai, 1965).

All this was amazing enough in itself. But perhaps even more amazing was that within a few years almost every monkey in Imo's troupe had chosen to adopt the new behaviors she initiated.

What happened with Imo and her troupe illustrates the movement in evolution toward creative innovations. It also illustrates how in the course of evolution behavior was increasingly transmitted through learning and conscious choice (e.g., Clark, 2002; de Waal, 2001).

This evolutionary movement toward creativity and conscious choice was not isolated. If we look more closely at the history of life on our planet, we see that there has also been evolutionary movement toward ever more extensive caring.

In contrast to most reptiles, birds and mammals care for their young. Some "higher" reptiles do care for their young, crocodiles for example. But most reptiles lay their eggs and leave them to hatch on their own. There are reptiles, such as the rainbow lizard, who eat their offspring instead of caring for them. If baby rainbow lizards do not run off and hide after they hatch, they risk becoming their parents' lunch.

It is only with the emergence of birds and then mammals—from mice, cats, and chipmunks to dogs, dolphins, and elephants—that we begin to see caring as a major evolutionary force. Both mothers and fathers care for their young in most bird species. Among mammals, the primary caregivers are mothers, although in some mammals, owl monkeys, marmosets, and tamarin monkeys, for example, caring goes beyond maternal to paternal caring (Eisler, 2000, 2007).

Among some species, this caring extends to other members of the group. Among elephants, for example, adults form a protective circle around the young when danger threatens. Empathy and caring by animals can even extend to other species, as illustrated by dolphins and dogs who save human lives (in the case of dogs, sometimes at the cost of their own).

Some mammals, such as elephants and primates, not only need prolonged physical care to survive, but they also seem to need love. Little chimpanzees have been observed to die of grief when their mothers are killed. And when human babies are denied love—like the children in Romanian and Chinese orphanages who just got rote physical attention—they too often die. And if they live, studies show that their brains do not fully develop, with lifelong adverse consequences (Perry, Pollard, Blakly, Baker, & Vigilante, 1995).

So the evolution from reptiles to mammals—and then to humans—brought with it a growing need, and capacity, for caring, as well as for learning, creativity, and conscious choice. This evolutionary movement was not linear. Nor did it mean that older evolutionary dynamics no longer were in play.

Like all other species, humans are still subject to the older laws of nature, including the laws of natural selection. But as Darwin and other major evolutionary theorists (e.g., Dobzhansky, 1968) recognized, human emergence—particularly the emergence of our powerful human brain—brought a new level of processes transcending earlier ones to bear.

## A Systems View of Evolution—and Human Nature

Our brain is not the only factor that distinguishes humans from other species. But it is an essential factor. (See also chaps. 8 & 11, this volume, on brain development.) The new structures of the human brain, in interaction with earlier ones, facilitate our empathic caring capabilities, allowing us to overrule more primitive short-sighted purely selfish ones. As Paul MacLean, Karl Pribram, and other brain scientists have shown (e.g., Miller, Galanter, & Pribram, 1986), the capacity for empathy and moral judgment is severely impaired when these new structures are injured.

With the emergence of our prefrontal cortex also came a vastly expanded capability for learning and problem solving. Many species are capable of these abilities, and use learning to modify their behavior. Anyone who has a dog knows this, and laboratory experiments on species ranging from pigeons and rats to cats and monkeys verify the capacity of many life forms for learning. There are other highly intelligent species, such as parrots, elephants, and apes. In some species we clearly see the cultural transmission of learned behavior, as illustrated by what happened after Imo washed her first yam. But with humans, learning, rather than genetic changes became the primary mechanism for both acquiring behaviors and changing them.

Humans learn all through life—both through experience (particularly when we are young) and instruction (from parents and other adults, schools, religious teaching, peer groups, and the mass media). Most important is that what we learn is typically not genetically determined. If what we learn were genetically determined, we would not see such variability of behaviors, beliefs, and customs in different cultures.

Another major evolutionary advancement was a growing capacity for consciousness, or awareness of what is happening within and around us. Damasio (1999) distinguishes between core consciousness (a rudimentary awareness) and extended consciousness (which includes consciousness of oneself in relation to others). Some degree of extended consciousness is found in other primates and a few other mammals. But it is most developed in humans, who are able not only to reflect on themselves but also on their environment, beliefs, and actions. This new level of consciousness is a necessary precursor for language, art, and other forms of symbolic expression and communication. It also makes possible our sense of past, present, and future, and thus our capacity to make long-range plans (Deacon, 1998; O'Manique, 2002).

Extended consciousness is a major factor in another key human capacity: the ability to make conscious choices. On some level, most living species make choices. But in many species these choices are primarily biologically preprogrammed and unconscious. Certainly humans make unconscious choices. But humans, more than any other species we know of, are capable of conscious choice—reflecting on various options and deciding what course to take. And in humans, choices are largely a function of learning.

Our capacities for innovation, planning, and creativity are other developments brought by the human brain. In combination with our erect posture, which freed our hands to craft ever more complex technological inventions, these abilities led to an enormous range of human-made material technologies as well as cultures.

And we do not just innovate and create in response to new environmental stimuli. We actively search and initiate change—and we do this almost from the moment we are born, as anyone who has watched a toddler actively explore and try to change its environment can attest. Loye (2000) notes scientific evidence that the human brain is active/initiating rather than just passive/responsive. We are able to plan ahead and to act on these plans. This is a crucial point. We are not just reactive, we are proactive. The capacity to imagine the future, plan for it, and work to create it, are key human characteristics.

Karl Pribram (Miller, Galanter, & Pribram, 1986) experimentally confirmed this "future sense orientation" in monkeys. When monkeys were asked to press different bars when they saw circles or stripes, Pribram found that the monkeys' brain waves registered intention and not just action. But, again, this future sense is most developed in humans.

Our more developed and complex human cortex connects to earlier brain and neural structures to guide behavior through what Pribram calls "feed forward" loops, moving from plans to actions, which affect both cognition and emotion (Miller, Galanter, & Pribram, 1986). When this feed forward connection is severed in lobotomized individuals, they manifest impaired capacity for self-regulation and long-range planning. They also exhibit loss of empathy and the capacity to care.

However, empathy, caring, consciousness, self-regulation, learning, and long-range planning are also often compromised in individuals who have not had brain injuries. As psychologists have long shown, abusive childhoods and even abuse in young adulthood may be equal to brain injury for its impact on a person's capacity for learning and for having healthy relationships later in life (e.g., Solomon & Siegel, 2003). In other words, empathy, caring, self-regulation, learning, and future planning are, up to a certain age in humans, dramatically affected by lack of love.

This takes us to the importance of caring and love on the human level—not only for survival but also for development—particularly for the full development of our capacities for caring, conscious choice, and creativity.


*The Evolution of Love and the Evolution of Human Nature*

Love is still generally considered something "soft" or "feminine." Hence, until recently, love has not been a subject of "hard" science.

Even today, caring in mainstream evolutionary theory is at best mentioned as a strategy that evolved to help pass on an individual's or related genes. But to fully understand the evolution of love, and its implications for the evolution of our species (and hence, for human nature), we need a new systems view of evolution.

As we have seen, love did not appear on the evolutionary stage full-blown. Indeed, the striving for oneness, for connection with another that we associate with love has ancient evolutionary roots. The impulse of complex molecules to come together led to the first self-maintaining and self-reproducing cells. Through symbiosis—an original form of partnership now being investigated by many biologists—these functionally simple cells joined to form the more complex bacteria that are the origins of all life. The observation of these behaviors in primordial life is the basis of biologist Margulis's (1981) theory of symbiogenesis and physicist Mae-Wan Ho's (1998) theory that the organism participates in evolution through a network driven more by linking than brutal struggle.

Of course, none of this was due to conscious emotions, much less love. But later in the history of life, this impulse for connection does assume a caring form. We already see some caring behaviors in worker ants, bees, and other social insects who bring food back to their group. But, as we have seen, it is not until the emergence of mammals and birds that we clearly begin to see the behaviors we associate with love.

Like all trends in evolution, the evolutionary movement in the direction of more caring and empathy was not a linear or straight-line movement. But it is a clearly observable progression. And with the appearance of humans, caring took an even greater leap, as without its further evolution, none of us would be here: Our species would not have emerged.

Consider how this may have happened. The development of the capacities that make us uniquely human required a much larger, more complex brain as well as a higher ratio of brain-size-to-body-size, both of which relate to intelligence. The average brain-mass-to-body-size ratio of mammals is ten to one hundred times larger than that of reptiles (Sagan, 1977). But the mammalian species with by far the largest brain-mass-to-body-size ratio is our species; it is dramatically larger than that of our closest primate relatives: the bonobos and chimpanzees. While the average chimpanzee brain weight is approximately 450 grams, the average human brain weight for the same body weight is approximately 1300 grams (Quartz & Sejnowski, 1997). This larger brain required a larger head. But the larger head cannot fit through the human birth canal. So the human brain continues to develop after birth—particularly during the first years, but also for many years after. During this time, unable to fend for themselves, human babies and children require extended caring to survive. This in turn requires that adults be motivated for caring through neurochemical rewards of pleasure (Quartz & Sejnowski, 1997).

Not only that but also rote physical care is not sufficient for children to fully develop their capacities. Indeed, children denied "positive bonds of affective attachment" may not even survive (Bradley, 2004, p. 105). So caring had to evolve further into the emotions and behaviors we call love.

In short, the emergence of our species would not have been possible without the emergence of caring and then love. This does not mean that the emergence of caring and love was the cause of the appearance of humanity on the evolutionary stage. But it was one of the prerequisites for our emergence in a synergistic evolutionary movement toward a new level of dynamics. The evolution of caring, culminating in love, was a prerequisite for our species' unique capacity for intelligence, symbolic thinking, learning, communication, consciousness, caring, planning, choice, and creativity.

At a 2001 meeting of the General Evolution Research Group (GERG), there was therefore a significant push for attention to the evolution of love, along with recognition of its past minimization. It was pointed out that in *The Descent of Man*, Darwin himself wrote of love 95 times, yet this has been generally ignored (see chap. 7, this volume).

But there is more. Once love came on the evolutionary stage, it developed its own dynamics, bringing new needs and motivations that surpassed earlier ones.

*Love as a New Evolutionary Dynamic*

The origins of our caring-rewarding neurochemistry can, of course, be explained in terms of gene transmission. Among others, neuroscientist Lucy Brown, anthropologist Helen Fisher, and psychologist Arthur Aron believe that the neural circuitry for adult male/female attachment evolved to motivate individuals to sustain affiliative connections long enough to complete species-specific parental duties (Fisher, 1994).

But romantic love and love for offspring are only two aspects of love. Once the capacity for loving appeared on the evolutionary scene, love became a motivation in many different kinds of relationships other than those connected with reproduction. As Brown put it, love seems to be a motivational drive in itself, not unlike the drive for food, sleep, and sex (L. Brown, personal communication, March 4, 2003).

Certainly our capacity to love and empathize is most often expressed with our own children and other family and community members. These are the people with whom we have bonded through ties of blood or friendship. But some people are extremely unloving to their own children—contradicting the claim that caring behaviors can be predicted by the degree to which we are genetically related (Dawkins, 1976). On the other hand, people who adopt children, including children of another race or country, often love and care for them well. And thousands of service organizations all over the globe are working to extend this empathic caring to humanity in general—even to people traditionally considered enemies.

These caring emotions and behaviors have no reproductive connection whatsoever. They can only be explained as a function of new motivational dynamics that arose in the course of evolution in addition to natural selection and sexual selection.

The striving for self-preservation and reproduction certainly plays an important part in human needs and motivations. But it cannot explain much that makes us uniquely human. It does not explain that we can care for total strangers—people utterly unknown and foreign to us, such as children hurt or orphaned by faraway wars. It cannot explain love for other species, as well as the idea at the core of the contemporary ecological movement—that all life is interconnected. Nor can it account for why our human yearning for a loving connection sometimes manifests itself in faith in a loving deity and in the belief that God is love (Eisler, 1995, 2007). This spiritual extension of love also transcends reductionist explanations of all human behaviors as ultimately motivated by a competitive struggle between genes.

All these are extensions of the evolutionary movement toward caring connection—and they are integral to human nature. Indeed, one could posit that they are even more so than our capacities for violence and insensitivity, as they are uniquely human. (See chap. 7, this volume, on love and Darwin's theory of evolution.)

As neuroscientists Quartz and Sejnowski (1997) note, recent brain studies support the conclusion that parent–child bonds, the pair bonds of romantic love, and the social bonds of friendship and caring may all have a common root, activating neurochemicals that make us feel good, some even perhaps resembling reward circuits for addictive behaviors (Keverne, Martensz, & Tuite, 1989; Young, Lim, Gingrich, & Insel, 2001). Love triggers neurochemical messages of well-being and pleasure—making us feel good both when we are loved and when we love others—be it a child, a lover, a parent, a friend, or a pet.

But loving bonds do more than that. As psychology, and more recently neuroscience, demonstrate, they are necessary for the full development of those capacities that are at the core of our humanity. In other words, love in our species is a new dynamic that must be taken into account not only for an understanding of human evolution but also for an understanding of how we can fully develop our unique human potentials.

### Love and Human Development

Reductionist evolutionary theories ignore that loving bonds are necessary for the full development of those capacities that are at the core of our humanity. Children who grow up in a loving and stimulating environment are able to develop their cognitive and emotional capacities much better than those who do not (e.g., Solomon & Siegel, 2003).

Even rats develop better if they are given loving care. A research team from McGill University reported that pups of attentive mothers who spent more time licking and nursing their young performed much better on tests for spatial learning and memory than pups whose mothers were less attentive. The favorable mental effects were obvious at a young age and endured through life. The study also found that affectionate care enhanced the rats' neural activity (Liu et al., 1997).

In a rat daycare component, the McGill study showed that the ill effects of lack of affection could be overcome by outside help. Pups born to low-care mothers and raised by high-care mothers were indistinguishable mentally from pups born to high-care mothers. They fared better in mazes, swam better, and had more synapses or neural connections in their brains than their less-loved classmates.

The difference in the physical and behavioral development of these animals was not a genetic one. It was due to experience—specifically, to the experience of affectionate caring or lack of caring (Liu et al., 1997). Researchers observed that even in nonhuman mammals loving care sets off a chain of biochemical and physical reactions that stimulate brain and memory development.

Liu et al. (1997) pointed out that these findings have important implications for children's development. They reinforce findings that children from emotionally and intellectually deprived homes benefit greatly from high-quality infant care programs. Lots of loving stimulates brain development, as does high-quality daycare. Beyond this, children who forge ahead, thrive, and become creative contributors often show enriched early environments or experiences, along with support and freedom to explore (Runco & Richards, 1997).

These kinds of findings also have important implications for evolutionary theory. They show that evolutionary theory must take into account the biologically rooted human need for caring, particularly during the early years, in any explanation of human development and human behavior, and what happens when it is both adequate and inadequate. Where limited emotional functioning becomes habitual, it influences the neurochemical development of the brain, and with this, as I will discuss later in Recreating Society, the kinds of traits and behaviors that become habitual.

The consequences of severe childhood abuse and effects on development have been well documented (Solomon & Siegel, 2003). In one tragic example during the 1980s, the Romanian dictator Nikolai Ceausescu prohibited family planning. He even required women to undergo monthly gynecological examinations to prove they were not avoiding pregnancy. As a result, thousands of children were abandoned by parents who could not, or would not, raise them. Many of these children ended up in orphanages staffed by overworked, underpaid attendants who had little time or inclination to give them emotional comfort and caring. Frequently these children died. And many of the survivors suffered lifelong developmental damage. This included survivors who were later adopted by compassionate families. Measures of frontal-occipital circumference (a measure of head size that in young children is a reasonable measure of brain size) were abnormally low in many of these orphans.

Other factors contributed to this tragedy, such as lack of proper nutrition and lack of stimulation of any kind; it was not just the absence of love. But, as neuroscientist Perry (2002) writes, "when early life neglect is characterized by decreased sensory input (e.g., relative poverty of words, touch and social interactions) there will be a similar effect on human brain growth as in other mammalian species" (pp. 92–93).

It takes years of skilled intervention and care to try to reverse some of this damage, plus massive investment of public resources (which are not often allocated to these ends), and intervention is not successful in every case. Ziegler (2002), a pioneering psychologist who developed such a residential care program, emphasized that the key to these efforts is love. So here again we see that the emergence of caring and then love was not only a prerequisite for the emergence of a human brain that supports our great capacity for learning, planning, consciousness, and creativity. Caring and love play a major role in the extent to which these human characteristics are developed and expressed or are stunted and distorted. Therefore, to support our fullest human development, we must create cultures that support our great human capacity for caring and love.

### Biology and Culture

The common argument about whether biology or culture shapes human behavior ignores what we know today. This is that human behavior—indeed, the development of the brain itself—is shaped by the interaction of biology and culture.

Which genetic potentials are or are not expressed is heavily influenced by our experiences. And our experiences, as detailed later in Recreating Society, are in turn heavily influenced by the kinds of cultures we grow up in.

I again want to note that the theory I am proposing is different from theories that attribute human traits, even cultures, to evolutionary imperatives programmed into our brains millennia ago. It is also different from the popular theory that all human behavior is motivated by "selfish genes" ruthlessly seeking to replicate themselves, or related genes (Dawkins, 1976).

As I have been developing, human motivations go beyond those of surviving and passing on genes. Clearly when Albert Schweitzer and Mother Teresa devoted their lives to caring for people on the other side of the world, or when Nelson Mandela reached out to the Whites who jailed him and oppressed his fellow Black Africans, their motivation went beyond helping people who share their genes. Behind their actions was our unique human capacity for loving, which, as we have seen, is reinforced by rewards of pleasure from neurochemicals in our brains.

Like love, creativity is also intrinsically motivated and self-reinforcing, with people in the throes of creativity—of writing, painting, or just thinking in innovative ways—often report feeling excitement, and well-being that spurs them on (Csikszentmihalyi, 1990; Deci & Ryan, 1975). Like love, it is tied to self-actualization, and is an important motivation in its own right.

Many human motivations—such as love, curiosity and explorativeness, search for meaning, striving for excellence and the realization of one's creative potentials—may or may not be helpful for surviving and passing on genes. The daring of explorers driven by curiosity has often led to their untimely demise. The motivation to excel can be so stressful that it adversely affects health and even survival; high achievers often have high blood pressure, heart attacks, and strokes.

In other words, and this is not a contradiction of the theory of natural selection, some human behavior is based on other motivations in addition to survival and reproduction. That human motivations extend way beyond survival and reproductive fitness has been demonstrated by psychologists (Deci & Ryan, 1975; Maslow, 1971). For example, Abraham Maslow's (1968, 1971) needs hierarchy begins with physiological needs, next followed by needs for safety and security. When these are met, social needs come next, including love and belongingness, followed by needs for esteem and recognition of contributions. All these are considered basic "deficiency needs." But once met, one can move on to "being" or growth needs, and most notably, self-actualization.

Maslow's model is largely consistent with my position, although I see the human need for love as even more basic, intertwined not only with survival but also with human development. But Maslow (1968, 1971) also saw love as a prerequisite to the truest emergence of creativity, which he showed is high in self-actualizing individuals. And like other psychologists, he recognized that whether we develop our capacities for caring, creativity, and altruism (which he also frequently found in "self-actualizers") largely depends on our life experiences.

In the next part of this chapter, we will see how these experiences are heavily shaped by the kinds of cultures or subcultures we grow up in. For now, I want to point out how conventional evolutionary theories themselves reflect a particular cultural perspective. They reflect, and reinforce, the cultural ranking of "hard" stereotypically masculine traits and behaviors such as conquest and domination, over "soft" stereotypically feminine ones such as love and empathy. And their battles between evolutionary opponents are basically a replay of old stories where "heroic" warriors slay their enemies before they can mate with the waiting princess.

In reality, of course, both men and women have the capacity for "soft" caring behaviors. For example, there is abundant evidence (Montuori, Combs, & Richards, 2004) that highly creative people tend to be relatively "androgynous." That is, they combine what are more stereotypically seen as female or male traits. They can be both assertive (male stereotype) and sensitive (female stereotype), whatever is needed.

Indeed, what is considered appropriate for men and women varies from culture to culture. In Africa, for instance, women are expected to carry heavy loads of fuel and water for miles, in sharp contrast with the Victorian ideal of weak, helpless "femininity." Similarly, the ideal for "masculinity" ranges all the way from the Hopi view that men should be peaceful and nonaggressive to the "macho" ideal that equates being a "real man" with violence and domination.

The norm for childcare also varies enormously from culture to culture. It ranges from habitual violence and strict controls, such as the swaddling that immobilizes infants and the beatings epitomized by adages such as "spare the rod and spoil the child," to the nonviolent, gentle, and responsive methods recommended by child development studies today. To understand human behavior, we have to look at what kinds of cultures people grow up in. We have to understand the interaction of biology and culture.

So, to answer the crucial question of whether our needs for love, meaning, and realization of our potentials are met, and whether our capacity for creating and loving is expressed or inhibited, we come to still another level of dynamics. We move from biological to cultural evolution.


## RECREATING SOCIETY

Just as we need a new conceptual framework for understanding biological evolution, we need a new conceptual framework to better understand the interaction between biology and culture.

Cultures consist of a society's inclusive beliefs, values, customs, and institutional infrastructure, from the family, education, and religion, to politics, economics, science, and technology. But conventional cultural categories such as Eastern/Western, religious/secular, rightist/leftist, technologically developed/undeveloped, and capitalist/communist do not fully describe cultures.

As a start, we need new categories that describe what kinds of human capacities, and what kinds of relations, a particular kind of culture supports. This is a critical question, particularly in our time when the direction of human culture is the most important factor in shaping our future and that of generations to come.

## A New Conceptual Framework for Society

As Robert Ornstein (1990) writes in *The Psychology of Consciousness*, every society's language provides categories that mold consciousness, and these categories play a major role in how we view the world—and how we live in it. For example, as long as people believed that monarchies were the only possibility, no other systems could be imagined.

Categories such as democracy, capitalism, socialism, and communism expanded the scope of our thinking. But none of these or other conventional social categories describe the totality of a culture.

Religious/secular and Eastern/Western only describe ideological and geographic differences. Right/left and liberal/conservative only describe political orientations. Industrial, preindustrial, and postindustrial describe levels of technological development. Capitalism and communism describe different economic systems. Democratic/authoritarian describes political systems in which there are, or are not, elections.

We need holistic categories that describe what configuration of beliefs and institutions—from the family, education, and religion, to politics and economics—support the expression of our capacities for caring, creativity, and consciousness, as well as relations based on mutual respect, accountability, and caring.

As I studied human societies cross-culturally and historically with this basic question in mind, I developed a new system of social classification. One distinguishing feature of this system is that it pays special attention to the primary human relations: the formative childhood relations and the relations between the male and female halves of humanity that, as we saw earlier in Rethinking Human Nature, are essential for human survival and development.

Using a multidisciplinary approach, I saw two basic social configurations. Since there were no names to describe them, I called them the *partnership model* and the *domination model*.

The partnership and domination models take into account the whole of a culture. They describe the core configuration of two contrasting ways of structuring institutions, beliefs, and relations that underlie cultures that are in other respects very different.

## The Partnership Model and the Domination Model

Hitler's Germany (a technologically advanced, Western, rightist society), Stalin's USSR (a secular leftist society), Khomeini's Iran (an Eastern religious society), and Idi Amin's Uganda (a tribalist society) were some of the most brutally violent and repressive societies of the 20th century. There are obvious differences between them. But they all share the core configuration of the domination model. They are all characterized by top-down rankings in the family and state or tribe maintained through physical, psychological, and economic control; the rigid ranking of the male half of humanity over the female half; and a high degree of culturally accepted abuse and violence—from child- and wife-beating to chronic warfare.

The partnership model has a different core configuration: a democratic and egalitarian structure in both the family and the state or tribe; equal partnership between women and men; and a low degree of built-in violence because it is not needed to maintain rigid rankings of domination. Cultures with this configuration can be tribal, such as the Teduray of the Philippines and the Mouso of China, agrarian, such as the Minagkabau of Sumatra, or industrial and postindustrial, like Sweden, Norway, and Finland. These are not ideal societies. But their beliefs and institutions support respect for human rights in families and the family of nations.

Nordic nations are democratic cultures where there are not huge gaps between haves and have-nots and a generally high living standard for all. They encourage gender equity in families and society. They pioneered the first peace studies programs, have laws prohibiting physical punishment of children, and have a strong men's movement disentangling "masculinity" from domination and violence.

Here women play important leadership roles and constitute approximately 40 percent of legislatures. As the status of women is higher, stereotypically feminine traits and activities such as nurturance, nonviolence, and caregiving are considered appropriate for men as well as women. These traits and activities are supported by fiscal policies such as funding for universal health care, elder care, child care allowances, and paid parental leave. The Nordic nations are leaders in environmental protection. And these nations are regularly at the top of the United Nations national quality of life charts—way ahead of nations that still orient closely to the domination model.

The tension between the domination and the partnership models reveals hidden patterns in our past and present. This tension goes way back into prehistory, shaping the course of cultural evolution and the possibilities for our future.

Based on data indicating that human cultural organization did not follow a single linear course, as assumed by many conventional accounts, the cultural transformation theory I introduced in *The Chalice and The Blade* (Eisler, 1987) proposes that from the beginning, cultures took a variety of paths—some orienting primarily to the domination model and others orienting more to the partnership model. This multilinear theory of cultural evolution (Eisler, 2004) is more congruent with a basic tenet of Darwinian and neo-Darwinian thinking: Behavior will adapt to a given environment within the limits of the organism's flexibility.

For most species, adaptation is largely unconscious, and unconscious motivations also shape human behaviors, and hence human cultures. But to the extent that our behaviors are conscious and intentional, adaptation can be influenced by our human creativity. Moreover, we humans are not just reactive. We can also be proactive. So for us, adaptation to different environments is not the whole story. We also have the capacity for conscious choice.

Certainly environmental factors seem to be implicated in the different cultures of our two closest primate relatives: the bonobos and the common chimpanzee. Until recent human incursions, the bonobos' forest habitat provided an abundant food supply. This more hospitable environment undoubtedly contributed to the fact that the bonobos' social organization is much more partnership-oriented than that of the chimpanzees: It is less rigidly hierarchical; it is not male-dominated; and it has a low degree of violence.

Likewise, archeological and mythical data suggest that partnership-oriented cultures developed in the more hospitable areas of the globe where the earliest agrarian cultures emerged. These data also suggest that dominator-oriented cultures developed in the more arid, inhospitable areas where nomadic herding cultures emerged (Eisler, 1987, 1995; Gimbutas, 1982; Mellaart, 1967; Min, 1995; Platon, 1966).

That domination or partnership cultures are likely to arise in different environments is further supported by cross-cultural data. To investigate the origins of male dominance, Sanday (1981) examined data from 156 societies distributed relatively equally among the six major world regions, spanning the period between 1750 BCE and the late 1960s. She found that societies in more fertile areas were more likely to be sexually egalitarian, whereas societies in less hospitable environments were more likely to be male-dominated. She also found that "sexually equal societies are less likely to be faced with periods of famine than sexually unequal societies" and that warfare was another source of stress found in male-dominant societies. That is, dominator-oriented cultures are more likely to be found in environments where the necessities of life are hard to come by, whereas more partnership-oriented cultures are more likely to be seen where life is not so harsh.

However, none of this is to say that the natural environment is the sole determining factor for the kind of culture we live in. As particular family structures, religions, education, art, law, economics, politics, and other institutional forms develop, they together become contributing elements of the human environment. As this occurs, a whole new set of dynamics comes into play.

Once cultural patterns become established, they acquire a life of their own. Cultures, like other living systems, seek to retain their basic patterns. In looking at cultural evolution, we therefore have to take into account principles of systems self-organization that maintain particular cultural patterns (Eisler, 2004).

Nonetheless, even the most entrenched systemic patterns can be altered during periods of disequilibrium. We therefore also have to take into account principles of discontinuity when systems disequilibrium makes possible foundational change (Gould, 1980; Prigogine & Stengers, 1984).

In *The Chalice and The Blade* (Eisler, 1987) and other publications (Eisler, 1995, 2000, 2004), I detail evidence indicating that during a chaotic time in prehistory a shift from a partnership to a dominator direction in the more fertile areas of the globe radically altered the course of civilization (e.g., Childe, 1958; Gimbutas, 1982; Min, 1995; Nash, 1978; Platon, 1966).

I also detail evidence showing over recorded history a periodic movement toward the partnership model countered by fierce resistance and periodic regressions. And I present evidence that in our time of mounting systems disequilibrium, the momentum toward partnership has been accelerating—offering the possibility of another fundamental cultural shift: this time from domination to partnership.

If we look at the past 300 years from this perspective, we see one organized social movement after another that challenges the entrenched traditions of domination. In the 18th century, the "rights of man" movement challenged the "divinely ordained right" of kings to rule over their "subjects." In the 19th century, the feminist movement challenged the "divinely ordained right" of men to rule over the women and children in the "castles" of their homes. In the 20th century, the civil rights, women's rights, indigenous rights, peace, and environmental movements continued and broadened the challenge to entrenched traditions of domination.

All these movements were driven by deep human needs and motivations for caring and equity. Yet they were (and are) also fiercely resisted. And their gains have periodically been pushed back by regressions to the domination model.

To better understand this resistance and regression, I moved my research into new areas. As I discuss next, this includes a new analysis of how the interaction of culture and biology affects the human brain.

## Changing Society and the Brain

I am now proposing that to prevent regressions and accelerate the shift to more equitable, peaceful, and sustainable world cultures, we have to look at how the experiences characteristic of dominator or partnership cultural environments interact with our brains. Specifically, I am proposing that to better understand and effectively change chronic violence, injustice, and oppression, we have to move beyond the idea that these are inevitable results of our evolutionary heritage and look at how the differences between the partnership model and the domination model not only influence beliefs and behaviors but also impact nothing less than the neurochemistry of our brains.

The human brain is remarkably flexible in youth and even in adulthood—so much so that it has been called a work in process. This flexibility allows us to learn and innovate but also has its drawbacks. If we grow up in dominator cultural environments, we tend to develop a brain neurochemistry that is adaptive to these environments.

Indeed, in rigid dominator settings people do not usually survive long if they fail to obey orders from above. They will be burned at the stake, stoned to death, shot, or at best imprisoned. Under such conditions, harsh parenting styles can be said to be adaptive, as they teach children to submit to those in control. But this adaptation requires that the human capacity for empathy and caring be dampened in certain respects, even suppressed, because it would interfere with these stressful styles of parenting. This is not to say parents who do this do not love their children, but their love becomes conflated with coercion, as is appropriate in social systems where relations are ultimately backed up by fear and force.

Scientists have found that traumatic or chronic stress is associated with high levels of the hormone cortisol and the neurotransmitter norepinephrine. Scientists have also found that these chemicals are in turn associated with problems of impulse regulation and propensity to violence. Conversely, free circulation of the neurotransmitters dopamine and serotonin, the hormones oxytocin and vasopressin, and other substances involved in bonding and empathy, is associated with the less stressful, nonviolent, caring experiences. These would be more characteristic of the partnership model (Eisler & Levine, 2002). Though there may be individual variations to any pattern, the key point is that there are central tendencies produced by different socialization processes.

Babies are born with a need for empathic love, validation, and stimulation. Yet to maintain a dominator culture, children have to be taught to conform as needed to top-down control. Patterns of childrearing are carried over into peer groups where even children not exposed to dominator parenting are socialized for dominator relations. And if mass socialization—religious or secular—presents these kinds of relations as normal, moral, and even fun, as many films, TV, and video games do, these patterns are further reinforced.

Such socialization can get in the way of meeting our most basic emotional needs, including love and caring, and also in the way of the inherent flexibility of the human brain, and potential for innovation, and risk taking. Montuori, Combs, and Richards (2004) identified "openness to experience" (rather than suppression or repression) and five other "core creative traits" which make awareness, questioning, and innovation more likely in an individual and, also, when possessed by groups of individuals, can further the ground-up evolution of healthy creative systems. These are independence of judgment, tolerance for ambiguity, from polarization to complex thinking, androgyny, and complexity of outlook. Each of these would be vastly more at home in a partnership than dominator cultural context. In fact, they could be a great threat to the stability of the latter.

## Dominator and Partnership Cultural Environments

Because the socialization required to impose and maintain relations of domination and submission is chronically stressful, people may develop neural and biochemical patterns that trigger fight-or-flight and/or dissociation responses that are not appropriate for the circumstances (e.g., Kaufman et al., 2004; Solomon & Siegel, 2003). When these patterns develop, they can constrict our capacity for independent thought and action, and lead to more abuse and conflict.

Economic conditions characteristic of dominator systems also contribute to chronic stress. Those on bottom are the most affected, but even those on top are affected by the domination system's self-perpetuating patterns of economic scarcity due to misdistribution of resources, lack of funding for health and education, diversion of resources into weaponry, and destruction of resources through environmental despoilation, war, and other forms of violence, all of which is stressful and creates a general sense of insecurity and fear (Eisler, 2007).

Studies also show that hierarchies of domination in themselves are a source of stress. This was dramatically shown by the "Whitehall Studies" of Marmot and his colleagues (Marmot, Rose, Shipley, & Hamilton, 1978) of the British civil service. Results showed that physical health, mental health, and even life spans, correlated significantly with an individual's position in the civil service hierarchy: Those higher up in the hierarchy were healthier and lived longer than those further down. These people were not poor. Yet these relatively well-off civil servants suffered disproportionately from stress-related problems—problems that the Whitehall study found derived from the domination hierarchy itself. And, as the Whitehall studies show, sooner or later this stress can lead to heart attacks, diabetes, depression, alcoholism, respiratory illness, or cancer.

By contrast, people in partnership-oriented companies, where workers have more autonomy and power to make decisions, report less stress and more job satisfaction. A more caring ethos manifests itself in supportive employee benefits—from good health care plans and parental leave to profit sharing and time off to engage in community service. This contributes to good health and longevity, and more highly motivated workers (Eisler, 2002, 2007). The brain effects would support greater flexibility, creativity, ability to work in teams, and other capacities that make for greater productivity and satisfaction. (Also see chap. 10, this volume, on new societal organization and interconnection.)

The socioeconomic gradient too is far less steep in partnership-oriented cultures. Even in the more partnership-oriented Nordic nations such as Sweden, Norway, and Finland there are statistical differences in health between higher and lower socioeconomic levels. But the average lifespan is 80 years. That these longer life spans are not due to genetics is shown by the fact that in the mid 19th century both adult and child death rates in these nations were very high. Nor are environmental conditions in these nations particularly conducive to health. The longer Nordic life spans are the more remarkable because of these nations' location in cold northern areas where winter days have long hours of darkness, known to lead to depression, health problems, and suicide. Yet despite this, the more caring policies of these nations generated a highly competent and educated workforce and social conditions that help people live longer. Not only that, the Nordic nations of Finland, Norway, Sweden, Denmark, and Iceland regularly rank at the top not only of the United Nations Quality of Life Indexes but also of the World Economic Forum's Global Competitiveness ratings (Trivers, 1975; World Economic Forum, 2005).

Of course, partnership-oriented cultures are not stress-free. And even in the strictest dominator cultural environments, some people maintain a countering independence and choose to relate in partnership ways. But to the extent that a significant part of the population is affected, negative patterns can be perpetuated from generation to generation.

On the basis of what we are learning from neuroscience, we can predict that many people living in dominator environments may develop habitual neurochemical patterns of fight-or-flight or dissociation to adapt to the constant stress inherent in rigid rankings backed up by fear and force. We can also predict that most people accustomed to accept human rights violations in their day-to-day relations are not likely to create institutions where human rights are respected. Nor are they likely to build the "culture of peace" envisioned by the United Nations, where children will be safe, loved, and supported in the full development of their human potentials.

Thus dominator environments tend to keep humanity stuck at a less advanced level of evolution, driven by deficiency rather than growth and actualization needs, interfering with the full development of qualities that make us fully human including, consciousness, creativity, empathy, and love.

## Using Our Creativity to Change the World

Like a vast engine of many parts, personal and cultural change are interactive processes. As we make changes in our personal attitudes, behaviors, and relationships, we empower ourselves as well as others to work for cultural change. If we make more room in our lives, and the lives of others, and in our immediate environments, for core creative traits such as independence of judgment, openness, tolerance for ambiguity, androgyny and valuing of complexity, it will affect all around us. It will help to free people. If we are more conscious and aware, we can sense the potential for "bifurcation," for when things can go one way or the other, personally and culturally, during periods of disequilibrium (Loye, 2004; Montuori, Combs, & Richards, 2004). And if we recognize the pivotal importance of empathy and caring in supporting our capacities for consciousness, creativity, and love, all this can build on itself.

Many people today are making great changes in the way they think and live, leaving behind traditions of domination and moving toward partnership (Eisler, 2004). But social policies have lagged way behind these changes in most world regions. Indeed, countering the powerful modern grassroots movement toward partnership, the last decades of the 20th century and the first decade of the 21st have been times of regression to the domination model.

And there are areas of blindness. While regressions to domination always include a return to an authoritarian, male-dominated, punitive family, sadly, many groups working for democracy and equality still view "women's rights" and "children's rights" as secondary, rather than as an integral part of the picture. Hence, we have lacked the solid foundations on which a better world can rest. The partnership and domination models provide important information for constructing more solid foundations. Unlike earlier social categories, this system of classification recognizes the central importance in molding attitudes and behaviors of the primary human relations.

It is in the formative childhood relations and the relations between the male and female halves of humanity that people first learn respect for human rights or acceptance of human rights violations as normal, inevitable, even moral. These relations also teach important lessons about violence. When children experience violence, or observe violence against their mothers, they learn it is acceptable to use force to impose one's will on others. If children grow up in families where females serve and males are served—and, as is the case in many world regions, where females get less food and healthcare—they learn to accept economic injustice in all spheres of life. Not only that, but we know from neuroscience that the brain's neural pathways are largely laid after birth—and that early experiences are key to whether neural patterns of flight-or-flight that perpetuate both intimate and international violence become habitual.

Many directions for potential change are detailed in Eisler (1995, 2004). One lever for fundamental change is stopping entrenched traditions of intimate violence—the violence against women and children that is the most prevalent human rights violation in the world, with yearly casualties far higher than the much more publicized violence from accidents, wars, and terrorism. This is why I cofounded the Spiritual Alliance to Stop Intimate Violence (SAIV—Web site: http://www.saiv.net), an international initiative of the Center for Partnership Studies to bring a strong—tragically still missing—moral voice to end violence against women and children. This critical assistance to women and children also helps to free males from dominator stereotypes of strength, denial of feelings, and constriction within their own gendered domain.

Another critical lever is changing the economic rules of the game to give visibility and value to the most foundational human work: the work of caring and caregiving still stereotypically considered "women's work." We need economic inventions that truly value this work; from measures of productivity that, unlike GNP, include the enormous economic contribution of the life-supporting activities performed in families, to economic inventions such as paid parental leave and social pensions for caregivers which give real support to this socially and economically essential work. Only if caring is given more value and visibility can we realistically expect the more caring policies so urgently needed in our world today.

Other levers for change include education for partnership rather than dominator parenting, mass media that model caring and sensitivity rather than violence and insensitivity, and curricula for schools and universities that point to the key importance in the evolution of human nature of traits, motivations, and behaviors such as empathy and caring, stereotypically viewed as "soft" or feminine—whether they reside in women or men.

We humans are the most creative life forms on our planet—amazing beings who can change not only our environments but also ourselves. With a clearer understanding of who we are, what we can be, and what is needed for a more sustainable, equitable, and peaceful global culture, we can use our enormous creativity to construct foundations for truly civilized cultures. As cocreators of our future, we can build cultures in synch with the direction of evolution toward the consciousness, caring, and creativity that are the true hallmarks of being human.

## REFERENCES

Bradley, R. T. (2004). Love, power, brain, mind, and agency. In D. Loye (Ed.), *The great adventure: Toward a fully human theory of evolution* (pp. 99–150). Albany, NY: SUNY Press.

Calvin, W. H. (1983). *The throwing Madonna: Essays on the brain*. New York: McGraw-Hill.

Childe, V. G. (1958). *The dawn of European civilization.* New York: Knopf.

Clark, M. E. (2002). *In search of human nature.* New York: Routledge.

Csikszentmihalyi, M. (1990). *Flow: The psychology of optimal experience.* New York: HarperCollins.

Csikszentmihalyi, M. (1993). *The evolving self.* New York: HarperCollins.

Damasio, A. (1999). *The feeling of what happens: Body and emotion in the making of consciousness.* New York: Harcourt.

Dawkins, R. (1976). *The selfish gene.* New York: Oxford University Press.

Deacon, T. W. (1998). *The symbolic species: The co-evolution of language and the brain.* New York: Norton.

Deci, E., & Ryan, R. (1975). *Intrinsic motivation and self-determination in human behavior.* Cambridge, MA: Perseus.

de Waal, F. (2001). *The ape and the sushi master.* New York: Basic Books.

Dobzhansky, T. (1968). Evolution VI: Evolution and behavior. In D. L. Sills (Ed.), *International encyclopedia of the social sciences* (Vol. 5, pp. 234–238). New York: Macmillan & Free Press.

Eisler, R. (1987). *The chalice and the blade.* New York: Harper & Row.

Eisler, R. (1995). *Sacred pleasure.* San Francisco: Harper Collins.

Eisler, R. (2000). *Tomorrow's children: A blueprint for partnership education in the 21st century.* Boulder, CO: Westview Press.

Eisler, R. (2002). *The power of partnership: Seven relationships that will change your life.* Novato, CA: New World Library.

Eisler, R. (2004). A multilinear theory of cultural evolution. In D. Loye (Ed.), *The great adventure: Toward a fully human theory of evolution* (pp. 67–98). Albany, NY: SUNY Press.

Eisler, R. (2007). *The real wealth of nations: Creating a caring economics.* San Francisco: Berrett-Koehler.

Eisler, R., & Levine, D. S. (2002). Nurture, nature, and caring: We are not prisoners of our genes. *Brain and Mind, 3*(1), 9–52.

Fisher, H. E. (1994). *Anatomy of love: The natural history of monogamy, adultery, and divorce.* New York: Ballantine.

Gimbutas, M. (1982). *The goddesses and gods of old Europe.* Berkeley: University of California Press.

Gould, S. J. (1980). *The panda's thumb.* New York: Norton.

Ho, M. W. (1998). Organism and psyche in a participatory universe. In D. Loye (Ed.), *The evolutionary outrider: The impact of the human agent on evolution: Essays in honour of Ervin Laszlo* (pp. 49–65). Westport, CT: Praeger Publishers.

Kaufman, J., Yang, B-Z., Douglas-Palumberi, H., Houshyar, S., Lipschitz, D., Krystal, J. H., et al. (2004). Social supports and serotonin transporter gene moderate depression in maltreated children. *Proceedings of the National Academy of Sciences, 101,* 17316–17321.

Kawai, M. (1965). Newly-acquired pre-cultural behavior of the natural troop of Japanese monkeys on Koshima Islet. *Primates, 6,* 1–30.

Keverne, E. B., Martensz, N., & Tuite, B. (1989). Beta-endorphin concentrations in CSF monkeys are influenced by grooming relationships. *Psychoneuroendoctrinology, 14,* 155–161.

Liu, D., Diorio, J., Tannenbaum, B., Caldji, C., Francis, D., Freedman, A., et al. (1997, September 12). Maternal care, hippocampal glucocorticoid receptors, and hypothalamic-pituitary-adrenal responses to stress. *Science, 277,* 1659–1662.

Loye, D. (2000). *Darwin's lost theory of love.* New York: iUniverse.com.

Loye, D. (Ed.). (2004). *The great adventure: Toward a fully human theory of evolution.* Albany, NY: SUNY Press.

Loye, D. (2004). What should it look like: Foundations and guidelines for building the fully human theory of evolution. In D. Loye (Ed.), *The great adventure: Toward a fully human theory of evolution* (pp. 252–268). Albany, NY: SUNY Press.

Margulis, L. (1981). *Symbiosis in cell evolution: Life and its environment on the early earth.* San Francisco: W. H. Freeman.

Marmot, M. G., Rose, G., Shipley, M., & Hamilton, P. J. (1978). Employment grade and coronary heart disease in British civil servants. *Journal of Epidemiological Community Health, 3,* 244–249.

Maslow, A. (1968). *Toward a psychology of being.* New York: Van Nostrand.

Maslow, A. (1971). *The farther reaches of human nature.* New York: Viking.

Mellaart, J. (1967). *Çatal Hüyük.* New York: McGraw-Hill.

Miller, G. A., Galanter, E., & Pribram, K. H. (1986). *Plans and the structure of behavior.* New York: Adams Bannister Cox.

Min, J. (Ed.). (1995). *The chalice and the blade in Chinese culture.* Beijing: China Social Sciences Publishing House.

Montuori, A., Combs, A., & Richards, R. (2004). Creativity, consciousness, and the direction for human development. In D. Loye (Ed.), *The great adventure: Toward a fully human theory of evolution* (pp. 197–236). Albany, NY: SUNY Press.

Nash, J. (1978). The Aztecs and the ideology of male dominance, *Signs, 4,* 349–362.

O'Manique, J. (2002). *The origins of justice: The evolution of morality, human rights, and low.* Philadelphia: University of Pennsylvania Press.

Ornstein, R. (1990). *The psychology of consciousness.* New York: Penguin.

Perry, B. D. (2002). Childhood experience and the expression of genetic potential: What childhood neglect tells us about nature and nurture. *Brain and Mind, 3*(1), 79–100.

Perry, B. D., Pollard, R. A., Blakley, T. A., Baker, W. L., & Vigilante, D. (1995). Childhood trauma, the neurobiology of adaptation, and "use-dependent" development of the brain: How "states" become "traits." *Infant Mental Health Journal, 16*, 271–291.

Platon, N. (1966). *Crete*. Geneva, Switzerland: Nagel Publishers.

Prigogine, I., & Stengers, I. (1984). *Order out of chaos*. New York: Bantam Books.

Quartz, S., & Sejnowski, T. J. (1997). The neural basis of cognitive development: A constructivist manifesto. *Behavioral and Brain Sciences, 20*, 527–596.

Richards, R. (1999). Everyday creativity. In M. A. Runco & S. R. Pritzker (Eds.), *Encyclopedia of creativity* (Vol. 1, pp. 683–687). San Diego, CA: Academic Press.

Runco, M. A., & Richards, R. (Eds.). (1997). *Eminent creativity, everyday creativity, and health*. Stamford, CT: Ablex Publishing.

Sagan, C. (1977). *The dragons of Eden: Speculations on the evolution of human intelligence*. New York: Ballantine Books.

Sanday, P. R. (1981). *Female power and male dominance: On the origins of sexual inequality*. Cambridge, England: Cambridge University Press.

Solomon, M. F., & Siegel, D. J. (2003). *Healing trauma: Attachment, mind, body, and brain*. New York: Norton.

Trivers, R. (1975). *United Nations human development reports*. New York: Oxford University Press.

World Economic Forum. (2005). *The global competitiveness rankings*. Retrieved March 15, 2007, from http://www.weforum.org/site/homepublic.nsf/Content/ NORDIC+COUNTRIES+LEAD+THE+WAY+IN+THE+WORLD+ ECONOMIC+FORUM%E2%80%99S+2004+COMPETITIVENESS+ RANKINGS

Young, L., Lim, M. M., Gingrich, B., & Insel, T. R. (2001). Cellular mechanisms of social attachment. *Hormones and Behavior, 40*, 133–138.

Ziegler, D. (2002). *Traumatic experience and the brain*. Phoenix, AZ: Acacia.

# III

## INTEGRATION AND CONCLUSIONS

# 13

# TWELVE POTENTIAL BENEFITS OF LIVING MORE CREATIVELY

RUTH RICHARDS

> I have listened. And I have looked with open eyes. I have poured my soul into the world, seeking the unknown within the known. And I sing out loud in amazement.
>
> —Rabindranath Tagore

This final chapter addresses 12 beneficial features, or characteristics, that may describe us if we are functioning more creatively. These are not to be taken as the 12 "main" or "flagship" features that describe everyday creativity. Furthermore, although each characteristic is embodied to varying extents in the preceding chapters, together they represent only one possible thematic integration of the material in *Everyday Creativity and New Views of Human Nature*. They do, however, reflect some major concerns of the contributors, and so are considered here along with the author's own additional comments and linkages to other literature. Beyond this, the 12 characteristics do not reflect, as one colleague joked, a 12-step program for recovery from lowered creativity! One, however, could do worse. These 12 features highlight important concerns in creative functioning and development, for both individuals and groups, and are presented here to help us think about them.

## TWELVE POTENTIAL BENEFITS OF LIVING MORE CREATIVELY

The 12 features are listed and defined in Table 13.1, and each is discussed subsequently. Do note that, although all 12 characteristics are

TABLE 13.1
Twelve Potential Benefits of Living More Creatively:
"When I'm Creative I Am . . ."

| Characteristic | Selected features |
|---|---|
| 1. Dynamic | Process-oriented, seeing change, and knowing oneself as process and part of a larger and evolving system. |
| 2. Conscious | Aware of and attentive to present experience, with attention to self (thoughts, feelings, actions, intentions, memories, imaginings), and environs (including creative opportunities) as per one's focus. |
| 3. Healthy | Following a lifestyle that helps engender sound and sustainable physical and psychological functioning, and internal balance and harmony, with active participation in life and creative coping with adversity. |
| 4. Nondefensive | Staying alert to unconscious, conscious, and environmental forces that can restrict our inner awareness, and working to limit these. |
| 5. Open | Welcoming new experience without, and unconscious material within; aware, intuitive, sensitive, bypassing preconceptions. |
| 6. Integrating | Functioning across multiple sensory modalities and states of consciousness; multiperspectival, enjoying complexity, integrating toward simplicity; aware of how much we miss in consensual reality. |
| 7. Observing actively | Whether physically passive or active, engaging in conscious, active mental participation as audience or observer; in dialogue with the observed, goal-related at times, and open to demands of the new. |
| 8. Caring | Guided by values and concerns rooted in love, compassion, and greater realms of meaning; aware of our interconnection and unity. |
| 9. Collaborative | Working with others toward broader goals, resolving conflicts, honoring uniqueness as part of a larger picture we cocreate. |
| 10. Androgynous | Bridging false dichotomies (e.g., both sensitive and assertive, intuitive and logical, gentle and strong); staying open to as yet unknown further possible ties for living beings, beyond stereotypes and societal limits. |
| 11. Developing | Aware that our personal development and species evolution (e.g., biological, psychological, cultural, biotechnological, spiritual) is ongoing; can be in part conscious; will involve us together as well as separately, and can contribute to a larger, dynamic picture of change and betterment which can persist across multiple generations. |
| 12. Brave | Accepting and even welcoming risks of exploring the unknown, ranging from sudden surprise to new and life-altering paradigms, with trust in the process and a greater good, embracing the mystery. |

related to everyday creativity, some represent specific characteristics of creativity (e.g., openness)—in which the creative product or process is defined, in terms of originality and meaningfulness. Other features represent correlates (e.g., observing actively), or preconditions (e.g., conscious awareness) for creativity, or potential consequences (e.g., health). Furthermore, many features fall into more than one category. Beyond this, some are universally linked with creativity (e.g., openness) whereas others, although relevant, depend in importance on one's creative direction and purpose (e.g., collaboration). Several contributors to this volume make the important suggestion that certain features (e.g., caring) may be more natural at higher levels of human and creative development.

For most people, these features seem positive in value as well as transformative in potential—for both individuals and groups. Hence the use of the term "benefits." Potential rewards include new purpose, connection, richness of experience, comfort with self and others, personal development, deeper knowing and life meaning, and enhanced well-being—both physically and psychologically. We might even come to see self and life in a whole new way.

## 1. Dynamic

Some say we think in terms of static snapshots. I am Jane, I am John. Here we are at the beach; here we are in the parlor with the kids. If this is the experience we have, what are we missing? Perhaps the entire rhythm of life.

We hear this from the contributors to this volume including Schuldberg (chap. 2), and Abraham (chap. 11) as well as Goerner (chap. 10) and Loye (chap. 7) because we do not live in a static world of snapshots. We are open systems of complex interacting processes in ongoing flux in relation to each other. It is remarkable when one thinks about it. We are constantly changing, with every breath, motion, and word we exchange. Indeed, when I hear you, my mind is altered. New neurochemical messengers, new dendritic connections, and new memories are created. This is about our creative process; let us not miss seeing it in action.

The "day-to-day" view of this process can teach us a lot, too, and it is sometimes amusing. Often, this process is regular and predictable, but not always. There is not a simple linear relationship in which "twice the effort gives twice the return." Sometimes it does give twice the return and sometimes it yields absolutely nothing at all. We have all had those days. At other times, we experience a sudden explosion of possibilities. Whole new realms open up. Here is the nonlinear butterfly effect of chaos theory, or the critical tipping point to a bifurcation toward creative change, as per Arons, Schuldberg, or Abraham (chaps. 8, 2, & 11, this volume, respectively), and at times it is the source of the "personal creativity" discussed by Runco (chap. 4, this volume). One sees these patterns occurring in day-to-day life (see Abraham & Gilgen, 1995; Richards, 2001; Robertson & Combs, 1995; Schuldberg, 1999). It is a thunderstorm, a family crisis, a stock market crash, or true love! Yet we never know exactly when such sudden changes will happen.

Meanwhile we can be "living well" and at ease, but with a touch of uncertainty, involving nonlinearity, "strange attractors," flexible guesses and best approximations, balancing within the flow of life, using the information that is available. Our information may be good, but it is incomplete—the whole is too large, and too complex to take in. If life is, as Schuldberg (chap. 2, this volume) says, "malleable but only indirectly steerable (p. 69)," we can still enjoy our jostling with the possibilities. We may even find, within it, "style" and "beauty" and feel awe in its complex patterns and fractal forms (Richards, 2001). We also find firsthand that we cannot control everything, although we can learn to be comfortable with this situation. Our rewards can include, Schuldberg (chap. 2, this volume) says, finding new "vitality, promise, and surprise" (p. 56).

This is not just about individuals in isolation. We are all part of multiple interconnecting systems, as Loye (chap. 7), Goerner (chap. 10), Eisler (chap. 12), and others tell us in this volume, and at all levels, including the physical and informational. It can seem hard enough to understand just one life, in isolation. Yet we are "in synch" with entire systems, extending endlessly. Sundararajan and Averill (chap. 9, this volume) speak of the energy and creativity of the Tao. We need to think, act, and create in terms of our deep interconnection with all of life, and know change as part of this complex system for the welfare of our world. Indeed, what happens next door, in Washington, DC, or on the moon is all part of your business and mine.

Beyond this, quantum mechanics and the new physics show us the instantaneous intertwining of events that are far apart (Ricard & Thuan, 2001). Can healing happen through heretofore unsuspected means and distant connections, as Richards poses in chapter 1 of this volume? What benefits may accrue if we are present with the flow of change? Perhaps we can have greater creative appreciation, as Pritzker suggests in chapter 5 of this volume, and better manage our possibilities as per Schuldberg (chap. 2, this volume). Perhaps we can see, at each moment, and all at once, from a multiplicity of perspectives as noted by Combs and Krippner (chap. 6, this volume). Indeed, a dynamic vision thrusts us more into the present moment, beyond ego, personal defense, and self-preoccupations, as Richards noted earlier (chap. 1, this volume). Here, colors are brilliant, aromas more intense, and we feel more truly alive.

Yet, do we not need to be consciously aware to take full advantage of all of this? The question leads to our next theme.

## 2. Conscious

We all know what it is like to be on automatic pilot and, in fact, spend much of our lives in habitual behavior patterns without great thought. We are driving, walking downstairs, opening a cupboard, and suddenly it strikes us that we have no idea why we are doing this, or even what we are looking for. It is mindless to an extreme. More often, we spend time in semihabitual behavior patterns without great attention to the choices we are making. Filing papers, making calls, answering e-mails—oops, what have we been doing? It is lunchtime already.

Our best creativity is different than this, not just active but very aware. As in Csikszentmihalyi's (1990) "flow," we may be present, focused, challenged, and know just what we are doing—creating a costume, let us say. We may not be aware of self, or self-conscious, thank heavens, and can kiss creator's "block" goodbye. Our sense of time may be skewed, but often it is such that we get more out of it. Should someone ask us later what we were experiencing, we can often tell them about it in detail, including our thoughts, feelings, and sensations. Even, sometimes, magnificently so, down to the sparkles of light on the last sequin we attached. This ability to recollect and report one's experience is one criterion for being "conscious."

In addition, our creative performance avails itself of "memory," "attention," and "controlled processing"—the presence of these functions fits another definition of consciousness (Farthing, 1992). Chapter authors in this volume speak to the need for an essential conscious presence in different ways, including Pritzker (chap. 5) on creative appreciation; Richards writing on "blocks in chapter 1," Sundararajan and Averill (chap. 9) on the subtleties of knowing, emotional awareness and expression; Eisler (chap. 12), on consciousness, creativity and caring; Zausner (chap. 3) on transforming illness; and Runco (chap. 4) on personal creativity, including issues of discernment. Personal creativity involves awareness of material that is new for the person, which triggers an adaptive response closer to Piaget's accommodation than a more automatic assimilation. Beghetto and Kaufman (in press) address the importance of their related "mini-c" creativity in our schools and elsewhere.

In interpersonal relations, empathy, and the I-Thou (vs. It) relationship ask us to be conscious and creatively present, just as a preliminary (Buber, 1970; Jordan, Kaplan, Miller, Stiver, & Surrey, 1991; Richards, in press-b). Only then can we authentically relate to another, and begin to create a genuine connection or mutuality so fundamental to human development and the fullest creative emergence, per Eisler and Loye (chaps. 12 & 7, this volume).

Plus there is more. Even when we believe that, now, we are finally and truly conscious, there are still worlds we are missing. Just look out the window and make a little sketch of what you see. Where did that tree come from? And that beige house with the skylight? Our filters kept them out. Can enlightened mind see everything? In chapter 6 of this volume, Combs and Krippner show us that, at our everyday level, there are "structures of consciousness" that consensually guide and channel us in our experience, structures we can learn a lot from—and also transcend.

This may sound good, but is the assumption valid that all of this is positive for us? The question leads to our next characteristic.

### 3. Healthy

Can writing creatively about our problems help us feel better? (Cameron, 1992). Many of us think so. We can make the problems conscious, and then transform them. Yet, impressions are one thing. How glad we are to have some "hard science," evidence of the healthy effects—in this case, to find that cathartic writing not only boosts health clinically—both physically and psychologically—but also can boost measures of immune function (Pennebaker, 1995). This is really important. Our T cells are now endorsing this creativity. If we have greater disease resistance, might we perhaps even live longer (Levy & Langer, 1999).

In fact there is evidence of creative activity being related to illness, including variants on bipolar mood disorders, as contributors to this volume note, including Schuldberg (chap. 2), Runco (chap. 4), and myself. This seems especially the case for artistic creativity, and at the eminently creative level more than the everyday level (Ludwig, 1995; Runco & Richards, 1998). Although this subject is complex, one can again, and paradoxically, find evidence supporting healthy effects of creativity in coping with psychological problems, even as with physical illness. One must ask how these creators would have done without their creative outlets.

Among the chapter authors in this volume, Zausner (chap. 3) powerfully shows the healing effects of creativity in physical illness as do I, along with Schuldberg (chap. 2) and others. Indeed, art and imagery can build a mind–body bridge of great power, as Zausner (chap. 3) and I both indicate. New routes to health may emerge (Cardena, Lynn, & Krippner, 2000) and possibly even in a distance healing context (Achterberg, Cooke, Richards, Standish, Kozak, & Lake, 2005). Notably, Sundararajan and Averill's (chap. 9) view of creative openness and Combs and Krippner's (chap. 6) "structures of consciousness" are consistent with Eastern approaches to greater knowing (e.g., Combs, 2002), and would also support the harmony, balance, and integration found in Eastern approaches to healing such as traditional Chinese medicine (Kaptchuk, 1983).

How interesting, too, if we think that our ideal leisure activity is sitting passively by a pool, sipping lemonade, only to find the greatest satisfactions can come from challenge, activity, and the chance to move ourselves to higher levels of competence and complexity (Csikszentmihalyi, 1993, 1996) while also, as other contributors show, cooperating, helping others, and contributing to a good cause (chaps. 7, 10, 12, this volume; Miller 1999). At the social level, Eisler's participatory "partnership" model is portrayed as more healthy for social organization (and certainly for individual creativity) than "domination" models. Here is health writ large, since effects now include the health and sustainability of cultures as well as individuals. One may ask for cultures that move, respond, breathe, and evolve in response to citizens at all levels, and which are created so this may continue.

If this healthy life has not stopped our running into upsets, problems, and surprises, we can now—recalling our dynamic and conscious themes—see that these are part of what we may call normal. We can then deal with the "bumps in the road" as part of an ongoing healthy process. Schuldberg (chap. 2, this volume), in fact, shows us that complete biological regularity can be lethal. Life is about infinite variation. Accepting this, we can be more in harmony, both within ourselves and the world, more open to change and surprise, and more alive.

If this sounds almost too good, are there not also painful problems to confront? This question leads to the next benefit of living more creatively.

### 4. Nondefensive

A friend was saying, "What bothers me about this 'creativity' talk is that it is too cheery, and light and fluffy. It just does not sound realistic. What about all the pain in the world?"

This comment is especially interesting, because one possibility for why our creativity may be underdeveloped or underrewarded, or miscast as light and fluffy, or even "orphaned" in psychology (Sternberg & Lubart, 1999), may be precisely because creativity can open our eyes. The issue, again, is creative process. We as creators are more willing to "let it come up," to see what is there, to face our shadow (Wilber, 2006) or what we often repress (Richards, 1993) and to "regress," productively, as some say, to primary process thinking (Martindale, 1999). If we live creatively, we are more apt to start looking without, and listening within. Suddenly we see a secret hidden deep within ourselves that we do not like at all, or we hear the world's pain as millions go without food. At times we may feel helpless, and overwhelmed.

Yet we are willing to pay the price (or, at least, pay it more often), because the benefits are so important. Not only will we look—and this may be really threatening to some people—but this time we may also ask some other people to take a look too. Authors in this volume, including Eisler, Loye, Goerner, Abraham (chaps. 12, 7, 10, & 11, respectively), and I (chap. 1) all see such a role for creativity. Once again, it is interesting how healthy creative awareness along with work to help others can nurture ourselves and the world (Miller, 1999; Runco & Richards, 1998).

Yet we sorely need to be less defensive, more in touch with ourselves and others. It is bad enough when we suppress "our own stuff." Beyond that, and hard for some to believe, is the extent to which we can become party to major public distortions in which we unknowingly collude on a large scale, affecting cultures and even history. In chapter 7 of this volume, Loye's case of "the lost Darwin" is particularly riveting. In chapter 1 I provide resonant examples such as the suppression of Dr. Ling's research. Humans think we know what we are doing, for instance, as citizens voting freely for national leaders, yet there may be unconscious factors biasing us toward certain features of dominance and influence of evolutionary significance (Ludwig, 2002). A psychiatrist I know (Richards, 1999a) said social groups might even be considered "psychotic" when they pull together and consensually reject some evident truth. If "psychosis" means being out of touch with reality, there may be a point here. It is a good thing many people are on a creative path which can also help them know themselves more fully.

The skeptical friend goes further: "If creativity brings about this healthy personal awareness," says this same friend, "How is it that creativity can be used for evil?"

This is a vital point, in the face of supposed nondefensiveness. Anyone who reads the history books or today's papers can think of many examples of creativity used to harm others. A knife, too, can be used for good or for evil—to make a salad or, alternatively, to murder someone. Creativity is a bit like the knife. It all depends. Runco, Loye, myself and others look at the values, choices, and costs involved in creativity versus conformity. The creative high road is not always easy. A special issue of the *Creativity Research Journal* (Gruber & Wallace, 1993), "Creativity in the Moral Domain," deals with some of the challenges and paradoxes. Indeed, creativity can be, and has been, used harmfully in certain endeavors in which there is dissociation from other areas of mind (Krippner, 1997).

Yet, all else being equal, time does seem to favor a movement toward health. Ongoing creativity does build a tendency to be increasingly nondefensive, open, broadly aware, and internally integrated, with other health benefits mentioned by contributors to this book including Zausner (chap. 3), Schuldberg (chap. 2), and myself (chap. 1). There are even transpersonal possibilities (Miller & Cook-Greuter, 2000). The creator can also move eventually from "deficiency" to "being" creativity (Rhodes, 1990), committing one's creations increasingly toward a greater good. We see this especially in some creative writers and playwrights who begin with their own unique conflicts but move outward toward more universal themes and concerns (e.g., Jamison, 1995; Morrison & Morrison, 2006). Noting it is defensiveness, including repression and suppression, not nondefensiveness, which predict for health problems (Singer, 1990), one can turn more hopefully to the next theme.

## 5. Open

Are we open to experience? We probably hope so. Openness can be defined as follows:

> [It] differs from ability and intelligence and involves the active seeking and appreciation of experiences for their own sake. Open individuals are curious, imaginative, and willing to entertain novel ideas and unconventional values; they experience the whole gamut of emotions more vividly than do closed individuals. (Costa & Widiger, 1994, p. 3)

This characteristic has been central to creativity over years of study (Barron, 1969; Feist, 1999; Helson, 1999), and it certainly finds resonance among many chapter authors of this volume, including Zausner (chap. 3), Pritzker (chap. 5), Runco (chap. 4), Sundararajan and Averill (chap. 9), Abraham (chap. 11), and myself (chap. 1). It helps us to heal, observe creatively, discern and make creative decisions, appreciate paradox and new realities, experience finely grained emotional distinctions, and be able to know more deeply and authentically. This characteristic is so central that psychological and psychobiological aspects will both be addressed later.

It is interesting that openness now also appears as one dimension of the increasingly popular "five factor theory of personality" (Costa & Widiger, 1994). The other factors, incidentally, are neuroticism, extraversion, agreeableness, and conscientiousness. Whether or not one believes that these five factors (or dimensions) explain most of the variance between you, me, and the next person, it is still nice to see a central creative characteristic make the cut.

The presence of openness also helps support the viewpoint that everyday creativity involves general ways of encountering the world (in addition to possible domain-specific ones), as seen in chapters in this volume by Zausner (chap. 3), Runco (chap. 4), Schuldberg (chap. 2), myself (chap. 1), and others. Aspects of openness emerged relevant to both Eastern and Western perspectives on creativity, as well, in Sundararajan and Averill's (chap. 9) reported research.

There is further evidence that some creative characteristics or traits do transcend particular domains of activity (Barron, 1969; Helson, 1999; Martindale, 1999; Plucker & Beghetto, 2004; Singer, 2004). In fact, one innovative university-level arts program in Wellington, New Zealand, The Learning Connexion (http://www.tlc.ac.nz)—where I have visited and lectured—actually works to help students transfer certain learnings and features of personal creative style from art-making to broader realms of their lives (Milne, 2007).

The Learning Connexion's approach is relevant to a major discussion about whether factors in creativity are "domain specific" or more general in nature (Sternberg, Grigorenko, & Singer, 2004), as addressed in this volume by Zausner (chap. 3), and myself (chap. 1), and assumed in some other chapters. To be sure, special skills and abilities also have their place in creativity (e.g., Amabile, 1996; Gardner, 1983), and one finds special characteristics for artists versus scientists (Feist, 1999), among others. Yet what is it that gives creativity its special flavor? Many artists can skillfully copy a painting. What is involved in actually creating one? Openness, now part of the five-factor theory of personality, speaks to more general aspects of creative orientation that can and should produce originality across domains.

Another issue, related to openness and to creative orientation, is whether creative generative processes are a result of ordinary mental abilities, found perhaps in routine problem solving, or can involve significantly more than this—notably altered mind states or "altered states of consciousness." Considering the benefits of creativity for health and even immune function, reported by myself (chap. 1), Zausner (chap. 3), Runco (chap. 4), and other contributors to this volume, or the potential for major shifts in structures of consciousness, per Combs and Krippner (chap. 6), one might think a more complex neuropsychology is involved. Altered states can be defined, "by specifying changes to the ordinary waking state along any number of dimensions . . . [for example] the stream of thoughts, feelings, and sensations" (Baruss, 2003, p. 8).

In creative openness, more than one state may be involved, including complexities of the more open "incubation" period before inspiration, the sudden creative insight, or the "ah-ha!" moment, and often a highly focused activity that follows. Martindale (1999) found three patterns to varying degrees during the more receptive phase of creative activity: (a) low levels of cortical activation; (b) greater right than left hemisphere activation; and (c) low frontal lobe activity on EEG, including slow theta waves. What may be happening subjectively? Attention is defocused, thought is associative, and there are many simultaneous mental representations.

Chapters in this volume by Combs and Krippner (chap. 6), and by Sundararajan and Averill (chap. 9), link creative activity with patterns reflective of Eastern models of consciousness. Arons (chap. 8), Abraham (chap. 11), and Zausner (chap. 3) raise related issues. One might wonder about specific processes and mental states when creativity becomes part of a tradition such as Zen (Pritzker, 1999) or itself provides a spiritual path (Miller & Cook-Greuter, 2000). Might some aspects of creativity, a defocused openness, for example, share features with subtle mind states found in some forms of meditation? Notably, meditative states also serve to quiet and open the mind toward the unknown, indeed toward ultimate transformation. Far from being a minor alteration in mind state, meditation in Tibetan Buddhism, for example, is one of the six major "bardos" or transitional states of our lives (and death). These are all "different states, different realities of mind" (Sogyal Rinpoche, 1994, p. 107). The further development beyond structures of consciousness noted by Combs and Krippner (chap. 6, this volume) may use meditation as one means of access (Combs, 2002).

As with creativity, meditation has different types and stages, but one finds on EEG "a 'second' rhythmic theta stage of meditation," before the deepest stage (Austin, 1998, p. 90), indeed recalling the theta activity found by Martindale (1999). What further patterns may be related to creative receptivity and openness? As Austin (1998) says, meditation may be "*teaching the person how to reach—and hold onto—one of several abilities to attend*" (p. 92). Walsh and Shapiro (2006) further stress that meditation has "major implications for an understanding of such central psychological issues as cognition and attention, mental training and development" (p. 227).

It is worth exploring more receptive, and also more active, phases of creating, in terms of openness and varied mind states. In fact, after incubation and first insights, and some active work, phases may continue to alternate, in recursive and iterative response to the work as it progresses, for example, in creating visual art (Zausner, 1996, 2007). Csikszentmihalyi (1996) seems to suggest an altered state in the active state of "flow," found in focused and absorbed creative activity. This state appears key, for example, both to Pritzker's (chap. 5, this volume) mentally active audience creativity, and Schuldberg's (chap. 2, this volume) suggestions for how to maneuver in real time within chaotic and somewhat complicated systems. Books such as Franck's *Zen Seeing, Zen Drawing: Meditation in Action* (1993), make a direct experiential connection between creativity and a more active meditation. Zen Master Sekida (1977) calls such productive periods *positive samadhi*, and Zen Master Loori (2004) shows how varied elements from Zen practice can awaken our everyday creativity. It is interesting to note that Krippner (1999) cites research showing elevated creativity in meditators.

How might creative openness tap into such altered states? It is worth exploring, because, among other things, a huge body of physical and psychological meditation data awaits (Murphy & Donovan, 1999). Might creative incubation phenomena, for example, move toward phenomena found in insight meditation, including mindfulness? Might more focused, absorbed, and one-pointed activity move toward absorptive stages (e.g., before and including the first jhana) on the path of concentration? (See Goleman [1977] and Wallace [2006] regarding these two major approaches to meditation).

Many interesting questions then follow. In what ways might mental state account for greater access to unconscious contents and primary process, or what has been called regression in the service of the ego (Richards, 1981), as well as in meditation? Are such creative states healthy, in the same ways reported for meditation (Murphy & Donovan, 1999)? Can blissful meditative states help explain the joys of "flow" (Csikszentmihalyi, 1990) or, for that matter, the ancient roles of "exuberance" in mammalian survival (Jamison, 2004)? What happens neurologically when creative experiences are transformative, even transcendent, as some individuals report, quite delightfully, during creative activity (e.g., Rogers, 1993)? Are such states relevant to keeping Arons's (chap. 8, this volume) spiritual and creative balance, to Zausner's (chap. 3, this volume) access to cross-cultural symbols and archetypes, to Pritzker's (chap. 5, this volume) proposed "audience flow" in viewer creativity? Can creative states help us engage new structures of consciousness per Combs and Krippner (chap. 6, this volume)? Finally, can we cultivate such potentially creative mind states deliberately through biofeedback, or mind training such as meditation—toward effects including greatly enhanced creative richness and power?

## 6. Integrating

This feature begins with humility. We learn there are many ways to perceive and to know. In chapter 10 of this volume, Goerner shows we are facing a situation of paradigm shift, from post-Enlightenment organization to a new and integral "web world" and knowledge ecology model, drawing on our interconnection, information flow, and self-organization (see also Goerner, 1999). This is no gradual change, but rather, a major paradigm shift, as Kuhn (1996) has described it. We will be aided by a coming together of web-based systems and scientific insights. The longer the change takes to get well underway, the greater the escalating risks.

For the most productive change, our "knowledge ecology" needs new forms of collaborative creativity, and new "partnerships" as well, as Eisler shows in chapter 12 of this volume. Loye (chap. 7, this volume), in reviving "the lost Darwin," shows the needed marriage of systems science with social science, and integration of concerns based on love, moral sensitivity, and self-organizing processes into our thinking, related to Eisler's call for greater consciousness, creativity, and caring.

Yet even as one talks blithely about creativity, Sundararajan and Averill (chap. 9, this volume) show us that creativity itself, among many other things, is culturally dependent (see also Montuori & Purser, 1999) and can transform dramatically across cultures. In this case, are we seeking the usual Western novelty, or seeking authenticity—its delicacy revealed here in the finest nuances of emotion in poetry, drawing us into the moment, and the truth of an experience. Our personal experience is further shaded by our level of "differentiation" and "involvement." The integral challenge is not to choose, however, but to encompass it all. Thus the creative person enjoys paradox, and goes beyond dichotomies, per Abraham (chap. 11, this volume), and seeks creativity in a higher form.

We also learn, per Runco (chap. 4, this volume), that our experience is constructed, but that we have a choice. Indeed, our sense of self is constructed as well. In chapter 6 of this volume, Combs and Krippner reveal how our experience is filtered through our "structures of consciousness." We miss worlds and haven't a clue. Different structures have predominated as cultures evolved, although some people are ahead of the curve. Artistic creativity, for one, can take different forms within each structure. Integral consciousness is particularly rich, fluid, multiperspectival, offers an unusually rich palette, and draws from all previous levels. According to some estimates, a small but significant fraction of our current population may be ready to make a transition to integral consciousness (Combs, 2002). This could connect us as a culture to larger visions and through this to each other in a violent and fragmented world. It might be well to further such development in our educational system.

Nor need integral consciousness be the end of the voyage. Recall Abraham Maslow (1971), who, in a different developmental model, went beyond "self-actualization" to look at further, transcendent, experience in a subset of these people. Combs and Krippner end chapter 6 of this volume with integral consciousness as per Gebser, but, drawing from world traditions, other structures can be said to follow this one (Combs, 2002). These have been linked with developmental stages going beyond those of Piaget, for example, stages which are similar across ancient cultures and traditions including Hindu and Buddhist (Wilber, 2006). These involve personal development of body–mind–spirit including higher mental powers many do not at present fully recognize.

An ultimate goal is enlightenment, so as to bring profound wisdom and compassion—and thus the highest creativity—back into our manifest reality and everyday life. Wilber (2006) views this sequence as a natural unfolding of our potential. He sees spirituality, broadly characterized, as central to this higher potential, and even, as he jokes, a "cosmic conveyor belt." Such a sequence is in no way presented as dogma but, rather, as a scientific experiment already tried by many contemplatives and world masters across traditions—and which one can try and experience for oneself. The data are complex, and include both objective and subjective assessments (e.g., Murphy & Donovan, 1999). Do we in the West know these data well enough? If so, can we accept them scientifically? It is worth finding out. In what ways might they help us to further our own development?

Finally, within any enduring "structure" of consciousness, we also have a symphony of temporary "phenomenal states," which come and go. Creative people may find many ways to experience and know themselves and the world more deeply through the use of these. Examples are reverie, meditation, and shamanic states of consciousness. In addition, these can further certain experiences. In chapter 3 of this volume, Zausner shows the power of art in religious ritual, as a doorway to universal archetypes, and presents uses of imagery in shamanic rituals and enactments. Such imagery can present powerful symbols which provide a mind–body bridge in healing, and move us toward other ends, including transformation. As Zausner points out, the image is an interior experience, similar to an actual encounter. It enters our body. It can change our consciousness. And having this occur is one of our most powerful creative options.

Thus, we human beings can "speak many languages" of our experience, nonverbal as well as verbal (e.g., Gardner, 1983), and from varied states of consciousness. We can learn to integrate experiences as well, for a fuller and more creative knowing and, often, healing.

It is of interest that we humans are, much of the time, quiet and listening, not making art or changing the world. Do we have creative options at those times? This leads to the next characteristic.

### 7. Observing Actively

We cannot believe it sometimes, that there is something creative actually happening. We get confused because we are looking so often for a tangible creative product. When there is creativity, we think something should emerge from it that we can see that is produced, written, carved, or otherwise fashioned. Yet, with creative process, we need not have a product (or alternatively the process is the product). Here, we consider waking life, and the ordinary things we may do.

What about watching television, one might wonder? Here is an activity that has a particularly bad reputation for engaging our minds actively, as Pritzker—psychologist and former prizewinning Hollywood sitcom writer—shows us in chapter 5 of this volume. Could watching television possibly be creative?

Surprisingly, at times, yes. Even if we seem completely passive, we can be changing and growing inside, and doing so creatively. We may be risking surprise and shock by opening our minds, pulling up unconscious material, dialoguing with the characters, forging new understandings. As an example from Pritzker (chap. 5, this volume) of active involvement and the personal change possible he recounts an episode of the *Mary Tyler Moore Show*. Here an entire creative process is carried out below the surface. This is not in conflict with certain creative qualities that may seem opposed to active watching, such as defocused attention—or at least no more than being in an actual creative conversation. All phases of the creative process can take their place at the viewer's end in the inner response and dialogue of the active audience member.

Does this really happen? It seems to depend on what and how entertainment is offered. It is all too easy to be mindless and passive, as Csikszentmihalyi (1990) says, with entertainment "that will structure the viewer's attention at a very low cost in terms of the psychic energy that needs to be invested" (p. 119). Many of us have had conversations like that, and even whole days of basic passivity. It can feel very bad. We are perhaps too much in Piaget's "assimilation" phase as discussed by Runco in chapter 4 of this volume, and not "accommodation." We are not intentional, discerning, and working toward creative understandings. If we are conscious and goal directed, we might be good "problem-finding" creators all of the time, as both Runco and Eisler (chap. 12, this volume) suggest—or at least much more of the time—thinking creatively and critically when no one has asked us to do it and questioning what we are given, be it news in the paper, a change at the office, or the latest trend in globalization or weapons sales.

Remember, with flow, there is active involvement, challenge, absorption, and full engagement of one's capacities. No one says this has to show on the surface. With bibliotherapy, videotherapy, teletherapy, we may struggle silently and intensely with a conflict and come out, in some ways, a different person.

From a systems perspective, we can be creative as active observers in everyday life—as we absorb and integrate information, be this watching movies, television, or a child's drama performance. We might even make dramatic new discoveries. Indeed, transformation is often the point in a different situation, and one in which the person may be as immobile as one ever is—in a state of meditation (Wilber, Engler, & Brown, 1986).

We are open systems, and are constantly engaged in a metabolism with our surroundings, whether we take in information, or nutrients (Arons & Richards, 2001; Richards, 2001). If we are what we eat, we can also be— in a very real way—what we watch on television. A show may embed itself into our neurons. Maybe the child—or adult—has nightmares about a movie. Or maybe the movie changes our life for the better.

In chapter 3 of this volume, Zausner reveals the dialogic process in engaging with works of art. The viewer completes the intentions of the artist. Beyond this, in encountering archetypal symbols, the viewer opens to deep and unconscious universal meanings that might otherwise stay hidden. In imagery for healing, as Zausner and I discuss in our respective chapters in this volume, the viewer bridges mind and body in ways that can affect the growth of tissues, the flow of blood cells. There is plenty of action—all inside. In meditating on sacred art, Zausner notes that the viewer's encounter can even create altered states that are transformative. Research has shown positive relationships between appreciation of creativity and actual creative production (e.g., Richards, Kinney, Benet, & Merzel, 1988). But perhaps that is not surprising; it may all be about the same thing.

Yet why are we creating anyway? Do we make our contributions just for ourselves or for others?

## 8. Caring

Surely it is shocking, frustrating, frightening, but at this time also empowering, to learn of the long omission of the more connecting and hopeful parts of Darwin's evolutionary message. Loye tells us, in chapter 7 of this volume, that in *Descent of Man* Darwin spoke of "love" a full 95 times and of "survival of the fittest" only twice, once actually to apologize for the term. Darwin also wrote numerous times about moral sensitivity, sympathy (mutuality), and cooperation. Darwin addressed human values, and their centrality to human progress. Some chapters of this volume including those by Loye (chap. 7), Eisler (chap. 12), Goerner (chap. 10), Runco (chap. 4), Sundararajan and Averill (chap. 9), Arons (chap. 8), Pritzker (chap. 5), and myself find values and human concern intrinsic indeed to our best use of creativity.

Regarding Darwin, Loye (chap. 7, this volume) celebrates the diverse scholars and researchers who have persevered and created, rather than conforming to a limited neo-Darwinian norm. These figures have returned our human heritage to us and also advanced it. Loye suggests collaborative academic structures and systems emphases whereby we may retain and further advance the best of our human potential. Notably, its flowering includes high levels of personal and interpersonal development, including self-actualizing creativity and an ongoing path to a still unfolding higher human development (Maslow, 1971).

Eisler (chap. 12, this volume), it is interesting to note, goes back as well as forward, showing us that consciousness, creativity, and caring are, first of all, part of our evolutionary and developmental heritage. Without love and attachment, for example, our brains would not have developed normally nor would we have anywhere near full capacity for creativity. Our so-called individuality is inextricably dependent on cultural conditions (Montuori & Purser, 1999) and particularly as the brain develops. It is of interest to note that love enters midway in Maslow's hierarchy of needs and only after physiological and safety needs have been met. Too late, says Eisler; it is needed much earlier and is more basic than that. And, knowing this, can we not design and build a world that works more fully with our fundamental connectedness and caring?

In our own time and place, actually, we might well ask why so many of the popular songs on so many radio stations are all about love. Why do we care so much? It is not just for hormonal teenagers. In fact, a fundamental caring and loving kindness is universal, central to the world's great wisdom traditions (Smith, 1991), and inseparable from the highest wisdom. It is worth remembering, in this context, that Darwin once trained for the ministry (White & Gribbin, 1997).

Do we all know a bit about this creativity and also this expansive love—whether one calls it Eastern or Western? "True love is born from understanding," said Vietnamese Zen Master Thich Nhat Hanh. Our deepest knowing may even at times bring intimations of infinity, beauty, and awe (Richards, 2001). In Ssu-k'ung T'u's poem, "*Hsiung-hun*," offered by Sundararajan and Averill (chap. 9, this volume), in the primordial principle of creativity, we know "ceaseless activity" flowing from "pure potentiality," in what must be an outer-inner false-binary, sacred nondichotomy. In its dynamic, "ceaseless," creative activity, and the final nondichotomy of absolute and relative, does it not endlessly overflow and give birth, one might say, all across the quadrants of Figure 9.1 (p. 200, this volume)? Inextricably within this is the most profound loving kindness and compassion.

Abraham (chap. 11, this volume) alights here as well, approaching what Thich Nhat Hanh (1993) refers to as relative and ultimate reality— neither separate nor the same, and not in any way expressible in words. One might attempt this, however, and find a wisp of a hint, or a "finger pointing to the moon," through creative arts, including poetry (Thich Nhat Hanh, 1993).

Creativity indeed returns, billows, leaps, Sundararajan and Averill tell us in chapter 9, and makes creator "at once the desert, the traveler, and the camel," per Flaubert (cited in chap. 9, p. 204). Creativity of the Tao is not mastery without, but integration within—within all creation and manifested endlessly, of and for us all. Attain the ultimate and partake of the greatest mystery, if we were ever parted. Find the source of the I–Thou relationship (Buber, 1970), and reunion and "at-onement" through love (Fromm, 1956). Neither Eastern nor Western this time, our deepest creative potential is speaking, not to separateness and hate, but in the most profound way, to underlying unity and love.

Yet, if we are so deeply connected, why don't we humans collaborate more? What gets in the way? This brings us to the next feature.

## 9. Collaborative

Good thing we humans do collaborate—that we are a "collaborative learning species"—although we still could do better. An example of collaboration: Someone discovers fire, and the word spreads. Suddenly each hearth has a fire burning. Eisler gives a related example for a macaque monkey and its community in chapter 12 of this volume. This is, by the way, how cultural evolution can work. We share a creative discovery, our lives change, and we pass it on to the next generation. This knowledge can affect our genetic as well as our cultural survival. In an icy and brutal winter, think of the tribe that has fire and the tribe that does not.

Not everyone today sees creativity in terms of sharing. Goerner (chap. 10, this volume) shows three possible root metaphors for cultures through Western history: Empire (Roman times), God's Design (medieval Europe), and Freedom (Reformation to the Enlightenment to New World and modern society). Now, what is next? Each period stagnates and then it is "learn or die." She says we are on the perilous verge of transition. To what? An "ecosystem" or "web" metaphor for life.

Chapters in the volume by Goerner (chap. 10), Eisler (chap. 12), Loye (chap. 7), Abraham (chap. 11), Schuldberg (chap. 2), Zausner (chap. 3), and myself (chap. 1) all include systems and self-organizing views of how we function in groups, and can evolve together, indeed in "webs" of mutual complex connection and influence. This is true in the smallest group (dyad) or across world civilization. The new research on "mirror neurons" underlines how two people may physically, as well as psychologically, relate to and reflect back their connection to each other. At the global level, how complex it becomes. If one considers large groups, instant communications, the Internet, global networks, and virtual worlds as imagined by Abraham, the complexity of our interconnection multiplies exponentially. We do not think enough yet in terms of systems, change, multiple influences, and our proactive role as well, in the greater picture. Yet we need to do so quickly. As creators, at home or in the White House, with small or large creative projects, we are affecting others. Let us work together.

Nonetheless, some still hold to neo-Darwinian "survival of the fittest" paradigms—"us or them"—perhaps with self-sufficiency, stalwart independence, and aggressor models of winning. They may idealize the "lone creator," and forget that, meanwhile, we "stand on the shoulders of giants." Some may want brutally to suppress or dominate the "other" (some hapless political, religious, or ethnic figure or group, or even country), when what we really need is to get along better with each other. Alas, one can see a part of this modeled in some schools. Take "grading on the curve," which may seem a benign practice. Yet the students are learning a "zero-sum game"—you win,

I lose—hide one's notes and compete with the others for scarce resources ("As and Bs").

In this volume, Goerner (chap. 10), Eisler (chap. 12), and others argue that greater pressures, needs, energies, and increasing problems require—not a top-down hierarchical solution that stamps millions of upstarts into place—but a living evolving structure and "heterarchy" (combining hierarchy with structures that reach in all directions and draw from everyone). At best, it is truly an egalitarian and democratic "partnership," from the lowest level to the top.

Surprisingly, perhaps, according to Goerner (chap. 10, this volume), as things get more complex there can be self-organization into even smaller units, highly active, profusely interconnected with each other. Here is an even greater chance for creativity, and not just when things are going smoothly. According to Simonton's (1997) historiometric research, certain kinds of social disruptions (but by no means all), notably civil disturbance, or political fragmentation, carry a predictive effect for increased creativity—albeit with a generational lag. In any case, we can surely learn to pull diverse creative components together more effectively in our shrinking globe (in which too many creative contributions now get lost). As we think large, we can increasingly honor our creative uniqueness too, as part of the greater whole, as we cocreate, perhaps, a new and participatory "society of mind."

One might ask if all this complexity in an evolving world could not also mean conforming even more, and being more boxed in by roles and by life. One may hope not. Enter the next theme.

## 10. Androgynous

Are you masculine or feminine? This is not the question here. There are certainly some gender differences, of complex biopsychosocial origin (Brizendine, 2006). Yet this discussion is more about the overlap between gendered groups—or how broad a range of functioning we, female or male, allow ourselves. It is about whether we can fully be ourselves, whatever that may mean for us, or whether we have been boxed in by culture with its many limitations and "dos and don'ts" or by false dichotomies based on gender polarization (Bem, 1993). There are implications for both individuals and cultures, even for information technological advances, as the chapters of Abraham and Eisler (11 & 12, this volume), in particular, show.

"Big boys don't cry"—there is one beginning of it, as young men encounter our present culture. By contrast, highly creative people of both sexes typically value and express their emotionality and it can be healthy to do so (Russ, 1999). In the creative arts in China, and in the value system of Confucius, according to Sundararajan and Averill, sensitivity to emotional nuance in both expression and appreciation is a sign of great personal cultivation. How often are we limited in our own lives, however, by false dichotomies, in which we cannot be (or think we cannot be) both sensitive and assertive, emotional and intellectual, intuitive and logical, gentle and strong, dependent and independent? See for example, Abraham's chapter (chap. 11, this volume; see also Richards, in press-a).

*Androgyny* is a term often used here, referring to people having "a higher than the average number of male and female elements in their personalities. . . . they are more likely to behave in a way this is appropriate to a situation, regardless of their gender" (Dacey & Lennon, 1998, p. 110). Research psychologist Donald MacKinnon (in Dacey & Lennon, 1998) said of highly creative male architects:

> The evidence is clear. The more creative a person is the more he reveals an openness to his own feelings and emotions, a sensitive intellect and understanding self-awareness, and wide-ranging interests including many which in the American culture are thought of as feminine. In the realm of sexual identification and interest, our creative subjects appear to give more expression to the feminine side of their nature than do less creative persons. (p. 109)

Conversely, we could say a highly creative female architect might appear to give more expression to the masculine side of her nature, on the basis of dominant stereotypes. Yet male and female high creatives would each, in Jung's (1974) terms, be comfortable with both their archetypal *anima* and *animus*.

In chapter 11 of this volume, Abraham notes our many false binary choices (e.g., emotion vs. intellect), our false dichotomies, in the context of chaos theory, and how rising above these can lead to new and better creative possibilities. Our future cyberworld may help as well. So may aspects of an information culture that are not gender or strength dependent (Richards, in press-a). Eisler (chap. 12, this volume) and other researchers (e.g., Montuori & Conti, 1993) offer models for new and more egalitarian societies, stressing fuller personal development and "partnership" between all parties. How interesting, as Eisler says, that in more egalitarian Nordic nations where women constitute 40% of the legislatures, stereotypically feminine qualities such as nurturance, nonviolence, and caregiving are seen as appropriate for men as well.

Freedom from gender stereotypes has long been seen as central for creativity (Barron, 1969). It is listed, for example, in one creativity textbook as one of ten key traits in the creative personality (Dacey & Lennon, 1998), and appears in even shorter lists in other contexts (e.g., Montuori, Combs, & Richards, 2004). One should note that related statements might also be made about distortions and limiting stereotypes involving race, creed, class, and color. Keep in mind, again, that this is not about homogenization; we can certainly enjoy our gender or our ethnic origins. We contribute most richly when we bring our creative uniqueness to the greater mosaic. Rather, this is about equality and participation, the fullest development for each of us, and our honoring all members in our family of humanity.

Now, what are our prospects for the future? Are we apt to achieve greater creative and personal possibility? One turns to the next benefit of living more creatively.

## 11. Developing

What is development about? Is it about the unfolding and training of mind and body for health, problem solving, abstract thinking, and emotional maturity, through time, diet, and experience at school and leisure? Does development mean growing up, getting a job, perhaps marrying and having children, then retiring? Well, these may be a part of it. But what if our development involves even more? What if this is the best part of all?

"Development" and "evolution" involve more than some people think. Consider large scale advances that have changed lives and cultures, including fire, spoken language, agriculture, and the Internet. In some chapters from this volume including Loye (chap. 7), Eisler (chap. 12), Runco (chap. 4), Combs and Krippner (chap. 6), Abraham (chap. 11), and Goerner (chap. 10), one learns about both individual development and, taking a further step, about biological and cultural evolution (even including technologically aided biological and cultural evolution). One sees how individual creative innovations, and a population's creative reception of these, can lead to cultural change, cultural evolution and even, at times, survival. Abraham's remarkable chapter (chap. 11) shows us how our technology of the future may cause us to forge new cyberidentities, rules, and even virtual worlds.

Have we a choice in where our societies are going? We do. It is more than a little interesting that human beings (when conscious and creative, as Eisler says in chap. 12) have the potential for conscious evolution—we can deliberately decide in which direction to go. Humans are aware and self-aware, planners, and proactive creators, as Runco stresses in chapter 4. We can see what has worked and not worked, and learn from the past (oh, that we would do so). We can take the future more into our hands.

Question: What if we humans are not as developed as we can still be? What if a more highly advanced human consciousness can lead, naturally, to greater caring for each other and the world, and to higher overriding purpose?

Could this be true? Humanistic psychologist Abraham Maslow thought so, on the basis of his interview research with exceptional people, and our troubled planet certainly needs these caring qualities today. Interesting that Maslow's (1968) "self-actualizing" (SA) creativity is mentioned in this volume by contributors including Loye (chap. 7), Eisler (chap. 12), Abraham (chap. 11), Runco (chap. 4), Arons (chap. 8), and myself (chap. 1). Self-actualizing creativity shares qualities with everyday creativity, but perhaps at a higher level, falling at the top of Maslow's needs hierarchy, at the "self-actualizing" stage. This creativity occurs naturally in many areas of life, marked by almost a "childlikeness . . . 'open to experience' and . . . easily spontaneous and expressive." The person's manner seems "effortless, innocent, easy, a kind of freedom from stereotypes and clichés" (Maslow, 1968, p. 138). Note we have met related qualities earlier, in the sections explaining conscious, open, and androgynous characteristics.

Can we still give love if we do not have enough to eat? It happens. The invariance of Maslow's levels has been debated (Wahba & Bridwell, 1976), and furthermore, in chapter 12 of this volume, Eisler argues that love and attachment are crucial from the beginning, from Maslow's physiological needs, on up. One also sees that everyday creativity, as defined here—in part a survival capability—appears at all levels, necessary for our physical and psychological survival and already bringing in its wake healthy benefits and creative resilience.

Is there, therefore, a higher variant of everyday creativity at the level of self-actualized creativity? An important question. Although somewhat different, one often finds as part of SA, temporary but momentous "peak experiences," mentioned by Arons, including ecstatic, rapturous moments, of awe, wonder, amazement, humility, reverence, or oceanic feelings of oneness; brought about perhaps by art, nature, music, love, or meditation. They are their own justification and reward. They may also help convince us that "there is more." In addition, Maslow (1971), similar to some of the contributors to this volume including Loye (chap. 7), Runco (chap. 4), Goerner (chap. 10), Eisler (chap. 12), and others, found that values are critical, at higher levels of development. "Being values" such as goodness, beauty, or justice can come forth because "self-actualizing individuals (more matured, more fully human) . . . are now motivated in other higher ways" (Maslow, 1971, p. 289). This includes a wish to contribute so as to honor these values. Here is a touch of the Christian saint or Buddhist bodhisattva, and of higher altruistic creative purpose, as touched on by contributors to this volume including Schuldberg (chap. 2), Runco (chap. 4), Combs and Krippner (chap. 6), and Arons (chap. 8). There is resonance this time with the features discussed earlier including the dynamic, integrating, and androgynous characteristics for process and complex thinking as well as caring and collaborative characteristics.

Maslow's is only one model, although influential. Humanistic and transpersonal psychology and the new field of positive psychology are exploring varied frameworks and models for "optimal human functioning" as Loye indicates in chapter 7 of this volume. The "structures of consciousness" discussed by Combs and Krippner, in chapter 6 this volume, not only show how one develops over a single lifetime but also how cultures too can develop and evolve. Evidence suggests this pattern can be followed to yet higher levels of consciousness and spirituality—promising, although still rather rare in modern society (Combs, 2002; Wilber, 2006).

Whatever the model, however, the main point is "there is more." That human potential is unfolding and still holds manifold new possibilities. We need further research and dialogue to understand these possibilities better in Western scientific terms (e.g., Ricard & Thuan, 2001; Walsh & Shapiro, 2006), what they mean, and how one might cultivate them.

But what about those who do not want such an adventure and the risk it involves? This question leads to the final theme.

## 12. Brave

Being "brave" is important in creativity. It is about more than risk taking. Risk taking is about a given situation and a choice. Bravery is about everything, and at any time; it is an attitude and a lifestyle. It says, "I'm committed to X, and to the inquiry involved, and unknown consequences that might occur, even if something fearful could happen. I'm open to new insights, chaotic bifurcation, personal revelations, new views of reality, and major social changes that could affect my whole life and everything I do."

Indeed, almost all chapters in this book deal with the need for creative courage either directly or indirectly, and within oneself, or in contact with others, with Loye (chap. 7), Goerner (chap. 10), Eisler (chap. 12), and myself (chap. 1) illustrating some immediate consequences of creativity which is stifled, be it in schools, homes, cultures, or the world, and the need to take initiative, collaboratively. Loye's chapter on Charles Darwin raises particular concern about external suppression of part of the creativity of a figure even as momentous as Darwin, and on a large and historical scale. Abraham presents visions of a future cyberworld that could be challenging to many, and has already spawned powerful science fiction. In chapter 8, Arons' creative balancing act suggests that we upright creatures may always be a little off center, hence insecure, and need to move bravely to stay upright, finding sources of inspiration, including the spiritual, to help buoy us up.

Even when creativity works to heal individual pain and illness, per Zausner (chap. 3, this volume), or serve psychotherapeutic purposes as in Pritzker's (chap. 5, this volume) teletherapy, there may be creative leaps that involve facing one's own inner process and, at times, one's demons (see also May, 1975.) I address access to the unconscious in chapter 1 of this volume while sharing Barron's (1969) well-known statement (see also Richards, 2006) about highly creative people, that they are "both more primitive and more cultivated, more destructive and more constructive, occasionally crazier and yet adamantly saner, than the average person" (chap. 1, p. 33). Unfortunately, this creative inner access can have its own social as well as personal consequences, when some creative persons end up being pathologized and subtly pressured to return to "normal." As Runco (chap. 4, this volume) says, they are by nature deviant. Yet not only is this version of "abnormal" not necessarily "pathological" but as Barron (1969) suggests, it may also even represent a pinnacle of health.

Here then are hard won benefits of our everyday creativity, despite its healthy promise for individuals and for cultures. Some of us assert this is because creativity can be so dangerous. It keeps us in constant motion, and challenges whatever we think we know for sure; in the flash of a butterfly ("butterfly effects") wing, our creativity can change everything. One may even wonder if some of the cultural diminution of our everyday creativity— for example, that creativity can only be truly taken seriously when practiced by eminent creative individuals—is to keep us creative upstarts back in our place (Richards, in press-a, in press-b).

Well, that's okay, someone says; it was too much creativity anyway. Too much of a challenge, too much stress. Maybe I will just practice my creativity a little bit.

Actually, even this is important. To change a social trend, for example (and perhaps turn the Titanic away from the iceberg in time) a little creativity may be all it takes, at least if we all do it, and do it together. Perhaps this is a turn toward a more integral, or "partnership" way of living. A little course change can, at times, make all the difference.

On the more positive side, our creative possibilities are actually happy ones—and not just fearsome ones. Our developed creativity can leave us more powerful, resilient, open, free to appreciate, and to go with what happens, to open to a greater unknown, and embrace the mystery. We are not so mired in the past, or guarding of our own territories. Our bravery can increase correspondingly. How interesting that the more open direction is also the healthier one for us, individually and together.

We may also find, together, if creativity is more central in our lives, new humility and willingness to learn—as well as a growing trust in the creative process, and in working with each other, as well as our greater human potential. This could enhance the joy, while lowering the factor of fear and the need for solitary bravery. There is surely much we have yet to learn. Yet in this realm of the unknown, rather than shiver with fear, one can find hope that what underlies our sometimes brutal and bloody reality may still be good and affirming. If we are spiritual, this work can draw deeply from, and strengthen, our beliefs and practices. If we are not spiritual, we may yet find greater respect for this realm of the yet unknown, which we may increasingly want to know.

## IN CONCLUSION

From the distance we have traveled, one can see the core of everyday creativity across domains, as a dynamic, conscious, open, and healthy way of encountering life, a complex process (or set of processes), and perhaps also a set of states of mind (embedded within our "structures of consciousness"), which hold for us all a means of coping, thriving, growing, seeing more complexly, finding deeper meaning, and working more harmoniously together in a rapidly changing world. We may also, perhaps, meet opportunities for new understandings and transformation that will amaze us.

Our creativity can happen at work or at leisure, and whether we are physically active or just sitting around watching television. It sees more, integrates more broadly, is open and nondefensive, reveals what some might wish to hide, and brings us vividly into the present moment, beyond our limiting self-preoccupations. It goes hand in hand with higher structures of consciousness, and levels of development.

Although creativity can be used for destructiveness and antisocial ends, it can at best improve psychological health and integration in the creator, breaking down inner and outer barriers. Along some creative paths, it can enhance connection with others, and advance caring and empathy, toward more peaceful and collaborative ways of working together. At best, it can resist structures that are rigidly hierarchical, and people and groups that are oppressive. At higher levels, per Maslow, or other related models, it may even help us develop into new and more (fiercely) caring forms of human beings.

Perhaps it is not surprising that such everyday creativity may seem, to some people, disruptive and dangerous. At the same time, and perhaps for similar reasons, our everyday creativity can also help us to live better and to thrive—toward ever widening life possibilities, meaning, and joy.

Let me end by sharing some wisdom from a former mentor, the late John David Miller, PhD, historian of science and science educator, at the University of California, Berkeley. Dave manifested, as much as anyone I know, the creative spirit, through his sheer exuberance, presence, and love of sharing "discovery"-based learning with others, in a science classroom. It was Dave Miller who introduced me to creativity studies that went beyond the arts, and to everyday creativity in particular.

Some years ago, Dave shared the one piece of science he said most moved him. This was the *anthropic principle* (Barrow, Tipler, & Wheeler, 1988). Here were amazing coincidences! The "big bang," fundamental constants of the universe, nuclear resonances of oxygen and carbon, chemical reactions in the centers of stars, all this and more showing exquisite fine tuning, and a set of almost impossible coincidences, that have made carbon-based life forms possible—that have made us possible.

The so-called strong anthropic principle of cosmologists including Fred Hoyle and John Wheeler (Russell, 1998) can even be used to imply—to extrapolate a bit—that it is no accident we are here, and that we are here for a reason. They say there can be no matter without an observer to convert the quantum mechanical probabilities into an actual manifest cosmos. We "intelligent" life forms bring a quantum mechanical universe (and ourselves) into existence along with our observations. Is it therefore to manifest this universe that we "intelligent" beings—as a necessary and intertwined part of it—have come forth?

What then about intelligent life that can self-reflect and even transcend our limited consciousness?

Humans have indeed come forth in our manifest cosmos. And humans, as evolving life forms and cultures, are surely not finished. How might we personally develop; how might life forms evolve? At this dangerous crossroads for planet Earth and our own individual futures, how can we better live for ourselves and for all of creation, while manifesting the underlying beauty of a cosmos that holds the mysteries of life? Perhaps everyday creativity can help show us the way.

## REFERENCES

Abraham, F. D., & Gilgen, A. R. (1995). *Chaos theory in psychology*. Westport, CT: Praeger Publishers.

Achterberg, J., Cooke, K., Richards, T., Standish, L., Kozak, L., & Lake, J. (2005). Evidence for correlations between distant intentionality and brain function in recipients: A functional magnetic resonance imaging analysis. *Journal of Alternative and Complementary Medicine, 11*, 965–971.

Amabile, T. (1996). *Creativity in context*. New York: Westview Press.

Arons, M., & Richards, R. (2001). Two noble insurgencies: Creativity and humanistic psychology. In K. J. Schneider, J. F. T. Bugental, & J. F. Pierson (Eds.), *Handbook of humanistic psychology* (pp. 127–142). Thousand Oaks, CA: Sage.

Austin, J. H. (1998). *Zen and the brain: Toward an understanding of meditation and consciousness*. Cambridge, MA: MIT Press.

Barron, F. (1969). *Creative person and creative process*. New York: Holt, Rinehart & Winston.

Barrow, J. D., Tipler, F. J., & Wheeler, J. A. (1988). *The anthropic cosmological principle*. New York: Oxford University Press.

Baruš, I. (2003). *Alterations of consciousness: An empirical analysis for social scientists*. Washington, DC: American Psychological Association.

Beghetto, R., & Kaufman, J. C. (in press). Toward a broader conception of creativity: A case for "mini-c" creativity. *Psychology of Aesthetics, Creativity, and the Arts*.

Bem, S. L. (1993). *The lenses of gender*. New Haven, CT: Yale University Press.

Brizendine, L. (2006). *The female brain*. New York: Morgan Road Books.

Buber, M. (1970). *I and thou*. New York: Touchstone.

Cameron, J. (1992). *The artist's way: A spiritual path to higher creativity*. New York: Tarcher.

Cardeña, E., Lynn, S. J., & Krippner, S. (2000). *Varieties of anomalous experience: Examining the scientific evidence*. Washington, DC: American Psychological Association.

Combs, A. (2002). *The radiance of being—Understanding the grand integral vision: Living the integral life*. St. Paul, MN: Paragon House.

Costa, P. T., & Widiger, T. A. (1994). Introduction. In P. T. Costa & T. A. Widiger (Eds.), *Personality disorders and the five factor model of personality* (pp. 1–10). Washington, DC: American Psychological Association.

Csikszentmihalyi, M. (1990). *Flow: The psychology of optimal experience*. New York: HarperPerennial.

Csikszentmihalyi, M. (1993). *The evolving self: A psychology for the third millennium*. New York: HarperCollins.

Csikszentmihalyi, M. (1996). *Creativity: Flow and the psychology of discovery and invention*. New York: HarperCollins.

Dacey, J. S., & Lennon, K H. (1998). *Understanding creativity: The interplay of biological, psychological, and social factors*. San Francisco: Jossey-Bass.

Farthing, G. W. (1992). *The psychology of consciousness*. Englewood Cliffs, NJ: Prentice Hall.

Feist, G. J. (1999). The influence of personality on artistic and scientific creativity. The concept of creativity: Prospects and paradigms. In R. Sternberg (Ed.), *Handbook of creativity* (pp. 273–296). New York: Cambridge University Press.

Franck, F. (1993). *Zen seeing, Zen drawing: Meditation in action*. New York: Bantam Books.

Fromm, E. (1956). *The art of loving*. New York: Harper Colophon Books.

Gardner, H. (1983). *Frames of mind*. New York: Basic Books.

Goerner, S. J. (1999). *After the clockwork universe: The emerging science and culture of integral society*. Edinburgh, Scotland: Floris.

Goleman, D. (1977). *The varieties of the meditative experience*. New York: Dutton.

Gruber, H., & Wallace, D. (1993). Special issue: Creativity in the moral domain. *Creativity Research Journal, 6*(1 & 2).

Helson, R. (1999). Personality. In M. A. Runco & S. R. Pritzker (Eds.), *Encyclopedia of creativity* (Vol. 2, pp. 361–373). San Diego, CA: Academic Press.

Jamison, K. R. (1995). *An unquiet mind*. New York: Knopf.

Jamison, K. R. (2004). *Exuberance: The passion for life*. New York: Vintage Books.

Jordan, J., Kaplan, A., Miller, J. B., Stiver, I. P., & Surrey, J. L. (1991). *Women's growth in connection.* New York: Guilford.

Jung, C. G. (1974). *Dreams.* Princeton, NJ: Princeton University Press.

Kaptchuk, T. J. (1983). *The web that has no weaver: Understanding Chinese medicine.* Chicago: Congden & Weed.

Krippner, S. (1997). *Broken images, broken selves.* New York: Routledge.

Krippner, S. (1999). Altered and transitional states. In M. A. Runco & S. R. Pritzker (Eds.), *Encyclopedia of creativity* (Vol. 1, pp. 59–70). San Diego, CA: Academic Press.

Kuhn, T. S. (1996). *The structure of scientific revolutions.* Chicago: University of Chicago Press.

Levy, B., & Langer, E. (1999). Aging. In M. A. Runco & S. R. Pritzker (Eds.), *Encyclopedia of creativity* (Vol. 1, pp. 45–52). San Diego, CA: Academic Press.

Loori, J. D. (2004). *The Zen of creativity: Cultivating your artistic life.* New York: Ballantine Books.

Ludwig, A. M. (1995). *The price of greatness.* New York: Guilford.

Ludwig, A. M. (2002). *King of the mountain: The nature of political leadership.* Lexington: University of Kentucky Press.

Martindale, C. (1999). Biological bases of creativity. In R. Sternberg (Ed.), *Handbook of creativity* (pp. 137–152). New York: Cambridge University Press.

Maslow, A. (1968). *Toward a psychology of being.* New York: Van Nostrand Reinhold.

Maslow, A. (1971). *The farther reaches of human nature.* New York: Penguin.

May, R. (1975). *The courage to create.* New York: Bantam Books.

Miller, W. R. (1999). *Integrating spirituality into treatment: Resources for practitioners.* Washington, DC: American Psychological Association.

Miller, M. E., & Cook-Greuter, S. R. (2000). *Creativity, spirituality, and transcendence.* Stamford, CT: Ablex Publishing.

Milne, J. (2006). *GO! The art of change.* Wellington, New Zealand: Steele Roberts.

Montuori, A., Combs, A., & Richards, R. (2004). Creativity, consciousness, and the direction for human development. In D. Loye (Ed.), *The great adventure: Toward a fully human theory of evolution* (pp. 197–236). Albany, NY: SUNY Press.

Montuori, A., & Conti, I. (1993). *From power to partnership: Creating the future of love, work, and community.* New York: HarperSanFrancisco.

Montuori, A., & Purser, R. (1999). *Social creativity* (Vol. 1). Cresskill, NJ: Hampton.

Morrison, D., & Morrison, S. L. (2006). *Memories of loss and dreams of perfection: Unsuccessful childhood grieving and adult creativity.* Amityville, NY: Baywood Publishing.

Murphy, M., & Donovan, S. (1999). *The physical and psychological effects of meditation: A review of contemporary research with a comprehensive bibliography, 1931–1996* (2nd ed.). Sausalito, CA: Institute of Noetic Sciences.

Nhat Hanh, T. (1993). *Call me by my true names: The collected poems of Thich Nhat Hanh.* Berkeley, CA: Parallax Press.

Pennebaker, J. W. (1995). *Emotion, disclosure, and health.* Washington, DC: American Psychological Association.

Plucker, J. A., & Beghetto, R. A. (2004). Why creativity is domain general, why it looks domain specific, and why the distinction does not matter. In R. Sternberg, E. L. Grigorenko, & J. L. Singer (Eds.), *Creativity: From potential to realization* (pp. 153–167). Washington, DC: American Psychological Association.

Pritzker, S. (1999). Zen. In M. A. Runco & S. R. Pritzker (Eds.), *Encyclopedia of creativity* (Vol. 2, pp. 745–750). San Diego, CA: Academic Press.

Rhodes, C. (1990). Growth from deficiency creativity to being creativity. *Creativity Research Journal, 3,* 287–289.

Ricard, M., & Thuan, T. X. (2001). *The quantum and the lotus: A journey to the frontiers where science and Buddhism meet.* New York: Crown House Publishing.

Richards, R. (1981). Relationships between creativity and psychopathology: An evaluation and interpretation of the evidence. *Genetic Psychology Monographs, 103,* 261–324.

Richards, R. (1993). Seeing beyond: Issues of creative awareness and social responsibility. *Creativity Research Journal, 6,* 165–183.

Richards, R. (1998). When illness yields creativity. In M. A. Runco & R. Richards (Eds.), *Eminent creativity, everyday creativity, and health* (pp. 485–540). Stamford, CT: Ablex Publishing.

Richards, R. (1999a). "Four Ps" of creativity. In M. A. Runco & S. R. Pritzker (Eds.), *Encyclopedia of creativity* (Vol. 1, pp. 733–742). San Diego, CA: Academic Press.

Richards, R. (1999b). Affective disorders. In M. A. Runco & S. R. Pritzker (Eds.), *Encyclopedia of creativity* (Vol. 1, pp. 31–43). San Diego, CA: Academic Press.

Richards, R. (2000–2001). Millennium as opportunity: Chaos, creativity, and J. P. Guilford's Structure-of-Intellect model. *Creativity Research Journal, 13* (3 & 4), 249–265.

Richards, R. (2001). A new aesthetic for environmental awareness: Chaos theory, the natural world, and our broader humanistic identity. *Journal of Humanistic Psychology, 41,* 59–95.

Richards, R. (2006). Frank Barron and the study of creativity: A voice that lives on. *Journal of Humanistic Psychology, 46,* 352–370.

Richards, R. (in press-a). Everyday creativity and the arts. *World Futures.*

Richards, R. (in press-b). Relational creativity and healing potential: Power of Eastern thought in Western clinical settings. In J. D. Pappas, W. E. Smythe, & A. Baydala (Eds.), *Cultural healing and belief systems.* Calgary, Albert, Canada: Detselig Enterprise.

Richards, R., Kinney, D., Benet, M., & Merzel, A (1988). Assessing everyday creativity: Characteristics of the Lifetime Creativity Scales and validation with three large samples. *Journal of Personality and Social Psychology, 54,* 476–485.

Rinpoche, Sogyal. (1994). *The Tibetan book of living and dying.* New York: HarperSanFrancisco.

Robertson, R., & Combs, A. (Eds.). (1995). *Chaos theory in psychology and the life sciences.* Mahwah, NJ: Erlbaum.

Rogers, N. (1993). *The creative connection: Expressive arts as healing.* Palo Alto, CA: Science & Behavior Books.

Runco, M. A., & Richards, R. (1998). *Eminent creativity, everyday creativity, and health.* Stamford, CT: Ablex Publishing.

Russ, S. (1999). *Affect, creative experience, and psychological adjustment.* Philadelphia, PA: Brunner/Mazel.

Russell, P. (1998). *Waking up in time.* Novato, CA: Origin Press.

Schuldberg, D. (1999). Chaos theory and creativity. In M. A. Runco & S. R. Pritzker (Eds.), *Encyclopedia of creativity* (Vol. 1, pp. 259–272). San Diego, CA: Academic Press.

Sekida, K. (Ed. and Trans.). (1977). *Two Zen classics: Mumonkan and Hekiganroku.* New York: Weatherhill.

Simonton, D. K. (1997). Political pathology and societal creativity. In M. A. Runco & R. Richards (Eds.), *Eminent creativity, everyday creativity, and health* (pp. 359–377). Stamford, CT: Ablex Publishing.

Singer, J. (2004). Concluding comments: Crossover creativity or domain specificity? In R. Sternberg, E. L. Grigorenko, & J. L. Singer (Eds.), *Creativity: From potential to realization* (pp. 195–203). Washington, DC: American Psychological Association.

Singer, J. (1990). *Repression and dissociation: Implications for personality theory, psychopathology, and health.* Chicago: University of Chicago Press.

Smith, H. (1991). *The world's great religions: Our great wisdom traditions.* New York: HarperSanFrancisco.

Sternberg, R., Grigorenko, E. L., & Singer, J. L. (2004). *Creativity: From potential to realization.* Washington, DC: American Psychological Association.

Sternberg, R., & Lubart, T. (1999). The concept of creativity: Prospects and paradigms. In R. Sternberg (Ed.), *Handbook of creativity* (pp. 3–15). New York: Cambridge University Press.

Wahba, M. A., & Bridwell, L. G. (1976). Maslow reconsidered: A review of research on the need hierarchy theory. *Organizational Behavior and Human Performance, 15,* 212–240.

Wallace, B. A. (2006). *The attention revolution: Unlocking the power of the focused mind.* Boston: Wisdom.

Walsh, R., & Shapiro, S. L. (2006). The meeting of meditative disciplines and Western psychology. *American Psychologist, 61,* 227–239.

White, M., & Gribbin, J. (1997). *Darwin: A life in science.* New York: Plume.

Wilber, K. (2006). *Integral spirituality: A startling new role for religion in the modern and postmodern world.* Boston: Shambhala.

Wilber, K., Engler, J., & Brown, D. P. (1986). *Transformations of consciousness: Conventional and contemplative perspectives on development.* Boston: Shambhala.

Zausner, T. (1996). The creative chaos: Speculations on the connection between non-linear dynamics and the creative process. In W. Sulis & A. Combs (Eds.), *Nonlinear dynamics in human behavior* (pp. 343–349). Singapore: World Scientific.

Zausner, T. (2007). *When walls become doorways: Creativity and the transforming illness.* New York: Harmony.

# AUTHOR INDEX

*Numbers in italics refer to listings in the references.*

Heisenberg, W., 142, *146*
Helson, R., 7, 9, *19*, 297, 298, *315*
Henning, B., 113, *126*
Heraclitus, 82, *87*
Herrick, C. J., 245, *257*
Hersch, P., 123, *126*
Hesley, J. G., 121, *126*
Hesley, J. W., 121, *126*
Heston, M. L., 119, *126*
Hewes, D. E., 116, *128*
Hewstone, M., *218*
Hirsh-Pasek, K., 9, *22*
Ho, M.-W., 267, *283*
Hoffman, E., 189, *191*
Hoffman, L., *145*
Hofschire, L., 116, *126*
Holloway, R. L., 245, 246, *257*
Homer, W. I., 80, *87*
Hornyak, T., 252, *257*
Houshyar, S., *283*
Houtz, J. C., *106*
Hughes, G. A., 65, *72*
Hui, A. N. N., *107*
Hull, C. L., 157, *171*
Hull, R. F. C., 87, *88*
Huntington, C. W., 132, *146*
Huston, A. C., 112, *126*
Hutcheon, L., 248, *257*
Hutchings, J. B., 121, *125*
Hutchinson, J. C., 77, *87*
Huyssen, A., 250, *257*

Inhelder, B., 133, *148*
Insel, T. R., 269, *285*
Ishiguro, H., 252, *257*
Ivcevic, Z., 210, *218*
Izquierdo, I., *21*

Jackson, P. W., 34, *50*
Jahoda, M., 66, *72*
James, V., 136, *146*
James, W., 157, *171*, 196, *218*
Jamison, C., 120, *127*
Jamison, K. R., 9, *19*, 32, *50*, 297, 300, *315*
Janis, I. L., *104*
Janssen, I., 112, 115, *127*
Jantsch, E., 159, 166, *171*, 230, *238*
Jedlicka, G., 80, *87*
Jerison, H. J., *148*, 245, *257*
Jerison, J., *148*
Johnson, K. M., 112, *127*
Jonas, D., 64, *73*

Jones, K., 99, *105*
Jordan, J., 293, *316*
Josett, B., *88*
Jung, C. G., 76, 83, 84, 87, 88, 308, *316*

Kahrman, G., 270, *283*
Kaku, M., 86, *88*
Kaplan, A., 293, *316*
Kapleau, P., *88*
Kaptchuk, T., 295, *316*
Kasof, J., 95, 97, *105*
Katzmarzyk, P. T., *127*
Kauffman, S. A., 159, *171*
Kaufman, J., 279, *283*
Kaufman, J. C., 5, *18*, 29, *49*, 77, *88*, *107*, 216, *315*
Kawai, M., 263, *284*
Kazantzis, N., 121, *127*
Kearney, R., 136, *146*
Kegan, R., 133, 134, 135, *146*
Keith, A. L., 116, *127*
Keleman, S., 176, 179, *192*
Kellogg, R., 133, 137, *146*
Kent, R., 120, *126*
Keverne, E. B., 269, *284*
Keyes, C. L. M., *72*
Kiecolt-Glaser, J. K., 8, *20*, 37, *51*, 103, *105*
Kinney, D., 4, 5, *19*, 21, 25, 27, 28, 29, 30, 32, 42, 44, *50*, 52, 62, 66, *72*, 176, *192*, 304, *317*
Klein, K., 38, *50*
Kloss, W., 77, *88*
Knyazeva, H., 164, *171*
Koestler, A., 104, *105*, 122, *127*
Kohlberg, L., 97, *105*, 133, 135, *147*, 161, *171*
Koplowitz, H., 134, *147*
Kosenko, R., *129*
Kotler, J. A., *125*
Kottman, T., 119, *126*
Kozak, L., 48, 294, *314*
Krieger, A., 121, *125*
Krippner, S., 8, *19*, 39, 40, 49, *50*, 132, 134, 138, 140, 142, 143, 144, *145*, *147*, 162, 164, 167, 167–168, *171*, *173*, 181, *192*, 294, 296, 299, *315*, *316*
Kris, E., 137, *147*, 187, *192*
Krystal, J. H., *283*
Kucich, G., 205, *218*
Kuhn, H. W., 237, *238*
Kuhn, T. S., 300, *316*
Kung, H., 161, *172*

Kuschel, K. J., 161, *172*

Lachlan, K., 116, *126*
Laing, F., 250, *257*
Lake, C., 80, 87, 294
Lake, J., *48, 314*
Lakoff, G., 180, *192*
Lam, P., 49
Lamberton, H. H., *147*
Lambie, J., 200, 214, *218*
Lampropoulos, G. K., 121, *127*
Lane, R. D., 214, *218*
Lang, F. R., 63, *72*
Lang, S., 36, *50*
Langer, E., 100, *105*, 134, *144*, 294, *316*
Langer, S., 38, 42, *50*
Lappe, F. M., 223, *238*
Larson, R., 61, *72*,
Laszlo, E., 138, *147*, 155, *172*
Lawlis, F., 38, 39, *49, 50*
Leakey, R. E., 246, *257*
Leary, W., 36, *49*
LeBlanc, D., *50*, 66, *72*
Lee, A. Y., 214, *217*
Lee, D., *129*
Lee, T. W., 120, *126*
Le Guin, U. K., 250, *257*
Lehman, D. R., *73*
Leifer, M., 121, *125*
Leman, P. J., 133, *147*
Lennon, K. H., 308, *315*
Lepore, S. J., 8, *19*, 37, *50*
Lerner, R. M., *146*
Levine, D. S., 278, *283*
Levine, E. G., 9, *19*
Levine, S. K., 9, *19*
Levi-Strauss, C., 55, 64, *72*, 140, *147*
Levy, B., 294, *316*
Lewin, K., 155, 160, *172*
Lewin, R., 246
Lewis, V. J., 120, *127*
Lewis-Williams, D., 84, 87, 137, 138, *145*, *147*
Lidren, D. M., 120, *127*
Lim, M. M., 269, *285*
Lindheim, R., 113, *127*
Lindzey, G., 220
Lipschitz, D., *283*
Liu, D., 270, *284*
Livingston, R. B., 245, *257*
Locke, S. E., 39, *50*
Long, C. R., 209, *218*

Loo, L. K., *147*
Loori, J. D., 5, 6, *19*, 299, *316*
Lopez, J. F. T., 162, *173*
Lordkipanidze, D., 246, *257, 258*
Lorenz, E. N., 255, *257*
Lovell, E. J., Jr., 205, 206, *217*
Low, J., 111–112, 115, *127*
Lowing, P., *50*, 66, *72*
Loy, D., 132, *147*
Loye, D., 153, 154, 155, 157, 160, 161, 164, 166, 168, 170, *172*, 258, 262, 266, 281, 282, 283, 284, *316*
Lubart, T. I., 215, 219, 295, *318*
Ludwig, A. M., 9, *19*, 32, *50*, 294, 296, *316*
Luminer, O., *218*
Lunde, I., 28, 32
Lynn, S. J., 40, 49, 294, *315*
Lyotard, J. F., 253, *258*
Lyubomirsky, S., *73*

MacLean, P. D., 245, *258*
MacKenna, S., 88
Magai, C., 199, *218*
Magoun, H., 245, *258*
Malchioiti, C., 87
Mannheim, R., 88
Manzo, K. K., 111, 115, *127*
Marcel, A., 200, 214, *218*
Marçol, G., 255, *258*
Margulis, L., 267, *284*
Marks-Tarlow, T., 41, *51*
Marmot, M. G., 279, *284*
Martensz, N., 269, *284*
Martin, F., 6, *22*
Martindale, C., 295, 298, 299, *316*
Marx, C. R., 83, 88
Maslow, A., 6, 8, 9, 10, 20, 27, 30, 41, *51*, 99, 103, *105*, 161, 161–162, 162, *172*, 176, 179, 181, 188, 190, *192*, 272, *284*, 301, 304, 310, *316*
Mathis, R., 116, *127*
Matt, D. C., 189, *192*
Mattevi, B., *21*
Maturana, H., 159, 166, *172*
May, R., *51*, 164, *173*, 249, *258*, 311, *316*
Mayer, J. D., 210, *218*
McCrae, R. R., 210, *217*
McCready, W., 132, *146*
McCullough, L., 121, *127*
McIlwraith, R. D., 113, *127*
McIntyre, T. M., 142, *147*

# SUBJECT INDEX

Baby boomers, 9
Bakst, Leon, 142
Balance and harmony
    and openness to experience, 188
    and pathology, 187
    and posture-related metaphors, 185
    psychological models of, 180–181
    spiritual paths to, 188–190
    and upright body stance, 176, 190–191
Baldwin, James Mark, 133, 154, 156, 157, 158, 159, 160
Baldwin effect, 159
Balsamo, Anne, 253
Barnard, J., 205
Barron, Frank X., 5, 7, 26, 33, 42, 63, 181
Baudrillard, J. 253
Bausch, Ken, 169
"Being" values or needs, 27–28, 162, 176, 181, 190, 272, 310
Beneficial features of creativity, 289–291
    active observation, 290, 302–304
    androgyny, 290, 307–309
    bravery, 290, 311–313
    caring, 290, 304–305
    collaboration, 290, 306–307 (see also Collaborative)
    conscious presence, 290, 293–294
    development, 290, 309–311
    dynamic vision, 290, 291–293
    health, 290, 294–295 (see also Health)
    integral consciousness, 290, 300–302 (see also Integral)
    nondefensiveness, 290, 295–297
    openness, 290, 297–300 (see also Openness to experience)
Benet, Maria, 27
Berkeley Institute of Personality and Research, University of California, 33
Bernard, Claude, quoted, 3
Bernard, Jessie, 161
Bertalanffy, Ludwig von, 165
Bibliocounseling, 119
Bibliotherapy, 119–120
Bifurcation, 255, 281
Biology, and psychology, 165
Biology vs. culture, 271–273. See also Nature and nurture
Bipolar mood disorders, 99
    and creativity, 28, 32
Blade Runner (film), 250, 251
Blake, William, quoted, 131
Blank Slate, The (Pinker), 165

Bloom, Howard, 35
Body, revived interest in, 176–177
Bohm, David, 85
Boiling-water example of self-organization, 231
Bomvu Ridge paintings, 138
Bonobos, cultures of, 276
Boulding, Kenneth, 166
Bounded ratonality, 70
Bradley, Raymond, 169
Brain, human, 245, 264
    and domination vs. partnership model of society, 277–279
    evolution of, 245–248, 264–266, 267
    flexibility of, 278
Bravery, as creativity characteristic, 290, 311–313
Broadcasting, limited choice vs. niche marketing in, 69
"Broaden and build" strategies, 69–70
Brown, Lucy, 268
Bruno, Giordano, 249
Buddhism
    "engaged," 68
    and interconnectedness, 86
    and Nirvana, 201–202
    See also Zen Buddhism
Buddhism, Tibetan
    and Gowan's developmental model, 134
    and meditation, 299
    on "three poisons," 143
    visualization in, 85
Burroughs, William S., 67–68
Business Alliance for Local Living Economies, 235
Butterfly effect, 14, 59, 181. See also Chaos theory
Byron, Lord (George Gordon), 213

Cannon, Walter, 58
Caring
    as creativity characteristic, 17, 290, 304–307
    as evolutionary force, 164, 262–263, 267, 282
Catastrophes, 68
Catharsis, 197
Cave paintings, 84, 137–138
Ceausescu, Nikolai, 270
Center for Partnership Studies, 282
Cézanne, Paul, 142
Chagall, Marc, 141

Chaisson, Eric, 230

*Chalice and the Blade, The* (Eisler), 275, 277

*Challenges* (Lang), 36

Change
    active attitude toward, 261–265
    creativity for, 312
    discourse of, 256
    human nature as restricting, 262
    as interactive process, 280–281
    levers for, 281–282
    and uncertainty, 255

Chao Mêng-fu, 78

Chaos, 56
    and health, 61
    and somewhat-complicated system, 58–60
    and "weaving," 71

Chaos theory (nonlinear dynamical systems theory), 14, 58, 155, 166, 167
    and artistic uncertainty, 82
    and free will, 65
    on instability, 179
    maximal ferment for, 167
    and model of complexity and paradox, 181
    as transcending problems, 164

Chaotic attractors, 255

Chaotic variability, 64

*Cheers* (television series), 123

Childcare, cultural differences in, 273

Children's Television Act (1990), 112

Chimpanzees, cultures of, 276

*Chinatown* (film), 114

Chinese tradition, 77–78, 203–205, 213, 214–215, 307–308. *See also* Confucianism and Confucius; Eastern tradition

Choice
    and evolutionary movement, 263
    and extended consciousness, 265
    as human capacity, 276

Christakis, Aleco, 169

Christian Rhineland mystics, 132

Chuang Tzu, 215

Cinematherapy, 120–121

Civilization
    global, 235–236
    in Integral synthesis, 229, 233–235
    Organic Learning Civilization, 236–237
    *See also* Western civilization

*Civilization and Its Discontents* (Freud), 160

Cixous, Hélène, 248, 249

Clubbe, J., 205

Cold-engine example, 61–62, 67

Collaboration, as creativity characteristic, 15, 16, 221, 228, 237, 290, 306–307

Collaborative culture and skills, 237

Collaborative learning, 221

Collaborative learning culture, 221, 228, 235

Collective, humanity as, 233

Collective creativity, 221, 223–224, 227, 236, 238

Collective learning, 223–224, 229

Collectivism
    vs. individualism, 200, 202, 210
    vertical vs. horizontal varieties of, 210, 211

Combs, Allan, 154, 162, 167, 169

Communication, art as, 82–83

Compensatory advantage, and creativity, 28, 32

Complexity, from simplicity, 61–64

Complexity-based interventions, 69–70

Complexity and paradox, emerging model of, 180–181

Complexity Theory, 227, 254

Computer environments, in learning, 84

Concrete operations period (Piaget), 134, 139

Conflict, creative and resilient response to, 10

Conformity
    vs. creativity in future, 169
    and moral development/evolution, 159
    and theory of evolution, 153–154, 155–157, 165

Confucianism and Confucius, 213, 254, 307–308

Connectedness, and art, 86

Conscious choice
    and evolutionary movement, 263
    and extended consciousness, 265
    as human capacity, 276

Consciousness, 17, 42, 131, 179, 262–264, 265, 281
    disembodied, 253
    extended, 265
    heightening of (May), 25
    in Piaget's stages, 135
    and posture, 179
    revived interest in, 176–177
    structures of, 15, 131, 135 (*see also* Structures of consciousness)

Conscious and unconscious mind, 33, 76

Conscious presence, as creativity characteristic, 290, 293–294
Constancy model, of balance and harmony, 180
Constructivist epistemology, 91
Contemporary music, 138
Convention, vs. creativity, 100
Coping, creative, 9, 104
Correspondence, theory of, 85
*Cosby Show, The* (television series), 116
*Courage to Be, The* (Tillich), 249
Creative class, 11
    and creative migration, 11
    *See also* Cultural creatives
Creative courage, 256, 311
Creative insights, 101–102
Creative potential, 92–93, 102, 104
Creative psychologists, and Darwin, 153
Creative self-expression, 99, 100
Creative students, 34
Creative thinking, 94
    and ambiguity, 249
    and androgyny, 249
    in apes, 178
    and imagination, 140–141
    and interpretation, 95
Creativity, 131–133, 242
    and androgyny, 273
    attributional theory of, 97
    as authenticity and novelty, 200
    benefits and results of, 8–11, 13
    broad experience needed for, 214–215
    clearing of mind for, 143–144
    collective, 221, 223–224, 227, 236, 238
    and collective learning, 223–224
    complexity and paradox in, 180–181
    vs. conformity in future, 169
    and culture, 16, 195–196, 261, 282
    definition of, *xi*
    as deviant, 103
    as dynamic, 66
    economic principle of, 215
    as effective surprise, 104
    and emotion, 195
        and novelty plus authenticity, 201
    and "empty" mind, 132
    for evil purposes (dark side), 98n, 296
    and evolution, 153–154, 155–157, 165, 247, 248, 264 (*see also* Evolution; Evolutionary theory)
    as fundamental, 76–77
    as government priority, 11

and health, 8, 9 (*see also* Health)
    psychological health, 187–188
humans preeminent in, 136
and integral consciousness, 141, 142, 221
and Integral society, 221
and interface of individual and culture, 241–242
as intrinsically motivated, 272
as life-path, 13
and love, 268 (*see also* Love)
and maturation (Piaget), 133
meaningfulness in, 5, 26, 176 (*see also* Meaning)
moral dimension of, 8 (*see also* Moral development and theory)
multifaceted, 77–78
and nature–nurture interplay, 100
negative implications of, 28
originality in, 5, 26, 42, 92, 176
    vs. assumptions and routine, 101
    and effectiveness, 91
    as path, 13
pathologizing of, 31–33
and peak experience, 188
personal, 5, 91–93, 94–96, 97–98, 99, 102, 103, 104
personality traits in, 186–187
personal reservoirs of, 75
in Piaget's model of development, 134, 135
proactive, 98, 103–104
and problem solving, 98, 99, 101, 104
questions about, *xi*
revived interest in, 176–177
from self-appreciation, 237
social, 11, 15, 97
small "c", *xi*
as solutions to life's problems, 55
stages of, 208–209
and structures of consciousness, 137 (*see also* Structures of consciousness)
in television, 123
tensions and balance in, 185–186, 190
and unknown, 312–313
and upright body posture, 175–176, 177, 190–191 (*see also* Upright body posture)
Creativity, eminent
and emotion, 196, 198
and everyday creativity, 44–45, 212–213

and dimensions of relationships, 200–202

and emotion, 197–198, 213–215, 215–216

evolution of, 276–277

hierarchical, 228, 234–235

new categories for, 273–274

heterarchy, 307

partnership model vs. domination model, 274–280

popular (emotional training from), 214

Culture vs. biology, 271–273. *See also* Nature and nurture

"Culture of peace," 280

*Curb Your Enthusiasm* (television series), 115, 123

Cyberculture, 17

Cybernetics (general systems theory), 58, 165

and humanistic psychology, 168

maximal ferment for, 167

*Cyberpunk* (Rockwell), 253

Cyberpunk fiction, 243, 252–253

*Cybersexualities* (Wolmark), 242, 243

Cybersexuality, 241–242, 250–254

Cyberspace, 241, 244, 254

Cyberworld, 254

Cyborgs, 241, 243, 244, 253

Dabrowski, Kazimierz, 161, 162, 164

Dali, Salvador, bizarre life of, 187

Damon, William, 154, 162

Dante, 197

Darwin, Charles, 15–16

depression of, 187

lost story or lost theory of, 15–16, 153, 155

on love, 268

and moral theory, 156, 162

on movements in evolution, 262

and psychology, 155–156, 157

quoted, 153

and "survival of the fittest" vs. humanistic themes, 156–157

and transcendent human processes, 264

*Darwin and After Darwin* (Romanes & Morgan), 158

*Darwin on Man* (Gruber), 156

Darwin Project, 154, 169

"Darwin Wars," 164

da Vinci, Leonardo, 77

quoted, 109

Deconstructionist perspectives, 142

Deficiency needs, creativity fueled by, 9–10, 12

Democracy, in Organic Learning Civilization, 236

Depression, bibliotherapy for, 120

Derrida, Jacques, 248, 255

Descartes, René 38

*Descent of Man, The* (Darwin), 16, 156

humanistic/creative themes dominant in, 156–157

and love, 268

and *Origin of Species*, 157

*See also* Darwin, Charles

Development

as creativity characteristic, 15, 16, 41–42, 133–135, 159, 190, 290, 309–311

and love, 169–271

and "empty" (open) mind, 132

Developmental bibliotherapy, 119–120

Developmental models, 133

of Kohlberg, 97, 161

of Piaget, 133–135

*See also* Structures of consciousness, historical

de Waal, Frans, 154

Dewey, John, 6, 27, 154, 160

Diaghilev, Serge, 142

Dichotomies, false, 308

Dick, Philip K., 251

*Dick Van Dyke Show, The* (television series), 117

Differentiation, as relationship dimension, 200, 201

Directional indicators, and values, 183–184

Discretion, 92, 94, 96, 102

and postconventionality, 98

Disequilibrium, 93

Distance healing, 40–41

Distributed intelligence and empowerment, 233

Divergent thinking, 7

Diversity, need for, 237

*Do Androids Dream of Electric Sheep?* (Dick), 251–252

Doane, Mary Ann, 250, 251

Dobzhansky, Theodosius, 6, 27

"DO EASY" (DE), 67

Domain-specificity or -differences, 93, 96n

of creativity, 7, 77–78, 298

Domination model of society, 274–277

and brain, 277–279

current regression to, 281
  stress generated in, 279–280
Donne, John, 102
Drama, in television, 123–124
*Dr. Phil* (television show), 124
Drug use, 67–68
Dürer, Albrecht, 77
*Dutch and Flemish Artists* (Van Mander), 77
Dylan, Bob, TV special on, 45
Dynamical systems theory, 14, 58–60, 155, 255. *See also* Chaos theory
Dynamic Evolution, 227
Dynamic vision, as creativity characteristic, 290, 291–293

Earth goddess, 139
Eastern tradition, 199
  artists of, 77
  authority emphasized in, 199–200
  as collectivist, 202
  and "empty" mind, 132
  images of deities in, 85
  intrapersonal orientation of, 201
  new interest in, 176
  and structures of consciousness, 15
  *See also* Buddhism; Buddhism, Tibetan; Chinese tradition; Zen Buddhism
Ecological Economics, 227
Ecology(ies), 227
  knowledge, 221, 223, 236
Economic development, three Ts of, 11
Ecosystem, civilization as, 233
Ecosystem vision of humanity, 221
Education, in Organic Learning Civilization, 236
Effective novelty, 237
  in cultural change process, 228
Egostrength, 100
Einstein, Albert, on intuition, 184
"Einstein on the Beach" (Glass & Wilson), 143
Eisler, Riane, 161, 169
Eleatics, 254
Emergence, 59
Eminent creativity. See Creativity, eminent
*Eminent Creativity, Everyday Creativity, and Health* (Richards & Runco), 12
Emotion(s)
  and culture, 197–198, 213–215, 215–216
  and expressive writing, 38
Emotional acuity, 207

Emotional creativity, 195, 196–199
  and culture, 213–215
    and criteria for creativity, 199–200, 208
  in the everyday, 208–212
  novelty plus authenticity in, 201
  in poetry, 202–208
Emotional Creativity Inventory (ECI), 209–210, 214
Emotional fundamentalism, 216
Emotional genius, 197, 213, 216
Empathy
  among animals, 264
  education for, 282
  in humans vs. androids, 251
  impairment of, 266
  and new brain structures, 264
*Encyclopedia of Creativity*, 7, 12
Enlightenment (historical period), 223, 226, 227, 229, 236
Enlightenment (state of mind), 301
Entertainment, 303. *See also* Radio; Television viewing
Epistemology
  constructivist, 91
  genetic, 93
Equilibrium, punctuated, 247
*E.R.* (television series), 124
*Everybody Loves Raymond* (television series), 123
Everyday, synonyms for, 57
Everyday creativity. *See* Creativity, everyday
*Everyday Creativity and New Views of Human Nature*, 8
*Everyday Creativity, Eminent Creativity, and Health*, 12
Everyday psychopathology, 65–66
Everyday spirituality, 65
Evolution
  toward creative innovations, 263
  and creativity, 247, 248, 264
  cultural, 233, 276–277
    from biological, 159
    multilinear theory of, 275
  direction in, 262
  favorable capacities provided by, 262
  higher abilities resulting from, 264
  of hominid brain, 245–248, 264–266, 267
  of human nature, 242, 263–269
  in Integral synthesis, 229, 230–231 (*see also* Life)

for Henri Matisse, 79–80
for Albert Pinkham Ryder, 80–81
Image, 302
Imagery, for physical health, 38–40
Imagination, and play, 9, 95
Immune function, and expressive writing, 8, 37–38
Imo (teenage monkey), 263
Imperial hierarchies or cultures, 228, 235
Impression management, 97
Individualism, 211
    vs. collectivism, 200, 202, 210
    vertical vs. horizontal varieties of, 210, 211
Information, art as, 82–83
Inquiry, tensions and balance in, 185–186
Insecurity, wisdom of, 182
Insights, 101
Institute of Personality Assessment and Research, University of California, 7
Integral consciousness, 141–143
    as creativity characteristic, 144, 290, 300–302, 305
    diaphanous quality of, 143
Integral framework, 222, 225
Integral science, 16–17, 221, 222, 227, 229, 230
Integral society, 221, 226–227
Integration, 97, 141, 290, 300–302
Intelligent design, 262
Intention(s), 92, 96
    and healing, 39
Intentionality, 94, 102
Intercessory prayer, 41
Interdependence, 43
International Society for Systems Sciences, 168
Interpersonal relationships, dimensions of, 200–202
Interpretation, 94, 95, 102
    and creative thinking, 95–96
Intuition, 184
Invention, Piaget on, 93–94
Involvement, as relationship dimension, 200, 202
Ishiguro, Hioshi, 252
I–Thou relationship, 305

James, William, 154, 156, 157, 158, 196–197
Jantsch, Erich, 166
Jesus, 65, 249
*Journal of Creative Behavior*, 7

Jung, Carl, 45, 76, 84

Karasvina, Tamara, 142
Katz, Elias, 45
Keats, John, 195
    on negative capability, 205–206, 212
    "To Autumn," 202–203, 204
Keleman, Stanley, 176
Kerr, Christine, 45
King, Martin Luther, 249
Kinney, Dennis, 27, 28, 44
Klein, Paul, 113
Knowledge
    adaptation in, 93–94
    constructivist view of, 91
Knowledge ecology(ies), 221, 223, 236
Koeck, Pieter, 77
Kohlberg, Lawrence, 97, 154, 161
Koyetsu, 78
Krippner, Stanley, 12, 154, 162, 167
Kubie, Lawrence, 6
Kung, Hans, 161
Kwan Yin, 85

Lacan, Jacques, 243
Lakoff, G., 180
Lang, Fritz, 250
Lang, Serge, 36
Lao Tze, 185
Lappe, Francis Moore, 223
Large-scale creative dynamics, of somewhat-complicated systems, 63–64
Lascaux cave paintings, 84, 137–138
Laszlo, Ervin, 166, 169
*Law and Order: Special Victims Unit* (television series), 118
Leakey, Louis and Mary, 246
Learning, 265
    television as means of, 115–117
Learning Connexion, New Zealand, 298
*Left Hand of Darkness* (Le Guin), 250, 251
Le Guin, Ursula, 250, 251
Leonardo da Vinci, 77
    quoted, 109
*L'Eve Future* (Villiers de l'Isle-Adam), 250
Levi-Strauss, Claude, 140
    quoted, 55
Lewin, Kurt, 154, 155, 160, 163, 166, 168
Lewis, Maud, 14, 75, 81–82
Liberty, Equality and Fraternity, in Organic Learning Civilization, 236

Life, in Integral synthesis, 229, 230–233
Lifetime Creativity Scales (LCS), 28–29
Li Lung-mien, 78
Limbic system, 247
Ling, Gilbert, 35–36, 40
Liu Chüeh, 78
"Living well," 56–57, 60
    as dynamic, 66
    as example, 59
Loori (Zen Master), 299
Lorenz attractor, 255
Love, 138, 305
    evolution of, 266–268
        nonreproductive dynamic in, 268–269
    evolutionary movement toward, 263
    and human development, 269–271
    impairment from lack of, 266
    mammals' need for, 264
    as new evolutionary dynamic, 268–269
Lovell, E. J., Jr., 205
Lyotard, J.-F., 253, 255

Machiavelli, Niccolò, 228
MacKinnon, Donald, 7
MacLean, Paul, 264
Madonna (performer), 143
Magic, 138
Magical consciousness, 137–138
Mandela, Nelson, 249, 271
*Man for Himself: An Inquiry Into the Psychology of Ethics* (Fromm), 161
*Manifesto for Cyborgs, A* (Haraway), 243
Mann, Thomas, 138
Margulis, L., 267
Marmot, M. G., 279
*Mary Tyler Moore Show, The* (television series), 111, 115, 123, 302–303
*MASH* (television series), 115, 123
Maslow, Abraham
    and basic needs, 181
    and caring, 313
    on deficiency needs, 9
    and higher purpose, 309
    and humanistic psychology, 161
        and vision of Good Person and Good Society, 163
    on needs hierarchy, 179, 272, 305
    on peak experience, 188, 190
    and "second Darwinian revolution," 154, 157
    on self-actualization, 6, 27, 190, 272

on self-actualizing creativity, 30, 41, 99, 309–310
and transcendent experience, 301
Matisse, Henri, 14, 75, 79–80
Maturana, Humberto, 166
May, Josephine S., quoted, 221
May, Rollo, 25, 249
Mayer–Salovey–Caruso Emotional Intelligence Test (MSCEIT), 210
McKibben, William, 69
Mead, George Herbert, 154, 160
Mead, Margaret, 166
Meaning
    and myths, 140
    revived interest in, 176–177
Meaningfulness, 5, 26, 176
Media
    limited choice vs. niche marketing in, 69
    *See also* Television viewing
Media literacy, 118–119
Medieval European society, 226
Meditation, 144, 299, 300
Memory, and expressive writing, 38
Mental consciousness, 140–141
Mental imagery, for physical health, 38–40
Merleau-Ponty, Maurice, 176, 184
    quoted, 175
Merzel, Ann, 27
"Metabolism of the new," 43
Meta-domain, 93
*Metropolis* (Lang film), 250
Migration, creative, 11
Miller, Jean Baker, 161
Miller, John David, 313
Mind–body dichotomy, 37–38
Mindfulness meditation, 144
Minoan civilization, 139
Mirror neurons or cells, 136, 306
Modern–postmodern dialogue, 185
Monet, Claude, 142
Monkeys, cultural learning of, 263
Montuori, Alfonso, 169
Mood disorders, and creativity, 28, 30, 32, 42
Mooney, 5, 26
Moral development and theory
    and Baldwin, 159
    and Darwin, 156, 162
    and humanistic psychology vs. biological view of evolution, 159–161, 162
    stages of (Kohlberg), 97, 133

Moral dimension of creativity, 8
Moravec, Hans, 253
Morgan, Lloyd, 154, 158
Morley, 143
Moronobu, Hishikawa, 78
Morse, Samuel F. B., 77
Mother Teresa, 271
Motivation, 96
Multifaceted creativity, 77–78
*Murphy Brown* (television series), 123
Music, contemporary, 138
Mystics, Christian Rhineland, 132
Mythic consciousness, 139–140
    mental consciousness seen as enemy of, 142
Myths, and meaning, 140

Nachmanovich, S., quoted, 241
Narrative, 58, and meaning, 140
Nash, John, 237
Natural selection, 264
    in Integral synthesis, 231
    and nonreproductive motivation, 272
    vs. organic selection, 158, 159
    *See also* Evolutionary theory; "Survival of the fittest"
Nature and nurture, 100–101
    as cyborg and cyberspace, 244
Neanderthals, 246–247
Negative capability, Keats on, 205–206, 212
Neo-Darwinians, 153, 156, 158, 159
    and biologists, 160, 163
    reversal of coming, 222
Neo-Freudians, 6
*Neuromancer* (Gibson), 243, 244
Neuroticism, and emotional creativity, 210
New Age spirituality, 164
Nhat Hanh, Thich, 13, 68, 305
Niche markets, 69
Nijinsky, Vaslav, 142
Nirvana, 201–202
"Nixon in China" (Adams opera), 143
No Child Left Behind Act (2002), 118
"No Direction Home" (Scorsese TV special), 45
Nondefensiveness, as creativity characteristic, 14, 31, 290, 295–297
Nonlinear dynamical systems theory. *See* Chaos theory
Nordic nations, 275, 280, 308
"Normal" life, 65
Novelty(ies), 199–200, 201

and authenticity, 211
in creativity, 195, 209, 210, 242
effective, 228, 237
and Keats, 206

Observation, active, as creativity characteristic, 14, 15, 43–45, 82–83, 109–110, 113–115, 290, 302–304
Occupational drift, 32. *See also* Migration, creative
Olduvai Gorge explorations, 246
Oligarchic hierarchies, 228, 235
Ontogeny recapitulates phylogeny, in structures of consciousness, 136
Openness to experience, 7, 11, 42, 186–188, 210
    as balancing and harmonizing, 188
    and clear mind, 144
    as core creative trait, 278–279
    as creativity characteristic, 290, 297–300
    and emotional creativity, 210
    in progression to self-actualization, 10
*Oprah* (television show), 124
Organic Learning Civilization, 236–237
Organic selection, 158–159
Originality
    vs. assumptions and routines, 101
    and clinicians, 6
    in creativity, 5, 26, 42, 91, 92, 176
    of everyday life, 26, 29
    and finite–infinite consciousness, 182
    opposing vectors of, 175, 186, 190
"Original sin," 261
*Origin of the Species* (Darwin), 157
    and *Descent of Man*, 157
    *See also* Darwin, Charles
Ornstein, Robert, 154, 274
Orphanage children in Romania, 270–271
Osborn, Henry, 158
Owen, S., 204, 207

Pandora's Box metaphor, 31
Parallel process, 64
Parenting
    and creativity of children, 100
    partnership vs. dominator, 278, 282
Parmenides, 254
Partnership model of society, 274–277
    and brain, 277–279
    and stress, 280
Pascal, Blaise, quoted, 175

Rashevsky, Nicolaus, 165
Rational choice theory, 70
    and maximizers, 63
Rationality, 70
Ray, Paul, 227
rDzogs-chen (supercompleteness) teachings, 132
Reason
    in Organic Learning Civilization, 236
    political oppression legitimized by, 255
Rebellion, and upright body posture, 179
Referral flow, example of, 59
Reflective abstraction, Piaget on, 94n
Reformation, 226
Reich, Wilhelm, 176
Relationships, dimensions of, 200–202
Religion, and mythic consciousness, 139–140
Religious symbolism, in art, 84–85
Rembrandt, 83
Research, on healing at a distance, 40–41
Resilience, 42
Richards, Keith, 70–71
Richards, Lauren, 46
Richards, Robert J., 156, 159
Richards, Ruth, 62, 169
Risk-taking, 16, 311
Rogers, Carl, 6, 99, 199
Roman Empire, 226
Romanes, George, 154, 158
Romanian children in orphanages, 270–271
*Room 222* (television comedy), 111
Roosevelt, Eleanor, quoted, 261
Rucker, Rudy, 253
Ryder, Albert Pinkham, 14, 75, 80–81

Salthe, Stanley, 169
Sartre, Jean-Paul, 140, 182
Satisficers, 63
Savoring, Ssu-k'ung T'u on, 206–208, 212
Schools
    and creative students, 34
    egostrength as priority in, 100
    "grading on the curve" in, 306–307
Schuldberg, David, 12
Schweitzer, Albert, 271
Science, in Integral synthesis, 229, 230
Science fiction, 243, 248, 250, 254
Scientific journals, suppression of letters to charged, 36
Scientific revolutions, of 1500 and current age, 222, 223
Scorsese, Martin, 45

Script theory, 155
S-curve cycle, 230, 234
Second-order awareness, 207
*Seinfeld* (television series), 115, 123
Sekida (Zen Master), 143, 299
Self, sense of
    and Keats on negative capability, 205
    in Piaget's developmental stages, 135
Self-actualization (Maslow), 103, 176, 190
    self-actualizing creativity, 6, 10, 27, 41, 99, 162, 272, 310
Self-expression, 99, 103
    creative, 100
Self-integration
    Chinese notion of, 204
"Self-interest rightly understood," in Organic Learning Civilization, 237
"Selfish genes," 271
Self-organization Theory, 230
Self-organizing processes, 159, 166, 230, 231
*Self-Organizing Universe, The* (Jantsch), 166
Self-reflexivity, in savoring, 207–208
Self-transcendence, 205–206
Sensorimotor period (Piaget), 134
Serlin, Ilene, 45, 46
*Sesame Street* (children's television show), 112
Sexual equality. *See* Gender equality
Shamanic traditions, 189
    and cave paintings, 84, 138
    new interest in, 176
Shinn, Everett, 77
Simplicity
    complexity from, 61–64
    and "easy" approach as substance abuse, 67–68
*Simpsons, The* (television series), 116
*Six Feet Under* (television series), 114, 116, 123
Skills
    collaborative, 237
    creativity-relevant vs. task-motivation and domain-relevant, 42
Skinner, B. F., 157
Small-scale improvisation, and somewhat-complicated systems, 62–63
Smith, Adam, 237
Social classification system, 274
    heterarchy, 307
    hierarchy, 228, 234–235
    partnership model vs. domination model, 274–277

and brain, 277–279
and importance of primary human relations, 281
and regression toward dominance, 281
and stress effects, 279–280
Social creativity, 11, 15, 97
Social evolution, 198, 233
Social influences on creativity, 35–37
Solzhenitsyn, Alexander, 249
Somewhat-complicated systems (SCS), 14, 56, 57–58, 61, 68–69
and active vs. passive approaches, 66
and "broaden and build" strategies, 70
and cold-engine example, 61–62, 67
large-scale creative dynamics of, 63–64
macroscopic properties of behavior in, 58–60
microscopic properties of, 60
and positive psychology, 66
and small-scale improvisation, 62–63
and solitary actor vs. "weaving," 71
*Sopranos, The* (television series), 116
Southam, Marti, 45, 46
"Spatialization of form hypothesis," 180
Spiritual Alliance to Stop Intimate Violence (SAIV), 282
Spiritual awareness, 144
Spiritual extension of love, 269
Spirituality
and balance and harmony, 188–190
everyday, 65
New Age, 164
and transpersonal psychology, 164
Spiritual values, in creative life, 8
Springer, Claudia, 252–253, 253–254
Ssu-k'ung T'u, 195–196, 202, 203–205
on art of savoring, 206–208, 212
Stability and instability, 242, 254
*State of the World 2004* (World Watch Institute), 223
*Stepford Wives, The* (film), 250
Stereotypes, gender, 308
Stewardship, necessity of, 227
Stoics, 197, 198
Strange attractors, 58–59, 60, 255
Straus, Erwin, 176, 179
Stravinsky, Igor, 142
Stress, 95
and dominator hierarchy, 278, 279
and socialization process, 278

and television viewing, 112
Structures of consciousness, 15, 131, 311
Structures of consciousness, historical, 135–136, 137, 301
archaic, 136
magical, 137–138
mythic, 139–140
mental, 140–141
integral, 141–143, 144
phenomenal states in, 302
Students, creative, 34
Subsidiarity principle, 233
Substance use, 67–68
Suppression of creativity
in scientific controversy, 35–37
in students, 34
"Survival of the fittest," 153, 154, 156, 159–160, 163, 164
Sustainability movement, 235
Sustainable future, 261
Symbiosis, 267
Symbolism, religious, art as, 84–85
Symbols, archetypes as, 84
Systems science, 155, 166, 167
evolutionary, 161, 165–167
psychology partnership with needed, 168
and World Congress of Systems Sciences, 168
Systems Theory, 227, 255–256
Systems view of evolution and human nature, 264–273

Tagore, Rabindranath, quoted, 289
Teletherapy, 110, 118–119, 122–124
Television viewing, 15, 109–113, 302
active vs. passive, 111, 113–115
learning through, 115–117
Thales, 140
Therapy sessions, videotaped replays of, 122
Thinking, creative, 95
Third-person effect, 117
*Thirtysomething* (television series), 123
Tibetan Buddhism. *See* Buddhism, Tibetan
Tillich, Paul, 249
Tipping, 68
"To Autumn" (Keats), 202–203, 204
Tolerance of ambiguity, 7
Tomkins, Silvan, 154, 155
Toronto Manifesto, 168
Torrance, E. Paul, 7
Torres, Margie, 45

# ABOUT THE EDITOR

**Ruth Richards, MD, PhD,** is a board certified psychiatrist and educational psychologist. She is a professor of psychology at Saybrook Graduate School in San Francisco, California; a research affiliate at McLean Hospital, Belmont, Massachusetts (psychiatric affiliate of Massachusetts General Hospital); and a lecturer in the Department of Psychiatry, Harvard Medical School, Boston, Massachusetts. For many years, Dr. Richards has studied everyday creativity in clinical and educational settings and has published on creativity and social action as well as spiritual development. She is the principal author of *The Lifetime Creativity Scales*, which broke new ground as a broad-based assessment of real-life everyday creativity in a general population. With Mark A. Runco, Dr. Richards coedited *Eminent Creativity, Everyday Creativity, and Health*. She served on the executive advisory board for the *Encyclopedia of Creativity* and is also on the editorial boards of three journals: *The Creativity Research Journal*; *The Journal of Humanistic Psychology*; and *Psychology of Aesthetics, Creativity, and the Arts*, the journal for Division 10 of the American Psychological Association (Society for the Psychology of Aesthetics, Creativity and the Arts), where she is also an at-large member of the executive committee. Personally, Dr. Richards draws, writes, plays three instruments badly, and learns even more about creativity from her teenage daughter.